Competitive Approaches to Health Care Reform

**RICHARD J. ARNOULD
ROBERT F. RICH
AND WILLIAM D. WHITE**
Editors

Competitive Approaches to Health Care Reform

THE URBAN INSTITUTE PRESS
Washington, D.C.

RA
395
.A3
C667
1993

THE URBAN INSTITUTE PRESS
2100 M Street, N.W.
Washington, D.C. 20037

Library of Congress Cataloging in Publication Data

Competitive Approaches to Health Care Reform/[Richard J. Arnould, Robert F. Rich, and William D. White, editors].

1. Medical policy—United States.   2. Insurance, Health—Finance—Government policy—United States.   3. Medical care—United States—Cost control.
4. Competition—United States.   I. Arnould, Richard J.   II. Rich, Robert F.
III. White, William Deacons, 1945–

[DNLM: 1. Delivery of Health Care—economics—United States.   2. Health Services—organization and administration—United States.   3. Health Policy—United States.   4. Economic Competition.   5. Delivery of Health Care—economics—Canada.   6. United States.   7. Canada. W 84 AA1 C64 1993]

RA395.A3C667   1993   93-1603
362.1'0973—dc20   CIP
DNLM/DLC

ISBN 0-87766-604-0 (alk. paper)
ISBN 0-87766-603-2 (alk. paper; casebound)

Urban Institute books are printed on acid-free paper whenever possible.

Printed in the United States of America.

Distributed by:
         University Press of America
4720 Boston Way   3 Henrietta Street
Lanham, MD 20706   London WC2E 8LU ENGLAND

THE URBAN INSTITUTE is a nonprofit policy research and educational organization established in Washington, D.C., in 1968. Its staff investigates the social and economic problems confronting the nation and public and private means to alleviate them. The Institute disseminates significant findings of its research through the publications program of its Press. The goals of the Institute are to sharpen thinking about societal problems and efforts to solve them, improve government decisions and performance, and increase citizen awareness of important policy choices.

Through work that ranges from broad conceptual studies to administrative and technical assistance, Institute researchers contribute to the stock of knowledge available to guide decision making in the public interest.

Conclusions or opinions expressed in Institute publications are those of the authors and do not necessarily reflect the views of staff members, officers or trustees of the Institute, advisory groups, or any organizations that provide financial support to the Institute.

ACKNOWLEDGMENTS

We would like to express our thanks to a number of organizations and individuals who helped with the symposium upon which this volume is based or provided helpful insights into the structure of the volume. The symposium was organized by the Program in Health Economics, Management and Policy at the University of Illinois at Urbana-Champaign (UIUC) under the auspices of College of Commerce and Business Administration (UIUC) and the Institute of Government and Public Affairs of the University of Illinois. Special thanks are due to those at the University who through the formation of this organization provided direct and indirect support to the symposium and continuing support to the coeditors. Thanks are equally due to Ameritech Foundation, The Carle Foundation, State Farm Insurance Companies, and the Illinois Hospital Association whose support permitted us to attract a number of the top experts in health policy. In addition, special recognition must go to the program discussants, who contributed greatly to the lively nature of the symposium: Gloria Bazzoli, HRET, American Hospital Association; Lawrence DeBrock, Department of Economics, University of Illinois/Urbana-Champaign; David Dranove, Kellogg Graduate School of Management, Northwestern University; Thomas Hoerger, Department of Economics, Vanderbilt University; Gerrit Knaap, Department of Urban and Regional Planning, University of Illinois/Urbana-Champaign; Willard Manning, Department of Health Services Research and Policy, University of Minnesota; John Pollard, Carle Clinic Association, Urbana; Jim Rogers, Center for Health Policy Research, American Medical Association; and Leonard Schifrin, Department of Economics, College of William and Mary.

We are also grateful for the help of Martha Green and Lori Williamson in the Bureau of Economic and Business Research, and Anna Merritt and Jean Baker in the Institute of Government and Public Affairs for their valuable assistance in planning and organizing the symposium. Craig Copeland provided valuable input for a number of chapters.

Two people must be singled out for very special thanks. The first is Marla Osterbur, who contributed beyond the call of duty to the symposium and has played an enormous role in the typing and processing of manuscripts included in this volume. The second is an anonymous referee, who not only provided helpful comments about each of the individual papers but also recommended a major reordering of the outline that substantially improved the entire volume.

CONTENTS

Tables

Figures

FOREWORD

Introducing more effective competition among health care providers appears to be one of the major currents in the evolving plans of the Clinton Administration for health care reform. That is the central issue the contributing authors to this volume address.

The advantages claimed for competitive approaches generally derive from the economic theory of perfect competition—achieving maximum efficiency through a market in which all demand is satisfied at a price that earns the most efficient producers only as much as they need to stay in business.

Few observers of the U.S. health scene would claim that it represents anything like the textbook picture of competition. So the challenge is to achieve the conditions of market efficiency without compromising access to care—a massive challenge. This book contributes to the debate about how best to meet it by reviewing the considerable experimentation with competitive approaches to health care delivery and financing that took place during the 1980s.

One of the many insights in the book is the recognition that these approaches did not actually evolve from the free market perspective. They were, rather, efforts to restructure the role of government to achieve the conditions that would obtain in a functioning market.

The experts represented in this volume discuss the dilemma posed by "competition" in health care delivery from a variety of perspectives, including those of Canada and Great Britain. The major messages of the book are three: that competitive forces can be successfully harnessed to improve performance in health care markets; that competitive mechanisms cannot be relied on to address equity problems; and that elements of competitive reforms are compatible with a wide range of alternative reform schemes.

Understanding the fundamental problems underlying our health care system and the keys to effective reform has always been high on the Institute's own research agenda. We are pleased to publish this contribution by other analysts pursuing the same goal.

William Gorham
President

PREFACE

The Program in Health Economics, Management and Policy (PHEMP) was established at the University of Illinois to respond to issues in one of the largest, most complex and controversial sectors in the United States: health care providers and affiliated industries. The Program is organized under the auspices of the Bureau of Economic and Business Research of the College of Commerce and Business Administration, University of Illinois at Urbana-Champaign and the Institute of Government and Public Affairs, University of Illinois. The purpose of PHEMP is to foster the development of interdisciplinary research, teaching, and service programs that involve issues in health economics and finance, the management of health care providers, and the development and evaluation of health care policies by bringing together people from academia, industry, and the public. The Symposium on Competitive Health Policy Reforms: An Appraisal and Prognostication, where earlier versions of most of the papers included in this volume were first presented, served as the kick-off for PHEMP. The timing of the event has proved to be fortuitous. The symposium took place the week that Harris Wofford defeated his rival in the Pennsylvania primary election, largely on a health reform platform. This volume comes out at a time when serious debates are occurring across the nation on health care policy reforms. We believe this volume makes a useful contribution to this policy debate.

Part One

CONTEXT AND FRAMEWORK

Chapter One

COMPETITIVE REFORMS: CONTEXT AND SCOPE

Richard J. Arnould, Robert F. Rich, and William D. White

As we enter the 1990s, the U.S. health care system faces deepening problems. Simply stated, these problems are cost and access. Expenditures on medical care are exploding, while millions of Americans lack financial access to care. Together, these problems are swiftly eroding the viability of our existing system of health care delivery and finance, generating growing pressure for reform. A central and controversial feature of debate over health care policy since the late 1970s has been proposals for competitive, market-oriented reforms.

While often identified with a "free market" perspective, the essence of competitive proposals for reform has not been to eliminate health care regulation, but to restructure the role of government to harness competitive incentives. Examples include promotion of more aggressive shopping by consumers and payers and limits on anti-competitive actions by providers. Early debate over market-oriented policies was necessarily largely theoretical; past experience offered little basis for evaluating them. We now have over a decade of experimentation with competitive programs behind us. However, competitive reforms are more properly labeled experimental than are broad scale reforms, because their nature differed *within* programs (under Medicare the possibility of enrolling in Health Maintenance Organizations [HMOs] was offered in some markets but not in others): *between* programs (direct contracting was used in some state Medicaid programs but never in Medicare programs); and finally because some of these and other programs were, literally, government sponsored experiments. It is appropriate to ask what we have learned from the competitive reforms of the 1980s that can help guide health care policy in the 1990s and beyond.

In fall 1991, a distinguished group of economists and political scientists gathered at the University of Illinois at Urbana-Champaign to consider this question from their respective disciplinary perspectives. This volume is an outgrowth of that gathering. It has two goals:

first, to help provide a basis for assessing the U.S. experience with competitive reforms in the 1980s; and second, to explore the future of competitive policies based on this experience as well as alternative policies from abroad. This introductory chapter examines the context and scope of competitive reform efforts and briefly considers issues involved in assessing these reforms. We then provide an overview of the remaining chapters in the volume.

COSTS AND ACCESS

Medical care costs have been increasing rapidly in the United States for decades. The cumulative result has been a dramatic rise in the share of national income spent on health care. In 1969, $1 in $14 of national income went to health care (around 7 percent) (National Center for Health Services Statistics 1992). In 1980 health's share of national income was over $1 in $10 (about 10 percent). Currently, expenditures on health care exceed $800 billion, comprising nearly 14 percent of national income, almost $1 in $7 (U.S. Congressional Budget Office 1992). This is the highest percentage of income devoted to medical care of any major industrial nation (National Center for Health Services Statistics 1992). By the year 2000, health's share in the United States is projected to exceed $1 in $6 (18 percent) (United States Congressional Budget Office 1992).

Growth in public spending on health care has been even more dramatic. One quarter of all health care expenditures was paid for by the public sector in 1965. In 1992, government's estimated share was 45 percent. By 2000, the government's share is projected to reach as much as 48 percent (U.S. Congressional Budget Office 1992). This rapid growth has been accompanied by sharp increases in the share of budgets going to health care at the state and federal levels. For example, 11.7 percent of the total federal budget went to health care in 1980 compared to 15.1 percent in 1990. Estimates of health's share of the federal budget in 2000 run as high as 24 percent (Sonnefeld et al. 1991).

Despite our high level of total spending on health care, and in contrast to most other major industrial nations, access to health insurance is far from universal in the United States (see Langwell and Menke, chapter two, this volume). An estimated 33 million Americans, or 13.6 percent of the population, lacked any form of health insurance in 1990. Although virtually all of the elderly are covered under Medicare, among those under age 65, 1 in 7 has no insurance. The percentage without insurance exceeds 25 percent for some groups, such as young adults ages 18 to 24 and very-low-income families (U.S. Congressional Budget Office 1992). Two other significant problems are continuity of coverage (a major issue for Americans changing jobs and/or temporarily unemployed) and "underinsurance" (coverage that is inadequate to cover the costs of a major illness).

There is, moreover, deep personal unease about the future of health care financing. In a recent survey, 82 percent of Americans expressed concern about one or more adverse future developments in their health care coverage, and 61 percent were specifically worried that health insurance would become too expensive to afford (Smith et al. 1992).

ERODING FOUNDATIONS OF U.S. HEALTH CARE SYSTEM

Escalating costs and problems with access are exerting mounting pressure on the existing U.S. system of health care delivery and finance. This system, which evolved in the decades following World War II, has had two goals: to provide affordable health insurance for those who can pay for care; and to assure at least a minimal level of health care for all. The system has been supported by three main pillars (Aaron and Schwartz 1984). The first pillar has been private insurance, which covers the bulk of Americans (some 68 percent), mostly provided through employment-based group plans. The second pillar has been public social insurance, provided primarily through the Medicare and Medicaid entitlement programs, but also through programs such as those of Veterans Affairs (VA), together covering 19 percent of the population. The third pillar has been charity care for the medically indigent by public and private providers, together providing uncompensated care for the 13 percent of Americans without insurance, as well as those with inadequate private (or public) coverage (U.S. Congressional Budget Office 1992). Such charity care is financed partly by direct public and private subsidies, but also through "cost shifting" to paying patients.

The level of care received through these different access routes has varied considerably, and there has always been a problem with individuals slipping though the cracks. Furthermore, sharp controversy has existed over what constitutes an appropriate minimum level of access (i.e., Should access for all be equal to that of private group insurance, or should there be a two-tier system?). However, the existing tripartite public/private, pay/charity system has successfully provided access to affordable coverage for the majority of the population, and, arguably, at least a minimal, if not an ideal, standard of care for all.

Now, in the face of intensifying cost pressures, there are signs of impending collapse. Cost and access problems are interacting in two ways to erode the three pillars on which the system is built: first, access to insurance coverage is growing increasingly difficult; and second, both public and private payers are seeking to trim costs by driving down payment levels to providers.

In the private sector, self-employed individuals and small firms are finding it increasingly difficult to obtain affordable coverage. Moreover, employment has been growing most rapidly in low-wage service occupations where coverage is especially problematic. Sharp reductions in private coverage also loom on the horizon for retirees. Meanwhile, public programs such as Medicaid are seeking to limit the scope of benefits as ways to contain costs.

The weakening of the first two pillars of the system, private and public insurance coverage, puts added stress on the third pillar, uncompensated care. Simultaneously, as reductions in the availability of coverage expand the potential pool of indigent patients, efforts to push down payment rates are limiting providers' ability to cross-subsidize uncompensated care through cost shifting. The health care system is thus experiencing a double squeeze on access as the availability of both affordable insurance coverage and charity care has come under rising pressure.

COST CONTAINMENT AND PUBLIC POLICY

Cost and access concerns have long dominated health care policy debate in the United States. Until the late 1960s, however, the primary focus of public policy efforts was on increasing patients' financial access to care in response to increases in the cost of care; increasing costs were not addressed directly. Thus, private employment-based health insurance was (and continues to be) implicitly subsidized through the tax system, while following World War II, the Hospital Survey and Construction Act of 1946 (Hill-Burton Act) supported new capital investment in the industry. After 1965, Medicare and Medicaid sharply increased financial access for major groups outside the existing system of private, employment based insurance—the elderly, the poor, and the disabled.

By the late 1960s, there was growing recognition that simply expanding financial access was not solving problems with rising costs that underlay access problems, but, indeed, was helping to fuel them. This recognition, coupled with an explosion of public expenditures on health care following the introduction of Medicare and Medicaid, led to the emergence of cost containment as an independent policy objective.

Cost containment as a public policy goal reshaped health care policy debate in two ways. First, it forced policymakers to explicitly address trade-offs between costs and access that have long been implicit in these debates. Second, it focused growing attention on policies to improve efficiency (i.e., the effectiveness with which health resources are used) as a means of improving cost/access trade-offs.

Economists have long argued that health care markets differ from other markets. In particular, health care markets experience "market failure," inefficiently allocating resources because of problems with imperfect information and with incentives associated with traditional cost-based reimbursement. Thus, on the demand side of the market, generous cost-based insurance blunts incentives for consumers to shop competitively for care on a cost basis. At the same time, problems with imperfect information also make it difficult for patients to evaluate the cost and quality of services even if they wished to, encouraging the use of providers as agents to make decisions about care. On the supply side, provider/agents have little incentive to contain costs under cost-based reimbursement because they are paid more the more they produce and are not accountable for total costs. The combined effect of traditional systems of reimbursement and problems with imperfect information is a bias toward "overutilization" of care (i.e., utilization of services whose costs exceed their benefits to consumers). This is reflected not only in the level of use of existing services but also in the rapid introduction and diffusion of costly new technologies (see Arrow 1963; Pauly 1987; Weisbrod 1991).

In the late 1960s and early 1970s, concerns about "overutilization" led to a variety of public-sector regulatory initiatives. The approach underlying these regulatory efforts was to leave the existing system of cost-based reimbursement intact while imposing centralized controls on prices and resource availability. There were three major types of public initiatives. First, price controls were imposed on health services, particularly hospital services, usually based on individual providers' costs of producing services. Second, centralized planning was imposed, for example through Health Service Agencies (HSAs) and Certificate-of-Need (CON) legislation, to regulate capital investments by hospitals. Third, utilization review (UR) was imposed to examine the appropriateness of services, for example by agencies such as Medicare's Professional Services Review Organizations (PSROs).

Concerns about rising costs also existed in the private sector. However, attempts by private payers to curb cost in the 1970s were minimal; basically, private insurers continued to serve as passive claims processors (Havighurst 1988).

The impacts of public regulatory initiatives in the 1970s were mixed. Implementation was not always complete. PSROs, for example, never really got off the ground (Ermann 1988). CON legislation, while generally successfully implemented, by the early 1980s was widely acknowledged as ineffective. Some, but not all, of the rate setting programs apparently helped to check the growth of hospital costs (see Sloan and Steinwald 1980; Phelps 1992). Economists continued to question long run incentives created by cost-based reimbursement schemes, while access problems remained and public and private health care costs continued to rise rapidly.

Proposals for the competitive health care reforms that are the subject of this book began to emerge in the late 1970s. Alain Enthoven's (1978) market oriented "consumer-choice" health plan is an important early example. These proposals did not emerge in isolation, but were part of a larger debate. In the late 1970s options for national reform ranging from tax credits to single payer systems were actively discussed. Competitive proposals may be seen as representing a particular agenda, adding to a list of specific "options" for reform. However, competitive proposals also more broadly represented an alternative perspective on regulatory reform.

Proposals such as Enthoven's (1978) did not eschew regulation per se. Rather they challenged past reliance on centralized controls and argued for the incorporation of market incentives into regulatory systems. It is this broad perspective, rather than any particular agenda, that provides a unifying theme for examining the various competitive reforms considered in this volume.

Competitive reforms occurred within the context of a growing interest in market-oriented approaches across many sectors of the economy in the early 1980s and they were accompanied by a waning interest in comprehensive reform in health care at the national level.

A consequence of the absence of comprehensive national reform was to encourage diversity and the implementation of competitive approaches on a piecemeal, experimental basis.

Market-oriented reforms were accompanied by mounting cost containment efforts in the private sector and the growth of what has come to be know as "managed care." Attempts to restructure the role of government in health care markets to harness competitive incentives and the growth of managed care have been closedly intertwined. But they are by no means synonymous. The term "managed care" is used broadly in this volume to refer to individual payer and provider strategies for cost-containment, in contrast to market level regulatory reforms.

Examples of managed care include Health Maintenance Organizations (HMOs), Preferred Provider Organizations (PPOs) and utilization review (UR) programs seeking variously to "manage" patients' use of selected providers and types of care through direct monitoring and economic incentives and to negotiate favorable payment rates (see chapter five of this volume).

The growth of managed care and expanding private cost containment efforts have lent increased credibility to market-oriented proposals. Conversely, regulatory reform efforts have played a major role in promoting important aspects of managed care. For instance, a central feature of PPOs is the use of economic incentives to "steer" patients to providers. Insurance enabling laws in many states in the past prohibited private insurers from "steering." Regulatory reforms eliminating these provisions helped make possible a rapid growth of PPOs in the late 1980s. In addition, significant aspects of managed care, such as selective contracting, have been incorporated in market oriented reforms of public programs, blurring our distinction between managed care and competitive regulatory reforms. The next section considers the scope of competitive reforms against this background of growing use of managed-care strategies by private (and public) payers.

SCOPE OF COMPETITIVE REFORMS

Proposals for competitive reforms have been diverse and have frequently entailed multiple strategies—for example, simultaneous reforms in the regulation of markets for medical care and health insurance. A useful starting point in examining the scope of competitive reforms is to classify individual strategies in terms of the types of "market failure" problems that they propose to "fix."

Competitive strategies can be divided into four broad types: (1) those that address problems with incentives on the consumer side of markets for health care services; (2) those that address incentive problems on the supply side of markets for health services; (3) those that address performance on the supply side of insurance markets; and (4) those that address problems with the costs of gathering and evaluating information on both the demand and supply sides of health care markets.

Proposals for altering demand-side incentives have focused on issues of consumer cost sharing. The underlying notion has been that if the consumer bears a larger share of the cost of the services used and the cost of his or her insurance, the consumer will be more cost-conscious in shopping for services and/or insurance. Higher deductibles and coinsurance rates and proposals to eliminate the tax deductibility of private health insurance are examples of competitive strategies to address demand-side issues (see Pauly 1988).

Competitive strategies that address the supply side of markets for health services have had two focuses. First, federal antitrust regulation has been used to limit provider collusion (e.g., price fixing) and hospital mergers deemed anticompetitive by the U.S. Department of Justice. Second, strategies have been adopted to restructure markets for provider services to replace "patient-driven" competition with "payer-driven" competition (see chapter four of this volume).

In private markets, payer-driven strategies have centered on shifting the locus of decision making about provider choice from patients to their insurers and facilitating the ability of insurers to shop for services on their enrollees' behalf. An example mentioned earlier is the elimination of restrictions in state insurance enabling laws on the ability of preferred provider organizations (PPOs) to negotiate prices selectively with providers and to use financial incentives to "steer" patients to particular vendors. Strategies that facilitate provider accountability through utilization review are other examples.

In the public sector, the use of competitive bidding and selective contracting by the California Medicaid program is an example of a competitive reform that addresses supply-side elements of market failure. In addition, Medicare's Prospective Payment System (PPS) for paying hospitals and its Resource Based Relative Value System (RBRVS) for paying physicians embody competitive elements. The basic approach in these schemes is, however, very different. Whereas strategies like selective contracting seek to directly harness competitive forces through competitive bidding, rate setting schemes such as the PPS and RBRVS adopt an indirect approach.

The underlying notion in the PPS and RBRVS is that even if direct competition is lacking in health care markets due to monopoly markets, or consumers' failure to shop effectively, or lack of consumer information, market forces can be brought to bear indirectly through a process of "yardstick" competition (Schleifer 1985). Under PPS, payment rates are set prospectively, based on the average costs of producing services nationwide for product lines defined by Diagnosis Related Groups (DRGs). With some adjustments, the amount a hospital is reimbursed for treating a patient is no longer based on the specific hospital's cost. If its treatment costs are less than the DRG payment, the hospital earns a surplus or profit. If its costs are greater a loss is incurred. Hence, incentives are created for hospitals to increase efficiency. Over time, DRG payments (i.e., the payment "yardstick") can be adjusted to reflect increases in average efficiency. "Yardstick" competition is implemented through the adjustment of the prices to "competitive" levels.

Competitive strategies in insurance markets have focused on expanding the range of options available to consumers and on permitting consumers to realize savings from selecting lower-cost options. Here, the underlying notion has been that through appropriate restructuring, "payer-driven" competition in provider markets may in turn be "driven" by competition among insurers for consumers (Enthoven 1978; Pauly et al. 1991).

Informational strategies have evolved significantly over time. Initially, the primary focus was on reducing consumer problems with imperfect information through elimination of restrictions on advertising and public provision of price and quality information (e.g., hospital prices, death rates, etc.) . The basic reasoning was that consumers would be able to shop more effectively for services if information costs were reduced.

Over the past decade, additional concerns have emerged about information on the supply side of the market for services. Early utilization review programs presumed that providers were well informed. The focus was on monitoring providers to prevent deliberate overutilization (or underutilization) of services. Evidence of high levels of variation in practice patterns led to growing concerns about the efficacy with which information is disseminated and used on both the supply side and demand sides of health care markets (see chapter seven of this volume). This concern has resulted in increased efforts to develop practice standards and to use utilization review as a vehicle for informing as well as monitoring providers.

ASSESSING COMPETITIVE REFORMS

Attempts to assess the success or failure of competitive reforms and examine their implications for the future raise several issues. The first concern is the need to determine the criteria to use to evaluate competitive reforms. The second is to assess the degree to which the experiences of the 1980s are applicable to the environment of the 1990s.

The rationale for competitive reforms, as previously mentioned, has been to improve efficiency. One obvious criterion for examining reforms is whether they, in fact, do so. There is also the broader question of the implications of these reforms for cost/access trade-offs. It is from this perspective that competitive reforms have been most controversial.

Implicitly, improving efficiency provides a basis for improving cost-access trade-offs. Thus, reducing "overutilization" should result in lower expenditures on care and/or potentially increase access to services. But restructuring markets along more competitive lines may also directly effect the distribution of services. For example, greater consumer cost sharing may reduce access at the same time that it encourages more prudent use of services. Hence, from a policy perspective, it is important to examine the full implications of competitive reforms for cost/access trade-offs and not just for their impact on efficiency.

It is also important to recognize that embedded in controversies over competitive reforms are longstanding disagreements about appropriate criteria for evaluating performance with respect to access. Thus, to what extent should free exercise of consumer choice about both the type and amount of services be an objective versus equality of access to care for all? Disagreement over these issues is reflected in essays by economists and political scientists in this volume, both in discussions of objectives and in the dimensions of performance to be examined by research.

Finally, on the issue of applicability, the competitive reforms of the 1980s shared a common rationale but no comprehensive plan for implementation. Experimentation occurred and, by default, implementation was piecemeal. Thus, generalization from the results of the experimentation is possible but requires caution. Now for the first time in over a decade, however, large-scale comprehensive health care reform appears a real possibility. This volume explores the relevance of past competitive reforms for the future we are now creating. The following is a brief overview of major points covered in succeeding chapters.

VOLUME OVERVIEW

The remainder of Part One of this volume examines the context of competitive reforms and industrywide trends in costs, expenditures, and access. Chapter two, by Kathryn Langwell and Terri Menke, reviews trends in health care costs and utilization in the 1980s and offers a range of international comparisons. The continued rapid growth of U.S. health care expenditures as a percentage of GDP contrasts sharply with trends in other industrialized countries. This leads Langwell and Menke to raise questions about the efficacy of competitive reforms. However, although macro-level comparisons are useful in describing general trends, the piecemeal implementation of reforms constrains the value of analyzing specific competitive reforms; micro-level analysis of specific measures are thus included in later chapters. Examining quite different issues, Deborah Freund, in chapter three, explores trends in utilization review and the emergence of standardized protocols as both a cost-containment tool and a vehicle for disseminating information to providers.

Part Two of the volume turns to an examination of competitive reforms with a primary focus on the impact of reforms on market performance. In chapter four, David Dranove presents the case for competitive reforms from an economic perspective. He argues that competitive reforms have successfully resulted in a shift from "patient-driven" to "payer-driven" competition in selected provider markets and offers a blueprint for successful reform of insurance markets. He points out, however, that adverse selection may pose continuing problems in these markets and that future reforms need to address cost issues associated with technological change as well as the current organization of the industry.

In chapter five, Richard J. Arnould, Robert F. Rich, William D. White, and Craig Copeland examine the interface between competitive reforms and "managed care." We argue that managed care is most usefully thought of in terms of payer-level strategies to control costs and utilization, through which important dimensions of competitive reforms may be implemented. We examine evidence on the impact of managed care at the level of individual organizations and systemwide. At the organization level, results vary with the form of managed care. Early studies questioned the systemwide impact of managed care. More recent evidence, such as that presented in this volume by Dranove (chapter four), Jack Zwanziger and Glenn A. Melnick (chapter six), and Roger Feldman, Catherine L. Wisner, Bryan Dowd, and Jon B. Christianson (chapter eight), suggests that the impact of managed care in conjunction with competitive reforms has been substantial.

In chapter 6, Zwanziger and Melnick analyze empirical evidence on the impact of competitive reforms in health care markets in California. The state of California has constituted a major experiment with "payer-driven" competition. Zwanziger and Melnick conclude that providers there are responding in ways consistent with economic predictions, greater competition leading to lower costs. They also present evidence suggesting that major problems have not emerged regarding access or quality.

In chapter seven, Charles E. Phelps and Cathleen Mooney explore geographic variations in medical interventions and estimate possible welfare losses resulting for patients. They find that common socioeconomic theory explains only a small part of observed variations. Their analysis also suggests that the welfare losses associated with these variations may be quite large. This raises significant questions about the ability to disseminate and use information on the supply side of health care markets.

In chapter eight, the final chapter of Part Two, Feldman and colleagues examine efforts to use HMOs to introduce competition into Medicare markets as an example of public-sector experimentation with market-oriented reforms. This picture is complicated by complex federal regulations, but the authors' findings suggest that competition has been largely successful in wringing out actual and potential excess HMO profits in Medicare markets.

A central message of Part Two is that there is a growing body of evidence that at a micro level, health care markets can be made to perform much like other markets. Part Three offers views on competitive reforms from an alternative disciplinary perspective in essays from political scientists James A. Morone (chapter nine), Lawrence D. Brown (chapter ten), and Theodore R. Marmor and David A. Boyum (chapter eleven). These discussions highlight both methodological differences between disciplines and differences in the scope of analysis based on varying judgments about appropriate criteria for evaluating these reforms.

In chapter nine, Morone examines the implementation of competitive reforms in the 1980s and the factors contributing to their piecemeal character. He then poses broad questions about the regulatory feasibility of using competitive principles as a basis for comprehensive reform. The thrust of his argument is that the regulatory burdens of successfully operating a system of health care delivery and finance based on "managed competition" may prove far greater than a comparable government-operated single-payer system because of incentives for individual payers to avoid poor risks. To the extent that government's ability to operate a single-payer system has been questioned, Morone suggests its ability to "manage" competition is even more questionable.

In chapter ten, Brown observes that in the course of embracing market principles and competitive reforms, the U.S. health system has become perhaps the most clinically regulated in the world. Brown examines both the makings of this paradox and the possible implications of recent trends for the future. In the process, he raises fundamental questions about appropriate criteria for the design of health care systems. In chapter eleven, the final essay in Part Three, Marmor reviews the political conditions leading up to experiments with competitive reforms in the 1980s. He then explores the prospects for success of further market-oriented reform based on this experience. He concludes that it is critical to look not just at the underlying soundness of proposals for reform but also at their political viability and the likelihood of their successful implementation.

Part Four of this volume examines options for future health care reform. Frank A. Sloan, in chapter twelve, examines the case for future government involvement in health care from the perspective of correcting problems of market failure. One possible underlying cause of failure in health care markets is that economic incentives simply do not function. Sloan argues, however, that the growing body of empirical research suggests that the issue is, instead, one of the markets' appropriateness. Based on past experience, Sloan sees the restructuring of market incentives as a powerful tool for improving efficiency. But he is pessimistic about the extent to which changed incentives can address equity issues. He ends the chapter with a discussion of possible policy options.

Kenneth E. Thorpe, in chapter thirteen, compares U.S. and Canadian experiences with cost containment using data disaggregated at the state/provincial levels. He argues that experiences in California compare favorably with those of a number of Canadian provinces. He contends that a single-payer system is not a necessary condition for checking growth in costs. However, he also argues that his findings point to public involvement in restructuring markets as an important component with implications for national reform.

In chapter fourteen, John Posnett describes experiments with competitive reform within the context of the English National Health Service (NHS). The thrust of these reforms, enacted in 1991, has been to create a quasi-market for care within the NHS. Their full impact remains to be seen. But reflecting on the first year, Posnett suggests that experiences have been largely consistent with economic predictions. In markets that contain multiple providers, reforms resulted in competition. But in markets which were monopolistic in structure, competitive reforms permitted providers to behave as monopolists.

The premise of chapter fifteen, by Mary Ann Baily, is that we lack the resources to provide beneficial medical care on an unlimited basis and hence must ration it. Comparing market and nonmarket mechanisms for doing so, she argues that deep contradictions surround Americans' current expectations from health care policy. Baily states that adopting a competitive approach as a basis for comprehensive reform is one way of resolving these contradictions. However, she suggests that such an approach is not necessarily the one the majority of Americans might favor if ways could be found to ensure efficient public provision at an acceptable level of care with some latitude for choice.

In Part Five, containing the final chapter of this volume, Arnould, Rich, and White assess the "state of the art" in competitive reforms. We conclude that competitive reforms can work. Through appropriate restructuring, major steps can be taken to resolve market "failure" problems in health care markets. Another important message is that there is no single competitive strategy. Rather, the experiments of the 1980s suggest a continuum in the scope and context of possible applications of competitive principles. Finally, the research reported in this volume suggests important caveats. The primary thrust of competitive reforms has been to restructure government regulation of health care markets, not eliminate it. Indeed, some of the essays in this volume suggest some aspects of competitive reforms could potentially increase rather than decrease regulatory demands on the government. At the same time, competitive reforms raise important distributional issues from an equity standpoint. With these lessons in mind, we conclude with a consideration of the possible role of competition-oriented strategies under a range of alternative types of policy scenarios.

References

Aaron, Henry, and William B. Schwartz. 1984. *The Painful Prescription: Rationing Hospital Care.* Washington, D.C.: Brookings Institution.

Arrow, K. 1963. "Uncertainty and the Welfare Economics of Medical Care." *American Economic Review* 53(3): 941–73.

Enthoven, Alain. 1978. "Consumer Choice Health Plans (Parts 1 and 2)." *New England Journal of Medicine* 298 (Part 1, Mar. 23): 650–58; and 298 (Part 2, Mar. 30): 709–720.

Ermann, D. 1988. "Hospital Utilization Review: Past Experience, Future Directions." *Journal of Health Politics, Policy and Law* 13(4): 683–704.

Havighurst, Clark. 1988. "The Questionable Cost-Containment Record of Commercial Health Insurers." In *Health Care in America,* edited by H. E. Frech. San Francisco: Pacific Research Institute for Public Policy.

Hoy, E. W., R. E. Curtis, and T. Rice. 1991. "Change and Growth in Managed Care." *Health Affairs* 10 (Winter): 18–36.

National Center for Health Services Statistics. 1992. *Health United States: 1991.* Hyattsville, MO: U.S. Public Health Service.

Pauly, Mark. 1987. "Lessons from Health Economics: Nonprofit Firms in Medical Markets." *American Economic Review* 77(2): 257–62.

————. 1988. "A Primer on Competition in Medical Markets." *Health Care in America,* edited by H. E. Frech. San Francisco: Pacific Research Institute for Public Policy

Pauly, Mark, Patricia Danzon, Paul Feldstein, and John Hoff. 1991. "A Plan for Responsible National Health Insurance." *Health Affairs* 10(1), Spring: 5–25.

Phelps, Charles E. 1992. *Health Economics.* New York: Harper Collins.

Schleifer, A. 1985. "A Theory of Yardstick Competition." *RAND Journal of Economics* 16(3): 319–27.

Sloan, Frank, and Bruce Steinwald. 1980. "Effects of Regulation on Hospital Costs and Input Use." *Journal of Law and Economics* 23(1): 81–110.

Smith, Mark, Drew E. Altman, Robert Leitman, Thomas W. Maloney, and Humphrey Taylor. 1992. "Taking the Public's Pulse on Health System Reform." *Health Affairs* 11(2): 125–33.

Sonnefeld, T., D. R. Waldo, J. A. Lemieux, and D. R. McKusick. 1991. "Projections of National Health Expenditures through the Year 2000." *Health Care Financing Review* 13(1): 1–28.

U.S. Congressional Budget Office 1991. *Selected Options for Expanding Health Insurance Coverage.* Washington D.C.: Author.

————. 1992. *Projections of National Health Care Expenditures.* Washington D.C.: Author.

Weisbrod, Burton. 1991. "The Health Care Quadrilemma: An Essay on Technological Change, Insurance, Quality of Care, and Cost Containment." *Journal of Economic Literature* 29 (June): 523–52.

Chapter Two

CONTROLLING COSTS OF THE U.S. HEALTH CARE SYSTEM: TRENDS AND PROSPECTS

Kathryn M. Langwell and Terri Menke

The U.S. health care system has many strengths. The substantial resources our nation devotes to medical research, as well as a financing system that encourages the rapid dissemination of new technologies, enable us to provide the highest quality care in the world. The great majority of the population—those with health insurance—have access to care without waiting, and there are few limits on our choices of providers, types of health coverage, and alternatives for treatment.

Yet, over the past two decades, criticism of the health care system has grown. Substantial numbers of people remain without health insurance, either private or public. In addition, health care spending per person is much higher than in other developed countries and is rising faster than the gross national product. Since policies to address one of these problems may cause a worsening of the other, we may anticipate further deterioration of insurance coverage or continued rapid increases in spending for health care.

This chapter discusses trends in spending for health care from 1965 to 1989, with emphasis on implications for developing cost-containment policies. Evidence on the effectiveness of selected strategies for controlling health spending—including approaches for increasing the competitiveness of the market for health services—is reviewed, and the potential for achieving effective cost containment in the United States is considered.

TRENDS IN SPENDING FOR HEALTH CARE

In 1989, the United States spent $604 billion on health care—or about $2,400 per person. The annual rate of increase in real per capita spending between 1980 and 1989 was 4.4 percent. Even if we assume that the annual rate of increase will be considerably lower in the

1990s—for example, 3.3 percent—we would spend almost $3,400 per person (in 1989 dollars) on health care in the year 2000. Moreover, as stated, the United States already spends much more on health than do other developed countries—11.8 percent of gross domestic product in 1989, compared with 8.7 percent in Canada, 8.2 percent in the former West Germany, 6.7 percent in Japan, and 5.8 percent in the United Kingdom (see figure 2.1).

As health spending has risen, its distribution by payer has also changed. The share of personal health spending that householders pay out of pocket declined from 39.5 percent to 23.5 percent between 1970 and 1989. By contrast, private insurance payers and governments have assumed an increasing share. Private insurance accounted for 23.4 percent of health spending in 1970 and 32.6 percent in 1989, while federal, state, and local governments together paid for 34.6 percent of health spending in 1970, before Medicare and Medicaid were enacted, but 40.6 percent in 1989 (see figure 2.2).

Impact on Consumers

Even though out-of-pocket spending has declined as a share of total health expenditures, it remained relatively stable as a percentage of after-tax income—just below 5 percent—over the past two decades (see figure 2.3). Medicare beneficiaries, however, not only spend a much higher proportion of their income on health care than the average household, but they have also seen this proportion rise fairly steadily—from 7.8 percent in 1972–73 to 11.5 percent in 1989.

In fact, a small fraction of the population each year accounts for an exceptionally high proportion of total spending for health care. In 1980, the 50 percent of the population with the lowest health bills accounted for only 2 percent of total health spending, while the 10 percent with the highest expenditures accounted for 75 percent. This pattern holds for the population under age 65, not just for the aged population, and poses a particular problem for design of effective cost-containment strategies.

Impact on Providers

During the decade of the 1980s, much of the effort to control health care costs was focused on hospital spending—both through managed care that attempts to control hospital admissions and lengths of stay

Figure 2.1 HEALTH EXPENDITURES AS PERCENTAGE OF GROSS DOMESTIC
PRODUCT: UNITED STATES AND SELECTED COUNTRIES, 1970–89

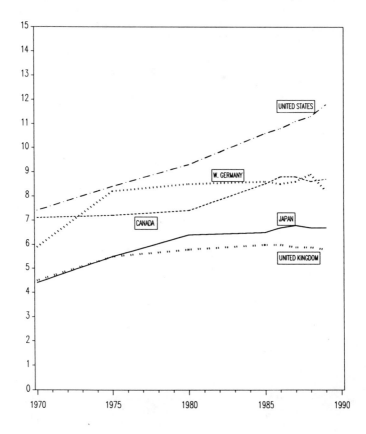

Source: U.S. Congressional Budget Office calculations based on data from Schieber
and Poullier 1991.

Note: Gross domestic product (GDP) equals gross national product less net property
income from abroad. Use of GDP for international comparisons of health spending
eliminates variations arising from differences in the role of foreign transactions in
different economies.

and through Medicare's Prospective Payment System (PPS). Nevertheless, during that period, hospital spending continued to rise. For
example, in 1980, $154 billion (in 1989 dollars) was spent on hospital
care, compared with $233 billion in 1989. This growth was the result

Figure 2.2 DISTRIBUTION OF PERSONAL HEALTH CARE EXPENDITURES IN
THE UNITED STATES BY SOURCE OF PAYMENT, 1965–89

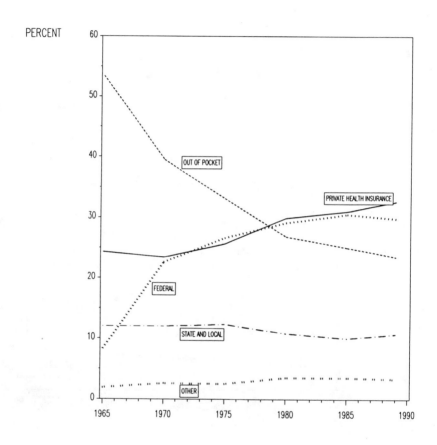

Source: U.S. Congressional Budget Office calculations based on data from Health Care
Financing Administration, Office of the Actuary, 1991.

Notes: Personal health care expenditures equal national health expenditures less
spending for research, construction and administrative costs. "Other" category
includes philanthropy and industrial in-plant spending for health.

of a striking 64 percent increase in real spending per admission
between 1980 and 1989, which more than offset the 13 percent drop
in admissions.

Higher spending for hospital care went hand in hand with higher
hospital margins on total revenues over much of this period.

Figure 2.3 DIRECT OUT-OF-POCKET SPENDING FOR HEALTH IN THE UNITED
STATES AS PERCENTAGE OF AFTER-TAX INCOME

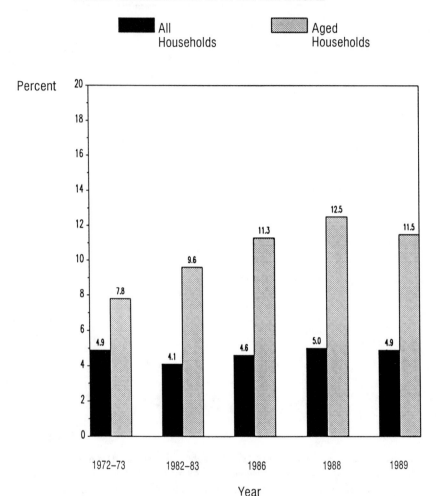

Source: U.S. Congressional Budget Office calculations, using data from Consumer
Expenditure Survey of Bureau of Labor Statistics.

Note: Data are tabulated by age of surveyed person. Aged households are those in
which the surveyed person is age 65 or over. Such households may includes some
individuals under age 65. The decline in direct out-of-pocket spending as a share of
after-tax income for aged households between 1988 and 1989 may be due, in part, to
the Medicare Catastrophic Coverage Act of 1988, which was partially in place in 1989,
but subsequently repealed.

Figure 2.4 U.S. HOSPITAL MARGINS BASED ON TOTAL REVENUES, 1965–90

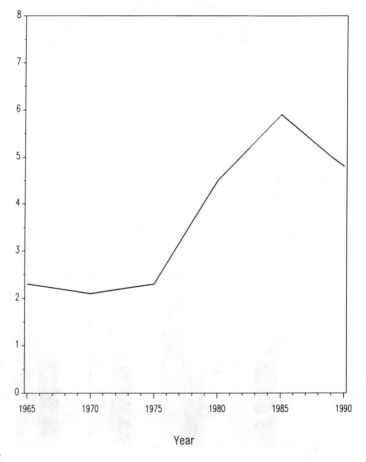

Source: U.S. Congressional Budget Office calculations based on data from American Hospital Association, National Hospital Panel Surveys, 1965–90.

Note: Total margin is defined as the ratio of aggregate total revenues minus aggregate total costs to aggregate total revenues.

Although hospital margins declined from 5.9 percent to 4.8 percent between 1985 and 1990, these margins are still substantially higher than those between 1965 and 1975 (see figure 2.4).

Spending for physicians' services increased even more rapidly than spending for hospital services over the decade of the eighties. In 1980, we spent $268 per person (in 1989 dollars) on physicians' services; by 1989, we were spending $458 per person—a 70 percent increase in real spending per person over a nine-year period.

Physicians' incomes, after expenses, also rose during the 1980s—nearly 20 percent in real terms between 1981 and 1987. U.S. physicians earn considerably more than their colleagues in other countries, both in absolute and relative terms—around 50 percent more than physicians in Canada and West Germany, and nearly three times as much as physicians in the United Kingdom and Japan. Although U.S. physicians earned five times the average compensation of all U.S. workers in 1986, physicians in other countries earned only two to four times the average worker's compensation (see figure 2.5).

Impact on Federal Budget

The rapid growth of national spending for health care, overall and per capita, also has significant implications for the federal budget. In 1970, spending on health constituted 7.1 percent of the federal budget. By 1990, that share had grown to 13.4 percent. Even more disturbing, the U.S. Congressional Budget Office (CBO) is projecting that health care will account for 20.5 percent of federal spending by 1996 (see table 2.1).

MEDICAID

The fastest-growing component of federal health expenditures is the Medicaid program. After taking general inflation into account, the CBO projected that real federal Medicaid expenditures will rise at an average annual rate of 10.5 percent between 1990 and 1996. The corresponding growth rates projected for Medicare and all other federal health expenditures are 6.1 percent and 4.4 percent, respectively. Consequently, Medicaid, which accounted for 24.5 percent of federal health expenditures in 1990, is projected to account for over 30 percent of federal health expenditures by 1996 (see table 2.1). Rising Medicaid expenditures also affect state budgets.

Several factors may have contributed to the recent rapid rise in Medicaid expenditures, including the options and mandates to expand eligibility for pregnant women, infants, children, the elderly, and the disabled, and state initiatives to enroll more eligible people. The recent recession also lead to increases in the eligible population.

Figure 2.5 RATIO OF AVERAGE INCOME OF PHYSICIANS TO AVERAGE
COMPENSATION OF ALL EMPLOYEES: UNITED STATES AND
SELECTED COUNTRIES, 1965–87

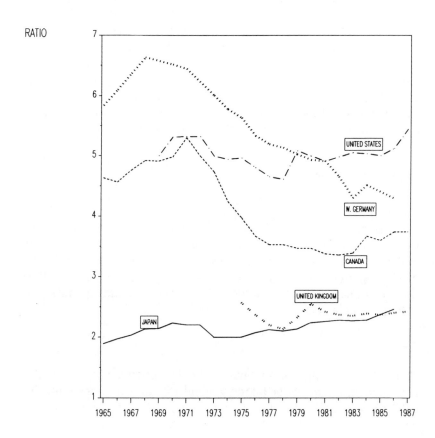

Source: U.S. Congressional Budget Office calculations based on data from Organization
for Economic Cooperation and Development, Health Data File, 1989, as reported in
the *Health Care Financing Review, 1989 Annual Supplement*.

Notes: Data for the following years were missing and values were imputed by the
Congressional Budget Office: 1971, 1976, 1980, and 1984 for the United States; 1966,
1967, 1969, 1970, 1972, and 1973 for West Germany; and 1985 for Japan. Data missing
at the beginning and end of the time periods were not imputed.

   The concepts and methods of estimating used to compile average compensation
per employee are not the same across countries, nor necessarily within each country
over time. Among the issues that cannot be taken fully into account are the regional
or national basis of the estimates, whether or not both salaried and self-employed
professionals are included in the figures, the exact nature of the professional groups
covered, the treatment of part-time workers, and whether or not the income definitions
used reflect income-tax, census, or national-accounts concepts.

Table 2.1 FEDERAL SPENDING ON HEALTH, FISCAL YEARS 1965–96

	1965	1970	1975	1980	1985	1990	1991	1992	1993	1994	1995	1996
In Billions of Dollars												
Total Federal Spending	118.2	195.6	332.3	590.9	946.3	1,251.7	1,337.1	1,503.7	1,501.2	1,533.5	1,533.5	1,604.8
Federal Health Spending:	3.1	13.9	29.5	61.8	108.9	168.0	187.7	216.5	239.5	265.0	293.9	328.4
Medicare	n.a.	6.2	12.9	32.1	65.8	98.1	104.5	117.6	129.1	142.5	158.0	176.6
Medicaid	0.3	2.7	6.8	14.0	22.7	41.1	52.0	61.7	70.7	81.1	92.4	105.3
Veterans Affairs	1.3	1.8	3.7	6.5	9.5	12.1	12.5	13.9	14.4	15.3	16.0	16.9
Other	1.5	3.2	6.1	9.2	10.9	16.6	18.7	23.3	25.3	26.1	27.5	29.6
As Percentage of Total Federal Spending												
Federal Health Spending	2.6	7.1	8.9	10.5	11.5	13.4	14.0	14.4	16.0	17.3	19.2	20.5
As Percentage of Federal Spending on Individual Health Programs[a]												
Federal Health Spending:	100.0	100.0	100.0	100.0	100.0	100.0	100.0	100.0	100.0	100.0	100.0	100.0
Medicare	n.a.	44.6	43.7	51.9	60.4	58.4	55.7	54.3	53.9	53.8	53.8	53.8
Medicaid	9.7	19.4	23.1	22.7	20.8	24.5	27.7	28.5	29.5	30.6	31.4	32.1
Veterans Affairs	41.9	12.9	12.5	10.5	8.7	7.2	6.7	6.4	6.0	5.8	5.4	5.1
Other	48.4	23.0	20.7	14.9	10.0	9.9	10.0	10.8	10.6	9.8	9.4	9.0

Source: U.S. Congressional Budget Office calculations and projections, August 1991.

Notes: Medicare expenditures are shown net of premium income. "Other" includes federal employee and annuitant health benefits, as well as other health spending. "Federal Health Spending" excludes spending for the CHAMPUS program.

The baseline numbers shown do not take into account discretionary caps. A small portion of the increase in the share of federal spending accounted for by health from 1990 to 1996 is the result of substantial spending for deposit insurance in the first years of this period, which will be recovered during the latter years.

[a] May not add to 100.0, because of rounding.

MEDICARE

The annual rate of real growth in Medicare spending per enrollee was also substantially higher than growth rates in health spending per person in the nation throughout the 1970s and in the first half of the 1980s. But Medicare's real growth in spending per enrollee moderated during the last half of the 1980s to 3.2 percent—a growth rate considerably less than the 4.6 percent annual increase in spending per capita that the nation experienced (see figure 2.6).

Most of the decline in growth in the last half of the 1980s stemmed from a substantial drop in the rate of increase in Medicare's spending for hospital services. Although the real rate of growth in physician spending also declined somewhat, it continued at a 7.2 percent annual rate per enrollee during the 1985–89 period compared with 0.5 percent annually for hospital spending (see figure 2.7).

The average annual real rate of growth of per capita spending for hospital care in the nation, however, was essentially stable over the 1980s, even though the rate of growth in Medicare's spending dropped substantially (see figure 2.7). This pattern illustrates a major factor in our inability to gain better control over health spending. In our multiple-payer system, successful efforts by one payer to reduce the growth in costs appear to be offset by more rapid increases in costs for other payers.

EVIDENCE ON COST CONTROL POLICIES

A number of policies have been proposed—and some implemented—with the goal of reducing the level of health spending and/or its rate of growth. They include both competitive and regulatory strategies and are as follows:

Competitive Strategies

□ Policies that increase consumers' price consciousness through greater cost sharing;
□ Policies that attempt to improve the efficiency of the health care market through incentives to choose more economical providers and delivery systems; and
□ Policies to encourage increased competition in the markets for health insurance and health services.

Figure 2.6 AVERAGE ANNUAL GROWTH RATES OF REAL NATIONAL AND
MEDICARE EXPENDITURES FOR HEALTH IN THE UNITED STATES,
TOTAL AND PER CAPITA, 1970–89

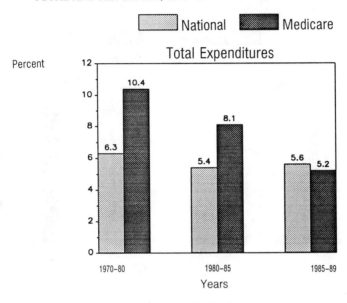

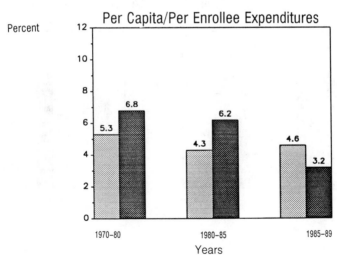

Source: U.S. Congressional Budget Office calculations based on data from Health Care
Financing Administration, Office of the Actuary, 1991.

Note: Real expenditures are calculated using the GNP fixed-weighted deflator.

Figure 2.7 AVERAGE ANNUAL GROWTH RATES OF REAL NATIONAL AND
MEDICARE EXPENDITURES FOR HOSPITAL AND PHYSICIAN
SERVICES IN THE UNITED STATES, TOTAL AND PER CAPITA,
1970–89

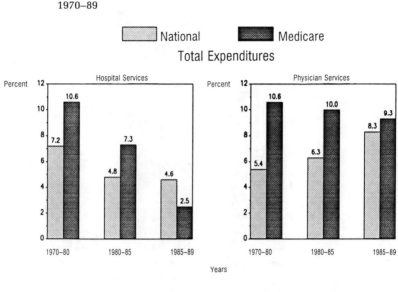

Total Expenditures

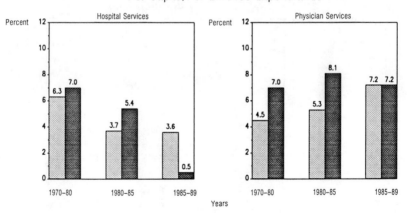

Per Capita/Per Enrollee Expenditures

Source: U.S. Congressional Budget Office calculations based on data from Health Care
Financing Administration, Office of the Actuary, 1991.

Note: Real expenditures are calculated using the GNP fixed-weighted deflator.

Regulatory Strategies

☐ Direct controls over prices;
☐ Controls over capital and technology; and
☐ Expenditure limits.

A decision to adopt effective strategies to control costs would require weighing the advantages of the current system against the disadvantages of a continuing increase in health spending relative to income. This section provides background information on the potential of these various strategies to achieve greater control over health care costs and the trade-offs that each implies.

Competitive Strategies

Controlling costs through strengthening market forces could permit consumers to retain more freedom to choose their individual insurance coverage, treatment modality, and provider. Competitive strategies for controlling health care costs rely upon strengthening the price consciousness of consumers and encouraging competition among insurers and providers.

STRENGTHENING PRICE CONSCIOUSNESS.

Many observers have cited the declining share of costs paid by consumers as a major cause of the rapid increase in spending for health services over the past two decades. The reduction in price consciousness of consumers leads them to purchase both more and higher-quality services. In addition, the modest cost sharing required for some services fails to provide consumers with adequate incentives to search for providers who charge less, and makes them relatively insensitive to price increases.

The most comprehensive study examining the response to varying cost-sharing provisions of insurance plans has been the RAND Health Insurance Experiment (RHIE), conducted during the late 1970s and early 1980s. The study found a significant relationship between the use of medical services and the amount paid out of pocket. Spending per person was 45 percent higher in a plan that required no cost sharing, compared with a plan that required 95 percent cost sharing up to an annual maximum.

Cost sharing did not affect all services and all consumers uniformly, however. For example, although cost sharing caused consumers to initiate fewer contacts with medical providers, there was little difference by plan in the number of services used once a contact was initiated (Manning et al. 1987). Effects also differed by type of service: nearly all the impact of cost sharing occurred in outpatient services, and there were no significant differences in hospital admissions or in spending for hospitalized people enrolled in the different insurance plans. This may, in part, result from the limited maximum out-of-pocket liability.

Cost sharing clearly has the potential to reduce spending for health services. The effects of a substantial increase in cost sharing, however, would vary among types of services and by characteristics of consumers. For example, ambulatory care services would be more responsive than other services to increased cost sharing, with consumers seeking fewer initial visits rather than receiving less-intensive visits. In addition, an across-the-board increase in cost sharing would have more impact on the poor than on other consumers—an outcome that might have adverse consequences for health status and access to care.

Over the 1980s, the share of health expenditures paid out of pocket by consumers in the United States declined from 24 percent to 20 percent. In part, this decline reflects the trade-off that insurers and consumers are making between managed care, which limits consumers' choices of providers and treatments, and lower out-of-pocket costs.

Although cost sharing is an effective strategy for reducing expenditures for health care, most other industrial countries impose only nominal or no cost-sharing requirements. Among countries in the Organization for Economic Cooperation and Development, only France imposes a level of cost sharing approaching that in the United States. In France, out-of-pocket payments comprise 20 percent of national health expenditures. In Canada's health system, provinces may impose user fees or allow providers to bill patients directly for amounts greater than the government-set payments on covered services, but none do so, because federal funding is reduced dollar-for-dollar for such amounts. The exception is that patients can be billed for room and board in long-term care facilities. In the former West Germany, out-of-pocket costs represent 7 percent of total health care expenditures. Patients pay primarily for over-the-counter drugs and to obtain better medical equipment than the sickness funds provide. In Great Britain, patient cost sharing represents about 3 percent of the cost of the National Health Service. Despite the lower levels of cost sharing in these other countries, each spends substantially less per capita on health than does the United States.

MANAGED CARE/UTILIZATION CONTROLS

Managed care has been widely advocated since the early 1970s as a strategy for controlling costs. The principal impetus for managed care is evidence that many of the health services provided to consumers are unnecessary or inappropriate. Managed care is directed toward intervening in the decisions made by care providers to ensure that only appropriate and necessary services are provided and that the services are delivered efficiently. Managed-care organizations base this intervention on information that is not generally available to consumers, and thus act on consumers' behalf.

Recent studies suggest that a high proportion of medical procedures performed are inappropriate. For example, one study of selected medical procedures provided to Medicare beneficiaries in eight states found that 17 percent of coronary angiographies, 32 percent of carotid endarterectomies, and 17 percent of upper gastrointestinal tract endoscopies performed were inappropriate (Chassin et al. 1987). To the extent that these patterns persist across all medical services, the loss to society from provision of unnecessary and inappropriate services may be substantial. Managed care, based on guidelines for appropriate care and employing utilization review and feedback to physicians about appropriate care, is expected to reduce this loss.

In addition, some managed-care organizations negotiate with providers to obtain the lowest price available for services. If this negotiated price leads to higher efficiency in providing services, then managed care may also reduce waste.

During the 1980s, managed care grew dramatically. The number of health maintenance organizations (HMOs) more than doubled after 1980, with nearly 35 million enrollees in 1989. Growth in the population covered by preferred provider organizations (PPOs) was also substantial during the 1980s. In 1984, only 1.3 million households were eligible to use PPOs; by January 1989, over 18 million households were eligible. Overall, about half of the population was subject to some type of managed care by 1989. Blue Cross and Blue Shield plans, for example, reported 52 percent of enrollees in managed care in 1989, including 6 percent in HMOs, 15 percent in PPOs, and 31 percent in managed fee-for-service plans (CBO 1991a).

Evidence for the effectiveness of managed care in reducing expenditures for health care is limited, and much of the research was conducted in HMOs with fully integrated financing and delivery systems that are quite different from the majority of today's managed-care organizations. These types of HMOs have been found to reduce hospital use by about 20 percent, after allowing for differences in the characteristics of HMO enrollees and nonenrollees (Manning et al. 1987). HMOs that are more loosely structured—and PPOs and managed fee-for-service plans—have much less effect on utilization, with research studies reporting impacts ranging from zero to about an 8 percent reduction in utilization (Brown 1987; Feldstein et al. 1988). Managed care's principal impact appears to be on hospital use, with ambulatory care either unaffected or increasing as services are shifted from inpatient settings to outpatient sites.

The actual reduction in spending for health services in managed-care organizations is less than the reduction in use, because the administrative costs of managed care are higher than those of unmanaged insurance plans. In addition, managed care, when it is successful in reducing spending, appears to have a one-time effect with no impact on rates of growth of health spending over time (Newhouse et al. 1985).

Other countries appear to monitor and review providers, rather than individual patients and procedures. In addition, they apply this process uniformly and comprehensively to all physicians in large geographic areas, unlike the uncoordinated review in the United States. For example, all Canadian provinces have systems to monitor physicians' practice patterns. These systems identify physicians who bring patients back when not clearly medically necessary, who order more laboratory work than other physicians, and who deviate in other ways from the expected pattern of care. In British Columbia, for example, physicians with statistical profiles more than two standard deviations from the average for the physicians' peer group (defined by specialty and geographic area) are reviewed by a committee that can recommend penalties for cause.

The former West Germany, like Canada, monitors on a subnational level. Each region maintains a data system that has the capability to create profiles of physicians' practices with respect to services provided, patient mix, and cost profiles of services provided. Physicians whose profiles deviate from those of their peer group may be reviewed by the regional committees and, if warranted, penalized.

In contrast, because comprehensive data on physicians' entire practices are not available to any one insurer in the United States, most utilization review and managed care involve review of specific patients' care and individual treatment decisions—for example, requirements for a second opinion before elective surgery is approved for payment. This type of review requires substantial resources to identify cases for examination and considerable clinical knowledge to assess the appropriateness of the decision. Moreover, the review standards vary from insurer to insurer. A physician may have patients who are subject to utilization review processes that differ greatly, depending on the rules of their particular payer. Further, because providers are subject to varying standards, they may not respond by changing overall practice patterns.

COMPETITION AMONG INSURERS AND PROVIDERS

In the latter half of the 1970s, concerns about the imperfections of the market for health services and the consequences for total and public expenditures for health care produced a number of proposals that were expected, if implemented, to increase competition among insurers and among providers. Increased competition, in turn, was expected to result in downward pressure on prices and greater efficiency in the provision of health services.

In the years since the concept of a competitive strategy for controlling health care costs was introduced, a number of changes have occurred in the market for health services. The growth in the number of HMOs, partly in response to federal law that required employers to offer an HMO option, has increased the competitiveness of the health insurance market. Employees, if they are offered health insurance, typically have more than one plan to choose among, sometimes with financial incentives to choose lower-cost, more efficient insurer-provider arrangements.

Competition among providers of health care has also increased over the past decade. The number of physicians relative to population size has grown, and physicians are now less able to control competition from other providers who perform overlapping services—and who generally charge lower prices for these services than physicians. For instance, optometrists now can perform diagnostic tests for a number of eye diseases and can provide follow-up care for cataract surgery and other medical conditions under the Medicare program. Chiropractors, too, have been successful in many areas in achieving an established role in health care and in obtaining reimbursement from third-party payers. The corporate practice of medicine—in HMOs, urgent care centers, walk-in clinics, and retail store dentistry—is now widespread. Advertising by physicians, hospitals, dentists, and other providers now is an accepted phenomenon that was prohibited by medical ethics and state regulations in the past.

In contrast, competition among health plans has not developed as originally envisioned, with health insurers contracting with a unique set of providers that serve only the insurers' enrollees. Instead, most of the rapid expansion in alternative insurer/delivery systems has occurred through PPOs and loosely structured HMOs that offer overlapping networks of noncompeting providers. To achieve greater competition, some observers argue that it would be necessary to establish discrete, nonoverlapping provider networks so that consumers would be offered choices that are clearly different.

Other proposals to increase the competitiveness of the health care market by expanding the cost consciousness of consumers also have not been implemented. In particular, the share of health insurance premiums paid by employers remains fully untaxed, and without dollar limitations. In fact, the development of cafeteria plans for fringe benefits now permits many employees to pay their own share of the insurance premium and other health expenses from pretax dollars.

Changes in the competitive nature of the market for health services would suggest that, if competition were an effective strategy, the rate of increase in health care costs in the United States would have declined during the 1980s, particularly in areas that have become more highly competitive. Although the number of studies on the impact of competition is limited (see Merrill and McLaughlin 1986; Hadley and Swartz 1989; Robinson and Luft 1989; McLaughlin 1988; and Melnick and Zwanziger 1988), the findings suggest that:

□ Competition can lead to product differentiation and higher costs, rather than to price competition and greater efficiency;
□ A higher HMO market share may not be associated with lower hospital expenses per capita in a market area—even if per capita hospital expenses for HMO members are lower—apparently because of offsetting increases in hospital expenses for patients not enrolled in HMOs; and
□ The effect of competition on hospital costs is uncertain, with some studies suggesting that competition lowers costs and other studies indicating that costs are unaffected or higher in more competitive markets.

Evidence on the growth rate in per capita spending for health care over the past two decades also suggests that the competitive strategy, to the extent it has been attempted, has had, at best, only a small impact on health care costs.

Regulation of the Market for Health Services

Some policymakers have argued that greater regulation of the market for health services is necessary because this market is not functioning properly in the United States; that is, strategies to increase competition among insurers and providers are ineffective or lead to even less-desirable outcomes.

Only some of the generic elements of regulation—control of entry, price regulation, prescription of conditions and quality of services, and the imposition of an obligation to serve all applicants under specified conditions—have been used in the United States in attempts to deal with the entire market for health services. Strategies applied to the market that is publicly financed include direct price controls, the federal health planning and certificate-of-need programs, and the state all-payer rate-setting programs for hospitals. In addition to examining these regulatory policies, this subsection also examines strategies to limit expenditures used in other countries.

PRICE CONTROLS

Expenditures for health care are determined jointly by the quantity and price of services used. Setting limits on prices that may be charged for services is another strategy for cost control that has been implemented in the U.S. health care system. Most recently, during the mid-1980s, the Medicare program imposed a freeze on physicians' fees.

In the absence of any changes in the quantity or mix of services, a reduction in the price of a service should lead to lower total expenditures for that service, but changes in the quantity or mix of services typically do occur. For example:

□ More services may be provided when prices are reduced;
□ Price controls on one type of service create incentives for providers to substitute other services for the controlled one;
□ Price controls implemented for a specific population group (such as Medicaid or Medicare enrollees) may result in higher prices charged to other population groups; and
□ When prices are controlled for only some groups, those groups may have less access to health care than others.

Studies of the effects of fee freezes or controls on physicians' prices indicate that they result in a pronounced volume offset that substantially reduces the anticipated savings from these policies. Under the Economic Stabilization Program (ESP) in the early 1970s, for example, the number of services delivered to Medicare patients increased by about 10 percent during the first year of the ESP and by 8 percent to 15 percent (depending upon physician specialty) during the second year. As a result, the ESP was not effective in curbing increases in Medicare's program costs (Gabel and Rice 1985). Similarly, increases in the volume of physicians' services during the Medicare physician fee freeze in 1984 to 1986 were associated with a continuing rate of increase in per enrollee physician expenditures of 10 percent or more during each of the years that fees were frozen (Mitchell, Wedig, and Cromwell 1988).

Most states limit reimbursement to hospitals and physicians under the Medicaid program. Before the Omnibus Budget Reconciliation Act of 1981, states were required to pay hospitals according to Medicare rules, which relied on a reasonable cost methodology. The 1981 act allowed states to pay hospitals an amount that would cover only the costs of economically and efficiently operated hospitals. The typical Medicaid hospital payment per day is about 80 percent of the average per diem cost for Medicaid patients. Physician reimbursement under Medicaid has also been restricted. In 1989, Medicaid paid physicians about 69 percent of Medicare rates.

There is general agreement that these relatively low reimbursement rates have helped to reduce access to care for Medicaid beneficiaries—but less access does not necessarily mean that total costs are lower. Only about 75 percent of physicians are willing to treat Medicaid patients, whereas nearly all physicians treat Medicare enrollees. For some specialties, the Medicaid participation rates are even lower. For example, one survey showed that only about 55 percent of physicians providing reproductive health services treat Medicaid patients. Some physicians have reported that hospitals have discouraged them from admitting Medicaid patients. Partly as a result of limited access to services in physicians' offices, Medicaid patients seek care in hospital emergency departments and outpatient departments—which typically are more expensive—to a greater extent than patients with other types of health insurance.

The effect of Medicare's Prospective Payment System (PPS) for reimbursing hospitals on spending for hospital services appears to indicate that price controls may be an effective strategy for controlling spending in the hospital sector, particularly in combination with increased monitoring of use. During the first five years of the PPS, the average length of stay for Medicare enrollees declined 10 percent.

Over the same period, partly because of the Medicare hospital utilization review process introduced concurrently with the PPS, admissions of Medicare enrollees fell 12 percent. Despite these dramatic declines in use of services, the average annual rate of increase of real Medicare spending for hospital services per enrollee was about 1.3 percent per year between 1983 and 1988. This was, however, considerably lower than the 6.9 percent annual rate of growth per enrollee between 1980 and 1983 (see CBO 1991b).

Although the Medicare program sets hospital payment levels prospectively and, beginning in 1992, now uses a fee schedule to reimburse physicians, reimbursement of providers in the United States has primarily been based on costs or charges. In addition, every provider has a unique set of charges, and each payer may negotiate a discount on these charges with individual providers. One consequence of these pricing arrangements is that vastly different prices can be paid for the same service, even when that service is performed by the same provider. In addition, substantial administrative costs are incurred by third-party payers and by providers in the effort to keep track of all the different price arrangements.

Some other industrial countries rely on negotiations to establish prices for specific services. In the former West Germany, for example, reimbursement for ambulatory care physician services is fee-for-service, based on a national relative value scale determined through negotiations between national associations of physicians and sickness funds. A conversion factor that translates the relative value scale into monetary terms is negotiated between regional associations of physicians and sickness funds to establish the fee that all physicians in the region will receive from the sickness funds for performing each procedure.

In Canada, physicians are also reimbursed on a fee-for-service basis, with payment rates established by a fee schedule negotiated by the provinces and physicians' associations. Similarly, in France, ambulatory care physicians are reimbursed on a fee-for-service basis, with the fees set by the government. In the former West Germany, France, and Great Britain, physicians who provide services as part of a public hospital episode are paid a salary, rather than a fee-for-service reimbursement.

In some countries, such as Canada and the former West Germany, these price controls for physicians' services are combined with utilization review mechanisms, as described earlier, that permit the identification of physicians and other providers who generate services above the norm. In the former West Germany, the relationship between price and volume is even more direct—when expenditures rise above the negotiated aggregate ceiling, fees paid to physicians are reduced proportionately.

Price controls may have greater potential for reducing health care costs when applied uniformly to the whole health care system, because cost shifting among services and payers is less likely to be an issue. In addition, access to care is not differentially affected if price controls are applied uniformly within a geographic area. Volume responses, however, would still be possible even within a national system of controlled prices, and could be large enough to reduce potential savings substantially, unless price controls were combined with systematic utilization monitoring and review of all providers.

HEALTH PLANNING AND CERTIFICATE-OF-NEED PROGRAMS

The Health Planning and Resource Development Act of 1974 required that all states receiving federal health resources enact certificate-of-need (CON) laws—providing for state review and approval of capital investments of health care institutions. Health planning, particularly with respect to capital investment in hospitals, was believed to be an important component of any effort to control rising health care costs. Research in the 1960s had shown a statistical relationship between the supply of hospital beds and the use of hospital beds. By 1980, all states except Louisiana had enacted CON laws.

Subsequent research on the effectiveness of CON laws consistently found them to be ineffective in restraining per diem, per case, or per capita hospital costs (Brown 1983). At the same time, concern was expressed about the new distortions of the market that were introduced by CON activities, particularly regarding the impact of CON on the potential entry of new competitors into the market (CBO 1991a). Since CON requirements were applied primarily to hospital investment decisions, there also was a perception that the requirements caused investment to shift from hospitals to other health care providers to which CON did not apply.

In 1986, federal CON requirements for states to receive funds were dropped. Supporters of health planning and certificate-of-need requirements, however, suggest that the experience of the 1970s and early 1980s did not reflect the full potential for health planning and CON laws as a strategy for cost containment. They argue that the rulings were applied in most states erratically, resulting in decisions about capital proposals that were inconsistent with cost-conscious expansion of health facilities and orderly adoption of new technologies. In the few states where CON requirements have been linked to hospital rate-setting and to statewide (rather than local area) health planning, proponents of CON laws suggest that they have been much more effective in reducing growth in health care costs.

The governments of many other countries control the capital acquisition of hospitals. In Canada, hospitals must make separate applications to the provincial ministry of health for capital expenditures, including facilities, equipment, and renovations. The provinces provide most of the financing for capital acquisition, but hospitals must provide some funding themselves. Although hospitals may acquire enough private money for capital investments, the provinces can refuse to provide the associated operating costs for capital purchased without provincial approval.

In the former West Germany, hospitals must submit a certificate-of-need application to the state government for capital spending, and state and local governments provide the funding. In France, the investment decisions of public hospitals are publicly controlled. Private facilities can make their own investment decisions, but prices are set by the government, which indirectly influences the amount of capital that can be acquired.

In Great Britain, the central government determines a national budget for capital costs. Decisions about capital acquisition are made at varying geographic levels, depending on the type of expenditure. For example, decisions about facilities or equipment that would be used by patients from a wide area, such as computerized axial tomography (CT) scanners or a new hospital, are made on a regional or national level.

Restrictions on capital acquisition in other countries have led to lower rates of technological diffusion of medical equipment in comparison to the situation in the United States; such restrictions keep costs down but also tend to limit access to new technologies and treatments.

STATE ALL-PAYER RATE-SETTING PROGRAMS

Four states—Maryland, Massachusetts, New Jersey, and New York—implemented statewide all-payer hospital reimbursement systems programs during the 1970s and 1980s. The effectiveness of these all-payer systems has been examined by a number of researchers, nearly all of whom have found that all-payer rate-setting is associated with lower costs, ranging from 2 percent to 13 percent lower, and with reduced rates of increase in hospital costs over time compared with the increases projected in the absence of an all-payer system (Hadley and Swartz 1989; Hadley and Zuckerman 1990; Rosko 1989).

Because of the perception that all-payer systems are an effective mechanism for controlling hospital costs, the federal government has allowed states to receive a waiver from the Medicare PPS if all payers are subject to regulation in the state and if Medicare outlays to hospitals in the state are less than or equal to what the expenditures would have been under the PPS. Initially, 14 states considered adopting all-payer systems in response to the waiver option. Only Maryland, Massachusetts, New Jersey, and New York, however, actually received waivers. New York and Massachusetts withdrew from the Medicare waiver program in 1985 and New Jersey allowed its Medicare waiver to expire in 1989. At present, only Maryland continues to operate an all-payer system that includes Medicare under its rate-setting program.

CONTROLS ON EXPENDITURE LEVELS

Another mechanism for controlling health care costs, within a regulatory framework, is to set prospective limits on spending. This may be done by global budgeting, under which the government sets in advance the operating budget for specific providers—most commonly hospitals—and by expenditure controls, under which the government establishes a target for or imposes a cap on aggregate spending for health services. Expenditure targets have been used in some industrial countries to control spending for physician services. If these targets are exceeded, physicians are paid less per unit in the current period or the future. Expenditure caps are a stronger version of this approach, with spending absolutely limited in the time period to the amount defined by the cap.

The United States, to date, has used neither global budgeting nor expenditure targets for cost containment, at either the federal or state level, with one exception. Under the Omnibus Budget Reconciliation Act of 1989, target rates of increase in physician spending under the Medicare program were implemented beginning in 1990. If the rate of increase in spending exceeds the target, physicians' fees under the Medicare program would be lowered in subsequent years.

Even if Medicare's physician expenditure targets are successful in constraining the rate of increase in that program, the impact they would have on physician spending in the nation is uncertain. The imposition of targets only for Medicare, which accounts for about 30 percent of physicians' revenues, may lead to changes in physicians' practice patterns that result in more—or more costly—services being provided to non-Medicare patients. In other words, Medicare could achieve savings at the expense of other third-party payers and individual consumers with less market power.

Unlike the United States, some other industrial countries have relied extensively on controls on expenditure levels, including national or area expenditure targets, annual global budgets for hospitals, and expenditure targets for physician services. Five of the Canadian provinces have established expenditure targets for physicians' services, which, if exceeded, lead to lower fees in the next round of fee negotiations. Quebec caps physicians' incomes for each quarter; if the income limit is exceeded, payments are greatly reduced during the rest of the quarter.

Operating costs for hospitals in Canada are reimbursed with global annual budgets that are negotiated between the provinces and individual hospitals. These global budgets vary with the number of hospital beds per capita, the ratio of hospital staff to patients, and the amount and types of services provided. Hospital administrators then allocate these funds at their discretion. However, these global budgets have not always been applied as intended, because cost overruns have often been paid by the provinces.

The Canadian federal government has also capped its contribution to national health spending. Until 1977, the federal government matched provincial spending dollar for dollar. Since 1977, the federal government has limited the growth in its contribution to health care costs by using a formula based on growth in the gross national product. Per capita payments are made to the provinces, regardless of the individual province's health care expenditures. This formula has forced the provinces to bear an increasing share of health care costs, since health expenditures have generally grown faster than gross national product.

The West German Health Care Cost Containment Act of 1977 established an annual assembly of health care providers, statutory and commercial insurance carriers, labor unions, employers, and state and local governments, which sets ceilings on the growth rates in national health care spending by type of service. A unique feature of the system is a negotiated expenditure cap that has been applied to spending for ambulatory physician services since 1985. If expenditures rise faster than expected, the fees for physician services are reduced to prevent total spending from exceeding the cap. Such global budgeting is not applied to hospital reimbursement.

Expenditures for hospital services in Britain's National Health Service are fixed by the national government within the framework of the entire government budget. Annual funding is allocated to the regions based on a formula that accounts for population size and the region's mortality rate. If a region overspends its allocation, less money is provided the next year. Generally, a hospital receives the same budget as the previous year, increased by an inflation factor, although individual hospitals can lobby for increased funding. France also instituted global budgeting for hospitals in 1983. Before that, the government reimbursed hospitals with preset per diem rates.

Global budgeting for hospitals' operating costs and expenditure caps for overall spending or specific types of spending could limit the level and rate of growth of health care spending, if they are strictly applied. If a specified amount of money is allocated, and no other source of funding is available, then the health care system is constrained to cost only that amount. Setting the budget or cap, however, requires careful planning to avoid detrimental effects on quality and access to care.

Expenditure targets for physicians' services may also be an effective mechanism for controlling health care costs, particularly if the system responds rapidly when it appears those targets will be exceeded. Immediate reductions in fees, when volume rises, to bring total spending down to the target is one effective approach. Similarly, a target associated with a substantial reduction in fees in future periods, or income limits tied to annual per-physician targets, may be effective. In general, though, expenditure targets are applied less rigidly than expenditure caps, and, therefore, produce less definite outcomes. Some countries also combine expenditure targets with ongoing monitoring of individual physician practice patterns, to reduce the potential for some physicians to increase their incomes at the expense of other physicians under the target.

POTENTIAL TO CONTROL RISING HEALTH CARE COSTS IN THE UNITED STATES

Control of health care costs—through either a one-time drop in spending or a lower rate of increase—is much more difficult to achieve in the United States than in countries that have a coordinated nationwide health care policy or have implemented a national health system. In the United States, attempts to control health spending in one segment of the market or for specific groups of consumers may be successful for the segment of the market affected. The overall impact on health spending may be much less, however, since providers and insurers may compensate for lower revenues from one segment of the market by increasing prices for, or the quantity of services provided to, other groups.

During the 1980s, a number of strategies to control health care costs were implemented. Managed-care and utilization review requirements spread rapidly to encompass a substantial portion of the population. Price controls were imposed on physicians under the Medicare program for an extended period. A new hospital payment system was inaugurated under the Medicare program that created incentives for greater efficiency in the provision of hospital services. Competition among providers and insurers increased. Although it is difficult to quantify the overall effects of each change separately, it appears that these efforts to contain costs have had little impact on total spending. The average annual rate of increase in real health spending per person was 4.3 percent between 1980 and 1985 and 4.6 percent between 1985 and 1989. And the share of gross domestic product (GDP) devoted to health spending rose from 9.2 percent in 1980 to 11.8 percent in 1989 (CBO 1991b).

Evidence from other countries, and from research, suggests that it may be possible to achieve greater control over health care spending in the United States than has been achieved in the past decade (CBO 1991a). Significant changes, however, would be required in the financing and delivery of health care.

If the competitive strategy were to be fully implemented, the current tax subsidy to employment-based health insurance would be reduced or eliminated. Employees then would no longer have incentives to purchase excessive insurance that offers coverage for routine predictable services and low cost sharing. The result would be that consumers would become more price conscious in choosing among providers and alternative treatments. Greater consumer price consciousness would presumably induce insurers to offer leaner packages, with lower premiums, and would encourage providers to become more efficient and price competitive. Adopting the competitive strategy to control health care costs would, however, result in consumers paying more out of pocket for health care and could result in reduced financial access to care for low- and middle-income people, unless government chose to subsidize services for the financially vulnerable.

An alternative strategy for controlling costs would rely on regulation of the health sector. These policies would include: prohibition of first-dollar coverage under insurance policies; mandatory uniform utilization monitoring and review applied to all physicians rather than to individual patients and specific procedures; direct controls over prices that apply to all payers (including a prohibition on additional billing by providers); health planning that establishes capital and technology targets relative to population at national and regional levels and that does not reimburse for services provided through unapproved purchases; and effective national and regional budgets for overall spending or expenditure targets for specific types of spending.

The available evidence suggests that the regulatory approach to controlling health care costs could achieve that goal with greater certainty than the competitive strategy. The regulatory approach, however, could result in more adverse effects on some of the desirable features of our current health care system. In particular, a major restructuring of the present system would probably mean less spent on research and development, longer waiting times for access to new technologies, and limitations on our existing choices of providers, health insurance coverage, and treatment alternatives. Whether these trade-offs are desirable depends upon the priority the nation places on controlling costs versus maintaining other characteristics of the health care system.

In the absence of significant changes in the structure of the health care system—whether through competitive or regulatory strategies—it is unlikely that the United States will be able to achieve much greater control over health care spending than was evident in the 1980s. The consequences of failure to control health costs are many. Health care spending will grow as a share of national income. Workers will receive a greater share of compensation as health insurance coverage, and less in the form of direct wages and salaries. As health care costs continue to rise at a rate that exceeds the rate of increase in wages and salaries, fewer workers—particularly lower-wage workers—will have employment-based group insurance. Governments, both federal and state, will spend a larger amount to maintain current health programs, exerting pressure on government budgets and potentially crowding out funds for other programs in the absence of higher taxation. Finally, failure to control health care spending will make it more difficult to address the other major failure of the health care system—the large and growing number of people in the United States without health insurance coverage.

References

Brown, L. 1983. "Common Sense Meets Implementation: Certificate-of-Need Regulation in the States." *Journal of Health Politics, Policy, and Law* 8(3): 80–94.

Brown, R. 1987. *Biased Selection in Medicare HMOs*. Plainsboro, N.J.: Mathematica Policy Research.

CBO. See U.S. Congressional Budget Office.

Chassin, M., et al. 1987. "Does Inappropriate Use Explain Geographic Variations in the Use of Health Care Services?" *Journal of the American Medical Association* 258(8): 1–5.

Feldstein, P. et al. 1988. "Private Cost Containment: The Effects of Utilization Review Programs on Health Care Use and Expenditures." *New England Journal of Medicine* 318 (20): 1310–1314.

Gabel, J., and T. Rice. 1985. "Reducing Public Expenditures for Physician Services: The Price of Paying Less." *Journal of Health Politics, Policy and Law* 9(4): 595–609.

Hadley, J., and K. Swartz. 1989. "The Impacts on Hospital Costs between 1980 and 1984 of Hospital Rate Regulation, Competition, and Changes in Health Insurance Coverage." *Inquiry* 26(2): 35–47.

Hadley, J., and S. Zuckerman. 1990. *Hospital Cost Variations under PPS: Final Report*. Prepared for Prospective Payment Assessment Commission, Washington, D.C.

Holahan, J., A. Dor, and S. Zuckerman. 1990. "Understanding the Recent Growth in Medicare Physician Expenditures." *Journal of the American Medical Association* 263(12): 1658–61.

Manning, W., et al. 1987. "Health Insurance and the Demand for Medical Care: Evidence from a Randomized Experiment." *American Economic Review* 77(3): 251–73.

McLaughlin, C. 1988. "The Effect of HMOs on Overall Hospital Expenses: Is Anything Left after Correcting for Simultaneity and Selectivity?" *Health Services Research* 23(3): 421–40.

Melnick, G., and J. Zwanziger. 1988. "Hospital Behavior under Competition and Cost Containment Policies." *Journal of the American Medical Association* 260(18): 2669–75.

Merrill, J., and C. McLaughlin. 1986. "Competition versus Regulation: Some Empirical Evidence." *Journal of Health Politics, Policy, and Law* 10(4): 613–23.

Mitchell, J., G. Wedig, and J. Cromwell. 1988. *Impact of the Medicare Fee Freeze on Physician Expenditures and Volume: Final Report*. Baltimore, MD: Health Care Financing Administration.

Newhouse, J., et al. 1985. "Are Fee-for-Service Costs Increasing Faster than HMO Costs?" *Medical Care* 23(3): 960–966.

Robinson, J., and H. Luft. 1988. "Competition, Regulation, and Hospital Costs, 1982–1986." *Journal of the American Medical Association* 260(18): 2676–81.

Rosko, M. 1989. "A Comparison of Hospital Performance under the Partial-Payer Medicare PPS and State All-Payer Rate-Setting Systems." *Inquiry* 26(12): 48–61.

Schieber, G., and J.-P. Poullier. 1991. "International Health Spending: Issues and Trends." *Health Affairs* 10 (Spring).

Schramm, C., S. Renn, and B. Biles. 1986. "Controlling Hospital Cost Inflation: New Perspectives on State Rate Setting." *Health Affairs* 5(3): 22–33.

U.S. Congressional Budget Office. 1991a. *Rising Health Care Costs: Causes, Implications, and Strategies.* Washington, D.C.: Author.

————. 1991b. *Trends in Health Expenditures for Medicare and the Nation.* Washington, D.C.: Author.

Chapter Three

OUTCOMES ASSESSMENT: MARKET INCENTIVES OR REGULATORY FIAT?

Deborah A. Freund

If it is fair to characterize the 1970s as a regulatory era in American health policy and the 1980s as the competitive era, then the 1990s promise to be called the "outcomes assessment era." Clearly, policy-makers and governments investing heavily in the regulatory and competitive initiatives of the 1970s and 1980s could not have foretold the limited success of these cost-containment initiatives. Like certificate-of-need in the 1970s and Diagnosis Related Groups (DRGs) and competition in the 1980s, outcomes research and medical practice guidelines have been sold to Congress as the solutions to our nation's health cost problems. The positive impact of the outcomes movement has been assumed before being empirically tested.

It is unlikely that outcomes research will be the panacea that so many anticipate; yet, the next 5 to 10 years will be decisive. For this movement to be a permanent and important fixture in American society and not just a passing "fad" requires that it meet the expectation of its progenitors by fundamentally changing the ways medicine is practiced and the health care system is organized in the United States. As Paul Ellwood stated in a 1988 Shattuck Lecture at Harvard, "If our logic is sound, the health-outcomes strategy could bring order and predictability to the American Health Care system."

This chapter examines what impact outcomes research may have on the health care delivery system and whether such research is likely to lead to a system that is more regulatory or more "competitive" than at present. The chapter is organized as follows: section two provides background information on outcomes research and its precursors, including the legislation creating the Agency for Health Care Policy and Research (AHCPR); section three describes the most important initiatives comprising the outcomes era—patient outcome research teams (PORTs) and medical practice guidelines; section four addresses whether outcomes research is part of a competitive or a regulatory strategy; and section five assesses the likely impact of outcomes research on the health care delivery system and briefly discusses future research needs.

OUTCOMES RESEARCH AND PRECURSORS

The outcomes era has its roots in several different strands of research, the most important of these being: (1) small-area variations analysis (SAA), brought to the fore primarily by John Wennberg of Dartmouth Medical School; and (2) appropriateness analysis, developed by Robert Brook and colleagues at the University of California, Los Angeles (UCLA) and at the RAND Corporation. The genesis of Wennberg's most recent work on outcomes grew out of the small-area variai tion research that he and Alan Gittelsohn conducted almost 20 years ago. In their landmark study, Wennberg and Gittelsohn (1973) studied the rate of performance of tonsillectomies in small New England counties and found variations that could not be explained by differences in the demographics or other characteristics of the population. Wennberg and colleagues have repeated SAAs for a variety of other measures of use of services or procedures in other locations since 1973 with similar results. For example, Wennberg, Freeman, and Culp (1987) found that the overall use of hospitals by an aged population in East Boston was higher than that by an equivalent population in New Haven after controlling for demographics and other variables; similar results held for the pediatric populations in these areas and in Rochester, N.Y. (Perrin et al. 1989). Since it appeared that health outcomes were the same in Boston and New Haven, the authors were able to simulate, for example, what would happen to expenditures in Boston if New Haven treatment practices were adopted. The estimated savings were on the order of $300 million per year.

Later, yet another Wennberg study documented the differential rate of performance of transurethral resection of the prostate (TURP) in New England communities (Wennberg 1990). Frustrated that the available variables were unable to explain why certain men underwent a TURP and others did not, the emphasis changed from recording variations in the rate at which certain procedures were performed to analyzing the true causes of the variation and implications for health status. There were several questions of interest: What roles did physicians and physician uncertainty play in treatment? What influence did treatment styles have on outcomes of care, including but not limited to mortality, functional status, and quality of life?

What is the role of patient preference? Wennberg's interviews with physicians suggested that some physicians preferred to operate on a prostate earlier in the course of the disease than others. The research team attributed this to a different underlying philosophy about when and why to perform the surgery. Similarly, interviews with patients showed that some preferred to elect the greater nightly discomfort associated with "watchful waiting" than the TURP, an intervention associated with greater relief of symptoms but a higher probability of death or complications.

In further work on treatment variations for benign prostatic hypertrophy, Wennberg, Roos, Sola, et al. (1987) performed cross-national comparisons of death rates following individuals who had their prostates removed by open excision versus a TURP. Cross-national comparisons were necessary because of the infrequent use of open prostatectomy in the United States. Much to the investigators' surprise, the men who had TURPs were more likely to die or to be rehospitalized following surgery than those who had open resections. Studies such as these, which highlighted not only that both individuals and their surgeons had different preferences about when to operate but that different outcomes are associated with different management strategies, served to introduce the world to outcomes assessment/outcomes research. More generically, outcome assessment studies investigate the benefits and costs (risks) of different strategies for managing a chronic or acute illness in order to: (1) provide better information to patients and their physicians on the menu of treatment options from which they may choose and (2) develop practice guidelines to assist such choices. It is hoped that making this information available in a way that patients understand, and sharing information on variations data with physicians, will reduce variation in the rate of performance of the index procedure.

Over much of the same time period, Robert Brook and colleagues at UCLA and RAND developed their pioneering methods of studying the appropriateness of medical care. Rather than focusing on variations in care, the Los Angeles group sought a way to measure the quality and appropriateness of care. Much of Brook's work was motivated by earlier experiences in the 1970s evaluating whether peer review had a positive impact on the quality of care given to Medicare patients (Brook and Williams 1976). Briefly, the UCLA/RAND methodology involves the following steps: (1) A procedure is selected for scientific evaluation and scrutiny; (2) An extensive literature review, aided by a technique such as a meta-analysis, is conducted to identify indications for use of the procedures and the attendant risks, benefits, and apparent effectiveness; (3) A specific list of indications is developed based on the literature, with input from expert physicians in the relevant area. Disease severity and comorbidity are taken into consideration in developing the lists; (4) After the list of indications is completed, an expert panel of nine nationally regarded physicians is appointed to review the results of the literature review and the indications list; (5) The expert panel ranks the indications based on their experience, giving a score of 1 for inappropriate and 9 for the most appropriate indications; (6) Results of the panel's ratings are collated and discussed in a face-to-face meeting with each other, at the end of which the panelists rerate the indications; (7) Retabulation of the results yields a set of medical guidelines with the following scores: 1–3 inappropriate, 4–6 equivocal, 7–9 appropriate (Kahn, Kosekoff, Chassin, et al. 1988). The RAND appropriateness methodology has been applied to a variety of procedures since its first development in 1984, including but not limited to carotid endarterectomy, and coronary artery bypass (Park et al. 1989).

With a strong push from both Dr. Wennberg and key support on Capitol Hill from Senate Majority Leader George Mitchell (D-Me.) and Senator David Durenberger (R-Minn.), and Congressman Willis Gradison (R-Ohio), these two research efforts resulted in authorization in 1986 and appropriation in 1987 for the first outcomes initiative, the Patient Outcomes Assessment Research Program, to be housed in the National Center for Health Services Research. Frustrated by the small size of the appropriation, however, Durenberger and Gradison, aided by a newly interested Congressman Henry Waxman (D-Ca.) and the Association for Health Services Research, led the charge to create the Agency for Health Care Policy and Research (AHCPR). It was envisioned that the AHCPR would be responsible for directing the nation's efforts in outcomes research and that such research, rather than the previous ineffective cost-containment strategies, would go a long way toward redressing our health system's cost and organization problems. Congress mandated that the agency would not only pursue long-term outcomes research activities but would also be responsible for developing medical practice guidelines for up to 20 different problems—the first 3 groups of guidelines were to be generated in the first nine months. In creating a new agency and thereby elevating the importance of its predecessor, the National Center for Health Services Research, rather than placing the outcomes initiative in the Health Care Financing Administration (HCFA), Congress made clear its determination to pursue the science of deriving national guidelines; it feared that the HCFA, in its "desperation" to cut costs, would have subverted the effort.

PORTs AND MEDICAL PRACTICE GUIDELINES

By mid-1991 the AHCPR, with a budget of over $50 million, had funded a large number of diverse grants (Agency for Health Care Policy and Research 1990). The agency also had commissioned an Institute of Medicine report on what constitutes good guidelines (Lohr and Field 1992). Although the AHCPR has a large program of general health services research, by far its largest area of concern is the medical treatment effectiveness program (MEDTEP), which includes the PORT initiative and the practice guidelines development program. In MEDTEP the focus is on *effectiveness* rather than *efficacy*, an important distinction. Efficacy refers to the outcomes of a procedure or medical management done by expert hands on an appropriate patient; generally, efficacy is determined in clinical trials conducted in a very controlled setting in a university teaching center. Effectiveness, on the other hand, refers to the outcomes that result when a procedure is performed in everyday practice (i.e., when it is disseminated into the community). Using an adaptation of the RAND model, the AHCPR currently is developing guidelines in the following areas: benign prostatic hypertrophy, urinary incontinence, pain management, pressure sores, cataracts, sickle cell anemia, depression, HIV, Alzheimer's disease, diabetic retinopathy, congestive heart failure, headache, cerebral vascular disease, low blood pressure, and otitis media. It has also funded PORTs covering the following topics: prostate disease, acute myocardial infarction, ischemic heart disease, low back pain, hip replacement, total knee replacement, cataracts, diabetes, Caesarean section, pediatric gastroenteritis, biliary tract disease, prevention of stroke, community-acquired pneumonia, low birth-weight, and others.

By design, all of the PORTs include a multidisciplinary group of investigators such as epidemiologists, biostatisticians, clinicians, economists, clinical decision analysts/decision scientists, as well as experts in large database manipulations, health status, quality-of-life measurement, and other fields. In addition, where possible, a common set of methodologies is employed starting with those that the Dartmouth and RAND teams found most useful (Salive, Mayfield, and Weissman 1990; Wennberg 1990). A typical PORT initiative includes the following components: (1) meta-analysis or in-depth literature review, (2) analysis of claims, (3) surveys of functional status, (4) clinical decision modeling, (5) and dissemination of findings (Freund et al. 1990). Similarly, each of the panels charged with developing guidelines includes participants from all of the relevant clinical specialties and health professions.

The use of meta-analysis, a scientifically performed literature review, has several purposes in the context of the PORTs (Rosenthal 1991). The first is to search the literature in areas of interest to identify clinical controversies and what is known about treatment effectiveness in these areas. Claims analysis permits illumination of variations in practice styles and outcomes by small areas. Outcomes are constrained to the crude measures available in insurance claims (e.g., death rates, readmissions, charges, etc.). Claims analyses can also be conducted to determine relationships among variables, including outcomes, the number and type of comorbidities, and hospital and demographic characteristics. Typically, small-area characteristics are merged from the area resource file, and hospital characteristics from the American Hospital Association. Although all PORT teams use Medicare claims, some also use claims databases from other countries, Blue Cross/Blue Shield, private insurance companies, and Medicaid.

The surveys that are conducted as part of PORTs are a means to obtain information on functional (both physical and emotional) status and quality of life associated with different treatment options. PORT teams also use surveys to elicit information on various aspects related to utilization that are not available from claims. Other methods are used to collect information on patient utility (preferences toward one outcome versus another), which are used in decision analyses. Based on patient preferences, the relevant outcomes can be entered into a decision analytic model and their probabilities of occurrence estimated from the meta-, claims, or functional status analyses. Dissemination studies investigate how to best inform physicians of optimal treatment guidelines and the effect (if any) on practice and on variation in performance of disseminating treatment guidelines. For the most part, large-scale dissemination to change prevailing practice behavior is beyond the scope of the PORTs; in fact, several teams do not anticipate getting as far as the dissemination studies in their first five years of funding from the AHCPR.

OUTCOMES RESEARCH: COMPETITIVE AND
REGULATORY CONTEXTS

Although we have moved into a time of high investment in outcomes research, vestiges of the 1970s and 1980s remain; health policymakers often are unable to give up older programs. Thus, it is important to ask whether the outcomes movement is inherently competitive and fits into a competitive strategy as explicated by Dranove in the next chapter in this volume, or whether it will be translated into a mandatory review strategy that is regulatory in nature, such as utilization review or professional standards review organizations. Even though the ultimate results of outcomes research will not be known for a number of years, and the supporters of the AHCPR legislation did not view it as part of a greater competitive strategy for health system reform, the answer to this question, as Lawrence Brown (chapter 10, this volume) contends, will either be "it depends" or "it's both." Outcomes research is consistent and can be useful in either context.

Assume for a moment that the desire really is to transform our medical delivery system into a functioning market. Then how does the outcomes movement address many of the fundamental tenents of competition? By "getting rid of flat-of-the-curve medicine" and by providing information and creating consumer choice (Enthoven 1980). Flat-of-the-curve medicine refers to the property of the production function for health when diminishing marginal productivity sets in (e.g., providing more units of medical care does not improve health status or it diminishes it, ceteris paribus). By studying which patients benefit from what procedures and under what circumstances, PORTs can gain a fundamental understanding of what the production function for health looks like for a specific underlying medical condition. Determining what medical practices are on the production function rather than outside it (presumed unattainable for the dollars available) or below it (implying great inefficiency in the use of available resources) and why is critical to making the health care market functional in an economic sense. This topic is addressed in greater detail by Phelps and Mooney in chapter seven of this book.

By the same token, markets do not function if not enough is known about the goods and services supplied and if there is no real fix on consumer preferences. Unlike fruit or wine, whose appearance, color, and taste can be described, good-quality medical care is hard to measure and describe. Investigators who participate in outcomes research attempt to measure quality by studying what interventions are likely to produce better results in patients and with what probability. Similarly, by also studying patients' preferences for certain outcomes versus others and the intensity of these preferences, researchers can begin to provide the ingredients to redress another important aspect of market failure. Thus, if health system reform is structured along market lines, outcomes research will undoubtedly contribute many of the elements necessary to making competition a reality.

Although rarely the focus of policymaking, creating consumer choice is thought by many to be a laudable goal in and of itself (Enthoven 1980). Though there is no evidence that the AHCPR legislation was intended to foster more choice per se, there was the clear notion that information used by physicians to marshal facts on the advantages and disadvantages of treatment options would also be of great use to patients/consumers, thereby allowing consumers to make more informed choices. In the managed competition debate, consumer choice refers to providing the opportunity for the insured individual to select among health plans or insurers who compete for the insured's business. In theory, health plans can compete across many dimensions, including, but not limited to: price, the diversity of practice styles represented by physicians associated with a given health plan, amenities, and location. An element of health plan choice is present if a patient may select a physician who practices a style that maximizes his or her utility (e.g., is more likely to present the options and suggest an intervention that matches the patient's preference for one health state over another, or one level of risk versus another). Forcing or regulating a given intervention on a patient is inconsistent with consumer choice. Little actually is known about the cost-effectiveness of medical and surgical management of patients.

Various methods have been devised to begin to measure quality and appropriateness, yet little emphasis has been placed on understanding how patient preferences for the type of care received fit into the definition of quality. This is a void that the PORTs will begin to fill. The discussion on cost-effectiveness often is based on using an appropriate intervention or achieving a good outcome from a physician's viewpoint without considering whether the intervention fits with the patient's preferences. Unless outcomes information affects the way physicians practice in organized settings, and some demonstrable difference occurs in outcomes that can be communicated to the public in the form of quality-adjusted prices, there is likely to be little, if any, positive impact. The risk that guidelines could be implemented in a way that runs counter to the notion of consumer choice should also be emphasized, however. For instance, if third parties pay only for one treatment regimen in similar patients, then guidelines will have been translated into a regulatory use.

OUTCOMES OF OUTCOME RESEARCH: IMPACT ON CONSUMERS, PHYSICIANS, AND THE DELIVERY SYSTEM

Much information will be derived from the medical practice guidelines development and PORT projects. But what impact are the findings likely to have on the U.S. health care system? This discussion is best organized by focusing on both the demand side of the equation, including agents of consumers, and on the supply side (e.g., the influence on physician behavior). The chapter ends with a discussion of system considerations.

As mentioned previously, each PORT has a subteam working to obtain patient utilities for given health states and to compare how elicited health state preferences may differ between those in a particular health state versus those who are currently healthy. The Dartmouth PORT team headed by Wennberg has shown that small samples of patients have clear preferences for different health states and might make different choices about if and when to undergo surgery if information on the probabilities of various outcomes were presented to them. However, if consumers are to be aided by PORTs, we must first ascertain whether outcome probabilities generated on these small samples are generalizable; and second, we must find a way to make outcomes information accessible to all patients. The Wennberg team has developed a videotape about alternative treatments for prostate disease that can be viewed in a physician's office (Wennberg 1990). The videotape features several patients with benign prostatic hypertrophy and their physicians talking about their experiences. Some of the patients interviewed in the video say they are glad they had the surgery because they no longer experience pain and frustration; others say they regret it. Although interactive video technology is still being evaluated formally, many PORTs are likely to try to make similar videotapes in the areas they are studying. However, it is unknown whether physicians on a large scale will be willing to show videos in their offices, how widely the videos will be circulated, or, most importantly, whether such discussions will be in a form most patients could understand. It is too early to know other approaches PORTs might use to disseminate guidelines to patients or prospective patients, but there is unlikely to be research by characteristics such as income, insurance status, or culture/ethnic status. PORTs are not, in general, testing the relative effectiveness of different dissemination strategies such as individual counseling, brochures, videos, and the like on patient satisfaction or on changing patient behavior.

At present, most PORTs are organized to provide information on the relative effectiveness of alternative treatments, although the more important question regards their cost-effectiveness. The assumption is that patient and physician behavior will change if information on treatment alternatives is provided. However, in the absence of complete information on total and out-of-pocket costs, it is impossible to tell whether consumers will choose the more or less invasive option on average or the less expensive. Thus, it is unclear what will happen to health care costs when outcomes data become available. If information is presented in terms of cost-effectiveness, consumers may change their choices, so long as their insurance plans do not neutralize the relative economic impact.

One possibility is that outcomes information will be less useful to consumers than to their physicians and purchasers of care (their employers). At present, few companies employ benefits managers who are better able to understand the practice of medicine than the employees they insure. A few companies, however, have highly placed medical directors in charge of negotiating payment arrangements with care providers. More companies are likely to follow suit, making such medical directors the direct consumers of outcomes information. Benefit managers can use guidelines from PORTs as a starting point in their own dissemination or price negotiation efforts. Outcomes information will improve if purchasers require it, and the market is more likely to function competitively if the providers from whom they get most of their data voluntarily provide it. Although PORTs will make every attempt to make their studies generalizable to all populations, it is unrealistic to expect this to be the case. Therefore, market-specific outcomes studies will be important, and there is already a trend in this direction. For example, a consortium of the largest corporations in Cleveland has been created and has mandated outcomes studies. It is unclear precisely how the resulting data will be used, but the findings will likely vary from national averages. Conceivably, in addition to disseminating this information to employees, the corporations will also use it to negotiate preferred contracts for certain procedures. The more benefits managers have medical or clinical backgrounds, the more conceivable that they can provide a consultative role in guiding an employee's choice of treatment.

Most PORTs are conducting their claims analyses using information from Medicare, claims that do not represent a cross section of the population. Thus, outcome studies derived from Medicare patients may not apply to others. Medicare beneficiaries also do not have benefits managers to intercede for them. Perhaps this is a role that the American Association of Retired Persons could assume, especially in their function as an underwriter/sponsor of supplementary insurance.

How will patient preferences be translated into the structure of insurance policies or managed-care entities, including health maintenance organizations (HMOs)? It is easy to envision outcomes information creeping into the hands of insurers, even though Congress's intent in creating the AHCPR was not to have outcomes research influence reimbursement practices. The HCFA, and private insurers, will not find outcomes research beneficial and are not likely to adopt the guidelines emanating for AHCPR and other organizations unless they are certain costs will be reduced. Guidelines research cannot promise this result. Similarly, hospitals and other health care providers will be hesitant to adhere voluntarily to the guidelines produced in outcomes research if such guidelines do not add additional profits to the "bottom line" (Nash and Markson 1992).

If PORTs indicate that one management approach is more cost-effective than the next, managed-care entities are likely to adopt guidelines mandating or suggesting its use. These entities are also likely to realign their contracting or reimbursement arrangements as a result. Absent other changes, such use of guidelines presage more regulation, not *less*. Ironically, insurers and managed-care providers will also not only find it easiest to incorporate outcomes information into utilization review but to abuse such information. They are likely to pursue aggressively such information. But outcomes research is meant fundamentally to empower consumers to make a utility-maximizing treatment choice, not to save their insurer money. Purchasers and consumers will be at odds if outcomes information leads the latter to mandate one treatment choice when the former (now armed with information) would make a different selection. In the marketplace, consumers should be able to choose plans that will allow them to effectuate their own choice and not simply steer them to the most cost-effective alternative. Will individuals be willing to pay for such flexibility to choose the more expensive treatment? Will they have the choice? It is likely they will have the choice and will pay more for less restrictive benefits in the privately insured market because health plans will respond, but such a scenario is doubtful under government sponsorship.

An equally salient aim of the outcomes movement is to reduce variation in medical practice through changing provider behavior. How will this be accomplished? Each PORT is charged with conducting small-area analysis (SAA) studies prior to embarking on effectiveness studies. Although many of the original Wennberg studies show that simply feeding back information to physicians reduces variation in the use of procedures, the weight of other literature on how physicians respond to education and feedback is less convincing. Eisenberg (1986) pointed out that educational efforts to provide information on best treatments not only must be evaluated separately from efforts aimed at feeding back information to physicians on their own practices but also should be evaluated seriously. Unfortunately, serious evaluations are scarce, and those that exist do not generalize to community practice, since they report findings of studies conducted in academic medical centers. Existing studies are furthermore limited because they concentrate on the influence of single dimensions of use, not total use. Similarly, Soumerai and Avorn (1984) point out in their studies on pharmaceutical therapy that education is a multidimensional intervention; if printed materials do not work, other strategies used in concert might. However, the precise form of the information is likely to impact upon how providers respond.

Many of the PORTs are extensively using the local medical community and national societies in their dissemination effort, an approach supported by the literature on the role of professional leadership. For example, several studies have found that when information is transmitted by mail, it is not as successful in changing physician behavior as when it is imparted personally (see, for example, Check 1980; and Geertsma, Parker, and Whitbourne 1982). In similar fashion, some PORTs' dissemination activities will involve feedback, a data strategy whose usefulness has been demonstrated. Physician practice patterns do change with feedback, but the duration and extent of the changes depend on the nature of the intervention (Wing, McCarron, and Shaw 1983). Recommendations of expert panels, however, are not widely adopted (Lomas et al. 1989).

As suggested earlier, compared to small-area variations studies, effectiveness studies may to lead to greater intrusiveness in the practice of medicine. Although national policymakers and regulators have been concerned that procedure rates are too high, it is too early to tell what the conclusions of the PORTs will be on this issue—in fact, it could be the reverse; it may be that PORTs will find that more people would benefit from a variety of procedures than are getting them now. Whatever the findings, the challenge will be to disseminate the results of PORT studies to practicing physicians in the hope that the implied behavior change will occur. However, to effect such behavior change will require further research on how best to communicate information to physicians. Similarly, there is the question of which physicians to provide information to. In the knee replacement PORT, for example, the primary focus is on understanding which patients benefit from total knee replacement versus osteotomy, and in what circumstances. Thus, the focus is first on amassing information of use to orthopaedic surgeons. However, such information will not be equally useful to referring physicians such as family physicians and rheumatologists. Thus far, there appears to be no sentiment to tie particular reimbursement practices to the referring physician, although presumably these physicians contribute to variations in rates of performance of procedures and therefore to their outcomes.

Another issue that many PORTs plan to study directly or indirectly is the relationship between outcomes and volume of performance by physician and hospital. Although outcomes by physician and by volume statistics are generally not yet reported, there has been a move toward publicizing outcomes by physicians. For example, the New York State Supreme Court recently ruled that information on patient mortality rates for each heart surgeon in New York be published (Ravo 1991). Demonstrating across a variety of conditions that "practice makes perfect" could have sweeping implications for both the organization of practice as well as reimbursement policy. Third parties and purchasers might negotiate exclusive provider relationships in unprecedented numbers, agreeing to only reimburse providers with the best outcomes. Hospitals might also actively try to woo the services of those physicians identified as best, resulting in the closing of entire services in other hospitals or markets.

In fact, states have begun to show an interest in outcomes research and guidelines. Mark Chassin, one of the original RAND investigators to work on appropriateness and now commissioner of health in New York State, has announced his intention to link reimbursement to hospitals to their outcomes (Lyall 1992).

Health Care Markets

Having discussed how both the demand and supply sides of the market are likely to be affected by outcomes research, it is logical to ask: What will happen to market outcomes and market structures? Zwanziger and Melnick (1988) have shown that as the market has become more competitive, the rise in hospital costs has slowed. It will be interesting to see whether outcomes information is adopted more quickly in relatively more competitive markets. It is important to note here that researchers conducting small-area analysis often define small areas in ways foreign to economists. The "plurality rule" is the most frequently used rule in such analysis (Wennberg and Gittelsohn 1973). Under this rule, providers are assigned to a small area if a plurality of patients in an area get care there. Areas are generally quite small and are not constructed taking into account the number of substitute providers; thus, providers who deliver the same service to similar patients may be assigned to different areas. Although it might be more difficult to measure the denominator necessary for the construction of rates when markets are the measure of small areas used, such economic analysis of small areas is likely to be very useful in further refining estimates of the extent of variation in small-area rates due to physician practice style versus other factors. The failure of most small-area analyses to account for market structure in regression analyses most certainly leads to estimates of variation due to treatment style that are too large.

In the long run, outcomes information may strengthen the market and make it more competitive. But it may also lead to greater regulation. Assuming that outcomes information on the differential performance of providers becomes available, it is likely that consumers truly will be in a better position to make choices about what providers to select, or which health plans to join. Similarly, the treatments they select will be closer to the utility-maximizing ones. Purchasers will also become more informed consumers and are likely to demand that third parties structure insurance arrangements to adhere to the medical practice guidelines, while encouraging patient choice. It is also conceivable that practice guidelines will lead the HCFA and other payors to change the basis of payment to physician packages and to adopt a new system of administered prices for episodes of care. Ultimately, whether the outcomes movement will have a demonstrable impact on the health care economy is pure speculation. Whatever occurs, much more research will be needed to measure the impact. In addition, PORTs are not designed to do any research on the impact of financial incentives on outcomes; as recently pointed out by Pauly (1992), this is yet another topic about which virtually nothing is known.

Note

This chapter is a revised version of a paper originally presented at a symposium on "Competitive Health Policy Reforms: Appraisal and Prognostication," at the University of Illinios at Urbana-Champaign in November 1991. I would like to thank Bernard Friedman and blind reviewers for their comments. Any errors are mine alone.

The research was funded in part by grant HS 06432 from the Agency for Health Care Policy and Research to Indiana University and sub-grantees to establish a Patient Outcome Research Team. Opinions expressed are those of the author and do not necessarily reflect the views of AHCPR.

References

Agency for Health Care Policy and Research. 1990. "Medical Treatment Effectiveness Research." *AHCPR Research Program Note.* U.S. Department of Health and Human Services, Public Health Service, Rockville, Md., March.

Brook, Robert, and Kathleen Williams. 1976. "Evaluation of the New Mexico Peer Review System." *Medical Care* (suppl.) 14(12, December).

Check, W. A. 1980. "How to Affect Antibiotic Prescribing Practices." *Journal of the American Medical Association* 244: 2594–95.

Eisenberg, John. 1986. *Doctors' Decisions and the Cost of Medical Care.* Ann Arbor, Mich.: Health Administration Press.

Ellwood, Paul M. 1988. "Shattuck Lecture—Outcomes Management: A Technology of Patient Experience." *New England Journal of Medicine* 318: 1549–56.

Enthoven, Alain. 1980. *Health Plan: The Only Practical Solution to the Soaring Cost of Medical Care.* Reading, Mass.: Addison Wesley.

Field, M. J., and K. N. Lohr. 1990. *Clinical Practice Guidelines: Directions for a New Program.* Washington, D.C.: National Academy Press.

Freund, D., R. Dittus, J. Fitzgerald, and D. Heck. 1990. *Health Services Research* 25(5): 723–26.

Geertsma, R. H., R. C. Parker, and S. K. Whitbourne. 1982. "How Physicians View the Process of Change in Their Practice Behavior." *Journal of Medical Education* 57: 752–61.

Kahn, K. L., J. Kosecoff, M. R. Chassin, M. F. Flynn, and A. Fink. 1988. "Measuring the Clinical Appropriateness of the Use of a Procedure: Can We Do It?" *Medical Care* 26(4): 415–22.

Lomas, J., G. Anderson, et al. 1989. "Do Practice Guidelines Guide Practice?" *New England Journal of Medicine* 321(19): 1306–11.

Lyall, Sarah. 1992. "Proposal Ties Hospital Reimbursement to Quality of Care." *New York Times.* Dec. 25: B1–2.

Meier, Barry. 1991. "Rx for a System in Crisis." *New York Times Magazine,* Good Health Section. October 6: 18–21.

Nash, D., and L. Markson. 1992. "Managing Outcomes: The Perspectives of the Players." *Frontiers of Health Services Management* 8(2): 3–51.

Park, R., A. Fink, R. Brook, et al. 1989. "Physician Ratings of Appropriate Indications for Three Procedures: Theoretical Indications vs. Indications Used in Practice." *American Journal of Public Health* 79(4): 445–47.

Pauly, Mark V. 1992. "Effectiveness Research and the Impact of Financial Incentives on Outcomes." In *Improving Health Policy and Management: Nine Critical Research Issues for the 1990s,* edited by S. M. Snortell and U. E. Reinhardt. Ann Arbor, Mich.: Health Administration Press.

Perrin, E., C. Homer, D. Berwick, et al. 1989. "Variation in Rates of Hospitalization of Children in Three Urban Communities." *New England Journal of Medicine* 320: 1183–87.

Ravo, Nick. 1991. "State Court Orders Disclosure of Surgeons' Mortality Rates." *The New York Times.* October 23: 3–12.

Rosenthal, Robert. 1991. *Meta Analytic Procedures for Social Research, 2nd ed.* Newbury Park, Calif.: Sage Publication.

Salive, Marcel., J. A. Mayfield, and N. Weissman. 1990. "Patient Outcomes Research Teams and the Agency for Health Care Policy and Research." *Health Services Research* 25(5): 697–705.

Soumerai, S. B., and J. Avorn. 1984. "Efficacy and Cost-Containment in Hospital Pharmacotherapy: State-of-the-Art and Future Directions." *Milbank Memorial Fund Quarterly* 62: 447–74.

Wennberg, J. E. 1990. "On the Status of the Prostate Disease Assessment Team." *Health Services Research* 25(5): 709–15.

Wennberg, J. E., and Alan Gittelsohn. 1973. "Small Area Variations in Health Care Delivery." *Science* 183: 1102–08.

Wennberg, J. E., J. L. Freeman, and W. J. Culp. 1987. "Are Hospital Services Rationed in New Haven or Over-Utilized in Boston?" *Lancet* 1(8543): 1185–89.

Wennberg, J. E., N. Roos, L. Sola, A. Schori, and R. Jaffe. 1987. "Use of Claims Data Systems to Evaluate Health Care Outcomes: Mortality and Reoperation following Prostatectomy." *Journal of the American Medical Association* 257(7): 933–36.

Wennberg, J. E., B. A. Barnes, and M. Zubkoff. 1982. "Professional Uncertainty and the Problem of Supplier-Induced Demand." *Soc. Sci. Med.* 16: 811–24.

Wennberg, J. E., L. Blowers, R. Parker, and A. M. Gittelsohn. 1977. "Changes in Tonsillectomy Rates Associated with Feedback and Review." *Pediatrics* 59: 821–26.

Wing, E. T., M. M. McCarron, and S. Shaw, Jr. 1983. "Ordering of Laboratory Tests in a Teaching Hospital: Can It Be Improved?" *Journal of the American Medical Association* 249: 3076–80.

Zwanziger, Jack, and Glenn Melnick. 1988. "The Effects of Hospital Competition and the Medicare PPS Program on Hospital Cost Behavior in California." *Journal of Health Economics* 7(4): 301–20.

Part Two

COMPETITIVE STRATEGIES AND MANAGED CARE

Chapter Four

THE CASE FOR COMPETITIVE REFORM IN HEALTH CARE

David Dranove

Since the 1970s, a range of policies has sought to foster market competition in the health care sector (e.g., Enthoven and Kronick 1991; Pauly et al. 1992). Competition in the health sector is not new, however. Nor would adoption of a centralized, Canadian-style health insurance plan eliminate competition. Providers will always compete for resources, and the form that competition takes will be a function of the institutional structure. At issue is the degree to which health care institutions can successfully be restructured to fully harness market forces in ways that promote policy objectives while also minimizing costs associated with marketing and, especially, adverse selection. The debate about national health insurance should be cast in these terms.

It is useful to begin by dispensing with the notion that the only way to reduce health care costs is by centralizing financing (i.e., the "Canadian option"). As a benchmark, suppose that a centralized financing scheme can reduce expenditures to $2,500 per capita. The same expenditure level can easily be achieved within a competitive environment. The government could simply provide each American with a $2,500 voucher toward the purchase of health insurance. By disallowing all other forms of payment for health services, health care costs would be held to $2,500 per capita. Rather than offer a fixed benefit package as typifies centralized plans, however, insurers would be free to structure benefit offerings in response to market forces. Thus, they could tailor benefits to the needs of specific consumers, and could innovate to gain a competitive advantage. This scenario is not beyond reality; many health maintenance organizations (HMOs) in the United States rival costs incurred in Canada, while offering a variety of benefits packages.

The main differences between the system just described and the Canadian option are as follows: (1) Private insurers, in conjunction with providers, would develop competing benefits packages, utilization review programs, organizational structures (e.g., HMOs), and so forth, to attract enrollees. As in all other consumer goods markets, there would be associated marketing expenses as providers attempted to inform consumers of their alternatives and to influence their choices. (2) Adverse selection may make it difficult for individuals with high expected costs to obtain coverage commensurate with their needs. This not only raises obvious concerns about equity but may lead to inefficiencies in both insurance and labor markets.

The benefits of competition are many, and are the focus of this chapter. The preceding example does point out several costs associated with competition. The first cost stems from having multiple sellers, resulting in foregone economies of scale—excessive paperwork, the subject of much outcry, is one example. The second cost is associated with marketing expenses. Of course, these two costs are present in virtually all monopolistically competitive markets. (Indeed, a fundamental result from the theory of monopolistic competition is that the equilibrium will entail excessive costs.) For example, advertising dollars as a percentage of sales for consumer goods such as beverages, games and toys, and cosmetics range from 9–14 percent ("Advertising to Sales Ratios, 1989," Advertising Age, Nov. 13, 1989, p. 32). Proffering savings associated with reduced paperwork and marketing expenditures as justifications for a regulated monopoly in health care is logically equivalent to offering the same justification for nationalizing the production of beverages, games and toys, and cosmetics.

The third cost associated with competition is that of selection. This cost is not usually found in other monopolistically competitive markets. It seems, then, that the debate about competition boils down to this: *Do the advantages accruing from private-sector competition in benefits design, utilization review, organizational structure, and so on, outweigh the costs of selection?* If not, can we take steps to minimize the latter while maintaining the former?

The former example also illustrates that the debate about costs should be divorced from the debate about competition. It is trivial to contain expenditures on health care without sacrificing the benefits of competition, and we can do it using the same tax system that will be necessary to support the Canadian or other option. Of course, it may not turn out that consumers really do wish to constrain expenditures. If individuals elect to spend more than $2,500 *out of pocket* for health care, then the argument for cost containment based on some external standard (in this case, $2,500) is specious. A voucher plan along the lines proposed by Enthoven and Kronick (1991) would permit additional spending by those who feel it is worth it. Perhaps individual consumers perceive that health care is more worthwhile than some of our political leaders. (Of course, what consumers want most of all is more health care and lower costs.)[1]

Beyond concerns about adverse selection and the specific cost issues discussed previously, opponents of competition offer two additional critiques. The first is that the theory of competitive markets does not apply to health care, because of the "special nature" of the product. The second is that empirical evidence purportedly shows that competition leads to perversely bad outcomes. In my estimation, these critiques stem from two sources. First, they are based on fundamental misunderstandings about the theory of competition, and second, they draw on empirical work that is outmoded and often incorrect.

The next section seeks to clarify what competition is and how it can work. Section three discusses competition between medical providers. I argue that restructuring of insurance markets has led to a shift from "patient-driven" to "payer-driven" competition between providers, with important resultant benefits in terms of prices and costs. Section four examines competition between different payers for insurance dollars. Theory and evidence about the salutary effects of competition between insurers is mixed, and provides the strongest argument against competitive reforms. Section five concludes by considering what I believe to be the key factor missing in most debates about health care reform—technological change.

WHAT IS COMPETITION?

Competition may be defined as rivalry between sellers for customers or markets. This is typically associated in the public mind specifically with price competition. For example, Benham (1972) showed that price advertising for eyeglasses is associated with lower prices. This narrow view of competition is appropriate when all product attributes other than price are standardized. One can certainly argue that eyeglasses are relatively standard products; hence, it is not surprising to see successful price competition. Many products are not standardized, however, and for these products competition can occur along multiple dimensions. In addition to price, competition may be based on technical quality, amenities, access, and so forth.

Whether based on price and/or other attributes, effective competition has at least three benefits. First, it forces sellers to provide the combination of price and other attributes that best meets the needs of consumers. Second, it forces sellers to find the most efficient way to deliver their goods and services. Third, it provides powerful incentives for innovation. Economists agree that, in general, the vast majority of long-term economic growth is attributable to innovation. It seems important, therefore, to explore the likely importance of innovation in health care markets; I address this later in the chapter.

The benefits of competition are not guaranteed, however. To realize them, conditions must be right. For competition to lead to appropriate levels of a particular product attribute, three conditions must be met. The first condition is that the attribute must be important to buyers. It is sensible to believe that technical quality is important. Price, on the other hand, may be less important, especially if patients are directly choosing providers and have generous insurance. The second condition is that sellers can take action to influence the attribute. In some cases, quality is largely beyond the control of the seller (e.g., flu vaccinations). In other cases, substantial quality differences may arise from differences in training and investments (e.g., open heart surgery [Luft, Hunt, and Maerki, 1987]). The third condition is that consumers must be able to detect differences between sellers. There is little doubt that sellers have substantial quality differences. For example, open heart surgery mortality rates differ by a factor of two or more between competing hospitals (Luft et al. 1987). Unresolved statistical issues currently affect the validity of the data on sellers quality. As the data and our ability to analyze it improves, the ability to identify high-quality sellers will also improve.

It is important to realize that the factors that may inhibit successful competition may also inhibit successful regulation. Indeed, for regulation to dominate competition, one must believe that regulators are better than consumers at dealing with problems of motivation and observation.

The next two sections discuss the two major arenas in which health care competition is played out. The first is competition between health care providers. Both theory and evidence suggest that market forces can lead to healthy competition between providers. The second is competition between health insurers (including vertically integrated "managed-care" systems). Theory and evidence are slightly less optimistic here, identifying a major cost of competition—that associated with adverse selection.

COMPETITION BETWEEN MEDICAL PROVIDERS: FROM PATIENT-DRIVEN TO PAYER-DRIVEN

The usual bemoaning of competition begins with the litany of concerns about the patient/consumer: the patient is not price sensitive; the patient faces high information costs and has questionable ability to use such information; the patient must make choices under duress; and so on. In essence, what is being described here can be called "patient-driven competition" (Dranove, Shanley, and White, forthcoming). Such competition does not necessarily lead to the desirable outcomes associated with competition. Indeed, there may be substantial inefficiencies (e.g., costs may be too high [see Robinson and Luft 1985], and low-quality/high-priced sellers may thrive).

Two problems underlie patient-driven competition. The first is that insured patients are not financially motivated to be good shoppers. The second is that patients lack the informational wherewithal to be good shoppers. The result of patient-driven competition is that those who foot the bill—insurers, employers and ultimately enrollees—are not receiving value for their insurance dollar. Inefficiencies like these create the opportunities for substantial gains from innovation.

This raises the question of why inefficiencies persisted. Perhaps employers and employees never cared enough about health care costs to do anything about them until the 1980s. Another reason is that government regulation impeded the innovations necessary to eliminate them. A key example is provisions in insurance-enabling laws that historically prevented insurers from negotiating discounts with individual providers or attempting to steer enrollees to these providers. Eliminating these restrictions played a major role in the emergence of new organizational forms, particularly preferred provider organizations (PPOs). In the past decade, PPOs and HMOs have shifted the locus of purchasing power from patients to payers, creating what can be called "payer-driven competition."

PPOs and HMOs, which dominate many markets across the nation, (i.e., Chicago, Denver, Los Angeles, Minneapolis and many others), seek to identify a subset of hospitals to be "preferred providers" and to steer patients to those hospitals through financial incentives such as lower copayments. Unlike patients, these payers are both motivated and capable price shoppers. They are motivated because they stand to keep any savings they obtain from lower prices. They are

capable because they enjoy the benefits of large size—they can negotiate on behalf of many patients and can systematically collect both
price and cost data, where costs reflect intensity of resource use.

Given the importance of information in selecting providers, it is
not surprising that the free market has generated a thriving industry
in information. Although it is unrealistic to expect an individual
patient to systematically gather and analyze data on hospital outcomes, large payers may readily do so. A good example is the Pennsylvania Corporate Hospital Quality Project, currently being conducted
by researchers at the University of Pennsylvania. Several large Pennsylvania companies approached these researchers and asked them
to develop hospital quality measures that they could use to help them
identify the best hospitals in the state. Such data will be influential in
future negotiations between payers and hospitals.

The government may also recognize the importance of cost and
quality information under a centralized health insurance plan. However, under competition, there are powerful private incentives to
both obtain and analyze data, as well as to improve upon current
techniques. The best role for the government is to enforce mandatory
information disclosure.

Empirical Evidence on Competition Between Providers

I recently participated in a local radio talk show in which an ardent
defender of Canadian-style health insurance commented that "we
know that competition does not work." That is, contrary to economic
textbook theory, competition in health care leads to higher prices
and higher costs. This is not the only forum where such a view has
been shared. A recent hospital merger in Virginia was approved by
a U.S. District Court judge (*United States versus Carilion Health
System and Community Hospital of Roanoke Valley, 892 F 2nd
1042*) who argued that unlike normal markets where competition
suppresses prices, competition in hospital markets is associated with
higher prices.

Those who share this view need to be updated with the facts. There
was a time under patient-driven competition when both economic
theory and empirical evidence might lead one to conclude that competition was ineffective. Substantial evidence now shows, however,
that where competition is payer-driven, prices are lower and quality
competition is constrained. In addition, where there are more sellers,
payer-driven competition is more effective.

Table 4.1 PRICE INDICES: 1983–88

Fiscal Year	Gross Price Index	Net Price Index
1983	100	100
1984	114.4	113.5
1985	122.3	119.1
1986	N.A.	N.A.
1987	150.3	130.8
1988	169.5	139.9

Source: Dranove et al. (1991).
N.A., data not available.

This subsection summarizes some of my own research on competition, using data from California (Dranove, Shanley, and Simon 1992; Dranove et al. 1991 and forthcoming). I analyze California both because the data are available and because trends in California tend to lead the nation. Related work, with similar conclusions, is summarized in this volume by Zwanziger and Melnick, chapter six.

My research indicates that one reason for the confusion about the effects of competition on price is that many early researchers did not have an appropriate measure of price. Early studies measured price as hospital charges (e.g., Noether 1988). These studies suggested that charges may be the same or higher in competitive markets. But under payer-driven competition, the charge is not the relevant price. What is relevant is what hospitals actually receive.

PPOs and HMOs are able to negotiate deep discounts from charges. I have heard one Los Angeles area hospital administrator quip that there are no private payers left in his market who pay charges. Price analyses based on list prices are meaningless. My own work evaluating hospital price inflation in California offers some insight into the magnitude of discounting. The standard measure of hospital price inflation is the Bureau of Labor Statistics (BLS) hospital price index. This index, based on charges, indicates that hospital prices have risen dramatically nationwide. My colleagues and I calculated a comparable index using charges for private California hospitals, as well as estimated discounted prices. Price indices are reported in table 4.1, and corresponding inflation rates are reported in table 4.2. These tables indicate the prevalence of discounting.

Discounting is having an effect on hospital profitability. Dranove et al. (forthcoming) estimate that hospital profit margins for privately insured inpatients fell from 20 percent to 10 percent between 1983 and 1988. Consistent with the idea that competition is the driving

Table 4.2   ANNUALIZED INFLATION RATES

Fiscal Years	Gross Price Inflation	Net Price Inflation
1984	14.4	13.5
1985	6.9	4.9
1986–1987	10.9	4.8
1988	12.7	7.0
1984–1987	11.1	7.0

Source: Dranove et al. (1991).

factor, they found that margins varied directly with the degree of market concentration. At the same time, price competition is leading to a reduction in the acquisition of costly medical technologies. Zwanziger and Melnick (1988) found that the so-called medical arms race had disappeared as long ago as 1985. Dranove et al. (1992) questioned the validity of evidence linking competition to excess medical technology in earlier years. Rather, they suggested that provision of technology is driven by economies of scale and scope, as would be expected under competitive pressures. Consistent with this view, both Zwanziger and Melnick (chapter six, this volume) and Thorpe (chapter thirteen, this volume) suggest that overall expenditures in California are rising less rapidly than elsewhere in the nation.

The bottom line that emerges from this literature is that under payer-driven competition, provider behavior closely approximates that associated with textbook markets. That is, competition leads to lower prices and lower costs. Based on these criteria, the evidence is that competition works.

What about Monopoly Providers?

A textbook source of market failure is monopoly. Local monopolies exist in all service markets with a geographical emphasis, including health care, ice cream vending, and dry cleaning. In industries other than health care, public policy has concluded that the cost of correcting these local monopolies exceeds the benefits of any major industry restructuring. This does not completely rule out the use of public policy to address monopoly issues. For example, the U.S. Department of Justice in recent years has vigorously enforced antitrust laws, particularly when local providers have taken steps to thwart competition (e.g., the Maricopa case (*Arizona v. Maricopa Medical Society 457 U.S. 332* [1982]) where physicians in the Phoenix, Arizona, area created a cartel for the purposes of fixing prices). As another example, the Health Care Financing Administration's Medicare Prospective Payment System uses a yardstick competition scheme to promote cost-consciousness among all hospitals, regardless of local market structure (Shleifer 1985).

Future Prospects for Competition between Providers

There is little question that markets for hospital services under payer-driven competition will have attractive features. Purchasers will be armed with ever-improving data on costs and quality, enabling them to secure better deals. Moreover, to more effectively compete, providers will be forced to produce more efficiently. Indeed, Dranove and Satterthwaite's (1992) model of price and quality competition under uncertainty suggests that the benefits of improving provider efficiency may vastly exceed the benefits to individual purchasers of obtaining better deals. Since improved performance may take more time than improved shopping, we likely have not yet begun to realize the full benefits of competition between hospitals.

Competition between other medical providers is more problematic. The key to successful competition is motivated and informed purchasers. Purchasers are only now beginning to gather systematic data on individual physician performance. The continuing growth of group practices may be viewed as a response to the demands of purchasers for performance information—it is probably cheaper to monitor groups than individuals. Admittedly, debate about the validity of performance data, often contentious when it comes to hospitals, may be even more so for physicians. This is because there will be less data per physician, introducing unwanted noise, and because medical services tend to be more idiosyncratic than basic hospital services. Of course, this also poses a problem for any public-sector effort to monitor physician performance. The advantage to the private sector is that there will likely emerge a multiplicity of approaches, with market forces singling out the best of these for long-term survival. Similar issues exist in areas such as long-term care, where again the public sector has also made little progress.

COMPETITION BETWEEN INSURERS

The previous section suggested that purchasers of medical care are able to bring about the benefits of competition between providers of care. But does competition work for the purchasers as well? Will the price of insurance approximate the cost? Will efficient insurance plans drive out inefficient insurance plans?

Insurance is not a commodity product—insurance plans differ according to coverage, monitoring and payments to physicians, administrative expense, and so on. Because of these differences, competition offers two benefits. First, individuals can tailor their insurance plan to their own tastes—those who are willing to bear more risk can assume higher copayments, for example. This is a fundamental characteristic of other insurance markets (e.g., automobile and home insurance) and should not be a source of concern in health insurance.

More importantly, the heterogeneity of the insurance product encourages insurers to innovate in ways that have the potential to generate substantial consumer benefits—consider the emergence of Kaiser Permanente in the 1940s and utilization review in the 1980s. Competition forces insurers to develop new and better insurance products. It often takes time to determine if new products are beneficial (e.g., utilization review), but in the long run the market serves as a powerful sorting mechanism.

As with provider markets, the key to success of insurance markets is the presence of motivated and capable purchasers. In the case of insurance, the purchasers are ultimately individuals. As Feldman and colleagues discuss in chapter 8 of this book, insurance purchasers are highly motivated, exhibiting large price sensitivity to different insurance plans. Ironically, it is government regulation that prevents even greater price sensitivity. Due to a historical accident associated with World War II price controls, employer-provided health insurance is a tax-exempt fringe benefit. For a typical worker, this has the effect of reducing the effective price difference between any two insurance plans by 25 percent to 35 percent.

Although our health care system would like to encourage workers to fully consider the cost of their insurance coverage, our tax system encourages the choice of more expensive plans.[2] This is like trying to encourage the purchase of fuel-efficient automobiles by providing a tax break for the purchase of gas guzzlers. Although it is hard to get economists to agree on many things, there is virtual unanimity that any efforts to improve the performance of the health insurance market must begin with reform of the tax code.

Some suggest that reforming the tax code would eliminate the provision of insurance. Perhaps these individuals are implying that insurance really is not worth much and that we only purchase it because of the tax subsidy. What is almost certainly true is that elimination of the tax subsidy would affect availability of insurance for workers in low-wage jobs. But this argues for targeted subsidies, rather than across-the-board tax breaks, as promoted by Pauly and colleagues (1992) and Enthoven and Kronick (1991). At a minimum, a ceiling on the tax exemption is called for, so that the most expensive plans do not receive the biggest subsidies.

For insurance markets to work, it is also necessary to have well-informed consumers. As a recent issue of Consumer Reports ("Are HMOs the Answer?" August, 1992) indicates, it is possible to obtain and provide systematic data on important dimensions of performance for insurers. Many large firms employ benefits specialists who are well-schooled in insurance alternatives. These firms work with their employees to identify the most desirable insurance plans in their markets. Presumably, if changes in tax laws cause consumers to have an even greater financial stake in their insurance, they will become even better shoppers. This will encourage providers to be even more efficient.

Even if consumers on the whole are well-informed about their insurance alternatives, questions remain regarding the ability of certain groups, such as the elderly, to make informed choices. Enthoven and Kronick (1991) have proposed that one role for government is to evaluate insurance plans prior to marketing and to ensure minimum-benefit packages. Private-sector firms analogous to Consumer Reports can be invaluable sources of information. This would be a natural area for a group like the Association for the Advancement of Retired Persons, as well as local community groups.

It should be emphasized here that the consumer groups perceived to be most at risk in competitive insurance markets are not guaranteed fair treatment under regulatory schemes. Interstate and intrastate differences in funding exist in almost all government programs, including Medicaid, public health, schools, transportation, and so on. The advantage of competition is that it promotes generation of information and enables all groups to leverage their purchasing power to obtain better products.

It is apparent that two necessary conditions for insurance markets to succeed—motivated and capable consumers—are within our grasp. But are they sufficient for insurance markets to succeed? As Rothschild and Stiglitz (1976) have demonstrated, a major remaining threat to insurance markets is adverse selection. Adverse selection is a threat whenever three conditions exist among buyers: (1) there is more than one type of buyer (e.g., high and low risks for needing medical care); (2) the seller's profits depend on the specific buyer with whom he or she transacts; and (3) the seller cannot distinguish buyers prior to fixing the terms of the deal.[3]

Under these conditions, a number of inefficiencies and inequities may emerge. First, as suggested by Rothschild and Stiglitz (1976), low-risk buyers may be unable to obtain complete insurance at fair prices, because sellers are afraid that such plans will attract high-risk buyers. Second, high risks will have to pay commensurately high premiums, raising issues of fairness, especially when the risks are through no fault of their own (e.g., genetic defects). Third, and perhaps most troubling, sellers may take steps to attract low risks and avoid high risks. In this sense, competition between insurers may be "selection-based," rather than based on efficiency or innovation.

Selection-based competition is not necessarily a problem. It may simply entail different risk groups paying different premiums, with equity being the only concern. However, it is clear that a number of inefficiencies can emerge from selection-based competition. For example, most insurers require waiting periods and exclude coverage of preexisting conditions on new enrollees. This reduces labor mobility, with consequent efficiency effects. As a second example, insurers usually extract price premiums from individual enrollees and small groups—the reasons include the law of large numbers, suspicions regarding hiring practices, and agency problems within insurance firms. This tilts product and service markets toward large groups.

Although this chapter's discussion has dismissed most of the problems allegedly associated with competition, I cannot dismiss the problems related to selection-based competition. My conversations with major insurers indicate that identification of good-risk groups is an important competitive tool. Although deemed essential by insurers, this practice may prove to be their undoing, since it argues for the elimination of private insurance markets.

The magnitude of any efficiency loss resulting from selection-based competition is debatable. Pauly and colleagues (1992) indicated that less than 1 percent of the population is currently uninsurable, in the sense that they are unable to obtain insurance through a group and unable, due to severe preexisting conditions, to obtain individual insurance. These individuals could be covered in a tax-subsidized high-risk pool to maintain equity without intruding into an otherwise well-functioning private insurance market. A key policy question is the extent to which the fraction of uninsurables would increase if we exposed the elderly and the poor to selection competition. Another major question is the magnitude of reductions in labor mobility or in small-firm effectiveness resulting from selection-based competition. Evidence on the costs of selection-based competition is needed, and I hope it will rapidly emerge.

Restatement of the Problem

The health care product is a tremendously difficult one to allocate efficiently. Providers have varying degrees of skill, and consumers are poorly informed about alternatives. Insurance opens the door to moral hazard. *These problems are fundamental to both private- and public-sector approaches.* Based on the findings of the past decade, the private sector seems well-equipped to deal with most of these problems. Innovative financing mechanisms are encouraging providers to produce efficiently and to charge prices in line with costs (see, for example, Zwanziger and Melnick 1988, and Dranove, Shanley and White 1993). Insurers are developing a variety of tools to evaluate performance and encourage further improvements in quality. Not all of these developments will lower costs—the market will determine if any cost-containment activities are worth the associated reductions in access and quality. Given motivated and informed buyers, however, we may be hopeful that the developments that emerge will be the ones most desired by consumers.

The cost of competition is largely associated with selection. Some current estimates suggest that selection factors will seriously affect a small minority of consumers (see Pauly et. al 1992). We need to be more confident in this assessment before discounting selection effects altogether.

A regulated approach will lock in existing institutional arrangements, with all future changes dictated by the whims of the political process, rather than by the demands of consumers. As with all other goods, if we move to a regulated environment, we will never know what we lost, because the greatest gains from competition result from innovation. Advances in treatment protocols, organizational structure, evaluation of providers and technologies, and so forth, can enormously improve the performance of the health care system. Competition is the best way to encourage these advances.

WHAT ABOUT TECHNOLOGY?

I conclude this essay by focusing attention away from the traditional areas of debate on health care reform and toward the issue of technological change. Economists generally agree that the major determinant of changes in costs and quality of medical care is technological change. This is true in competitive markets and regulated markets alike. Any fundamental reform of a health care system must address the issue of technological change. Weisbrod (1991) has argued that the forms of technological change that have emerged in the past 40 years have been largely cost enhancing. (Needless to say, there have been enormous improvements in quality as well.) He submits that this need not have been the case. Consider the treatment of polio. One hundred years ago, this treatment was costless—there was no established therapy. Treatment 50 years ago involved the iron lung—it was better than previous treatment but also very costly. Today, the Salk vaccine renders "treatment" at minimal cost and maximum effectiveness. Weisbrod has suggested that nowadays we have too many "iron lung" treatments and not enough "Salk vaccine" treatments.

Weisbrod also contends that the emergence of high-cost treatments was a direct result of incentives in the regulatory and competitive environments. Cost-based reimbursement in the United States made cost-enhancing technologies easy to sell to providers. At the same time, a hostile tort system discouraged the development and testing of vaccines. During the 1980s, both public and private payers have moved away from cost-based reimbursement. Medicare's prospective payment system discourages adoption of technologies that increase inpatient costs. For example, contrast the slow diffusion of the positron emission tomography (PET) scanner with the high rates of diffusion of earlier scanning technologies. As another example, HMOs have become increasingly reluctant to include costly technologies such as organ transplants in their covered benefits. The upshot is that suppliers of new technologies are no longer assured an eager market for their cost-enhancing innovations. In spite of recent changes in public and private reimbursement in the United States, we continue to lead the world in the rate of adoption of new medical technology, and we continue to experience higher costs as a result.[4]

Any restructuring of our health care system must necessarily affect the incentives to adopt and develop new technologies. Whether this leads to an appropriate level of technology depends largely on whether consumers can rationally evaluate choices. If individual consumers on their own or through their insurer/employer agents cannot do this, then it is debatable whether their government agents can do any better. On the other hand, even if consumers can rationally evaluate choices, it is entirely possible that the resulting rate of adoption of technology and associated costs may be perceived as too high from a societal perspective. This may simply be a result of unrealistic consumer expectations, or it may instead reflect an unwillingness on the part of individuals to offer equal access to technology for all.

Restructuring health care in the ways discussed here will affect providers' incentives to adopt new technologies, and will thereby indirectly affect the forms of technological innovation offered by basic researchers. However, one can question whether this alone is sufficient to redirect the course of basic research toward finding cost-reducing technologies. I offer two approaches directly targeting basic research that may lead much more rapidly to reductions in medical costs. Ironically, both approaches involve public funding. However, it is recognized by even ardent free-market economists that basic research is an appropriate domain for public funding.

First, the National Institutes of Health (Bethesda, Md.) could require a "cost-impact statement" with each grant application, giving preferential treatment to proposals with the potential to lower cost, ceteris paribus. Second, the Health Care Financing Administration and the private insurance industry could offer substantial prizes each year to the innovation or innovations with the greatest potential to lower health care costs without compromising quality. Other industrial nations could do the same.

The idea of using prizes to promote innovation is not new. The modern clock was a response to a prize offered by Great Britain's Royal Academy of Science, which was seeking a reliable method of determining longitude at sea. More recently, the refrigeration industry offered a multimillion dollar prize for a substitute for fluorocarbons. Were the health care industry to offer a prize of comparable size, in terms of percentage of overall industry budget, it would be in the billions of dollars. That would garner the attention of more than a few researchers!

Notes

1. Concerns about consumer sovereignty may be offset by concerns about equity—is it fair to allow wealthy people to obtain more generous health insurance coverage? This concern can be addressed by enforcing a common standard for the voucher.

2. Elimination of the tax deductibility of health insurance would easily fund the expansion of coverage to the 37 million uninsured.

3. An analogous set of circumstances may exist for buyers facing diverse sellers, such as in used-car markets.

4. Many new innovations would not be profitable were it not for profits earned in the United States. The United States has become the testing ground for new technologies, with other countries picking and choosing among them. Any radical restructuring of our health care system could significantly affect diffusion of new technology worldwide.

References

Benham, L. 1972. "The Effect of Advertising on the Price of Eyeglasses." *Journal of Law and Economics* 15(2): 337–52.

Dranove, D., and M. Satterthwaite. 1992. "Monopolistic Competition When Price and Quality are Imperfectly Observable." *RAND Journal of Economics* 23(4): 518–534.

Dranove, D., M. Shanley, and C. Simon. 1992. "Is Hospital Competition Wasteful?" *RAND Journal of Economics* 23(2): 247–62.

Dranove, D., M. Shanley, and W. White. 1991. "How Fast Are Hospital Prices Really Rising?" *Medical Care* 29(8): 690–696.

————. Forthcoming. "Price and Concentration in Local Hospital Markets: The Switch from Patient-Driven to Payer-Driven Competition." *Journal of Law and Economics.*

Enthoven, A., and R. Kronick. 1991. "Universal Health Insurance through Incentives Reform." *Journal of the American Medical Association* 265(19): 2532–36.

Kaplan, R. 1992. "Utility Assessment for Estimating Quality Adjusted Life Years." University of California, San Diego. Photocopy.

Luft, H., et al. 1987. "The Volume-Outcome Relationship: Practice-Makes-Perfect or Selective-Referral-Patterns?" *Health Services Research* 22(2): 159–82.

Noether, Monica. 1988. "Competition Among Hospitals." *Journal of Health Economics* 7: 259–84.

Pauly, M., et al. 1992. *Responsible National Health Insurance.* Washington, D.C.: Enterprise Institute.

Robinson, J., and H. Luft. 1985. "The Impact of Hospital Market Structure on Patient Volume, Average Length of Stay, and the Cost of Care." *Journal of Health Economics* 4(4): 333–56.

Rothschild, M., and J. Stiglitz. 1976. "Equilibrium in Competitive Insurance Markets: An Essay on the Economics of Imperfect Information." *Quarterly Journal of Economics* 90: 629–650.

Shleifer, A. 1985. "A Theory of Yardstick Competition," *RAND Journal of Economics* 16(3): 319–27.

Weisbrod, B. 1991. "The Health Care Quadrilemma: An Essay on Technological Change, Insurance, Quality of Care, and Cost Containment." *Journal of Economic Literature* 29(2): 523–52.

Zwanziger, J., and G. Melnick. 1988. "The Effects of Hospital Competition and the Medicare PPS Program on Hospital Cost Behavior in California." *Journal of Health Economics* 7: 301–20.

Chapter Five

THE ROLE OF MANAGED CARE IN COMPETITIVE POLICY REFORMS

Richard J. Arnould, Robert F. Rich, William D. White,
and Craig Copeland

Competitive reforms in health care have been closely linked to managed-care mechanisms, the latter of which grew rapidly during the 1980s. However, the tendency to use the terminology of competitive reforms interchangeably with that of managed care has led to confusion. The two terms are not synonymous, even though there is much overlap in their policies and actions. This chapter has three goals: first, to clarify the relationship between competitive reforms and managed care; second, to identify and describe the scope of efforts to implement managed-care strategies; and third, to survey evidence on the impact of managed care in the context of competitive reforms.

COMPETITIVE REFORMS AND MANAGED-CARE SYSTEMS

The term competitive has been used to describe many of the health policy reforms of the 1980s. Chapter one defined competitive reforms as efforts to improve the performance of health care markets by harnessing competitive forces. In this broad context, competitive reforms have attempted to reduce the level of "market failure" either through direct imposition of competition or through the use of competition incentives or indirectly through application of "yardstick competition." These have been achieved in some cases through the restructuring of the regulatory framework. Attempts have thus been made to increase reliance on market mechanisms. Yet misconceptions persist because high levels of regulation continue to exist even with the competitive reforms. The key to understanding the nature of the reforms is that regulation has been restructured but not eliminated.

Consider three types of policies: those involving purely market outcomes, those involving purely regulatory outcomes, and those involving a combination of market and regulatory outcomes. Clearly in the United States the number of examples of purely market and purely regulatory policies is limited, with the largest number of policies in health care markets combining both market and regulated outcomes.

Systems of managed care are mechanisms through which policy reforms—some competitive and some regulatory—may be implemented. They can be used as mechanisms to enhance competitive policy reforms, or purely regulatory policies, or socialized policies. For this reason, some types of managed care have been instituted in Great Britain's socialized National Health Service as well as in the market-oriented U.S. system.

Managed-care systems may be viewed as payer-level mechanisms to contain costs by actively "managing" the patient's choice of provider and care. Langwell and Menke (chapter two, this volume) state that "managed care is directed toward intervening in the decisions made by care providers to ensure that only appropriate and necessary services are provided and that these services are provided efficiently." Thus, whereas interventions could be in the form of efficient incentive contracts, they could also be in the form of regulatory or administrative directives such as utilization review and protocols. Lynn (1991) has contended that the essence of managed care is providers becoming accountable to patients and their employer/insurance representatives for the quality, effectiveness, and cost of care.

The basic features of managed care are: (1) contractual arrangements with selected providers to furnish a comprehensive set of health care services to members, usually at negotiated prices; (2) significant financial incentives to "steer" patients toward providers and procedures within the plan; and (3) ongoing accountability of providers for their clinical and financial performance through formal quality assurance and utilization review.[1] All forms of managed-care plans do not display all of these characteristics. Moreover, similar characteristics receive differing emphasis across various plans. The importance of the extent of this definition is that it permits the concepts of managed care to be fit within the conceptual framework of competitive reforms and regulatory reforms referred to earlier in this chapter.

If managed-care systems are viewed as the operators through which many types of policy reform can be initiated, the confusion over the differences between managed care and competitive reforms is reduced. Clearly, not all strategies associated with managed care necessarily entail either competition or decreased regulation. Neither do all policies seeking to promote market competition necessarily entail managed care. PPS (Prospective Payment System) is one such example. Through "yardstick competition" it attempts to harness competitive forces. But it is not managed care as defined here. Thus, as stated at the outset, although closely related, managed care and competitive reforms are not one and the same. A review of developments in managed care is valuable in evaluating the context and impact of competitive reforms.

The next section examines organizational innovations that have emerged to implement managed-care strategies for selective contracting and "steering," and for establishing provider accountability. Developments have occurred in private health care markets where there is a clear separation between implementation of these strategies and the competitive reforms facilitating their implementation. An example of this is the voluntary entrepreneurial establishment of preferred provider organizations (PPOs) versus regulatory changes in insurance-enabling laws making PPOs possible, as discussed by Dranove in chapter 4 of this volume. Public-sector initiatives have also occurred where elements of managed care have been directly carried out by government as mechanisms for competitive reforms. The use of selective contracting by some state Medicaid programs is an example.

Managed-Care Systems and Other Competitive Reforms

Health maintenance organizations (HMOs), PPOs, competitive bidding arrangements, direct negotiations, selective contracting, and utilization review (UR) all entail elements of managed care. HMOs and PPOs satisfy the previously mentioned first two features of managed care (contractual arrangements with providers to provide comprehensive health care to members plus financial incentives to steer patients toward providers in the plan). All of the above mechanisms are intended to satisfy the third feature (increasing the accountability of providers with respect to decisions that affect clinical and financial performance). HMOs and PPOs accounted for 25.3 percent of group health premiums in 1990, a hefty increase from 0.3 percent in 1982 (Hoy et al. 1991). In 1990, 90 percent of all employees covered by employer-based private health insurance plans contained some characteristic of managed care (Hoy et al. 1991). During the rapid growth of the 1980s, the character and details of many of the traditional forms of managed care changed, blurring the distinction between them. These changes generate problems when categorizing and evaluating plans. Past literature has focused mostly on performance of general categories of managed-care plans, such as HMOs compared to traditional fee-for-service (FFS) medicine. Clearly, research must turn to characteristics of plans such as financial incentives, organizational characteristics, and ownership, to develop more consistent and meaningful results. Research reported elsewhere in this book (namely, by Freund in chapter three, Dranove in chapter four, Zwanziger and Melnick in chapter six and Feldman and colleagues in chapter eight) reflects moves in this direction. However, much of the results of analysis of managed care systems reported in the following overview is plagued with this shortcoming.

HEALTH MAINTENANCE ORGANIZATIONS

Current concepts of managed care generally have their origins in prepaid group practices (PGPs) of the 1930s and 1940s, (e.g., Kaiser-Permanente Health Plan, Health Insurance Plan of New York, and Group Health Cooperative of Puget Sound). These PGPs later became known as HMOs, a change in emphasis to gain support or alleviate resistance from physicians who opposed the notion of prepaid plans. The HMO Act of 1973 (Public Law 93-222) provided financial support to develop new HMOs and mandated that employers also provide an HMO alternative if they offered a traditional health plan and if a federally qualified HMO operated in the area (Langwell 1990). The purpose of the Act was to stimulate development of HMOs.[2]

Luft (1981) includes the following five points in his description of HMOs:

1. The HMO assumes a contractual responsibility to provide or assure the delivery of a stated range of health services. This includes at least ambulatory care and inpatient hospital services.
2. The HMO serves a population defined by enrollment in the plan.
3. Subscriber enrollment is voluntary.
4. The consumer pays a fixed annual or monthly payment that is independent of the use of services. (This does not exclude the possibility for some minor charges related to utilization).
5. The HMO assumes at least part of the financial risk or gain in the provision of services.

Later a sixth point was added—that the enrollee is restricted to providers specified by the HMO.

HMOs are organized according to four models—staff, group, Independent Practice Association, and network, as described by Christianson et al. (1991):

Staff: An HMO that delivers services through a group practice to provide health services to HMO members (generally restricted to serving HMO enrollees); physicians are salaried members of the staff of the HMO.

Group: An HMO that contracts with a group practice to provide health services (these groups generally provide services to non-HMO enrollees); the group usually is compensated on a capitation basis.

Independent Practice Association (IPA): An HMO that contracts with an association of physicians from various settings (some solo practitioners, some small groups) to provide health services; physicians are usually reimbursed on a contractually negotiated fee-for-service basis, although the IPA may be capitated.

Network: An HMO that contracts with two or more group practices or IPAs, or any combination thereof to provide health services; the groups are usually compensated on a capitation basis.

The predominant types of early HMOs were staff and group models. However, the IPA models experienced tremendous growth in the 1980s, becoming the predominant model. In 1990, IPAs had 67.1 percent of HMO enrollees, group and network HMOs followed with 21.6 percent of the HMO enrollees, while staff HMOs had only 8.8 percent (Hoy et al. 1991).

In recent years the distinction between the models has blurred. A mixed model has emerged with any combination of at least two of the four HMO models, but usually involves an HMO that adds an IPA component to its staff or group model. In addition, HMOs have developed an option to allow enrollees to use providers outside the HMO provider network at less than the usual 100 percent copayment. This open-ended arrangement combats the criticism that HMO enrollees lack choice.

As previously indicated, HMOs grew dramatically in the 1980s. In 1982 there were 265 HMOs with 10.8 million enrollees (U.S. Congressional Budget Office 1990); by 1990 there were 652 HMOs with 34.6 million enrollees (Hoy et al. 1991), a 246 percent increase in plans and a 221 percent increase in enrollment. HMOs with an open-ended option grew by 46 percent in 1989 and 48 percent in 1990, a period in which closed-paneled HMOs grew by less than 5 percent per year. The percentage of HMO enrollees in open-ended HMOs was only 3 percent in 1990 (Hoy et al. 1991).

PREFERRED PROVIDER ORGANIZATIONS

The generic definition of the PPO is a contract between various health care providers, mostly hospitals and physicians, and buyers of health care services. The contracts generally specify that providers supply services on a discounted fee-for-service basis subject to complying with the PPO's utilization review program. Discounts often are based on volume of business. Buyers generally are self-insured employers or commercial insurers. Plan subscribers are permitted to choose providers outside the PPO, but are given economic incentives such as reduced cost-sharing or expanded benefits to use the preferred providers (Gabel et al. 1986). PPOs focus on a variety of cost-control options such as prospective price discounts, utilization review, or "steering" enrollees to providers that have proven to be cost-efficient. Confusion has once again been added to the nomenclature with the evolution of a new PPO model, the exclusive provider organization (EPO). This model resembles an HMO because enrollees are locked into using the network of providers (Marion Merrell Dow 1991).

The growth in PPOs has been substantial. Enrollment has grown from 1.3 million individuals eligible to use PPOs in December 1984 to 38.1 million individuals eligible in 1990 (Marion Merrell Dow 1991).

BLENDED PLANS

A recent innovation in managed care, the point-of-service plan, combines characteristics of HMOs and PPOs to balance demands for cost containment and freedom of choice. These plans contract with a network of providers. Generally the enrollee is required to choose a primary care physician "gatekeeper" who is under contract with the HMO and who controls specialty referrals. Copayments are minimal if the enrollee chooses a referral physician in the HMO's network. However, unlike traditional HMOs, the enrollee is not required to pay a 100 percent copayment if he or she chooses an out-of-plan provider after receiving prior approval from the gatekeeper physician. Providers generally are reimbursed on either a capitation or fee-for-service basis. Moreover, there are financial incentives that discourage out-of-network utilization (Hoy et al. 1991; U.S. Congressional Budget Office 1992).

Another development, the previously mentioned open-ended HMO, is even less distinct from a standard PPO when the open-ended HMO pays physicians on a discounted fee-for-service basis. There are open-ended HMOs for which enrollees are allowed to receive some amount of reimbursement when using out-of-network providers. Providers for these plans usually are subject to utilization review programs.

The point-of-service and open-ended plans frequently are located close along a continuum of managed fee-for-service plans. These latter plans often are used by indemnity insurance plans and are properly identified as managed-care plans because of their stipulation that providers and enrollees be subject to constraints such as various forms of utilization review and second opinions.

In reality, the distinction between plan types has become so hazy that it probably is not an exaggeration to say that the present categorization of any plan depends on whether the original plan was a more discrete HMO or PPO.

UTILIZATION REVIEW

As mentioned previously, the third feature of managed care is to shift the locus of accountability. Under traditional insurance arrangements, providers typically were accountable for their clinical and financial performance only to individual patients; third-party payers played a passive role. HMOs and PPOs are mechanisms that provide competitive financial incentives for providers and patients to reduce market failure resulting from inefficient production and consumption of health care services. Since the early 1980s, third-party payers have become increasingly active in directly monitoring providers' performance and in using results of monitoring as a basis for determining reimbursement. Direct monitoring or intervention usually assumes some form of utilization review (UR). Financial incentives are less-direct methods of influencing provider behavior. UR is commonly used in conjunction with financial incentives of HMOs and PPOs. The growth in the use of UR by traditional insurance plans has been significant. In 1991, conventional insurance plans that used some form of UR covered 91.9 percent of those covered by conventional insurance plans, compared to 43.8 percent in 1987 (Hoy et al. 1991).

Unlike the financial incentives discussed so far, UR is an administrative mandate, not an incentive. UR programs, developed to determine if specific health care services are medically necessary and are provided at an appropriate level of intensity and cost, fall into two classifications (Ermann 1988). Service-specific UR, the first classification, applies to particular services such as nonemergency services and ancillary services. The most widely used service-specific program is for second opinions for nonemergency surgery. Second-opinion surgery programs may reduce costs by preventing unnecessary surgery; they may alter a physician's practice patterns by exposing him or her to peer review; and they may emphasize seeking the most economical setting for the surgery (Ermann 1988).

The other major classification of utilization review programs is according to the timing of the review relative to the delivery of services. Preadmission reviews evaluate the necessity of a potential hospital admission, much like second opinions. Concurrent reviews determine if a patient continues to need current levels of inpatient care. Retrospective reviews identify questionable patterns of care and at times result in refusal to cover excessive charges. Retrospective review also is being used to profile physicians. Outlier physicians usually are informed of their deviation from plan norms and/or dropped from the plan (De Lissovoy et al. 1987).

FINANCIAL INCENTIVES

A variety of financial or competitive incentives is embedded in the contractual arrangements between providers, third parties and patients. A brief description of these arrangements is provided here along with their intended effects. We concentrate on the arrangements used in the more traditional forms of HMOs and on plan-provider contract characteristics to limit the nature of principal-agent relationships to the plan-principal and physician-agent. Some financial incentives, such as copayments, may be directed more toward enrollee behavior, and utilization review may fall somewhere in between, affecting both patient and provider behavior.

Clearly, the contractual arrangement with the provider physician[3] must be among the most prominent of the financial arrangements. One well-developed theorem of principal-agent asymmetric information models is that the agent's behavior may become compatible with the objectives of the principal if the agent's risk and reward are dependent upon the outcomes (Sappington 1991). This applies to managed-care systems in the following manner. The insurer usually cannot observe the "level of sickness" nor the effort required from the physician agent to treat the patient. The traditional fee-for-service (FFS) contract increases the reward to the agent without increasing the risk borne by the agent, and reduces the reward to the principal if more services are delivered by the agent. Figure 5.1 simplifies this by assuming that there are two possible patient states: the patient is either slightly ill or very sick. Profits of the insurer are measured on

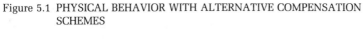

Figure 5.1 PHYSICAL BEHAVIOR WITH ALTERNATIVE COMPENSATION
SCHEMES

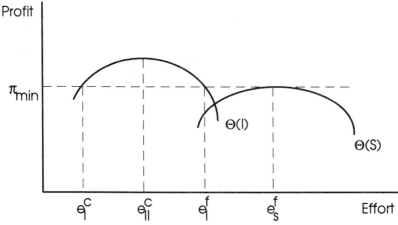

the vertical scale and the level of effort expended by the physician
is measured on the horizontal scale. The profit stream to the insurer
is represented by $\Theta(I)$ if the patient is only slightly ill and $\Theta(S)$ if
the patient is very sick. In each state, I or S, profits to the insurer
increase as the physician expends more effort, e.g., office visits or
lab tests, but ultimately a level of effort is achieved beyond which
profits to the insurer decline. Possibly in this range the cost of the
efforts exceeds the benefits to the patient. If the patient is only slightly
ill, the insurer's profit is maximized with the physician expending
effort level e_{II}^c; if the patient is seriously ill, the insurer profits are
maximized at effort level e_s^f. The two profit functions are constructed
such that the insurer potentially can earn more profits if the patient
is only slightly ill; thus $\Theta(I)$ has a higher maximum than does $\Theta(S)$.
Also, assume there is some form of quality assurance such that effort
levels of the physician must be at a level that maintains profits at or
above Π_{min} regardless of the state of illness of the patient. Finally,
for simplicity, the profit function for the serious ill, $\Theta(S)$, has been
constructed so that the physician has only one effort level that satisfies the minimum level of quality, Π_{min}, regardless of reward incentives.

The FFS physician earns more income by expending more efforts.
Therefore, the FFS physician will provide effort level e_s^f in the sickness case and e_i^f in the minor illness care. He or she has no choice
in the former situation, but maximizes his or her income by providing

more services than are consistent with profit maximization of the principal in the latter. (Note that the same result will occur with discounted FFS, so long as the marginal revenue from effort exceeds the physician's marginal disutility from effort).

Now assume the physician's reward is a salary(S) or capitation(C) and does not depend on effort, so long as minimum quality levels are achieved. S and C payment schemes have emerged that place providers at varying levels of risk for the cost of producing services. Again, quality standards require effort to be the same under all types of compensation in the state of severe illness. However, the C or S physician will provide a lower level of effort in the minor illness state than would the FFS provider. In fact, the S or C provider will locate at or between effort levels e_I^c and e_{II}^c. Lower effort levels, e_I^c, result from higher disutility from effort relative to positive utility from professionalism, which would move the provider toward e_{II}^c.

Additional actions can be taken by the plan administration to encourage the movement of C and S physicians up to and FFS down to e_{II}^c. A common mechanism is to stipulate that the providers will receive a bonus, the amount based upon the extent to which actual profits exceed Π_{min}. Alternatively, administrators can withhold partial payment to providers quarterly or semi-annually and redistribute it ex post the determination of profit achievements. The principal agent models predict that the intended outcomes of the withholds and bonuses are more likely to be achieved if the distribution back to the agents is based on individual rather than group performance.

Managed-care plans use similar contractual arrangements to generate appropriate financial incentives with hospitals. HMO and PPO hospital arrangements often share common characteristics. Three prospectively determined payment mechanisms are typical. Probably the most frequently used is a negotiated fee schedule resembling to a discounted fee for services. Per diems are another popular arrangement, often based on levels of care. Finally, contracts may adopt either the actual hospital's Medicare Diagnosis Related Group (DRG) prices or negotiated prices based on the DRGs. These mechanisms provide varying incentives for hospitals to produce services efficiently. However, an important question is whether the hospital has any control beyond that of the physician over the utilization levels.

Under all of these risk-based compensation schemes, providers are potentially at risk for financial loss if they are inefficient. Conversely, by improving efficiency, they stand to gain. However, beyond this, a provider may be at risk for reasons beyond its control. Thus, a provider may stand to suffer a large loss due to a few unusually costly patients. Although incentive effects will be stronger, the greater the risk borne by individual providers (e.g., individual physicians), the risk of high costs for reasons beyond a providers' control creates incentives to pool risk.

STRUCTURE AND OWNERSHIP

In evaluating the performance of alternative organizational (incentive and control) forms, it is important to consider variations in the external environment within which each form of managed care operates. Arnould and DeBrock (1992) contend that lack of recognition of variations in exogenous conditions and the resulting differences in endogenous conditions may be the cause of some of the debate over the impact of managed care. Luft (1981) identified the following organizational factors as important for the performance of managed-care plans: managerial structure and skills, sponsorship, and profit versus nonprofit orientation. The greater the centralization of management, the more effective are utilization control and incentive schemes. Luft (1981), Trauner and Tilson (1989), and Feldman et al. (1990) all found that centralization of management in group and staff HMOs was better able to achieve cost savings than the decentralized Independent Practice Association. Sponsorship of the managed-care plan also can affect the performance of the plan. Consumer-sponsored plans can perform very differently from plans sponsored by providers or private insurers (Luft 1981). Finally, goals of for-profit plans may produce results that vary greatly from the goals of nonprofit plans (DeBrock and Arnould 1992; Hillman, Pauly, and Kerstein 1989). A for-profit plan may have greater access to capital markets that could permit more rapid growth and development (Christianson et al. 1991; Langwell 1990; Luft 1981).

Environmental factors surrounding managed-care plans can also influence plan performance. Christianson et al. (1991) identified legal and regulatory constraints. In addition, sociodemographic factors and structure of the medical care market can alter performance; an area must be large enough to support the necessary enrollment for a successful managed-care plan (Luft 1981). Moreover, physician opposition can restrict the development for HMOs (Morrison and Luft 1990).

The competitive environment within which the managed-care plan operates may influence the contractual arrangements used and the spread of risk between insurers, providers, and patients. Most research to date has assumed that the type of financial incentives chosen by an HMO is exogenously determined and randomly distributed among HMOs (e.g., competitive environment has no impact on choice of capitation versus fee-for-service). If this were true, HMOs seemingly would always reimburse physicians with salary or capitation. But clearly, this is not the case. Thus, the type of contract must be endogenously determined by such factors as levels of supply and excess capacity, existence of group practices, willingness of providers to accept or substitute financial risk for administrative controls, and competition from other managed-care mechanisms. Were this not the case, the coexistence in a common market of HMOs with FFS and capitation schemes would signal either (1) massive market failure or (2) alternative complementary controls being used by HMOs to bring utilization and cost in line. Arnould and DeBrock (1992) have provided empirical evidence to suggest the latter. Alternatively, the entry of an HMO into a monopolized physician or hospital market is not likely to result in the acceptance of incentive schemes or controls that reduce the monopoly rents flowing to these physicians or hospitals. Thus, the choice of managed care and its organizational characteristics as well as its impact on market outcomes are influenced by a complex set of market conditions including provider and patient utilities, relative bargaining power, and transactions costs.

COMPETITIVE CONTRACTING

HMOs, PPOs, and UR have been used extensively in the private sector to contain health care costs where there has been no governmental regulation or mandate for their adoption. These types of managed care also are used to varying degrees by the Medicare program and some Medicaid programs. Three types of competitive constructing have been used widely by various state Medicaid programs and the federal Medicare program. These are selective contracting, competitive bidding, and the Medicare Prospective Payment System (PPS). Implementation of these programs has come about through public mandate or regulation.

Selective contracting and competitive bidding often are linked. These are processes through which efficient providers or ones who are willing to accept some or all of the financial risk are identified. Enrollees either are restricted to use these providers or are required to pay a substantial penalty for freedom of choice. Obviously, these exclusive arrangements are the sum and substance of HMOs and PPOs. Selective contracting, however, has been widely adopted by public agencies such as the state of California as a tool to reduce the costs of its Medicaid program. Through a process of bidding often followed with direct negotiations between hospitals and the state, contracts to provide services to MediCal recipients were awarded to a restricted number of hospitals. In some cases, hospitals that had been providing substantial quantities of services to MediCal enrollees lost that business to other hospitals who agreed to provide the services at a lower cost. Other states have engaged in similar, although less comprehensive, methods to use market negotiations to control cost. For example, the ICARE program, used by the state of Illinois for a short time, required hospitals to bid to provide a specified number of hospital days to Medicaid recipients at a per diem price. Clearly these actions fit within the description of managed care, because choice of provider is being managed. Equally as clearly, these actions represent competitive reforms in so much as they entail restructuring of regulations to facilitate market competition.

The Medicare PPS has taken a different form. It is not properly labeled a form of managed care because the prices are not the result of negotiated contracts nor does the program attempt to steer patients. However, it is a competitive reform as stated in chapter 1 because it is an example of the application of "yardstick competition." Clearly, prices are not determined through a competitive process but are set prospectively by an oligopsonistic buyer—The Health Care Financing Administration. The notion underlying the PPS rate-setting scheme is, however, to place providers in indirect competition in the absence of direct competition. Thus, the PPS seeks to create incentives for providers to behave as though the market were competitive and to attempt to minimize their costs. Prior to the PPS, hospitals were reimbursed on a modified cost-plus system that contained no incentive to reduce costs because doing so would decrease the "plus." Initially based on a mix of national, regional, and hospital-specific costs, DRG prices under the PPS have come to depend on national costs with some regional and hospital adjustments for differences in input costs and hospital case-mix severity. Incentives exist under the PPS/DRG system for hospitals to reduce cost because rents earned as a result of reduced cost either reduce losses or increase the earned surplus of those hospitals, where over time "yardstick competition" may be implemented by adjusting DRG payment rates to reflect any resulting decreases in national costs.

Selective contracting, competitive bidding, and the PPS are important health reforms in the public and private sectors. Although the role of "competition" may vary in each instance, the reform clearly is carried out through the market and with the exception of PPS through some mechanism that fits within this chapter's definition of managed care.

EFFECTS OF COMPETITIVE REFORMS AND MANAGED-CARE SYSTEMS

We turn now to cataloging the results of research directed primarily at documenting the effectiveness of various competitive reforms and managed-care systems. Although not necessarily inclusive, this survey is intended to place conflicting evidence in perspective and to show that managed care generally has had the intended hypothesized results particularly in studies where market penetration of the changes has been greater. This also sets a stage for the results reported by Dranove (chapter four), Zwanziger and Melnick (chapter six), Phelps and Mooney (chapter seven) and Feldman and colleagues (chapter eight) elsewhere in this volume. We divide empirical studies into two categories: those concentrating on the effects of managed care on those participating directly in that form of managed care; and those concentrating on the impact of managed care on broader health care markets (i.e., the spillover effects). The results of the two categories could differ substantially owing to self-selection bias or other forms of market failure. Finally, we provide evidence of the effects of yardstick competition used in PPS.

Two caveats relate to most of this research. First, many of the studies rely on data from the late 1970s and early 1980s, during which the market penetration of managed-care plans was still quite limited. Also, many of the modified organizational characteristics of these plans did not appear in substantial volume until the mid-to late 1980s. Second, data relating to certain aspects of managed-care plans are weak such as those identifying the location of plan enrollees. Yet these data are necessary to accurately describe market shares of managed-care plans in meaningfully defined geographic markets. Also of concern are the limited extent and quality of data identifying the organizational characteristics of plans, especially nonfinancial utilization controls. These shortcomings, although a good point of departure for studying market effects, result in many very limited or specialized findings and underscore the value of results reported elsewhere in this book by Langwell and Menke (chapter two), Dranove (chapter four), and Zwanziger and Melnick (chapter six), each using more current data and representing broader-based analysis of market impacts.

Direct Effects of Managed Care

This section concentrates on evidence relating to the direct impact of HMOs, PPOs, UR, selective contracting, and the PPS on individuals enrolled in those programs. Contrary to the discussion in the previous section, we utilize this subdivision here because most of the true blending of these programs has occurred quite recently and data do not permit more detailed breakdowns. Finally, the dimension of impact most commonly measured is the impact of the program on resource utilization and cost.

HMOs

Luft (1981), in one of the early analyses of HMOs, reported that HMOs saved as much as 30 percent on the treatment of enrollees compared to those treated under the more traditional FFS model. The most identifiable area of savings was the reduction of up to 40 percent in the number of hospital days and admissions. These results have survived the test of time with only minor qualifications (Hornbrook and Berki 1985; and Manning et al. 1987). The first qualification is that the results are much stronger for staff and physician group HMO models than for IPA models (Rice 1992).

Second, the early studies were criticized for not adequately accounting for biased selection of enrollees (i.e., do healthier people who have greater disutility toward being hospitalized more frequently enroll in HMOs?). Various measures that have been used to identify biased selection include comparisons between prior and current utilization of new HMO enrollees, and between FFS and HMO enrollees adjusted by health status indicators and demographic variables such as age, gender, and marital status. Others have made comparisons of use, cost, and health status of disenrollees compared to those remaining in the HMO. Finally, probably the best test of biased selection comes from the RAND Health Insurance Experiment (RHIE), in which people were randomly placed in various types of plans so that comparisons could be made among these random groups.

Surprisingly, Luft and Miller (1988) generally discounted studies based on demographic variables. HMO administrators frequently contend that age and gender are the best predictors of utilization.

There is limited evidence of favorable and unfavorable selection in studies that compared prior utilization to HMO utilization (Ellis 1985, Price and Mays 1985). Most of the other studies that used time comparisons of utilization did so with Medicare patients. Hellinger (1987) and Langwell and Hadley (1989) found evidence of favorable selection. Lichtenstien et al. (1992) found favorable selection using time comparisons in conjunction with other measures of health status. Clearly, the major weakness of time comparisons is the storing-up effect. Individuals who plan to shift to a more generous coverage "next year" delay medical procedures.

An accurate measure of health status probably is the ideal method for measuring the presence of adverse selection. In its absence, the next best alternative is the random assignment of enrollees to various plans, as was the case for those participating in the RHIE. Manning et al. (1984) and subsequent research generated from RHIE (Manning et al. 1987) provided evidence strongly refuting the argument that HMO savings in resource costs result from favorable selection.

Reduction in hospital admissions appears to be a more important factor than reduced average length of stay (ALOS) in explaining the reduced utilization of hospital days by HMOs. Luft (1981) found shorter ALOS in 30 of the 51 plans he analyzed. Welch (1985) found no significant differences in ALOS between HMO and FFS patients. Langwell, Rossiter, et al. (1987) found that ALOS for Medicare IPA HMO enrollees was 8.5, days compared to the national average for aged Medicare patients of 8.4 days. Bradbury, Golec and Stearns (1991), on the other hand, found that IPA members had a 14 percent shorter ALOS than traditional insurance patients. At a somewhat more micro level, Wilner et al. (1981) and Arnould, DeBrock, and Pollard (1984) found no significant differences in ALOS between HMO and FFS patients within a limited selection of diagnostic categories; Johnson et al. (1989) found shorter ALOS in 6 of 10 diagnostic categories for network (PGP) HMOs, but IPAs had shorter ALOS in only 1 of 10 diagnostic categories; and Dowd, Johnson, and Madson (1986) found that both IPA and PGP patients experienced lower ALOS than traditional insurance patients in 5 of the 7 DRGs studied. The evidence is very mixed, but generally supports reduced or certainly no greater ALOS for HMO patients.

Concentrating on inpatient resource use, Arnould et al. (1984) found that appendectomy HMO patients had lower charges than FFS patients, but that there were no significant differences between HMO and FFS patients admitted for hysterectomies, cholecystectomies (removal of the gallbladder), and herniorrhaphies. Johnson et al.

(1989) found that hospital charges were lower for network (PGP) HMO enrollees than for commercial insurance patients in 6 of 10 diagnostic categories studied. The network HMOs were better able to control surgical diagnoses, with 4 of 5 having lower charges, as opposed to the medical diagnoses, where only 2 of 5 had lower charges. IPAs were found to have charges indistinguishable from traditional insurance charges. Johnson et al. (1989) found that network HMOs had lower ancillary charge ratios (ACRs) than commercial insurance in 6 of 10 categories, whereas IPAs had lower ACRs in only 2 or 10 categories when compared to commercial insurance.

Three recent articles focus on the fact that organizational features generate significant differentiation among HMOs and, therefore, may explain the differing results found in the studies reported here as well as in those investigating the impact of HMOs on broader market performance. Langwell and Nelson (1987) found utilization of hospital services by Medicare enrollees to be 33 percent lower than for similar patients treated in an FFS setting, but reported no systematic relationship between utilization and type of HMO. Hillman, Pauly, and Kerstein (1989) found utilization of hospital and physician services to be significantly lower for enrollees in HMOs that used salary or capitation arrangements to reimburse physicians. The same was found true for proprietary HMOs when compared to not-for-profit HMOs. DeBrock and Arnould (1992) extended these results by finding that the payback or bonus further reduced utilization when based on individual performance, rather than when based on aggregate group behavior. Also, the impact of capitation arrangements on utilization almost disappeared in provider-owned HMOs. The empirical evidence supports arguments that variations in research findings on the impacts of HMOs can be attributed to the diversity of those organizations.

There may be concern over the impact of the financial incentives directed to providers on quality of care. Quality generally is measured by process (quality and quantity of inputs and procedures) and outcomes (mortality and morbidity rates). Luft (1981) found that HMOs tended to score higher than FFS plans when judged by process of care, and to have morbidity and mortality rates similar to those of FFS providers for equivalent populations. Cunningham and Williamson (1980) examined 27 process and outcome studies of HMOs and found that none of the HMOs studied was lacking in quality, while 19 were judged superior in quality to FFS providers. RHIE (Manning et al. 1985) focusing on Group Health Cooperative of Puget Sound, found the HMO to score very high in technical and interpersonal dimensions of care. Thus, there is no general evidence to suggest that HMOs are lower in quality than FFS providers.

PREFERRED PROVIDER ORGANIZATIONS

Evidence on the impact of PPOs on resource utilization of those enrolled in the plans is much more limited than for HMOs. Rice and colleagues (1990) questioned the ability of PPOs to have a significant impact on utilization (compared to FFS plans) because PPOs generally reduce out-of-pocket expenses for enrollees. Also, so long as the marginal discounted price exceeds marginal provider cost, providers have an incentive to increase utilization. However, PPOs could reduce unit price of services. Hosek et al. (1990) and Garnick et al. (1990) found charges for PPO users to be from 11 percent to 38 percent lower than for FFS users for four out of five employers studied, and 5 percent higher for one out of five. The source of the savings is not as obvious as was the case for HMOs.

Hester, Wouters, and Wright (1987), examining one employer, found total cost of a standardized visit to providers within the PPO network to be 33.7 percent less, but PPO users tended to be healthier and used the PPO network for less-severe problems. Finally, Diehr and colleagues (1990) that found employees of the city of Seattle, who were exclusive users of the PPO, utilized services less than those who were sometime users but no less than those who never utilize the PPO. Self-selection out of the PPO for severe illnesses may explain this finding.

UTILIZATION REVIEW PROGRAMS

Studies of the impacts of UR programs concentrate either on the efforts of single employers or single insurers. Richards (1984) found that one Illinois employer reduced ALOS by 18 percent and another reduced admissions by 21 percent, the latter relative to previous periods resulting in a cost savings of $2.5 million. Shahoda (1984) found that UR programs used by Blue Cross and Blue Shield reduced hospital use by 13 percent in northeastern Ohio, and 15 percent in both Kansas City and North Carolina. An experiment by Radio Corporation of America, Inc. (O'Donnell 1987) resulted in a decrease of 3.8 percent on medical claims by employees subject to UR and a contemporaneous increase of 6 percent in the claims of those not subject to UR.

In a study of University of Michigan employee groups, Feldstein, Wickizer, and Wheeler (1988) reported that, for 1984 and 1985, UR reduced admissions by 12.3 percent, inpatient days by 8 percent, hospital routine (room and board) expenditures by 8 percent, hospital ancillary expenditures by 14.8 percent, and total medical expenditures (including all inpatient and outpatient expenditures) by 8.3 percent. When 1986 was included, UR reduced admissions by 13.1 percent, inpatient days by 10.7 percent, hospital routine expenditures by 6.7 percent, hospital ancillary expenditures by 9.4 percent, and total medical expenditures by 5.9 percent (Wickizer, Wheeler, and Feldstein 1989). The authors did not find any meaningful evidence of selection bias.

In more recent work Wickizer (1992) reported that most of the impacts of UR occur in the quarters immediately following its implementation. Furthermore, effects of UR differ across diagnostic areas. The largest decrease in expenditures occurred in surgical diagnoses, compared to medical and mental health diagnoses (Wickizer 1990). A large percentage increase associated with utilization review occurred in hospital outpatient service expenditures (Wickizer 1990). However, hospital outpatient services still accounted for only a small percentage of the total medical expenditures.

These results are confirmed by at least two other studies. Scheffler, Sullivan, and Ko (1991) found that the combination of preadmission review and concurrent review reduced payments by about 4 percent for enrollees of Blue Cross and Blue Shield plans from 1980 to 1988. Khandker and Manning (1992) found that inpatient hospital spending fell about 8 percent and that total medical expenditures dropped by about 4 percent for another population.

MEDICARE PROSPECTIVE PAYMENT SYSTEM

As stated earlier, we categorize the Medicare PPS as a form of competitive reform because it attempts to correct inconsistencies in provider incentives. The incentives embedded in the PPS should increase provider efficiency and reduce excess utilization.

There are a variety of measures of the success of the PPS. Length of stay declined from an average of 10 days in 1983, one year before the phase-in of the PPS, to 8.5 in 1987, a decrease in ALOS in excess of 15 percent (Phelps 1992). Russell and Manning (1989) predicted that the PPS resulted in a reduction in government spending in Medicare Part A of $18 billion over what would have been spent in the absence of the PPS. Over a five-year period hospital admissions fell by 13 percent. Phelps (1992) contends that the PPS resulted in the use of a more efficient mix of services as well. Langwell and

Menke (chapter two, this volume) stated that during the last half of the decade of the 1980s, after the introduction of PPS, the real growth in Medicare's spending per enrollee was 3.2 percent, compared to 4.6 percent for the nation. Most of the decline in the growth rate was attributable to the drop in the rate of increase in expenditures for hospital services. In the first three years of the PPS, outpatient surgeries increased dramatically and use of skilled nursing facilities increased by over 25 percent. These impacts do not attempt to measure possible benefits of the system that go beyond Medicare recipients. Some private payers have adopted the Medicare DRG rates or a modified version of these rates.

BIDDING AND SELECTIVE CONTRACTING

Limited analyses have been conducted of selective contracting schemes used by states. The most publicized and oldest program probably is the California MediCal program, in which 92 percent of Medicaid hospital expenditures are to hospitals under direct contract with the state. Johns (1985) estimated that MediCal savings in 1983–84 exceeded $700 million. McCombs and Christianson (1987) reported on the successful implementation of a bidding process in certain Wisconsin counties to set capitation rates for Medicaid eligibles. Finally, Paringer and McCall (1991) estimated that, under a bidding system, Medicaid equivalent costs in the state of Arizona increased by 34.2 percent from 1983 to 1989, compared to a 60.7 percent increase for traditional Medicaid programs. The results of the use of selective contracting and bidding in pubic programs are clear and consistent with contentions that competitive reforms have achieved success.

Managed Care—Spillover Effects

The impact of managed-care programs on cost and utilization in the entire enrollee market—those who are enrolled in managed-care programs as well as those who are not—is important to trace. If cost containment has public goods characteristics, the existence of managed-care plans should reduce total market spending. Managed-care plans should have an impact upon market outcomes because of the growing importance (share) of these programs in the market and because competitive forces generated by these plans (or public goods aspects of provider behavior) stimulate better performance in the remaining segment of the market. Alternatively, the overall impact of managed care might be minimal to negative if providers can shift the impact of reduced revenues from managed-care patients to others (i.e., does managed care simply shift patients from plan to plan along with costs?). If the latter occurs, cost may be shifted, but total cost may not be reduced.

Several prior studies are mentioned here as evidence of the conflicting and weak evidence for the impact of managed care on "total markets." Luft, Maerki, and Trauner (1986) were unable to relate trends in health care cost in three markets (Hawaii, Rochester, and Minneapolis/St. Paul) to levels of HMO market share. Johnson and Aquilina (1986) and Feldman et al. (1986) drew similar conclusions. Welch (1991) found contrary evidence for Medicare patients; he found that average Medicare expenditures decreased by 1.2 percent for each Medicare HMO market share increase of 10 percent. McLaughlin (1987) and Hadley and Swartz (1989) found that HMO market share had a very limited impact on total market hospital costs.

As stated at the outset of this section, the foregoing studies are plagued by shortcomings that restrict the generalizability of the findings. First, as mentioned, the data apply largely to a time period prior to the major influx of managed-care plans on the market. Second, per capita total health care expenditures probably is the most obvious yardstick of the impact of managed-care plans on markets. Yet studies using this yardstick (e.g., McLaughlin 1987) are restricted to data collected prior to 1980. Third, those not using a marketwide measure of per capita expenditures generally resorted to expenditures for a limited population (e.g., Medicare recipients) or a limited measure of resource costs such as hospital costs.

Fourth, it is important to look at possible interactions between different types of managed care (e.g., HMOs and PPOs), a particularly important issue since the mid-1980s.

We believe many of these drawbacks are overcome in research reported in this volume. Langwell and Menke (chapter 2) cite clear evidence of the impact of the PPS on the rate of growth in spending for the Medicare population. Dranove (chapter 4) documents a variety of measures of the positive impact of competitive reforms on markets. (Elsewhere, Robinson (1991) and Melnick and Zwanziger (1988) find strong evidence that increases in the market share of HMO significantly reduce hospital costs.) Finally, Zwanziger and Melnick (chapter six) provide three forms of evidence that competitive reforms have had the predicted positive effects on market outcomes, and Feldman et al. (chapter eight) show similar evidence for Medicare HMO enrollees.

CONCLUSIONS

The confusion about the relationship between competitive reforms and managed care can be alleviated if competition is thought of as a process and managed care as a set of tools, some of which can be used to implement the process. In this context, elements of managed care create incentives which may result in more competitive outcomes in health care markets.

Empirical evidence shows the effects of various competitive reforms and forms of managed care to be consistent with expectations. Every form of managed-care plan and the PPS has the expected impact on patients subject to those plans. The total market effects are less clear from the earlier studies, but are becoming more obvious as the market significance of the plans increases. Elsewhere in this book, Dranove (chapter four), Zwanziger and Melnick (chapter six), and Feldman et al. (chapter eight) provide compelling evidence that competitive reforms do move health care markets toward greater efficiency. However, data sets used to analyze these reforms remain narrow. Dranove, in part, and Zwanziger and Melnick, in total, concentrate on the state of California. Feldman et al. concentrate on Medicare patients. Thus, generalizations from these studies should come with some caution. Finally, many of the tools of managed care described in this chapter are not limited to use in competitive health policies. They are being incorporated into the United Kingdom's highly socialized National Health Service (see Posnett, chapter fourteen, this volume), and figure prominently in most versions of managed competition now being considered as a basis for national health policy in the United States.

Notes

1. This definition draws heavily on Hoy, Curtis, and Rice (1991) and U.S. Congressional Budget Office (1992).

2. Competitive medical plans (CMPs), not treated elsewhere in this volume, are closely related to HMOs. Essentially they are 'at-risk' plans that experience-rate rather than community-rate and may not provide as many services as federally qualified HMOs.

3. We let the physician represent all providers.

References

Arnould, R. J. 1988. "OBRA 1986: The Influence of Physician Financial Incentives on Health Care-A Review." Draft report to the U.S. Department of Health and Human Services, Washington, D. C.
_____. 1992. "Strategic Choices of Internal Compensation Arrangements in HMOs." Unpublished Manuscript, University of Illinois. Program in Health Economics, Management and Policy.
Arnould, R. J., and L. D. DeBrock. 1986. "Competition and Market Failure in the Hospital Industry." *Medical Care Review* 43 (2, Fall): 253–92.
Arnould, R. J., L. DeBrock, and J. Pollard. 1984. "Do HMOs Produce Specific Services More Efficiently?" *Inquiry* 21 (3, Fall): 243–53.
Bradbury, R., J. Golec, and F. Stearns. 1991. "Comparing Hospital Length of Stay in Independent Practice Association HMOs and Traditional Insurance Programs." *Inquiry* 28 (1, Spring): 87–93.
Christianson, J. B., S. M. Sanchez, D. R. Wholey, and M. Shadle. 1991. "The HMO Industry: Evolution in Population Demographics and Market Structures." *Medical Care Review* 48 (1 Spring): 3–46.
Cunningham, F., and J. Williamson. 1980. "How Does the Quality of Health Care in HMOs Compare to That in Other Settings? An Analytical Literature Review: 1958–1979." *Group Health Journal* 1 (Winter): 4–25.
DeBrock, L. D., and R. J. Arnould. 1992. "Utilization Control in HMOs." *Quarterly Review of Economics and Finance* 32 (3, Autumn): 31–53.
de Lissovoy, G., T. Rice, J. Gabel, and G. Gelzer. 1987. "Preferred Provider Organizations: One Year Later." *Inquiry* 24: 127–35.
Diehr, P., N. Silberg, D. P. Martin, V. Arlow, and R. Leickly. 1990. "Use of a Preferred Provider Plan by Employees of the City of Seattle." *Medical Care* 28 (11 November): 1073–88.
Dowd, B., A. Johnson, and R. Madson. 1986. "Inpatient Length of Stay in Twin Cities' Health Plans." *Medical Care* 24 (8): 694–710.
Dranove, D., M. Shanley, and W. White. 1991. "How Fast Are Hospital Prices Really Rising?" *Medical Care* 29 (8, August): 690–96.
Ellis, R. P. 1985. "The Effect of Prior Year Health Expenditures on Health Coverage Plan Choice." *Advances in Health Economics and Health Services Research* 6: 149–171.
Ermann, D. 1988. "Hospital Utilization Review: Past Experience, Future Directions." *Journal of Health Politics, Policy, and Law* 13 (4): 683–704.
Feldman, R., J. Kralewski, and B. Dowd. 1989. "HMOs: The Beginning or the End?" *Health Services Research* 24 (2, June): 191–211.
Feldman, R., B. Dowd, D. McCann, and A. Johnson. 1986. "The Competitive Impact of Health Maintenance Organizations on Hospital Finances: An Exploratory Study." *Journal of Health Politics, Policy and Law* 10 (4, Winter): 675–97.

Feldman, R., J. Kralewski, J. Shapiro, and H-C. Chan. 1990. "Contracts between Hospitals and Health Maintenance Organizations." *Health Care Management Review* 15 (1): 47–60.

Feldstein, P., T. Wickizer, and J. Wheeler. 1988. "Private Cost Containment: The Effects of Utilization Review Programs on Health Care Use and Expenditures." *New England Journal of Medicine* 318 (May): 1310–14.

Francis, A. M., L. Polissar, and A. B. Lorenz. 1984. "Care of Patients with Colorectal Cancer: A Comparison of a Health Maintenance Organization and Fee-for-Service Practices." *Medical Care* 22: 418–29.

Frank, R., and W. P. Welch. 1985. "The Competitive Effects of HMOs: A Review of the Evidence." *Inquiry* 22 (2, Summer): 148–61.

Gabel, J., D. Ermann, T. Rice, and G. de Lissovoy. 1986. "The Emergence and Future of PPOs." *Journal of Health Politics, Policy and Law* 11 (2, Summer): 305–22.

Garnick, D. W., H. S. Luft, L. B. Gardner, C. M. Morrison, M. Barrett, A. O'Neil, and B. Harvey. 1990. "Services and Charges by PPO Physicians for PPO and Indemnity Patients: An Episode of Care Comparison." *Medical Care* 28 (10, October): 894–906.

Hadley, J., and K. Swartz. 1989. "The Impacts on Hospital Costs between 1980 and 1984 of Hospital Rate Regulation, Competition, and Changes in Health Insurance Coverage." *Inquiry* 26 (1, Spring): 35–47.

Hellinger, F. 1987. "Selection Bias in Health Maintenance Organizations: Analysis of Recent Evidence." *Health Care Financing Review* 9 (2, Winter): 55–63.

Hester, J., A. Wouters, and N. Wright. 1987. "Evaluation of a Preferred Provider Organization." *Milbank Quarterly* 65 (4): 575–613.

Hillman, A. 1991. "Managing the Physician: Rules versus Incentives." *Health Affairs* (Winter): 138–46.

————., M. Pauly, and J. J. Kerstein. 1989. "How do Financial Incentives Affect Physicians' Clinical Decisions and the Financial Performance of HMOs?" *New England Journal of Medicine* 321 (July): 86–92.

Holmstrom, B., 1979. "Moral Hazard and Observability." *Bell Journal of Economics* 90: 74–91.

Hornbrook, M. C., and S. E. Berki. 1985. "Practice Mode and Payment Method—Effects on Use, Costs, Quality, and Access." *Medical Care* 23: 484–511.

Hosek, S., M. S. Marquis, K. Wells, D. Garnick, and H. Luft. 1990. "The Study of Preferred Organizations: Executive Summary." Santa Monica, Calif.: The RAND Corporation, June.

Hoy, E. W., R. E. Curtis, and T. Rice. 1991. "Change and Growth in Managed Care." *Health Affairs* (Winter): 18–36.

Johns, L. 1985. "Selective Contracting in California." *Health Affairs* 4 (Fall): 32–48.

Johnson, A., and D. Aquilina. 1986. "The Impact of Health Maintenance Organizations and Competition on Hospitals in Minneapolis/St. Paul." *Journal of Health Politics, Policy and Law* 10 (4, Winter): 659–74.

Johnson, A., B. Dowd, N. Morris, and N. Lurie. 1989. "Differences in Inpatient Resources Use by Type of Health Plan." *Inquiry* 26 (3 Fall): 388–98.

Khandker, R. and W. Manning. 1992. "The Impact of Utilization Review on Costs and Utilization." *Health Economics Worldwide*, edited by P. Zweifel and H. Frech. Kluwer Academic Press.

Kralewski, J., R. Feldman, B. Dowd, and J. Shapiro. 1991. "Strategies Employed by HMOs to Achieve Hospital Discounts." *Health Care Management Review* 16 (1): 9–16.

Kralewski, J., T. Wingert, R. Feldman, G. Rahn, and T. Klassen. 1992. "Factors Related to the Provision of Hospital Discounts for HMO Inpatients." *Health Services Research* 27 (2, June): 133–53.

Langwell, K. M. 1990. "Structure and Performance of Health Maintenance Organizations: A Review." *Health Care Financing Review* 12 (1): 71–79.

Langwell, K. M., and J. Hadley. 1989. "Evaluation of the Medicare Competition Demonstrations." *Health Care Financing Review* 11 (2, Winter): 65–80.

Langwell, K. M., and L. Nelson. 1987. "Physician Incentive Arrangements and Use of Hospital Services: A Framework for Analysis." Washington D.C.: Mathematica Policy Research.

Langwell, K. M., L. Rossiter, R. Brown, L. Nelson, S. Nelson, and K. Berman. 1987. "Early Experience of Health Maintenance Organizations under Medicare Competition Demonstrations." *Health Care Financing Review* 8: 7–55.

Lichtenstein, R., J. W. Thomas, B. Watkins, C. Puto, et al. 1992. "HMO Marketing and Selection Bias: Are TEFRA HMOs Skimming?" *Medical Care* 30 (4, April): 329–46.

Luft, H. S. 1981. "Health Maintenance Organizations: Dimensions of Performance." New York: John Wiley & Sons.

Luft, H. S., and R. Miller. 1988. "Patient Selection in a Competitive Health Care System." *Health Affairs* (Summer): 97–119.

Luft, H. S., S. Maerki, and J. Trauner. 1986. "The Competitive Effects of Health Maintenance Organizations: Another Look at the Evidence from Hawaii, Rochester, and Minneapolis/St. Paul." *Journal of Health Politics, Policy and Law* 10 (4, Winter): 625–58.

Lynn, J. T. 1991. "The Promise of Managed Care: An Insurer's Peropective." *Health Affairs* 10 (4, Winter): 185–88.

Manning, W. G., A. Leibowitz, G.A. Goldberg, W. H. Rogers, and J. P. Newhouse. 1984. "A Controlled Trial of the Effect of a Prepaid Group Practice on Use of Services." *New England Journal of Medicine* 310 (23): 1505–10.

Manning, W. G., A. Leibowitz, G. Goldberg, W. Rogers, and J. Newhouse. 1985. "A Controlled Trial of the Effect of a Prepaid Group Practice on the Utilization of Medical Services." Santa Monica, Calif: RAND Corporation, September.

Manning, W. G., J. P. Newhouse, N. Duan, R. B. Keeler, A. Leibowitz, and M. S. Marquis. 1987. Health Insurance and the Demand for Medical Care. Evidence from a Randomized Experiment." *American Economic Review* 77(3): 251–77.

Marion Merrell Dow, Inc. 1991. *Managed Care Digest, PPO Edition.* Kansas City, Mo.: author.

McCombs, J., and J. Christianson. 1987. "Applying Competitive Bidding to Health Care." *Journal of Health Politics, Policy and Law* (Winter): 703–22.

McCusker, J., A. Stoddard, and A. Sorenson. 1988. "Do HMOs Reduce Hospitalization of Terminal Cancer Patients?" *Inquiry* 25: 263–70.

McLaughlin, C. 1988. "Market Responses to HMOs: Price Competition to Rivalry?" *Inquiry* 25 (2, Summer): 236–47.

_____. 1987. "HMO Growth and Hospital Expenses and Use: A Simultaneous-Equation Approach." *Health Services Research* 22 (2, June): 183–205.

McLaughlin, C., J. Merrill, and A. Freed. 1984. "The Impact of HMO Growth on Hospital Costs and Utilization." *Advances in Health Economics and Health Services Research*, vol. 5. Edited by R. Scheffler and L. Rossiter.

Melnick, G. and J. Zwanziger. 1988. "Hospital Behavior Under Competition and Cost Containment Policies." *Journal of the American Medical Association* 260 (18, November): 2669–75.

Morrison, E. and H. Luft. 1990. "Health Maintenance Organization Environments in the 1980s and Beyond." *Health Care Financing Review* 12 (1, Fall): 81–90.

Newhouse, J., W. Schwartz, A. Williams, and C. Witsberger. 1985. "Are Fee-for-Service Costs Increasing Faster than HMO Costs?" *Medical Care* 23 (8, August): 960–66.

O'Donnell, P. 1987. "Managing Health Costs under a Fee-for-Service Plan." *Business and Health* 4 (March): 38–41.

Paringer, L. and N. McCall. 1991. "How Competitive is Competitive Bidding?" *Health Affairs* 10 (4, Winter): 220–30.

Phelps, Charles E. 1992. *Health Economics*. New York: Harper Collins.

Price, J. R. and J. W. Mays. 1985. "Selection and the Competitive Standing of Health Plans in a Multiple-Choice Multiple-Insurer Market." *Advances in Health Economics and Health Services Research*, vol. 6: 127–149.

Rice, T. 1992. "Containing Health Care Costs in the United States." *Medical Care Review* 49 (1, Spring): 2–4.

Rice, T., J. Gabel, S. Mick, C. Lippert, and C. Dowd. 1990. "Continuity and Change in Preferred Provider Organizations." *Health Policy* 16: 1–18.

Richards, G. 1984. "Business Spurs UR Growth." *Hospitals* 58 (5, March): 96–97.

Robinson, J. 1991. "HMO Market Penetration and Hospital Cost Inflation in California." *Journal of the American Medical Association* 266 (19, November): 2719–23.

Russell, L. B. and C. L. Manning. 1989. "The Effect of Prospective Payment on Medicare Expenditures." *New England Journal of Medicine* 320: 439–44.

Sappington, David E. M. 1991. "Incentives in Principal-Agent Relationships." *Journal of Economic Perspectives* 5 (2, Spring): 45–66.

Scheffler, R., S. Sullivan, and T. Ko. 1991. "The Impacts of Blue Cross and Blue Shield Plan Utilization Management Programs, 1980–1988." *Inquiry* 28 (3, Fall): 263–75.

Shahoda, T. 1984. "Preadmission Review Cuts Hospital Use." *Hospitals* 58 (15, August): 54.

Trauner, J., and S. Tilson. 1989. "Utilization Management and Quality Assurance in Health Maintenance Organizations: An Operational Assessment." In *Controlling Costs and Changing Patient Care?* edited by B. Gray and M. Field, Appendix B: 205–245. Washington, D.C.: National Academy Press.

U.S. Congressional Budget Office. 1990. "Managed Care and the Medicare Program: Background and Evidence." Staff Memorandum. Washington, D.C.: Author, May.

————. 1992. "The Effects of Managed Care on Use and Costs of Health Services." Staff Memorandum. Washington D.C.: Author, June.

Welch, W. P. 1985. "Health Care Utilization in HMOs: Results from Two National Samples." *Journal of Health Economics* 4: 293–308.

————. 1991. "HMO Market Share and Its Effect on Local Medicare Costs." Washington, D.C.: Urban Institute.

Welch, W. P., Hillman, and M. Pauly. 1990. "Toward New Typologies for HMOs." *Milbank Quarterly* 68 (2): 221–43.

Wickizer, T. 1990. "The Effect of Utilization Review on Hospital Use and Expenditures: A Review of the Literature and an Update on Recent Findings." *Medical Care Review* 47 (3, Fall): 327–63.

————. 1992. "The Effects of Utilization Review on Hospital Use and Expenditures: A Covariance Analysis." *Health Services Research* 27 (1, April): 103–21.

Wickizer, T., J. Wheeler, and P. Feldstein. 1989. "Does Utilization Review Reduce Unnecessary Care and Contain Costs?" *Medical Care* 27 (6, June): 632–46.

Wilner, S., S. C. Schoenbaum, R. Monson, and R. N. Winickoff. 1981. "A Comparison of the Quality of Maternity Care between a Health Maintenance Organization and Fee-For-Service Practice." *New England Journal of Medicine* 304 (March, 26): 784–86.

Yelin, E., M. Shearn, and W. Epstein. 1986. "Health Outcomes for a Chronic Disease in Prepaid Group Practice and Fee-for-Service Settings: The Case of Rheumatoid Arthritis." *Medical Care* 24: 236–47.

Chapter Six

EFFECTS OF COMPETITION ON THE HOSPITAL INDUSTRY: EVIDENCE FROM CALIFORNIA

Jack Zwanziger and Glenn A. Melnick

Until the early 1980s, the U.S. hospital industry operated within a relatively placid environment marked by regulation and by passive insurers acting largely as claims adjusters. This environment changed dramatically in the 1980s as a result of policies developed to attempt cost containment during this period of unprecedented growth in health care costs. Cost-containment measures primarily took the form of changes intended to introduce competition into the hospital industry. As one might expect, repercussions resulting from changing from a price-insensitive health care system to one based on free-market principles have been felt throughout the system.

A complete evaluation of these changes must await observation of their full effects. However, sufficient time has elapsed to study the changes in the California health care market subsequent to the passage in 1982 of the nation's first preferred provider organization (PPO) legislation. This chapter summarizes our research into the effects on the hospital industry of this fundamental change in the health insurance market. Competitive effects are likely to be larger in California because managed-care plans rapidly have grown to dominate the private insurance market and because the state's hospitals have low occupancy rates. In addition, California has good and easily accessible hospital data.

The most striking change in the California health care market in the last 10 years has been the restructuring of the market for private health insurance. Selective contracting plans—PPOs and health maintenance organizations (HMOs)—are now clearly the dominant form of private health insurance. By the end of 1989, there were 152 PPOs operating in California with 9.23 million eligible subscribers. There were also 54 HMOs with an additional 9 million enrollees, for a total of over 18 million enrollees in managed-care plans. After excluding Medicare, Medicaid, and the uninsured from the total state population of 29 million, managed-care plans cover more than 85 percent of the privately insured population.

This growth in managed health care has taken place in three distinct phases:

1983–85: When managed-care plans were first introduced in California, subscriber enrollment was sparse, but provider interest in the plans was substantial. Since extensive provider networks enhanced insurers' credibility and the attractiveness of their product to potential subscribers, plans tended to have large provider networks.

1986–88: During this period, managed-care plans grew explosively. Both providers and insurers developed a more sophisticated understanding of their relative bargaining power.

1989–present: Currently, as total enrollment approaches a plateau, plans have started to prune their networks. Hospitals have intensified efforts to increase their market power.

The remainder of this chapter is organized into three sections. The first section outlines a conceptual framework for understanding the insurance, physician, and hospital markets, and the intricate relationships between these markets. The second section explores the results of a series of analyses of the California hospital industry's responses to selective contracting, based on hospital and insurance data. The final section formulates conclusions and discusses the implications of the analysis for future policy decisions in health care markets nationwide.

CONCEPTUAL FRAMEWORK

The purchase of health care involves a complex set of interactions among many parties. For example, the market for hospital services involves at least four, and often five, players: the patient, the insurer, the physician, and the hospital, with the employer often playing a role as well. Patients obtain hospital care by initiating contact with physicians with admission privileges or by proceeding directly to hospital outpatient clinics and emergency rooms. Physicians influence the demand for hospital services through admissions of their patients and specification of services to be provided once admitted. Hospitals attempt to attract physicians and their patients by offering higher-quality services and more amenities than other institutions.

Hospitals also try to attract selective contractors by providing price discounts. Insurers play an important role as well, since they pay the largest portion of the hospital charges. Less directly, employers influence the process via their selection of the insurance plans offered to their employees.

Hospitals in Traditional Competition

This section examines both the traditional environment in which hospitals and insurers operate and the competitive market of selective contracting.

The centerpiece of our framework is the hospital.[1] In general, hospitals compete for patients through variations in services, in technology, and in amenities available for patient care. These choices attract physicians and therefore patients. Physicians' ability to deliver quality care and to compete for patients, therefore, depends in part on hospitals' investments in the necessary specialized equipment and staff. In negotiating with hospitals, physicians can increase their bargaining leverage by threatening to shift their patients to a credible alternative. Hospitals can respond by revoking admitting privileges among physicians who admit fewer than some threshold number of patients; physicians who cannot admit patients to the highly regarded hospitals in the area are likely to be at a competitive disadvantage.

The amount by which hospitals need to improve service, technology, and amenity availability to attract more patients depends on the competitiveness of both the hospital and physician markets. The more competitive the hospital market, the easier for physicians to shift their patients to other hospitals when they become dissatisfied. One hypothesis to draw from this amenity-based model of hospital competition is that the number of hospitals in an area is a good measure of the relative bargaining strength of hospitals with their medical staff. A finding that hospital expenditures increase with the number of area hospitals competing for physicians would support this theory (see Robinson and Luft 1985). A converse hypothesis would be that as physician markets become more competitive—as the number of physicians increases—hospitals are not as dependent on any group of physicians for patients and can reduce the intensity of costly quality- or amenity-based competition.

Introduction of Selective Contracting

The introduction of selective contracting by third-party payers changes the economic incentives faced by both insurers and providers. Third-party payers, competing with one another for subscribers, have both the economic incentives and the economies of scale required to gather and analyze data on both the price and quality of care, in order to identify high-quality and low-price providers. In theory, effective use of the selective contracting mechanism can generate savings for third-party payers that can lead to price advantages over payers who pay "too much" in a competitive insurance market. On the other hand, payers who use price as the primary criterion in selecting their preferred providers may lose subscribers owing to perceptions of unacceptable quality or insufficient accessibility. Thus, payers must assess the relative attractiveness to consumers of hospitals before choosing which hospitals to exclude according to price competitiveness.

Providers faced with price pressure generated by competition in selective contracting must also balance trade-offs in negotiating with third-party payers. A provider must assess: (1) its relative status in a payer's network, and therefore the likelihood of being excluded if it does not meet requested price concessions, and (2) its ability to keep patients should the contract not be offered.

Hospitals, in particular, must change their competitive behavior. Their ability to raise the quality and quantity of amenities they offer to attract more patients must be modified by the pressures to contain costs imposed by third-party reimbursement policies. Under cost-based reimbursement methods, it is easy for hospitals to compete based on quality, since they can recover their costs from third-party payers. The ability to compete on the basis of quality is restricted as insurers begin to exert their market power and limit payments through prospective reimbursement and selective contracting.

DETERMINING BARGAINING POWER UNDER SELECTIVE CONTRACTING

The degree to which selective contractors can obtain price discounts and better services depends on the relative bargaining positions of these contractors, physicians, and hospitals. Relative bargaining positions depend essentially on the combination of these parties' perceived credibility in threatening to move their customers, beneficiaries, or patients, respectively, to a competitor, and on the financial damage such a move would cause.

Several factors contribute to each party's perceived credibility. The first factor is the competitiveness of the various markets for hospital and physician services and for health insurance. The more competitive the hospital market, as shown both by the presence of other hospitals serving the area and by the availability of the needed spare capacity, the less dependent are insurers on any particular hospital and the more credible their threat to shift beneficiaries. As a result, the insurers' bargaining position is strengthened. Analogously, the more competitive the insurance market, the less dependent are hospitals on any particular source of patients and consequently the better the hospital's bargaining position. Finally, in competitive physician market areas, hospitals may be able to offer greater price discounts because they can reduce nonessential expenditures without fear of losing physician loyalty.

A more subtle factor, and one over which hospitals have much greater control, is the relationship between the hospital and its medical staff, particularly with the important primary care physicians in its market. Since patients are likely to be most resistant to switching their primary care physician, a hospital negotiating as a unit with its medical staff is likely to be best able to withstand pressure from selective contractors. Hospitals, then, can invest profitably in "bonding" their staff to them, even when that effort increases their costs, because they would expect to increase their negotiated prices and patient volumes.

MARKET POWER AS FUNCTION OF SWITCHING COSTS

To understand more fully the relative market power of physicians and hospitals, it is important to appreciate the significance of "switching costs." These are any costs borne by patients either when they change insurers to maintain a relationship with a particular physician or hospital, or change providers so that they may continue to use the same insurer. In general, the patient will make those adjustments that incur the lowest costs. The relative size of these costs is determined primarily by insurance options available to patients at their place of employment, and by the bonds between the patient and his or her physician(s) and hospital and between the patient's employer and the insurance plan.

The question of patient loyalty to a particular provider has not been studied extensively. However, it is likely that the bond between patients and their primary care physicians is stronger than that between patient and insurer in employment situations where another insurance plan is available that allows patients to retain current physicians. If the consumers' primary loyalty is to their primary care physicians, then switching costs will depend on the ability and willingness of these physicians to shift their practice from one hospital to another if a contract is not signed with their primary hospital. In the extreme, failure to achieve a contract could result in a patient's changing physicians or insurance plans, according to his options and preferences. Alternate possibilities include patients pressuring their physicians to join the medical staff of a network hospital in order to continue to see them in network hospitals, or patients going to out-of-network hospitals to maintain their physicians, while retaining their affiliation with the PPO, despite the higher out-of-pocket costs. In general, the stronger the patient bond with the physician, the greater the market power of the physician relative to that of the insurer.

Although the relative strength of the bond between patients and hospitals is unclear, hospitals are likely to develop stronger bonds with patients over time as stable referral patterns become established. The issue of switching costs becomes particularly relevant after a payer has established its network of preferred providers and during renegotiation of contracts. A hospital with low patient volume may initially accept a lower price from a payer. However, if the hospital's share of the payer's total volume in the area grows, its importance to the payer also grows, and therefore, it may be able to gain higher prices if the payer expects to lose too many subscribers who want to maintain relationships with their existing providers. Therefore, as with the physician, the greater the patient loyalty to a hospital, the greater the bargaining position of the hospital.

To summarize so far, hospital performance—price, costs, and quality—is linked to the structure of hospital, physician, and insurance markets and to other (noninstitutional) factors determining switching costs. Hospitals must still attract patients through nonprice competition by competing for the loyalty of admitting physicians. Selective contractors put pressure on hospitals to constrain costs in order to provide price discounts. The outcomes of this process depend on the relative bargaining positions of the three major parties, which in turn depend on the competitiveness of the three markets and on the relationship between physicians and hospitals.

Two potential downsides to price competition are the potential for a fall in the quality of care (Shortell and Hughes 1990) and a decrease in access to health care. Selective contracting provides incentives for hospitals to reduce costs through competition to provide the contractors with price discounts. Selective contractors also provide incentives to reduce costs by paying hospitals a fixed price instead of paying costs. Since hospitals keep the difference between prices and costs, there is an incentive to reduce costs to maximize profits or surpluses available for charity care and the expansion of services. Hospitals can reduce costs by reorganizing so that they deliver services more efficiently, but they may also reduce the level of services provided. One danger is that hospitals may cut costs by reducing services to the point of producing adverse health outcomes. Another danger is that the measures undertaken to reduce costs will involve reduction in charity care, reducing access to hospital services for the uninsured to the point that their health is adversely affected. Finally, there is the danger that selective contracting may impose hidden costs, such as increased travel costs. The empirical issue to resolve is whether the result of the increasingly competitive environment is greater efficiency or decreased quality.

Several related research questions arise from this primary concern:

☐ Is competition widespread enough to make it a viable cost-containment strategy?

☐ Are hospital revenues in more-competitive areas rising more slowly than in less-competitive areas?

☐ Does competition lead to lower prices?

☐ How are hospital costs in more- and less-competitive areas changing?

☐ How are cost savings being realized? Through concentrated or diffuse cuts? Or through greater efficiency in the provision of services? Or by increased specialization? Or all of these?

☐ What effect, if any, is the change in hospital costs having on outcomes of care?

These questions are addressed in the following section.

THE RESEARCH RESULTS

To answer the questions raised in the previous section, we looked primarily at 1980s hospital and insurance data from the state of California.

How Competitive Is the Industry?

A basic objection to the use of selective contracting and competition to control costs is that it can be effective only in areas with more than one hospital. A hospital that has a monopoly has little to fear from selective contracting.

Table 6.1 PROPORTION OF CALIFORNIA POPULATION IN AREAS WITH GIVEN HHI RANGES

HHI Range	Number of ZCAs	Percentage	Mean ZCA Population (1987 est.)	Total Population (1987 est.)	Percentage
HHI <= .15	157	9.3	39,498	6,201,221	23.2
.15< HHI <= .25	291	17.2	29,815	8,676,141	32.5
.25< HHI <= .35	272	16.0	19,820	5,391,009	20.2
.35< HHI <= .45	253	14.9	13,194	3,337,982	12.5
.45< HHI <= .55	273	16.0	7,987	1,892,856	7.1
.55< HHI	450	26.5	2,738	1,232,255	4.6

Notes: HHI, Hirschman-Herfindahl Index; ZCA, ZIP code area. See text for explanation.

To obtain a direct measure of the degree to which people have alternative hospitals available to them, we constructed a measure of concentration known as a Hirschman-Herfindahl Index (HHI) for each ZIP code area (ZCA) in California. The higher the HHI, the greater the degree of market concentration. The ZCAs with similar degrees of concentration are combined into the six HHI categories delineated in table 6.1 (Zwanziger and Melnick 1991c).[2]

Table 6.1 shows that 75.9 percent of the population live in ZCAs with an HHI of .35 or lower. Although this degree of concentration is high for most industries, it is equivalent to three-quarters of the population having a choice of being admitted to three or more equally sized hospitals, a reasonable degree of choice given the minimum effective hospital size required to provide a full range of services. While most of the population live in competitive areas, and thus these areas generate the most hospital costs, most counties, or ZCAs, are relatively non-competitive. This disparity between population and counties may explain the prevalence of the erroneous impression that competitive markets are the exception rather than the rule.

The impression that California hospitals are generally located sufficiently distant from one another so as to preclude competition results from the use of political boundaries for market areas (see number and percentage of ZCAs, table 6.1). However, patient-origin-based measures show that in fact the vast majority of the California population lives in areas served by more than one hospital. California is highly urbanized compared to other states, and thus its hospitals may be somewhat more competitive in that respect. Since health care expenditures are likely to be disproportionately concentrated in urban areas, owing to the higher average complexity of the care

Table 6.2 NET REVENUE TO GROSS REVENUE IN CALIFORNIA HOSPITALS

Year	1980	1981	1982	1983	1984	1985	1986	1987	1988
Ratio of net revenue to gross revenue	0.84	0.83	0.80	0.77	0.77	0.76	0.72	0.67	0.64

urban hospitals provide, even a larger proportion of total expenditures will occur in areas with a reasonable degree of competition.

Is Competition Constraining Revenue?

Selective contracting *must* constrain the rate of growth in hospital revenue if it is going to succeed. One indicator of the competitive and cost-containment pressures hospitals experience is the amount of discounts they provide to payers, since selective contracting usually results in negotiated prices below hospital charges.

A measure of these discounts is the difference between gross revenues (billed charges) and net revenues (the amount actually collected by the hospital). An increase in hospital discounts, especially a large increase, would generally indicate that fewer payers are paying hospital charges and/or that the discount each is receiving is increasing.

As shown in table 6.2, the ratio of net to gross revenue has decreased steadily in California since 1980, when charges were discounted 16 percent on average across all payers. Given that the public payers, Medicare and Medicaid, were paying the lower of costs or charges at that time, private payers were paying essentially full charges. This ratio fell gradually until the end of 1985, followed by a sharp drop. This table suggests that the pressure on hospital revenues followed a similar pattern.

The next test of this hypothesis occurred when we examined time trends in net real patient revenue in the period 1980–87 for hospitals in environments of differing competitiveness and subject to differing degrees of financial pressure from the Medicare Prospective Payment System (PPS) (Melnick, Zwanziger, and Bradley 1989). We found that after 1982, hospital revenues grew more slowly in the more competitive areas and that the average rate of growth in hospital revenue, for all hospitals, had fallen dramatically. Since the cohort of hospitals in each area remained the same during the entire period, we were able to trace differences in the rate at which revenues increased. The main weakness of this approach is its inability to separate out the effects of other factors such as changes over time in patient volumes, in the mix of inpatient and outpatient services, and in case mix from the direct revenue effects of competition.

We have developed a formal multivariate revenue model along the lines of the cost model used in Zwanziger and Melnick (1988) to provide detailed estimates of the effects. The preliminary results of this calculation show that hospital revenues have risen far more slowly in more-competitive areas than in less-competitive ones from 1983 to 1990. Competition *has* proven capable of reducing the rate of increase in hospital revenues (Melnick and Zwanziger 1991).

These results suggest that selective contracting has had a substantial (and since 1983, statistically significant) reducing effect on the total growth rate in hospital revenues, including a dramatic shift to relatively unconstrained outpatient services. *Total* hospital revenue, the sum of revenue from inpatient and outpatient services, has been increasing far more slowly in competitive areas of California than in concentrated ones.[3]

Does Competition Lead to Lower Prices?

Despite the rapid growth in health plans that base their payments on the prospective reimbursement approach, little is known about the effects of these plans on hospital prices. Some researchers have voiced concern that in markets for which one insurance carrier has a substantial share of the health insurance market, this market position can be exploited to gain greater discounts (Pauly 1987). Several articles have addressed these issues both theoretically and empirically (Staten, Dunkelberg, and Umbeck 1987; Staten, Umbeck, and Dunkelberg 1988). We tested these issues empirically using better measures and data than previous studies (Melnick, Zwanziger, Bamezai, and Pattison 1992). In addition to utilizing actual hospital pricing data from one of the oldest and largest PPOs in the country, our data are from 1987, several years after formation of the PPO, and thus reflect a more stable pattern of adjustment.

Blue Cross of California provided data on the prices they negotiated with their network of hospitals in 1987. In addition, they provided us with the number of inpatient days accounted for by each network hospital. We used data for 214 of the 226 general acute care hospitals in the Blue Cross preferred provider network.[4]

To examine the role of market structure in the determination of PPO prices, the final contract price between Blue Cross and providers was regressed (using ordinary least squares) on a vector of covariates that include market and provider characteristics as well as provider ownership dummy variables. Of the variables included to control for hospital differences, only the cost index (the predicted value of lagged relative costs) was statistically significant; hospitals providing a more expensive mix of services received a higher price. Of greater significance for our study, we found that hospital market structure, defined by degree of competition, is an important (and highly significant) determinant of the final price that Blue Cross pays its network hospitals.

After controlling for product differences, the estimated coefficient for the HHI is positive and statistically significant, suggesting that hospitals located in less-competitive markets are able to secure higher prices. A concrete implication of the results is the estimate for the long-run effect on market prices of a merger that leads to a reduction in the number of competitors from three to two equal competitors. In this case, the HHI would increase from 0.33 to 0.50, an increase of 50 percent. Our results would predict that this reduction in the level of competition would lead, on average, to an increase in prices of 9 percent.

It is important to note that this estimate of the price effect of a merger is likely to be an underestimate for at least two reasons. First, our analysis uses the HHI to measure the competitive structure of the market. The HHI used here is based on admissions by all payers, whereas the dependent variable is the price paid by an insurance plan for patients with private insurance. The HHI will measure the market's competitiveness with some error, since it is intended to measure the presence in the market of feasible alternative providers of hospital services. Thus, the HHI should be calculated using the discharges of privately insured patients only. Such an error in the measurement of a variable will tend to result in an underestimate of the magnitude of its coefficient (and the level of its significance), leading to an underestimate of the effects of competition on price.

A second reason for potentially underestimating the price effects of competition relates to the structure of our model. We utilized relative costs in the prior year to control for case-mix and other product differences across hospitals before estimating the effects of competitive structure on price. Our previous analyses of hospital competition found that hospitals in more-competitive markets were more successful in restraining their price increases over time in California. If competition leads to lower rates of cost increases, then hospital administrators, presumably aware of their cost-containment plans, would anticipate lower costs in the following year in more-competitive markets. If, based on the results presented here, lower costs lead to lower prices, then by including costs in our model, the estimated coefficient for the HHI will not capture the full effects of competition on price. For both of these reasons, the estimated coefficient on the HHI presented here should be considered a lower bound of the effects of competition on price.

We also found two other intriguing features of the data. First, the estimated coefficient of the variable measuring the share of the hospital's total patient days covered by Blue Cross is negative and marginally significant (at the .10 level). This suggests that the greater the share of the hospital's business derived from a single payer, the greater the leverage that payer has over the hospital and, therefore, the greater the discount the hospital must provide. The second feature is that the estimated coefficient of the variable that measures the Blue Cross market share held by a hospital in its area is positive and highly significant. This suggests that as a hospital's importance in the PPO network increases relative to the average competitor in its market, its leverage over the payer increases and the hospital is able to negotiate a higher price.

Our results illustrate some of the subtleties involved in developing hospital networks. In general, it pays for plans to contract with mid-sized hospitals, where they can gain greater leverage with the same number of patient days than they can in larger hospitals. This observation is due to the fact that larger hospitals have the ability to absorb a greater share of total Blue Cross days in the market without becoming too dependent on a single payer. In addition, these findings suggest that increased consolidation among plans would lead to greater hospital cost savings, since the importance of any single hospital is lower for larger plans with a greater number of patient days.

Most importantly, we find strong evidence that competition in the hospital sector can lead to lower prices to purchasers. Third-party plans that utilize selective contracting (PPOs and HMOs) can leverage competitive market conditions to negotiate lower prices from hospitals. However, the ways in which these insurance plans design and manage their hospital networks are important in determining the benefits they derive from competitive market conditions.

Are Costs Being Controlled?

Although, conceptually, selective contracting enables payers to constrain revenues to induce cost-effective behavior on the part of hospitals, we focused our initial assessment of the effects of competition on hospital costs. This apparently paradoxical choice was based on the fact that behavior is influenced by expectations as well as by current experience. Even before there were enough patients in PPOs to have a discernible effect on revenues, hospital administrators could begin to control costs in anticipation of competition's effects.

The main objective of several previously published studies has been to test the hypothesis that, with the enactment of selective contracting legislation, hospital competition changed in California from a force that tended to increase hospital costs to one that tended to decrease them. Several approaches were used, including a complex multivariate model used to examine real expenses, one based on ANACOVA for the year-over-year percentage increases, and percentage-change trends for different hospital cohorts (Luft and Robinson 1988; Melnick and Zwanziger 1988; Melnick, Zwanziger, and Bradley 1989; Zwanziger and Melnick 1988).

Although the methods utilized were very different, they all showed a dramatic slowing of the rates of increase in costs for hospitals in more-competitive areas relative to those in less-competitive ones. For example, the multivariate model found a significant cost-reducing trend for hospitals operating in competitive markets. The difference in total hospital expenses between hospitals in highly competitive markets and those in low-competition markets fell by an estimated 7 percent between 1983 and 1985. We have recently updated this model through the end of 1990, and the preliminary results show that this trend has continued (Melnick and Zwanziger 1991).

Did Hospitals Cut Costs in Selected Areas or Across the Board?

Previously cited research has shown that price-based competition has led hospitals to reduce the rate of growth in their costs (Melnick and Zwanziger 1988; Zwanziger and Melnick 1988; and Robinson and Luft 1988); however, the strategies employed to cut costs remain unclear. One cost-cutting mechanism, shifting patients from inpatient to outpatient services, is certainly not the answer. Melnick and Zwanziger (1988) have shown that there has been a decrease in total patient days and an increase in outpatient visits over time in California. They hypothesized that cost reductions could be achieved by substituting outpatient services for inpatient care, but found little difference in these changes across hospitals by market competitiveness (see also Melnick, Zwanziger and Bradley [1989] for supporting data through 1987).

Figure 6.1 DIVISION OF CALIFORNIA HOSPITALS INTO FIVE GROUPS
ACCORDING TO MARKET COMPETITIVENESS AND DEGREE OF
FINANCIAL PRESSURE FROM MEDICARE'S PROSPECTIVE PAYMENT
SYSTEM (PPS)

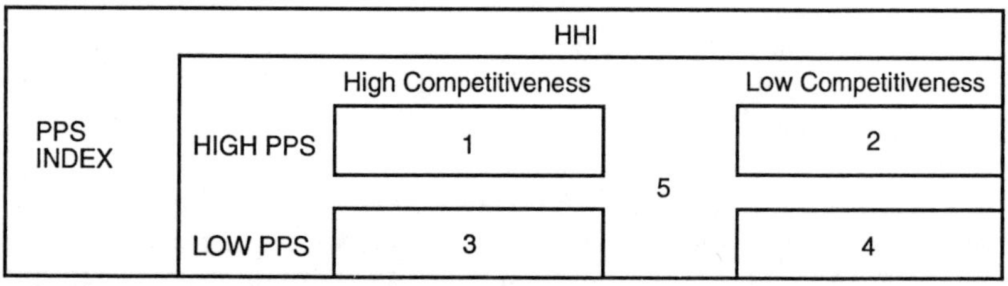

		HHI		
		High Competitiveness		Low Competitiveness
PPS INDEX	HIGH PPS	1		2
			5	
	LOW PPS	3		4

Notes: HHI, Hirschman-Herfindahl Index; see text for explanation.

Next, we looked at costs and resource use on a more disaggregate level. Using the California hospital cost reports filed with the Office of Statewide Health Planning and Development, we examined both expenses and a measure of output for each of 11 revenue centers (see Appendix 6.A for a definition of these cost centers). The cost-center outputs are measures of service units produced, such as x-rays, laboratory tests, and surgical procedures, and can be thought of as intermediate products in the overall production of a hospital discharge or outpatient visit. These cost-center outputs are quantified in terms of a standard unit of measure (SUM). Because a single cost center may have multiple outputs, the SUM is designed to reflect the level of resource use required to produce each type of output relative to a chosen standard for the cost center. The total number of SUMs produced by a cost center corresponds to its total output.

We constructed three measures of resource use at the cost-center level: (1) total expenses, (2) total SUMs, and (3) a measure of unit cost or efficiency in production, the expense per SUM. We calculated these measures for each of the 11 types of cost centers listed in Appendix 6.A. The 1982 value is used as a baseline representing the years prior to policy changes, and measures in subsequent years are examined as a percentage change from this period. Each measure is evaluated based on the level of competitiveness within the hospital market. Competition and PPS indices were defined as previously described by Melnick and Zwanziger (1988) and Feder, Hadley, and Zuckerman (1987). Hospitals were divided into five groups according to the competitiveness of their markets and the degree of financial pressure they face from the Medicare PPS program (see figure 6.1.)

The preliminary results of these analyses can be summarized as showing that hospitals in more-competitive areas cut expenses across most cost centers, rather than concentrating deep cuts in a few areas (Zwanziger and Melnick 1991a). The expense reductions also tended to result primarily from efficiency gains (the changes in expenses/SUM), rather than from reductions in the volume of services (the number of SUMs for each revenue center). The one major exception is in the area of therapeutic services, the growth of which has been cut dramatically in competitive areas.

These results suggest that through 1988, dramatic changes in the outcome of care were not a probable effect of hospital expense pruning. One central question raised by this analysis is how close hospitals are to cutting muscle rather than accumulated fat.

Is Hospitals' Service Mix Becoming More Specialized?

Specialization attained through hospitals focusing on a narrower range of services would be a particularly desirable consequence of selective contracting, in that specialization would be expected to reduce costs and increase quality. It would mark a fundamental shift in strategy from the "medical arms race" often blamed for the cost spiral (Feldstein 1977), in which advanced technology acted as a quality proxy and pacifier of the medical staff, to one centered on cost-effectiveness.[5]

Intuition tells us that underutilized services increase average costs substantially as fixed costs are spread over fewer patients (see Farley and Hogan [1990] for results supporting this intuition). Service rationalization leads to hospitals having greater service-specific volumes, and such hospitals tend to experience lower associated mortality, particularly for surgical procedures (see, for example, Flood, Scott, and Ewy 1984; Hannan et al. 1989; Hughes et al. 1987; Luft, Bunker, and Enthoven 1979; Roos et al. 1986; Showstack et al. 1987).

However desirable service rationalization might be from a public policy perspective, hospitals will move only grudgingly toward an increasingly concentrated service mix. Three factors are likely to impede specialization. The first is that the services a hospital provides serve to define it, and hospitals are loath to change critical components of their identity. Second, there are likely to be financial incentives to retain unprofitable services, since the revenue they generate still tends to exceed marginal costs. The decrease in volume would reduce profits, in the short run at least. Finally, hospitals use their service mix as an important part of their competitive strategy.

We hypothesize two related, but distinct and strategic dimensions in a hospital's development of its service mix. The first dimension is internal, in that a hospital evaluates its goals and resource constraints in deciding the range of services to offer. The second dimension is directly competitive and externally oriented, and consists of a hospital's comparison of the service mix it offers to that of its competitors.[6]

We constructed two measures of these strategic dimensions to determine whether or not hospitals have indeed changed their service mix over time or if the level of competitiveness of the hospital market in general is related to the service mix. The first, a measure of concentration, is an extension of the Hirschman-Herfindahl Index (HHI). The Service Mix HHI (SHHI) is defined as the sum of the squares of the discharges from a service category as a proportion of all discharges from the hospital. Therefore, we have defined an SHHI for each hospital as follows:

$$\text{SHHI}(1) = \text{Sum over all services offered } (P_{1i}^2), \quad (6.1)$$

where P_{1i} is the proportion of hospital 1's discharges accounted for by the ith service category.

This measure is analogous to the HHI used for measuring market concentration, with a hospital providing only one service having an SHHI of 1.0 and a hospital having its discharges equally divided among the 47 service categories having an SHHI of 0.021. The more discharges accounted for by a smaller range of services, the higher the SHHI.

The second measure of strategic dimensions, a measure of differentiation (DIFF), examines how different a hospital's service mix is from the average of its direct competitors. The measure is calculated using the proportion of discharges from each service category as follows:

$$\text{DIFF}(1) = \text{Sum over services } (P_{1i} - P_i)^2, \quad (6.2)$$

where P_i is the corresponding average proportion for the hospitals in a hospital's peer group and P_{1i} is the proportion of hospital 1's discharges accounted for by the ith service. Hospitals with a service mix similar to their competitors will have a small value for this measure relative to other hospitals; hospitals that have unusual service mixes will have larger values for this measure.

The results suggest that, at least through 1988, the change in the form of competition from amenity- to price-based competition has had no significant influence on either measure of hospital service mix (Zwanziger and Melnick 1991a). Contrary to the traditional view that hospitals compete by matching services, these results suggest that it is internal hospital factors such as size, ownership, and teaching status, plus external ones such as location and market size, that most strongly influence service mix. These findings are not surprising for data from 1983, the first year of the study, which largely reflect the preselective contracting, pre-PPS state of affairs. What is more surprising is that hospitals still had not changed their service mix strategy by 1988 despite several years of experience under the two cost-containment policies.

Do Cost Controls Reduce the Quality of Care?

Having established that hospitals in more competitive areas have slowed the rate of increase in costs, the question is whether this involves a loss of "fat" or of "bone and muscle." Luft and Robinson attempted to detect a deterioration in the quality of care associated particularly with hospitals in highly competitive areas. After preliminary analysis, they decided to focus their study of the relationship between competition and patient care outcomes on the mortality rates for three medical conditions: Acute Myocardial Infarction (AMI), stroke, and pneumonia (Luft 1991). They estimated expected mortality based on patient characteristics such as age, sex, and the presence of secondary diagnoses. They then examined the relationship between actual and expected mortality rates for Medicare and private insurance patients separately.

To remove the effects of overall trends, such as the shift from inpatient to outpatient services or technical improvements, Luft and Robinson adjusted expected outcomes in each year to the averages observed in that year. This focused the analysis on the question of outcomes in competitive areas versus those in less-competitive ones. They estimated 24 separate hospital-level regression models: 3 conditions (AMI, stroke, pneumonia) × 2 payers (Medicare, private insurance) × 4 years (1983–86). Each regression model was estimated using a weighted least-squares method, with the square root of the number of patients in the hospital used as the weight. The dependent variable was the inpatient mortality rate. Independent variables included payer mix and a competition measure (1—Hirschman-Herfindahl Index), the "policy" variables; and, as controls, hospital teaching status, type of ownership, and the diagnosis-specific volume (Luft and Robinson 1991).

In 13 of 24 regressions, a higher level of competition meant a higher mortality rate. (For the other 11 regressions, the results were statistically insignificant.) However, there was no clear indication that it was the time period (1983–86) that made the difference, there-fore providing no evidence of a time trend. On the other hand, Luft and Robinson (1991) found that there was a strong, but unclear, relationship between the percentage of Medi-Cal (California's Medic-aid program) patients at a hospital and the outcomes for Medicare and privately insured patients at that hospital. For most categories in most years, a greater percentage of Medi-Cal patients was associ-ated with a higher mortality rate for both groups, other things being equal. Finally, Luft and Robinson found no consistent pattern between the percentage of Medicare patients and patient outcomes.

These findings can be intepreted in several ways, each of which, at least initially, seems plausible. The fact that outcomes tend to be worse than expected in highly competitive areas suggests either that hospitals in these areas have had persistent quality problems or that the competition measure is correlated with significant, omitted patient characteristics that influence outcomes. The strong relation-ship between the percentage Medi-Cal patients and outcomes for non-Medi-Cal patients suggests, again, that hospitals with large Medi-Cal loads have had a persistent quality problem, or may suggest the presence of omitted variables that correlate closely with high Medi-Cal volume, or that low Medi-Cal reimbursement rates have squeezed hospitals and caused them to cut back on services that improve outcomes. The absence of a corresponding relationship between the percentage of Medicare patients and outcomes is consistent with a national study of the effects of the Diagnosis Related Group (DRG) payment system (Kahn et al. 1990; Rogers et al. 1990). It may reflect the fact during the period being studied, Medicare patients were generally profitable for hospitals.

The results of the current study are suggestive at best. Further research will enable more definite conclusions. On the simplest level, the analysis could be extended to include later years when hospitals found themselves under greater financial pressure. Such analysis would enable us to try to define more sensitive measures of quality of care such as complication rates, which would allow us to extend our study to include surgical procedures with low mortality rates. Finally, we could develop more hospital-specific measures of the intensity of cost-containment efforts, presumably the actual causal mechanism, and use them as explanatory variables.

Access to Care

The distance traveled for hospital care can be considered to be an aspect of accessibility. It is also the one aspect of cost of care that is borne entirely by patients (and their families). It is important to see

Table 6.3 AVERAGE DISTANCE TRAVELED TO HOSPITAL FROM ZIP CODE
AREAS OF DIFFERING COMPETITIVENESS IN CALIFORNIA

			HHI Range			
Year	<.15	.15–.25	.25–.35	.35–.45	.45–.55	>.55
1983	6.9571	7.6668	10.3007	13.1086	15.5073	19.3859
1984	6.9737	7.8529	10.2554	13.3548	16.8418	19.9284
1985	7.0932	7.5996	10.7505	12.9404	16.2241	19.4788
1986	6.8596	7.8062	10.4388	13.2925	16.2596	18.8233
1987	7.0611	7.8362	10.6186	12.5502	16.9187	18.8748

Notes: Columns in table represent (l. to r.) hospital markets of increasing concentration
as measured by the Hirschman-Herfindahl Index (HHI).

whether the explosive growth in plans that use a subset of hospitals
has led to a significant increase in the distance that Californians
travel for care.

Table 6.3 shows the number of miles traveled in California for
hospital care from 1983–87. The columns represent, from left to right,
hospital markets of increasing concentration (decreasing competitiveness) as measured by the HHI.[7]

Insurance plans that contract selectively have tended to avoid areas
with highly concentrated hospital markets, since they have little
ability to extract concessions in such areas (Zwanziger and Melnick
1991). As a result, areas served by several alternative hospitals are
those in which one might expect to see increases in travel distance.
However, it appears that this tendency is not observed. We found
no significant trends in travel distance even in relatively competitive
ZCAs. Alternatively, one might argue that it is in areas highly dependent on a single hospital where selective contracting could have a
significant effect on travel distance, since the exclusion of that local
hospital would force patients to travel to a distant one. Again, the
travel distance data provide no evidence of such developments. Overall, selective contracting has not appeared to cause a significant
change in the distance traveled by patients for hospital care. These
results are consistent with the observations that selective contracting
plans have tended to tread warily in limiting their provider networks,
because they have a relatively small ability to force patients into
changing providers.

CONCLUSIONS

These results show strong differences over time in the behavior of
hospitals in more-competitive versus less-competitive areas. One

Table 6.4 AVERAGE ANNUAL GROWTH RATE IN HOSPITAL EXPENSES PER
CAPITA: CALIFORNIA VERSUS THE UNITED STATES

Period	United States (%)	California (%)
1965–82	13.3	13.3
1983–88	7.2	5.5

could downplay the significance of these results by arguing that
competition will affect only a few atypical hospitals in the most
highly competitive areas. However, aggregate data prove that these
reductions did not occur at a few isolated hospitals. Rather, competition affected the rate of increase in total hospital costs (inpatient and
outpatient) for the entire state.

Aggregate Expense Data

To supplement our hospital-level analysis, we have strong aggregate
evidence that a significant change has occurred in California since
passage of selective contracting legislation in 1982. A comparison of
the rates of increase in hospital expenses between California and the
nation in general shows a dramatic change in the historical trends
after 1982.[8]

Table 6.4 shows that per capita spending, which had been growing
at the same rate in California as in the entire United States from 1965
to 1982, has been increasing at a substantially slower annual rate in
California since 1982 (5.5 percent in California compared to 7.2 percent nationally). We find differences in the rate of growth in expense
per adjusted day and per adjusted discharge (tables 6.5 and 6.6 respectively) because of California's dramatically shorter length of stay
relative to the rest of the nation.

Tables 6.5 and 6.6 provide partial measures of changes in treatment
intensity, the cost per unit of hospital output. In both cases, California
hospitals have reversed longstanding relationships between their

Table 6.5 AVERAGE ANNUAL GROWTH RATE IN HOSPITAL EXPENSES PER
ADJUSTED DAY: CALIFORNIA VERSUS THE UNITED STATES

Period	United States (%)	California (%)
1971–82	11.5	13.4
1983–88	9.0	7.3

Table 6.6 AVERAGE ANNUAL GROWTH RATE OF HOSPITAL EXPENSES PER
ADJUSTED DISCHARGE: CALIFORNIA VERSUS THE UNITED STATES

Period	United States (%)	California (%)
1971–82	11.4	13.7
1983–88	10.2	8.0

rates of growth and the national rate. Whereas prior to the advent of
selective contracting, California hospitals tended to increase their
costs/adjusted discharge and costs/adjusted day at a higher rate than
the national average, since 1982 their costs have annual increases
that are almost 2 percent below the national rates.

Finally, an examination of the most complete measure of demand
in California and the United States—per capita spending as a percentage of per capita income (table 6.7)—shows almost identical increases
between 1965 and 1982 (both measures increased by 129 percent);
between 1982 and 1988 the percentage increase in the United States
was 6 percent, while it decreased by 3 percent in California. These
aggregate data clearly indicate the significant changes that have
occurred in hospital behavior in California since 1982, changes that
are not evident in the United States as a whole. These data, combined
with the previous cross-sectional results, show the powerful effect
of competition on hospital costs.

The most important conclusion found in this study is that hospital
revenues are being constrained by the growth of managed-care plans,
and that these hospitals are restraining the rate of growth in their
costs. The results reported here differ from those of previously published studies that found that hospitals in comparatively competitive
markets tended to have higher costs than those in less competitive
markets (Farley 1985; Joskow 1980; Luft et al. 1986; Robinson and
Luft 1985, 1987; Wilson and Jadlow 1982). All of these studies used
hospital data from the 1970s and early 1980s, before selective contracting became an important aspect of the market for hospital insurance. The results of all of these studies are consistent with the theory

Table 6.7 HOSPITAL EXPENSES PER CAPITA AS PERCENTAGE OF PER CAPITA
INCOME: CALIFORNIA VERSUS THE UNITED STATES

Period	United States (%)	California (%)
1965	1.72	1.61
1982	3.94	3.78
1988	4.16	3.68

that during this period hospitals competed on bases of quality and amenity, rather than price (Held and Pauly 1983). The results reported here are for a period when the dramatic growth in selective contracting resulted in increasingly intense price competition among California hospitals. This was not a one-time reduction in costs but a continuing cost-cutting process. It remains unclear how these cost savings have been accomplished.

In addition, we conclude that:

□ Hospitals' cost cutting seems to have been "across the board" rather than concentrated in a few revenue centers.

□ There appears to have been no systematic change in hospitals' service mix, a critical element in achieving a hospital's mission and in carrying out its competitive strategy. Cutting costs while retaining the same basic strategy is clearly attractive in the short run to those concerned about keeping costs low, since a cost-reduction program based on structural changes such as a narrower service mix is much harder to reverse than one consisting of small changes in staffing ratios. Data from the end of the 1980s will show whether hospital administrators were able to maintain this strategy over a sustained period of growing financial pressure.

□ Competition appears to have had no impact on outcomes of care.

□ Data regarding distance traveled for hospital care suggest that health care plans have extensive hospital networks. As a result, there is no evidence of increased patient costs for health care associated with increased travel time.

Policy Implications

Our results provide strong evidence that competition in the hospital sector can lead to lower prices (and lower total expenditures) to purchasers. Insurers are often able to leverage competitive market conditions to negotiate lower prices. However, it is critical that third-party plans that utilize selective contracting (PPOs and HMOs) have alternatives when designing their hospital networks. It is important to keep in mind that the effectiveness of selective contracting as a cost and price control method is highly dependent on there being sufficient competition in the market. It is, therefore, incumbent upon both third-party payers, through their contracting activities, and government agencies such as the California attorney general, the Federal Trade Commission, and the U.S. Department of Justice, through regulatory oversight, to ensure that market conditions remain competitive. This will provide the opportunity to assess more fully the relative advantages and disadvantages of competition.

However, cost containment is a necessary, but insufficient, condition to recommend policies that increase price competition. After all, regulatory policies can also lower the rate of increase in costs (Robinson and Luft 1988) when applied with sufficient political will. It is the "costs" of cost containment that becomes the central issue, because in the long run, cost control that degrades quality or access excessively will become unacceptable, both politically and otherwise. The study of the evolution of the health care systems in states with distinctively different policies will provide further insight. Research in this area is not yet complete. The following analyses will shed additional light on the consequences of competition.

1. We have to identify more precisely how cost reductions were achieved. We could then use this information to develop better measures for investigating the implications of competition on outcomes of care.
2. We have to incorporate differences in physician and insurance markets and trace these differences to variations in prices, utilization and costs.
3. We plan to investigate the effects of selective contracting on physician behavior.
4. Ultimately, we are interested in the degree to which consumers benefit from price and quality competition brought about by selective contracting. One of the main ways in which consumers may benefit is if selective contractors pass savings in payments to providers on to consumers through reductions in premiums and/or increases in insurance benefits.

APPENDIX 6.A: AGGREGATION OF COST CENTERS

1. Routine Daily Services (RDS): Medical Surgical Acute, Pediatric Acute, Psychiatric Acute, Psychiatric Acute—Adolescent and Pediatric, Obstetrics Acute, Rehabilitation, Other Acute Care.
2. Intensive Daily Services (IDS): Medical/Surgical Intensive Care, Definitive Observation, Coronary Intensive Care, Pediatric Intensive Care, Neonatal Intensive Care, Burn Care, Psychiatric Isolation, Other Intensive Care.
3. Sub-Acute Daily Services (SADS): Nursery Acute, Psychiatric Long-term, Intermediate Care, Residential, Other Daily Services.
4. Visits (VISSUM): Emergency Room, Psychiatric Emergency Room, Surgical Day Care, Clinics, Home Health.
5. Other Ancillary Services (OAS): Ambulance
6. Laboratory (LABSUM): Lab—Clinical, Lab—Pathological, Blood Bank, Lab—Pulmonary Function.
7. Pharmacy (PHASUM): Central Services, Supply and Pharmacy.
8. Diagnostic Services (DX SUM): Electrocardiology, Cardiac Catheterization Lab, Electromyography, EEG.
9. Therapeutic Services (TX SUM): Inhalation Therapy, Physical Therapy, Occupational Therapy, Dialysis, Other Physical Medicine.
10. Radiological Services (RADSUM): Radiology—Diagnostic, CT, Radiology—Therapeutic, Nuclear Medicine.
11. Surgery (SURSUM): Labor and Delivery, Surgery and Recovery, Anesthesiology.

Notes

This study was partially supported by grants from the Office of the Assistant Secretary for Planning and Evaluation, U.S. Department of Health and Human Services; the

Agency for Health Care Policy and Research; and the Robert Wood Johnson Foundation.

1. Many theoretical models exist of how hospitals make decisions (e.g., Ellis and McGuire 1986; Harris 1977; Newhouse 1970; Pauly and Redisch 1973). Most of these models are empirically indistinguishable in terms of identifying the variables that are chosen and the determinants of those choices. In other words, although structurally different, these models do not provide important differences in terms of the specification of the reduced-form equation.

2. The HHI is remarkably stable over time. We used the value of the HHI in 1987 to define the six categories.

3. We present some aggregate data in the next section to further support this argument.

4. For proprietary reasons, Blue Cross did not give us the price data in dollars. Instead, they converted the dollar amounts into a relative price index by dividing each hospital's per diem rate by the overall average per diem rate.

5. The fact that hospitals could attract patients in this way, by constantly increasing quality and amenities with no regard for costs, was the straightforward result of the incentives built into cost- or charge-based reimbursement policies before 1982. Luft et al. (1986) found, in fact, that during this period there was a significant tendency for hospitals to mirror their competitors in their choice of specialized services.

6. Hospitals can use two generic competitive approaches in choosing the mix of services to provide: differentiation or imitation. Differentiation would involve a conscious effort to create a unique identity by offering a different set of services from competing hospitals; imitation would lead the hospital to match the services offered by its competitors. Luft et al. (1986) suggested that hospitals have generally engaged in an imitation strategy, matching the services provided by their competitors.

7. We also examined the travel distance for each of 47 service categories. They revealed no clear pattern of changes over time.

8. The change in trends would be even more dramatic if we compared California and the United States minus California, since California hospitals accounted for approximately 10 percent of the U.S. total.

References

Ellis, Randall P., and Thomas G. McGuire. 1986. "Provider Behavior under Prospective Reimbursement: Cost Sharing and Supply." *Journal of Health Economics* 5: 129–151.

Farley, Dean E. 1985. "Competition among Hospitals: Market Structure and Its Relation to Utilization, Costs, and Financial Position." Research Note 7, Hospital Studies Program. Rockville, MD: U.S. Dept. of Health and Human Services, Office of the Asst. Sec. for Health, National Center for Health Services Research and Health Care Technology Assessment.

Farley, Dean, and C. Hogan. 1990. "Case-Mix Specialization in the Market for Hospital Services." *Health Services Research* 25 (5 December): 757–782.

Feder, Judith, Jack Hadley, and Stephen Zuckerman. 1987. "How Did Medicare's Prospective Payment System Affect Hospitals?" New England Journal of Medicine 317: 867–873.

Feldstein, Martin. 1977. "Quality Change and the Demand for Hospital Care." Econometrica 4: N7.

Flood, Ann B., W. R. Scott, and W. Ewy. 1984. "Does Practice Make Perfect? Part I: The Relation between Hospital Volume and Outcomes for Selected Diagnostic Categories." Medical Care 22 (2): 98–114.

Hannan, E. L., J. F. O'Donnell, H. Kilburn, H. R. Bernard, and A. Yazici. 1989. "Investigation of the Relationship between Volume and Mortality for Surgical Procedures Performed in New York State Hospitals." Journal of the American Medical Association 262 (4 July): 503–10.

Harris, Jeffrey. 1977. "The Internal Organization of Hospitals: Some Economic Implications." Bell Journal of Economics and Management Science (Autumn).

Held, Philip, and Mark Pauly. 1983. "Competition and Efficiency in the End Stage Renal Disease Program." Journal of Health Economics 2 (Summer): 95–118.

Hughes, Robert G., Sandra S. Hunt, and Harold S. Luft. 1987. "Effects of Surgeon Volume and Hospital Volume on Quality of Care in Hospitals." Medical Care 25: 489–503.

Joskow, Paul L. 1980. "The Effects of Competition and Regulation on Hospital Bed Supply and the Reservation Quality of the Hospital." Bell Journal of Economics 11 (Autumn): 421–27.

Kahn, K. L., E. B. Keeler, M. J. Sherwood, W. H. Rogers, D. Draper, S. S. Bentow, E. J. Reinisch, L. V. Ruberstein, J. Kosecoff, and R. H. Brook. 1990. "Comparing Outcomes of Care Before and After Implementation of the DRG-Based Prospective Payment System." Journal of the American Medical Association 264: 1984–1988.

Luft, H. S. and J. R. Robinson. 1991. "Research and Analysis Pertaining to the Effects of Competition on Hospital Performance." Project Report. Photocopy.

Luft, H. S., John P. Bunker, and Alain C. Enthoven. 1979. "Should Operations Be Regionalized? The Empirical Relation between Surgical Volumes and Mortality." New England Journal of Medicine 301 (25: 1364–69).

Luft, Harold S., James C. Robinson, Deborah Garnick, Susan C. Maerki, and Stephen J. McPhee. 1986. "The Role of Specialized Clinical Services in Competition among Hospitals." Inquiry 23 (Spring): 83–94.

Melnick, G. A. and J. Zwanziger. 1988. "Hospital Behavior Under Competition and Cost-Containment Policies: The California Experience, 1980 to 1985," Journal of the American Medical Association 260: 2669–2675.

Melnick, G. A., J. Zwanziger, and T. Bradley. 1989. "Hospital Behavior under Competition and Cost Containment Policies in California, 1980–1987." *Health Affairs* 8 (2, Summer): 129–39.

————. 1991. "The Effect of Selective Contracting on Hospital Costs and Revenues, 1980–1990." Working Paper. Photocopy.

Melnick, G. A., J. Zwanziger, A. Bamezai, and R. Pattison. 1992. "The Effects of Market Structure and Bargaining Position on Hospital Prices." *Journal of Health Economics* 11: 217–233.

Newhouse, Joseph P. 1970. "Toward a Theory of Nonprofit Institutions: An Economic Model of a Hospital." *American Economic Review* 60 (March): 211–226.

Pauly, Mark V. 1987. "Monopsony Power in Health Insurance: Thinking Straight while Standing on Your Head." *Journal of Health Economics* 6: 73–81.

————. 1988. "A Response to 'Market Share/Market Power Revisited.' " *Journal of Health Economics* 7: 85–87.

Pauly, Mark, and Michael Redisch. 1973. "The Not-For-Profit Hospital as a Physicians' Cooperative." *American Economic Review* 63(1, March): 87–99.

Robinson, James C., and Harold S. Luft. 1985. "The Impact of Hospital Market Structure on Patient Volume, Average Length of Stay, and the Cost of Care." *Journal of Health Economics* 4: 333–356.

————. 1987. "Competition and the Cost of Hospital Care, 1972 to 1982." *Journal of the American Medical Association* 257 (23, June 19): 3241–3245.

————. 1988. "Competition, Regulation, and Hospital Costs, 1982 to 1986." *Journal of the American Medical Association* 260: 2676–2681.

Rogers, W. H., D. Draper, K. Kahn, E. B. Keeler, L. V. Rubenstein, J. Kosecoff, and R. H. Brook. 1990. "Quality of Care Before and After Implementation of the DRG-Based Prospective Payment System." *Journal of the American Medical Association* 264: 1989–1994.

Roos, Leslie L., S. M. Cageorge, N. P. Roos, and R. Danzinger. 1986. "Centralization, Certification, and Monitoring: Readmissions and Complications after Surgery." *Medical Care* 24(11): 1044–66.

Showstack, Jonathon A., K. E. Rosenfeld, D. W. Garnick, H. S. Luft, R. E. Schaffarzick, and J. Fowles. 1987. "Association of Volume with Outcome of Coronary Artery Bypass Graft Surgery." *Journal of the American Medical Association* 257 (6): 785–89.

Shortell, Stephen M., and E. F. Hughes. 1990. "The Effects of Regulation, Competition, and Ownership on Mortality Rates among Hospital Inpatients." *New England Journal of Medicine* 318 (17): 1100–07.

Staten, Michael, W. Dunkelberg, and J. Umbeck. 1987. "Market Share and the Illusion of Power." *Journal of Health Economics* 6: 43–58.

Staten, Michael, J. Umbeck, and W. Dunkelberg. 1988. "Market Share/Market Power Revisited: A New Test for an Old Theory." *Journal of Health Economics* 7: 73–83.

Wilson, George W., and Joseph M. Jadlow. 1982. "Competition, Profit Incentives, and Technical Efficiency in the Provision of Nuclear Medicine Services." *Bell Journal of Economics* 13 (Autumn): 472–82.

Zwanziger, J., and G. A. Melnick. 1988. "The Effects of Hospital Competition and the Medicare PPS Program on Hospital Cost Behavior in California." *Journal of Health Economics* 7: 301–20.

————. 1991a. "The Effects of Selective Contracting on Hospital Service Mix." Working Paper. Photocopy.

————. 1991b. "How Hospitals Managed Their Cost Savings, 1980–1987." Working Paper. Photocopy.

————. 1991c. "Selective Contracting and California Hospital Markets." Working Paper. Photocopy.

Chapter Seven

VARIATIONS IN MEDICAL PRACTICE USE: CAUSES AND CONSEQUENCES

Charles E. Phelps and Cathleen Mooney

The phenomenon of geographic variations in medical care use has drawn increasing attention over the past decade, a resurgence that has had an important influence in the passage of new legislation providing for substantial amounts of research into the study of the consequences of various medical care interventions. (See Freund, chapter 3, this volume, for the history and purposes of some of this legislation and Brown, chapter 10, this volume, for policy perspective on these issues and alternative approaches to dealing with problems caused by variability.) Although some variability in resource use is both inevitable and desirable, systematic variations are common and not easily explained by random variability, differences in disease incidence, or standard socioeconomic phenomena. The policy audience in Washington, D.C., and elsewhere has taken substantial notice of the phenomenon (Bowen 1987; Roper et al. 1988), yet economists have seemed more eager to dismiss the variations literature as irrelevant, or else briefly to explain it away. This chapter examines the various "dismissals" of the variations and shows why, even after accounting for these issues, variations remain a real and important phenomenon. We offer new empirical results regarding one possible explanation of variations—substitution between various medical interventions—and clarify their role in understanding regional variations.

We also develop a model of how variations can persist, based on the idea that physicians and patients must acquire and use costly information. We show how divergent "schools of thought" persist in the use of medical interventions, and we present new evidence to suggest that such "schools" have limited boundaries that do not extend to "all" medical practice, but rather, extend probably only within a single specialty or even a single disease. These results have implications for the degree of aggregation that one can safely use to study variations.

Finally, based on this information-cost model, we calculate the welfare losses associated with variations. This analysis contains an important addition to the variations literature—the measure of variation in the use of specific procedures *within* hospitalizations of the same diagnostic category. The welfare losses from this type of variation appear in our preliminary analysis to be nearly as large as (and add to) the welfare losses associated with variations in the rate of hospital admissions themselves.

To place our discussion in perspective in terms of other essays in this volume, Freund (chapter 3) argues that information (in the same sense that we discuss) "may both strengthen the market and make it more competitive. . ." while at the same time "may also lead to greater regulation." Brown (chapter 10) argues that this type of information provides a source of control for regulators to use. Both acknowledge that information about variations in medical care use can provide the basis for regulators to set "target" rates of use of medical interventions, and to detect deviant regions or individual providers.

Our perspective remains somewhat broader; we view the central questions more in terms of diffusion of information. For reasons not thoroughly understood, it seems that providers of medical care comprehend relatively poorly the proper ways to use many medical interventions. Furthermore, this lack of understanding seems to pervade the production of medical care independently of the regulatory environment or even of the financial and legal incentives of a health care system. Perhaps the problems associated with "keeping up" in medicine are nearly insurmountable, but the issues we address may more fundamentally involve the process of initial and continuing medical education than the functioning of health care markets themselves.

THE PHENOMENON OF VARIATIONS

To talk meaningfully about variability in use of medical care, one needs an appropriate measuring stick. The most common measure, and, as shown here, one that is economically meaningful, has been the coefficient of variation (COV), the ratio of the standard deviation (σ) of the distribution of rates of use divided by that distribution's mean (μ). Here, σ measures how "spread out" the pattern of use rates actually is, while μ provides the "yardstick." The COV also has the advantage that one can readily determine statistically significant differences from "no" intrinsic variability (Diehr et al. 1990, 1992). Traditionally in the relevant medical literature, "low variation" means a COV on the order of 0.1 to 0.15, and "high variation" means a COV of 0.4, 0.5 or higher. For two distributions of the same mean, a COV of 0.4 has a variance (σ^2) 16 times as large as one with a COV of 0.1, and a COV of 0.6 implies a variance 36 times larger.

The study of medical practice variations began in 1938, when Sir Alison Glover, a British physician, read a paper before the evening meeting of the Royal Society of Medicine. In that work, he showed that the rates at which school children had their tonsils removed varied greatly across regions of Britain. Using Glover's data, we have calculated the cross-county COV in the tonsillectomy rate as .66. Subsequent studies (Glover 1948; Lembcke 1952; Lewis 1969; Wennberg and Gittelsohn 1973) included a handful of surgical interventions, and several international comparisons of variations also appeared (Dyck et al. 1977; Vayda 1973). The rate of appearance of variations studies has increased rapidly since then, to the point that such study has now become a small industry, and the existence of variations seems well documented and stable across both time and national boundaries.

This literature may be summarized as follows. For some procedures where the reasons for medical intervention seem very clear (e.g., hip fracture, acute myocardial infarction), cross-regional variations are always quite low, with COVs ranging from .1 to .15 or even lower. Other interventions routinely show high variability across regions (e.g., hospitalization for back injury, back surgery, diabetes, hypertension, gastroenteritis, otitis media, etc., and several psychiatric admission categories), with COVs in the range of .4 to .6 or larger. Variations appear larger for nonsurgical hospital admissions than for most surgical admissions (Phelps and Mooney 1992; Phelps and Parente 1990; Wennberg, Freeman, and Culp 1987; Wennberg, McPherson, and Caper 1984; Roos, Wennberg, and McPherson 1988). Hospital care for cardiac and mental illness conditions seem to predominate in lists of hospital admissions with high variability.

"EXPLANATIONS" FOR VARIATIONS

The study of variations was hardly an hour old when the first attempt to explain away the phenomenon appeared: In discussing Sir Alison

Glover's 1938 paper on tonsillectomy variations, one physician in the audience said that "some of the strange facts presented by Dr. Glover . . . might be explained by a psychological factor—namely, maternal anxiety. . . . This factor alone was sufficient to explain the higher incidence . . . in boys than in girls and in well-to-do as compared with the poorer classes." Since then, attempts to dismiss variations have become more sophisticated. We summarize them here, and show why they cannot meaningfully explain the observed variations.

Economic Factors—Demand Side

Most studies of variations adjust for the age and gender composition of the populations under consideration, but do not control for other differences in such variables as income and price. (These studies presume that the age and gender mix of a region importantly determine aggregate illness rates.) Although a few studies have used direct controls for economic variables, little is known about the effect of these variables on variations in medical care use.

The ability of economic variables to explain medical care variations depends in part on the variability of those economic variables across regions, and these are not large. Intuitively, even if income or price "mattered" considerably in determining quantities demanded, these economic forces could not account for cross-regional variability in medical care use if the level of income and prices (insurance coverage) were relatively similar across regions.

In fact, these traditional economic variables do not differ much across regions. Per capita income across New York State counties has a COV of only .2 (data from New York State Statistical Yearbook 1989). Similarly, the fraction of various areas' population covered by health insurance varies by only a little. Across counties in New York State, the proportion of hospital admissions without any insurance coverage (private or government) has a COV of only .026 (calculations available from authors). With some arbitrary assumptions about the degree of coverage offered by these plans, we can calculate the COV in net price across counties at about .08.[1] Similarly, insurance coverage varies only a little across states. With the same assumptions as before, the estimated COV in net price to consumers across states is .11 (data from Health Insurance Association of America 1989, table 1.2). The cross-state estimate is higher than the previous within-state measure because Medicaid eligibility varies across states.

How does variability in income or price affect observed variability in use of a medical intervention? The change in the COV in a dependent variable (y) is *at maximum* $\mid \eta \mid$ times the change in the COV of an explanatory variable (x), where η is the elasticity of y with respect to x (see proof in Appendix 7.A). This provides an upper bound on the ability of income, price, and other variables to explain COVs in medical care use rates.

Keeler et al. (1988) estimated the income elasticity of demand for medical care, particularly for hospital episodes, which we summarize as about .1. Thus, variability in income should add to the COV of hospital use by approximately $.1 \times .2 = .02$. The price elasticity of demand for hospital care has been estimated at $-.1$ to $-.2$ (Keeler et al. 1988; Manning et al. 1987). Thus, the cross-region COV in net medical care price (COV = .08 to .11) will increase the hospital-use COV by about .016 to .022, using an estimate of $\eta = -.2$. Combined, these estimated income and price effects should add to an underlying COV in medical care use across regions by about .04. Thus, income and price variability cannot explain more than a small fraction of the total observed variability in medical care use, particularly for high-variation activities (COV = .4 to .6 or higher).

Other data show the lack of importance of income and price as major contributors to variations. Most notably, similar patterns of variations occur both in countries with national health care systems such as Canada and Great Britain, where the marginal money costs to patients are zero, and in the United States, where nonzero prices exist. This fact alone seems to refute the idea that "standard" demand-side phenomena account for the variations in any comprehensive way. Also, within the United States, the same insurance coverage applies across diseases where variations range over the entire spectrum of observed values (e.g., from .1 or smaller to .8 or larger).

Economic Factors—Supply Side

Two major arguments exist about supply-side factors as an explanation for variable rates of use of medical interventions. The first idea depends strictly on a classic "inducement" model (patients' demands shifted for pecuniary advantage) wherein different rates of medical use depend on different rates of inducement. The second depends on an availability idea (procedures are done where the facilities exist to undertake them).

Consider first how variations might be caused by inducement. For this to hold, either the market opportunities for inducement must differ across regions, or doctors must be willing to exploit inducement opportunities to a different degree in different regions. Neither possibility seems plausible on its face. The same economic forces that alter normal demand for care also would alter opportunities for demand inducement, and much variation remains even after controlling for such variables. The idea that different regions have different degrees of equilibrium inducement seems greatly at odds with the standard literature on inducement, which emphasizes that demand inducement will occur at the maximum possible rate by maximizing physicians (see Dranove 1988, Farley 1986, and references in Phelps 1992, p. 211 for more details). Finally, the presence of variations in Great Britain and elsewhere that are similar to those in the United States presents a considerable embarrassment to those who would explain away variations as an inducement phenomenon, since no incentives exist to induce demand in the British or similar systems.

A second hypothesis says that the availability of beds (or other specialized resources) accounts for the variations. Here, the evidence is mixed, and the problem of inference looms large: does demand follow supply, or conversely? The standard "Roemer's Law" model says that demand follows supply, whereas the standard economic interpretation says that supply follows demand (Roemer 1961).[2] Given the latter possibility, even finding a positive correlation between beds and hospital use rates would not confirm causation. Some studies find positive correlations between surgery rates and the number of surgeons and/or hospital beds in a region (Lewis 1969; Wennberg and Gittelsohn 1973), while others show no relationship (Roos, Roos, and Henteleff 1977; Vayda, Mindell, and Rutkow 1982).

More troublesome for a straight "Roemer's Law" interpretation, even within a single specialty such as cardiology or orthopedics, where relevant per capita resources are held constant, is that large differences in regional variations exist across procedures. For example, in cardiology, the COV for acute myocardial infarction hospital admissions is about .1, but for "chest pain" or "angina pectoris" hospitalizations (relatively less severe and more poorly defined ailments) the COV is as high as .3. In orthopedics, hospitalization for hip fractures has only small variability, but COVs rise to much higher levels for hospitalization for fracture of the ankle and fracture of the forearm, in part because more alternatives exist (e.g., ambulatory surgery or direct treatment in an emergency room [Wennberg 1987]). Since essentially the same resources combine to produce these different treatments, their presence or absence cannot explain regional differences in rates of treatment either for specific diseases or using specific interventions.

Intrinsic Differences in Illness Patterns

It is clearly important when comparing inter-area variations in medical care use to know the underlying patterns of illness. Almost all of the hundreds of studies of regional variation use age and sex standardized rates of medical care use. Blumberg (1987) has challenged the idea that age adjustment accounts for much variation in health status, showing considerable variations across cities in direct measures of illness (such as bed-disability days) even after adjusting for age and sex mix. Blumberg did not, however, show how these illness differences affect hospital use, if at all.

Wennberg (1987) responded by showing that hospital use patterns are unrelated to those illness differences (see also Wennberg and Fowler 1977). We have estimated a regression using Blumberg's (1987) data that shows only a very weak association between bed days and hospital days (t = 1.18), even though about one bed day out of every six is a hospital day. When we remove the hospital days from the bed-day measure, the remaining "home-bed days" are completely uncorrelated with hospital days (t = .19, R^2 = .0013). Thus, one direct measure of illness (bed days) has no association with aggregate rates of hospital use. However, this study focuses on broad patterns of illness and medical resource use, not disease- or procedure-specific approaches, as is common in the variations literature.

A study by Roos and Roos (1982) also addressed this question. Using data on a 5 percent sample of the elderly in Manitoba, they assessed both the health status characteristics of individuals and rates of surgery in 56 rural regions. Their measures included self-reported health status, disability measures, and mental status, as well as standard socioeconomic variables. Overall age/sex adjusted surgery rates varied by a factor of 2.7 from high to low regions; elective surgery rates varied by a factor of 3.2; cataract surgery rates varied by a factor of 4.2. Strikingly, none of the surgery rates was more than very weakly correlated with any of the health indicators, and in most cases, they were in the opposite direction to "need" models of medical use.[3]

None of these studies has a health indicator that directly corresponds to a specific medical procedure. Rather, each uses "general" indicators of illness. Only a small handful of studies provide such direct tests where the illness indicator focuses on a specific illness. One study of tonsillectomy in Manitoba (Roos, Roos, and Henteleff 1977) found no relationship between tonsillectomy rates and the prevalence of respiratory morbidity in a pediatric population. Using these authors' data, we have estimated an elasticity of tonsillectomy surgery rates with respect to their measure of respiratory disease of .4 (t = .96), so although a positive relationship exists, it is very weak, and normally we would not indicate it as differing from zero.

Another study directly measuring something closely akin to "fixable illness" found little or no association between such illness rates and rates of several interventions. In this study, Leape and colleagues (1990) used reviews of medical records in 23 regions to measure the appropriateness of three interventions (carotid endarterectomy, upper gastrointestinal endoscopy, and coronary angiography). They found substantial variations in the underlying rates of use of each of these procedures (COV = .49 for angiography, .41 for endarterectomy, and .21 for endoscopy). Rates of inappropriate use ranged from 8 percent to 75 percent for coronary angiography, 0 to 67 percent for carotid endarterectomy, and from 0 to 25 percent for endoscopy. For coronary angiography, inappropriate use accounted for 28 percent of the variations in use, but for the other two procedures, no significant correlations appeared (R^2 = .03). Leape and colleagues concluded that "little of the variation in rates of use of these procedures can be explained by inappropriate use." Given their definitions of inappropriateness, this provides a good test of how illness rates affect variations; they found little if any relationship for these procedures.

Random Noise

Several authors have noted that some of the data used to demonstrate variability in medical care use has potentially dubious statistical support (Diehr 1984; Diehr et al. 1992). First, some variability would exist simply owing to random chance, even if each observed region produced observations from the same underlying process. The smaller the region under study, the more likely this will occur. In addition, some of the variations literature uses the ratio of highest to lowest observations; the distribution of this "extremal quotient" is unstable when small numbers of persons reside in each area under study.[4]

One approach to assessing the importance of this phenomenon assumes that the event under study (e.g., hospitalization) occurs as in a Poisson process (McPherson et al. 1981). This allows the calculation of the "systematic" component of variation (SCV) that remains independent of chance events. In eight surgical procedures studied by McPherson and colleagues, the random component was only 1–4 percent of total variance in Canada, and averaged about 15 percent in England and Wales (McPherson et al. 1981, table 3). Diehr et al. (1990) have also studied the distribution of the coefficient of variation in "typical" variations data, and provided methods to estimate the 95 percent confidence intervals for coefficients of variation under the null hypothesis of equal rates of use in each region. Diehr et al. (1992) proved the relationship between a population-weighted COV measure and the chi-square statistic, thus providing precise tests for the significance of COV measures. We have applied this test systematically to our studies of variations across counties in New York State, and have found that virtually all of our measures of variability, even after using regression models to adjust for age, gender, income, employment, and other differences across regions, differ significantly from zero. We are not dealing with random noise.

Physician Differences

Scattered evidence suggests that individual physicians develop a practice style that predictably alters resource use, independent of patient illness characteristics. These patterns may depend upon the type of training a physician has received. Some of this evidence (Daniels and Schroeder 1977; Pineault 1977) looks at small numbers of doctors within a single health maintenance organization (HMO). Other work (Kissick et al. 1984) has examined doctors' decisions on a set of "paper patients" regarding doctors' decisions on hospitalization.

Several studies have looked directly at individual doctors' propensities to use hospital medical resources. The first of these (Wolfe and Detmer 1984) found systematic differences across doctors on length of stay (LOS) in two particular operative procedures (appendectomy and herniorrhaphy). McMahon and Newbold (1986) studied length of stay within Diagnosis Related Groups (DRGs) showing that physician practice patterns accounted for more variation than did severity of illness.

Using Manitoba data, Roos and colleagues have made three important contributions to this literature, "assigning" patients to doctors on the basis of frequency of contact in the previous two years. One study (Roos 1984) identified "hysterectomy-prone" obstetricians/gynecologists, and compared the relative odds of a patient of such doctors having either a hysterectomy or a dilatation and curettage (D&C). The relative risk of a hysterectomy for such doctors' patients was 1.6, and for a D&C was 1.8.

A second study (Roos et al. 1986) compared the use of hospital resources for primary care patients by doctor, standardizing for case mix. They showed that 70 percent of variation across physicians in per-patient hospital use was systematic. Further, they found negatively correlated average length of stay (ALOS) and admission rates ($r = -.38$). Case-mix adjustment removed some, but not all, of the variations. Specialization of the doctor had little apparent effect on hospital use, but experience and teaching hospital affiliation reduced hospital use, as did larger numbers of primary care patients in a doctor's practice.

Most recently, Roos (1989) calculated doctors' propensity to hospitalize patients in one sample, and then estimated the risks of hospitalization in another independent sample of those same doctors' patients. Using multiple logistic regression, she calculated the relative risk of hospitalization as 2:1 to 3:1 for patients whose doctors were medium and high on the overall propensity to hospitalize, compared with patients of those doctors who had a low propensity to hospitalize.

In a study still underway, Phelps et al. (1992) have shown strongly significant differences across primary care physicians' resource use for their patients. This study aggregates across all illnesses (of necessity, to obtain sample sizes sufficient to detect differences across doctors), and uses two separate measures to standardize the case mix and illness severity of patients across doctors' practices. In that study, for example, ranked on per-patient resource use, the highest decile of physicians spent over three times as much as the lowest decile.

Substitution in Production

Doctors can diagnose or treat some illnesses with more than one intervention. Thus, observed variations in the use of any one of those procedures would potentially overstate any welfare losses. Indeed, variations in any single procedure might have no associated welfare losses. For some patients, one approach may be preferred to another, but on a population level, we can think about combinations of any of these procedures to produce "cures" in a standard production function approach. Let Q_1 represent the number of cures attempted in figure 7.1; combinations of therapies T_1 and T_2 can produce Q_1 attempted cures along the isoquant. Depending on the substitution possibilities, even small differences in the relative prices of the two interventions could create significant differences in observed patterns of use. A unidimensional estimate of variability in the use of

Figure 7.1 SUBSTITUTE VS. COMPLEMENT TREATMENTS FOR THE SAME
ILLNESS

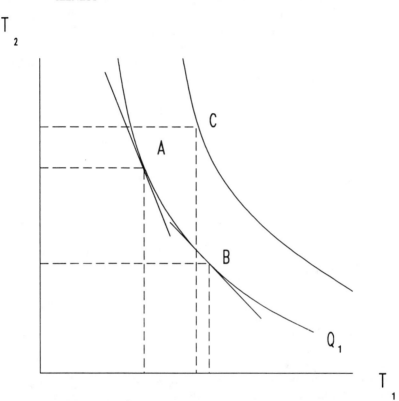

T_1 might show large variation, as would a separate estimate of the
variability for T_2.

One could envision communities with different relative prices for
procedures operating at points like A and B on the Q_1 isoquant (figure
7.1) in ways that were fully appropriate, with no welfare loss arising
at all (assuming that Q_1 was the appropriate overall rate of treatment).
Even if two communities faced the same relative prices, the welfare
loss might only reflect the additional expense in community B, say,
from not operating at the combination used in A. By contrast, seeing
communities like A and C would imply a "pure" variations issue,
namely, that differing and unexplained rates of treatment represented
mistakes on the extensive margin in at least one of the communities.

The correlation between use rates of interventions that potentially serve as substitutes provides a key test on this matter. If appropriate substitution is occurring, then large unidimensional variations could be observed with no welfare loss resulting. For this to hold, the competing interventions would have to show negative correlations in rates of use of. If positive correlations exist, they would indicate something like points A and C (figure 7.1), requiring different overall rates of treatment. Note that one could observe negative correlations and still have important differences in overall treatment rates. We next provide information about two alternative types of substitution: substitution of one form of treatment within the hospital for another, and substitution of inpatient for outpatient therapy.

SUBSTITUTION AMONG INPATIENT TREATMENTS

Within the hospital, we have identified a series of procedures that clearly have the potential to serve as substitutes.[5] We analyzed utilization rates for these procedures in New York State using data from hospital discharge abstracts contained in the Statewide Planning and Research Cooperative System (SPARCS) data (details from authors). These data provide considerable detail on diagnoses, procedures, and patient characteristics, including (importantly for our work) the county of each patient's residence. All of the New York State data cited in the following subsections assemble these records into county-of-patient origin, and calculate use-rates per capita for various interventions. In every case, results rely on residuals from reduced-form regressions that explain 30–90 percent of the raw variability.

Table 7.1 shows our basic results regarding substitution among procedures. This analysis provides the first results concerning substitution in production of health in the variations literature for more than a single procedure.[6] In every case except one that we investigated, the correlations are positive and usually significant at least at the .1 level. In all of these cases, the underlying illnesses and their treatments (cardiac disease, uterine disorders, back injuries) rank high on the list of apparent welfare losses when the procedures are ranked individually. The finding of *positive* correlations between the rates of interventions increases the welfare losses beyond those estimated in the unidimensional analysis. We summarize these results here:

Low-Back Injury. In hospital treatment of low-back injury, the correlation of nonsurgical and surgical admissions was .20. Among those patients, the use of alternative diagnostic tests (myelogram and computed tomography [CT]) was also positively correlated (.44).

Table 7.1 CORRELATION OF SUBSTITUTABLE PROCEDURES/ADMISSION
         RATES

Medical back admissions and surgical back admissions, for low-back problems	.20
Myelogram and CT[a], for low-back problems	.44*
Vaginal hysterectomy and total abdominal hysterectomy, for nonmalignancy	.29*
Total abdominal hysterectomy and myomectomy for nonmalignancy	.19
Extracapsular and intracapsular lens extraction	.33**
Arch- and carotid arteriogram for CVA[b]	.49**
CABG[c] and PCTA[d]	.62**
SV[e] CABG and SV PCTA	.50**
SV CABG and MV[f] CABG	.70**
Admission for pacemaker insertions and medical admissions for selected arrhythmias	.16
Admission for angina with and without arteriogram	.08
Admission for MI[g] with and without arteriogram	−.18
ICU[h] and non-ICU LOS[i] for MI	−.64**
ICU and non-ICU LOS for angina or chest pain	−.37*

Notes:
a. CT, computerized tomography.
b. CVA, cerebrovascular accident (stroke).
c. CABG, coronary artery bypass graft (bypass surgery).
d. PCTA, percutaneous transluminal angioplasty.
e. SV, single vessel.
f. MV, multiple vessell.
g. MI, myocardial infarction.
h. ICU, intensive care unit.
i. LOS, length of stay.
*Significant at $p < .10$.
**Significant at $p < .05$.

Coronary Artery Disease. One of the highest variability procedures, and the one with the single highest welfare loss index, is coronary artery bypass grafts (CABG), a major surgical intervention. An alternative procedure commonly used is a "balloon angioplasty" (technically known as percutaneous transluminal angioplasty, PCTA), in which a catheter threaded into the coronary artery is then inflated, compressing the plaque clogging the artery. For single-vessel procedures, CABG and PCTA have a .50 correlation. For multiple-vessel procedures, they have a .62 correlation. Surgeons also have the choice of conducting bypass surgery on a single blood vessel or multiple vessels. These procedures have a correlation of .70 in our data.

Nonsurgical Heart Disease. For patients with angina pectoris (chest pain due to insufficient blood supply to the heart), alternative interventions include hospitalization and supportive care versus hospitalization with an arteriogram, an expensive and invasive diagnostic test. These hospitalizations have a correlation of .08 in our data. For patients with an acute myocardial infarction (MI, heart attack), admissions with and without an arteriogram had a negative but insignificant correlation (-.18).

Cardiac Arrhythmias. For patients with selected cardiac arrhythmias, alternative interventions include hospitalization with "watching" versus surgical implantation of a cardiac pacemaker to stimulate the heart electrically to beat in proper rhythm. These have a correlation of .16 in our data.

Uterine Disorders Other than Cancers. For women with various uterine disorders, removal of the uterus is commonly recommended. Two approaches exist, one with an abdominal incision and the other with the surgery done vaginally. These two interventions have a correlation of .29 in our data.

Uterine Fibroid Masses. For women with fibroid masses on their uterus, alternative interventions include a complete removal of the uterus (hysterectomy) or removal of only that portion with the fibroid masses (myomectomy). These two surgical interventions show a correlation of .19.

Cataracts. For patients with vision clouded by cataracts, surgical removal of the lens of the eye allows the return of vision. Two alternative approaches to this surgery, extracapsular and intracapsular extraction of the lens, have a correlation of .33 in our data.

Diagnosis of Stroke. Patients hospitalized for a cerebrovascular accident (a stroke) can receive one of two diagnostic studies, an arch-arteriogram or a carotid arteriogram. These procedures have a correlation of .49 in our data.

Intensive Care Days—A Case of Actual Substitution. We actually found two cases where substitution does occur—the use of intensive care versus nonintensive care beds for patients with angina pectoris and acute myocardial infarction, where we found correlations of −.37 and −.64, respectively.

Table 7.2 SUBSTITUTION OF INPATIENT AND OUTPATIENT CARE?

	Correlation of Use Rates, Inpatient vs. Outpatient		
Procedure	Total	Urban	Rural
Cataracts	38	.43	.00
Glaucoma	.44	.40	.99
Tonsillectomy and Adenoidectomy	.09	.18	−.17
Varicose veins	.48	.81	−.22
Hemorrhoids	−.09	.13	−.34
Knee procedures	−.25	−.72	.12

Source: Parente (1989).

SUBSTITUTION BETWEEN INPATIENT AND OUTPATIENT CARE

An alternative form of substitution could occur between inpatient and outpatient treatment or diagnosis. One study has assessed this possibility using insurance claims data in the Rochester, N.Y., area. The insurance plans providing the data (Blue Cross and Blue Shield of the Rochester Area) cover about 75 percent of the under-65 population. Parente (1989) defined 19 service areas in this six-county region, and calculated the rates of various ambulatory and inpatient surgery for residents of those regions. Table 7.2 shows his results. In many cases, the overall correlation coefficient was positive. Only for knee procedures did statistically significant substitution appear to take place, and then primarily in the urban subregions. As with substitution among alternative inpatient treatments, substitution between inpatient and outpatient interventions does not seem to explain a great part of the observed variability in hospital use. Rather, when two alternative sites for therapy might substitute for each other, we more commonly found positive, rather than negative, correlations in the rates of use across regions.

Summary

It would appear from the available evidence that the extent of geographic variations can be explained only partially by standard economic phenomena such as price, income, and (using limited evidence) the distribution of illness across regions. Substitution in production of health does not seem to occur; rather, we systematically found positive correlations among procedures that could serve medically as substitutes. Thus, none of the standard explanations for the cause of variations can be considered plausible. We thus turn our attention to the one remaining concept—differences in beliefs about the efficacy of treatment and decisions about which patients should receive treatment.

TOWARD A MODEL OF PHYSICIAN LEARNING ABOUT TREATMENT EFFICACY

This section begins to build a model that explains the observed variations in medical care use.

Consider an obstetrician, who must decide with each delivery whether or not to perform a Caesarean section (C-section). The indications will differ across patients. The decision will individually balance the benefits, risks, and costs of normal delivery with those of a C-section. Given a specific distribution of patients' characteristics, we can summarize an obstetrician's beliefs about the efficacy of that procedure by the fraction of all patients delivered by C-section. The doctor wants to select the correct rate to perform the intervention. (We ignore here any incentives for demand inducement.)

The model we develop next corresponds to a simple "learning by doing" approach. Intuitively, it says that doctors "learn" an approach during their training (their "prior" belief) that they carry into their actual medical practices. This "prior" belief gets modified by observing the behavior of colleagues who may hold different beliefs, perhaps because they trained in different places where they learned different "truths." In this simple model, doctors' actual behavior will blend their training and subsequent experience. The "blend" of information will increasingly depend on "experience" as it accumulates over time. A mathematical version of this model follows:

Let θ define what the doctor believes as the "correct" rate for performing a procedure such as a Caesarean section, given a set of patients with particular signs and symptoms. We can conveniently summarize a doctor's prior beliefs about θ using a beta distribution:

$$h(\theta) = \frac{\Gamma(\alpha+\beta)\theta^{\alpha-1}(1-\theta)^{\beta-1}}{\Gamma(\alpha)\Gamma(\beta)} \quad 0 < \theta < 1. \tag{7.1}$$

The doctor's prior experience will come, say, from residency training plus self-education in journals, textbooks, and so forth. The size of the parameters α and β summarize the extent of that experience. The parameters $\alpha+\beta$ summarize the "equivalent" number of events that a doctor has previously experienced, and $\alpha/(\alpha+\beta)$ represents the "correct" rate of applying the intervention as defined by prior knowledge.

If the doctor "learns" from ongoing experience and has a quadratic loss function regarding the divergence from his or her prior beliefs and the "correct" parameter θ, then cumulative experience will move the doctor toward the community norm. If any individual doctor "samples" from colleagues' behavior regarding the right rate, then the sample of cumulative deliveries *seen* by an obstetrician will constitute additional experience beyond residency training. The relative costs of various sorts of information may make this a major source of information for most doctors.

For simplicity, suppose that a doctor values the expertise of each colleague similarly. The sample of deliveries (done by colleagues and observed by the doctor in his current community) $X_1. \ldots .X_N$ grows with time, and $y = \Sigma_N X_i$, where $X_i = 1$ when the delivery is by Caesarean section, $X_i = 0$ for normal delivery, and the doctor observes N deliveries cumulatively during his or her practice. The expected-loss-minimizing solution to estimate the "right" rate of C-sections is given by:[7]

$$w(y) = \frac{(\alpha+y)}{(\alpha+\beta+N)} = \frac{(\alpha+\beta)}{(\alpha+\beta+N)}\frac{\alpha}{\alpha+\beta} + \frac{N}{(\alpha+\beta+N)}\frac{y}{N} \quad (7.2)$$

(i.e., a weighted average of the prior "rate" $\alpha/(\alpha+\beta)$ and the observed rate y/N, the relative weights being $\alpha+\beta$ for the prior and N for the data). Thus, the Bayesian estimate behaves as if the doctor had previously seen $\alpha+\beta$ deliveries, α of which were C-sections, and blended that information with N new deliveries, y of which were C-sections. As N accumulates, the weight on community observation dominates the weight of experience and knowledge acquired during a residency training. The weights should also depend upon the success of a doctor's own patient outcomes, compared with prior expectations. We have not yet incorporated this factor into our model.

Figure 7.2 shows the path of a hypothetical doctor's expected-loss-minimizing estimate of the correct rate of C-sections, assuming that the doctor's residency accumulated 5000 deliveries' worth of experience, 20 percent of which were C-sections ($\alpha = 1,000$, $\beta = 4,000$); that 2,000 deliveries (circles) are observed annually in a "new" city where the C-section rate is 30 percent; and that there are 10,000 deliveries (triangles) per year. With the higher rate of observed deliveries, convergence to the new community norm of 30 percent Caesarean sections occurs more rapidly.

Figure 7.2 BLENDING OF TRAINING STYLE WITH COMMUNITY PRACTICE

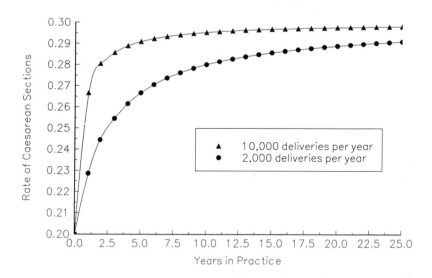

Years in Practice

These graphs show the main idea of the Bayesian learning model; the more the community norm differs from a doctor's training, and the larger the experience he or she gains during practice, compared with the cumulative experience in training, the faster will the doctor converge to the community norm.

Of course, other sources of information will affect a doctor's beliefs. Reading journals and attending professional meetings provide alternative information sources, but these appear relatively expensive compared with the ability to talk to colleagues while in hospital scrub rooms, or on the golf courses, and so forth. We anticipate that doctors would acquire information in a pattern such that the marginal costs of new "bits" of information equate across all sources. The preceding model demonstrates what happens when most of that information comes, in equilibrium, from colleagues in the same community.

Binomial event models like this are most appropriate when considering doctors' decisions on the extensive margin (e.g., whether or not to undertake a treatment for a patient). A growing body of evidence shows that this extensive margin has by far the most importance in issues of medical practice variability.[8] (For example, see Roos et al. [1986], regarding the role of hospitalizations versus length of stay in assessing variability of hospital use by physicians. See also the results of the RAND Health Insurance Experiment [RHIE], where most of the effects of insurance came through the decision to enter treatment, rather than the intensity of treatment) (Manning et al. 1987, Keeler et al. 1988.) However, this same general concept holds in any Bayesian learning model, no matter whether the underlying process is binomial (like C-sections) or continuous, as would be more appropriate for decisions on the extensive margin.

Consider the case of the intensity of use of a procedure, where a doctor has prior beliefs about the correct intensity distributed as $n(\mu, \tau^2)$. The doctor accumulates experience from a process distributed $n(\theta, \sigma^2)$ according to a sample $X_1, X_2, \ldots X_N$, with mean $y = \Sigma_N X_i / N$, where the X_i are observations taken from surrounding doctors' treatment of similar patients. Thus $g(y \mid \theta)$ is the conditional density function of y, distributed $n(\theta, \sigma^2/N)$. Again for quadratic risk functions, the expected-loss minimizing estimate of the correct intensity is distributed normally with mean $\omega\mu + (1-\omega)y$, where $\omega = (\sigma^2/N)/(\sigma^2/N + \tau^2)$. Thus, as the sample accumulates (with a doctor's experience in a community), the weight on the prior mean μ (presumably formed during residency training) diminishes, and the weight on y, the community norm, increases asymptotically toward 1 as N grows large.

These ideas were neatly summarized by Dr. Robert Mullin, a physician from New Haven, commenting on a study by Wennberg, Freeman, and Culp (1987) that showed that Boston residents were much more likely than New Haven residents to be hospitalized: "The academic flavor in Boston, the teaching atmosphere, has a much stronger tradition of bringing people into the hospital . . . . . [When Boston-trained physicians relocate in New Haven] they bring their bad habits with them, but peer pressure changes that" (in Knox 1987, p. 1).

Physician location, choice, and migration further reinforce these phenomena. Many physicians locate into a new community by joining an established practice partnership. Selection effects by both parties will probably ensure a similar approach to medical intervention among the established doctors and the new entrant. Even those entering solo practice will have some incentive to know about any predominant local practice styles before migrating, if for no other reason than that "conformance" reduces the risk of medical malpractice suits. Thus, physician migration patterns will tend to reinforce local practice patterns.[9]

Patient Beliefs

Equilibrium rates of treatment depend not only on the beliefs and values of doctors but also on those of patients. Patients' beliefs about the efficacy of an intervention may be shaped as much or more by "local" sources as will doctors' beliefs. If a patient "doctor-shops," then any "community" style will tend to support the beliefs of the patient's own doctor. Further, if the patient samples from other similar patients in the same community to learn about their therapy, those patients' experiences will also reflect the style of the community. Thus, a community norm about medical interventions will influence not only a doctor's recommendations but patients' willingness to accept those recommendations.[10]

Why Do Teaching Centers Differ in Beliefs?

The preceding model rests on the presumption that medical schools provide different versions of "truth" to their students. If each student received the same information about the efficacy of a medical intervention, then each resident would hold the same prior beliefs about the efficacy of an intervention. In such a world, no variations would exist. How do such differences emerge and persist?[11]

The question seems odd on its face, yet just as there are "schools" of thought in economics and other disciplines, so also are there schools of thought in medicine. In medicine, the opportunity for "schools" to arise comes even easier than in economics, for example, because the theory and research underpinnings of much of medicine are specialized by organ systems (nervous, musculoskeletal, endocrine, digestive, etc.). Thus, an orthopedic department may be an "aggressive" school in using arthroscopic knee surgery, whereas in the same medical school, an internal medicine department may cultivate a conservative approach to treating cardiac disease. No logical reason exists for "aggressive" approaches to correlate strongly across specialty, although they may within specialties, since an overall approach to using interventions may pervade a single specialty at a particular medical center. "Schools" arise easily in modern medicine primarily because astonishingly few interventions practiced have ever been subjected to carefully controlled scientific trials at a clinical level (outside the laboratory).

There are numerous reasons for this lack of scientific support. Prominent among them is that if an intervention (for whatever reason) has entered common practice, it becomes unethical to conduct a randomized trial on that intervention, because such a trial would involve withholding the procedure for some patients. The only realistic source of funding for such trials, the National Institutes of Health, will not fund studies that involve withholding of procedures in common use.

In addition, from an economic perspective, the normal functions that include good commodities and exclude bad commodities in the marketplace do not exist in much of medicine: no property rights exist for a good surgical technique, or for an excellent plan for treating diabetics. Further, no systematic liability exists for the damage wreaked by a bad surgical technique or treatment strategy, since each medical malpractice case stands on its own under the law. Thus, the incentives to produce information about the efficacy of an intervention differ considerably from those that normally operate in the marketplace. In such a setting, haphazard evidence can have strong sway, creating local pockets of enthusiasm or dismay for a particular intervention. Proponents and opponents of a particular medical intervention (neither side commonly possessing strong clinical evidence for its beliefs) can dominate the local approach in both a medical school and in various practice communities. The Bayesian learning approach previously set forth here shows how, once established, such pockets of belief can and will persist.

HOW COMPREHENSIVE ARE "SCHOOLS" OF THOUGHT?

One common suggestion about patterns of medical care use says that "supply creates its own demand," which, if true, has important welfare implications and leads to a specific set of regulatory and policy recommendations. This viewpoint predicts that high hospital bed supply in a region (relative to population) will *uniformly* lead to increased use of medical care across all diagnoses and therapies. The alternative we suggest here says that schools of thought within a given community do not necessarily arise because of specific resource availability, and may be unrelated across various areas of medical intervention. High rates of hip surgery may well not mean high rates of knee surgery, even though both would use the same sets of resources in general. Thus, the patterns of high and low use of various medical interventions can help distinguish between a model of "Roemer's Law" versus a model of limited information diffusion.

The patterns of medical care use formed by "schools" also affect the way analysis of medical practice variations should occur—in particular, the desirable level of aggregation across procedures. It is easy to show that the COV of the sum of a series of partly correlated random numbers falls as the number of summed variables rises, and that it falls faster, the smaller the correlations.[12] Thus, aggregation across a large enough number of procedures can eventually produce a trivially small COV in the aggregate use rate. We can safely aggregate procedures for variations analysis only when correlations are high across procedures. Studies of variations that aggregate across procedures run a considerable risk of producing misleading results.[13]

The earlier-mentioned study by Wennberg et al. (1987) suggested that the "Roemer's Law" model may have only limited applicability. Their study compared the relative use of various medical and surgical interventions in Boston and New Haven, two cities where hospitalization is dominated by faculty from prestigious medical schools. Overall, Boston uses much more hospital care on a per capita basis than New Haven. However, for major surgical procedures, the two cities show no apparent patterns. In some cases, Boston has greater use than New Haven, and in a comparable number of other cases, the reverse holds. The greater bed supply in Boston does not alter the overall rate of major surgery, and for specific interventions, one cannot predict readily which city will exhibit the higher rate. Wennberg and colleagues did show that the big differences between Boston and New Haven in nonsurgical admissions mostly occur for procedures where observed variations are quite high in many studies.

We have calculated the correlation of counties' use of various types of hospitalization to assess how uniform a region's patterns of use appear. If a region is "high" in all hospitalizations, the correlations will appear large, and conversely. Our model of physician learning suggests that, if anything, correlations will be higher among activities carried out by the same specialists, but will likely have little if any correlation across specialties.

Our results (see table 7.3) provide reasonable support for the belief that the use rate across various procedures is only weakly correlated.[14] Medical and surgical treatment of back injury are essentially uncorrelated. Pacemaker insertions are completely uncorrelated with the two other types of heart disease admissions (acute myocardial infarction and coronary artery bypass graft), although most of the significant positive correlations occur with two types of admissions showing correlations with other procedures. These correlations may merely demonstrate inadequate adjustment (in our regression models) for the age mix of these counties.

Testing the Model

The preceding model offers several refutable hypotheses that can be used to test its usefulness. A separate research project, now under-

Table 7.3 CORRELATIONS BETWEEN PROCEDURES/ADMISSIONS RATES PERFORMED BY SPECIALISTS

	Chole.	Hyster.	Cataract	Surgback	Medback	MI	CABG	Pace
Chole (cholecystectomy—removal of gallbladder)	1.0							
Hyster (hysterectomy)	-0.42	1.0						
Cataract (cataract surgery)	0.17	0.24	1.0					
Surgback (back surgery)	-0.07	0.07	0.56	1.0				
Medback (medical back)	0.11	0.02	-0.07	0.04	1.0			
MI (myocardial infarction—heart attack)	0.52	0.56	0.36	0.03	0.02	1.0		
CABG (coronary artery bypass graft—bypass surgery)	0.27	0.32	0.32	-0.04	-0.03	0.21	1.0	
Pace (pacemaker insertion)	-0.03	0.06	-0.02	0.95	-0.13	0.04	-0.01	1.0

Notes: Data weighted by county population. Critical values for rejecting Ho: r=0: 80 percent confidence level: $r >= .11$; 90 percent confidence level: $r >= .168$; 95 percent confidence level: $r >= .214$; 99 percent confidence level: $r >= .30$.

way,[15] offers us the capability of testing at least some of these ideas. The project uses data from a large independent practice association (IPA) that assigns each patient to a primary care doctor, identifying with certainty the relationship between patients and doctors. This allows calculation of a doctor's rates of use of various medical resources. From that standpoint, we can test the information model in various ways. For example:

□ The deviation of a doctor's propensity to treat from the community norm should diminish with a doctor's time in the community.
□ Doctors who trained in the community should begin their practices closer to the community norm than those who trained elsewhere.
□ Doctors with more extensive specialty training should move toward the community norm at slower rates than those with less-extensive training.
□ Hospital-specific norms should develop just as do community norms.
□ Patterns of use will correlate better within specialties (e.g., back surgery and knee surgery) than across specialties (e.g., hysterectomy and cataract removal).

We hope to be able to report the results from these types of analyses over the next several years of our new research project.

WELFARE LOSSES FROM VARIATIONS

If we accept that variations in medical practice depend on incomplete information, then we can calculate the welfare loss associated with those variations. The basic premise is that provision of information alters people's behavior. Their demands when "misinformed" lead to too much or too little consumption, and commensurate welfare losses. Compared with the "right" rate of use of an intervention, communities with "not enough" use miss out on use of some interventions where the benefits exceed—perhaps greatly—the costs. This creates one source of welfare loss. For communities with "too much" use, the costs exceed the benefits for some of the procedures performed, thus creating additional welfare losses to consumers. The "fully informed" demand curve provides the metric with which we

Figure 7.3 WELFARE LOSS FROM VARIATIONS WHEN AVERAGE RATE IS
CORRECT

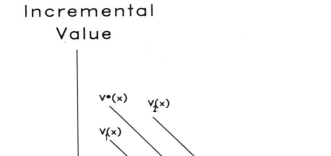

Incremental
Value

$V^*(x)$ $V_2(x)$

$V_1(x)$

Cost

Rate
of
Use

X_1 X^* X_2

calculate welfare losses—these "fully informed" demand curves
allow calculation of the "right" rate.

Figure 7.3 shows how we calculate welfare losses. Suppose two
communities (A and B) with otherwise comparable populations
exhibit aggregate marginal value functions $V(m)$ for a particular medical intervention according to V_1 and V_2 respectively. Suppose that
this procedure has constant per-unit cost C, and that the differences
in demand arise because of differences in beliefs about the efficacy
of the intervention. The communities will exhibit, respectively, consumption rates m_1 and m_2 with optimizing behavior, given the beliefs
in each region. Suppose further that the average rate of consumption
$M = (\Sigma X_i/N)$ is the rate that each community would use if fully
informed. We relax both of these assumptions momentarily. The
welfare losses are the triangles A and B, of size $L_i = .5 (X_i - M)(V(X_i)$
$- C)$. We can estimate $\Delta V = (V(X_i) - C)$ using information from

demand studies: $\Delta V = (X_i - M)dV/dX$. Thus, the welfare loss $L_i = .5(X_i - M)^2 dV/dX$. Adding up these welfare losses across all communities shows that

$$
\begin{aligned}
WL &= .5\ \Sigma(X_i - M)^2 dV/dX \\
&= .5N\mathrm{Var}(X)dV/dX \text{ for } N \text{ communities.} \quad (7.3)
\end{aligned}
$$

Algebraic manipulation shows that

$$
WL = .5\ \mathrm{COV}(X)^2 NCM/\eta, \quad (7.4)
$$

where $\mathrm{COV}(X)^2 = \mathrm{Var}(X)/M^2$ and η is the elasticity of demand evaluated at M.[16] Thus, the welfare loss is proportional to the product of (a) total spending ($N \times C \times M$), (b) the squared coefficient of variation, and (c) the inverse demand elasticity.[17] Of course, the COV should reflect systematic, not random, variability; we use regression analysis to make this adjustment. This provides a method to estimate welfare losses due to variations in medical care use, under the assumption that the variations are due to informational differences across regions. We use only unexplained residual variance in our measure of the welfare loss; the appendix in Phelps and Parente (1990) describes the precise relationships we employ here.

In these estimates, we arbitrarily assigned *all* residual variation to "disagreement" among physicians, and calculated the welfare loss accordingly. Although this is clearly incorrect—some variation is desirable because of variability in some unmeasured explanatory variable—we believe that the evidence presented in the subsections following confirms the economic importance of "variations," even if we discount a substantial fraction of the welfare losses calculated here.

Welfare Loss with Current Average Use Too Large or Too Small

This analysis also assumes that the average rate of use is "correct." We next prove that the welfare loss is larger if the average rate of use is biased away from the true welfare-maximizing mean. Suppose that instead of the average rate M, the "correct" rate is $X^* \neq M$. Then we would have overstated the welfare loss A for region 1, and understated it for loss B in region 2 (in figure 7.3). Then:

$$
\begin{aligned}
WL &= .5\ \Sigma_n (X_i - X^*)^2 dV/dX \\
&= .5\ \Sigma_n [(X_i - M) + (M - X^*)]^2 dV/dX \\
&= .5\ \Sigma_n [(X_i - M)^2 + (M - X^*)^2] dV/dX. \quad (7.5)
\end{aligned}
$$

Figure 7.4 WELFARE LOSS FROM VARIATIONS WHEN AVERAGE RATE IS
BIASED

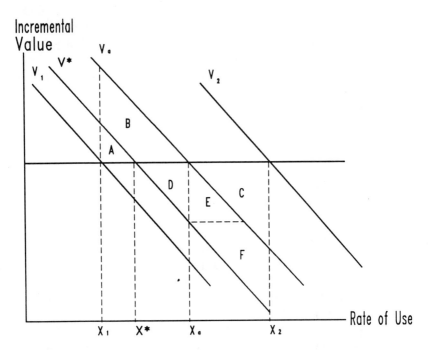

Thus, the added welfare loss due to a systematic bias is $.5N(M-X^*)^2$ dV/dX. Defining %Bias $= (M - X^*)/M$, then this added loss equals $.5(\%\text{Bias})^2 NCM/\eta$, $(.5 \times [\text{total spending}] \times \%\text{Bias}^2 / \eta)$, and this is true whether M exceeds or is less than the optimal rate of use X^*. Figure 7.4 shows this phenomenon in a two-city world. Most likely, our health care system leads to too much medical care use, if anything, so $M > X^*$ because of the pervasive effects of insurance, which drives the marginal cost of care to near zero for many consumers, so we can anticipate some effects of bias on welfare loss in general.

Our empirical estimates of "welfare loss" due to variations could provide an estimate of actual welfare loss that is too high or too low, and we have no obvious way of determining which is the case. By assumption, we have modeled all deviations from "the norm" as due to disagreement about the productivity of medical interventions. We use regression analysis to eliminate systematic variability (including age, sex, income, etc.), but other unmeasured variables could cause "appropriate" variability. If so, we will overstate welfare losses due to variable use rates.

Conversely, we may understate the welfare loss from variations because we ignore within-region variability. Our information acquisition model suggests that doctors in a single hospital can develop a "style" specific to the hospital, in which case variations will exist within regions that we have not measured, and variability across individual doctors, even on the same medical staff, seems potentially important (McMahon and Newbold 1986; Phelps et al. 1992; Roos et al. 1986).

Estimates of Welfare Losses Due to Variations in Hospital Admissions

We begin by estimating welfare losses due to variations in hospital admission rates, the aspect of variability that has almost uniformly been considered in the variations literature. We have calculated these welfare losses from using previous estimates (Phelps and Parente 1990), and adding an estimate of the physician fees associated with the hospitalizations. Details regarding data sources and methods are available from the authors. These results reflect only residual variance from regressions estimating reduced-form models for each of 110 modified DRG groups. The R^2 in these regressions commonly falls in the .4 to .6 range, although in some cases, part of that explanation of variance comes through age and sex variables, since our data are not age-sex adjusted by normal epidemiologic methods. Estimates by Phelps and Parente (1990) using two years of data showed that (through decomposition of variance) the behavior is quite stable through time; only a small proportion of the observed variance for any procedure (under 5–10 percent for almost every hospital admission type) is due to cross-year variation in county-specific means; the remainder (usually 90–95 percent) is due to variation across counties.

We have also tested to determine if the coefficients of variation that we observe might be due to chance. Following Diehr et al. (1990), we simulated a large number of "years" of New York State data (using actual county populations) under the null hypothesis that every county had identical rates of use, and then empirically derived the 95th percentile cutoffs for various underlying rates of admission (assuming a binomial model generating hospitalizations). For various underlying probabilities in the binomial model, the cutoff rates are shown in table 7.4. The rate of 5/10,000 corresponds to some of our more rare (but important) events like coronary artery bypass grafts, low-back surgery, and so on. Most of the other hospitalizations occur

Table 7.4 CRITICAL VALUES FOR DETERMINING "SIGNIFICANT" VARIABILITY
IN REGIONAL RATES OF HOSPITAL ADMISSIONS

Rate per 10,000	Ninety-fifth Percentile Cutoff for COV (Test of Null Hypothesis)
5	.095
10	.068
15	.055
20	.048

Notes: COV, coefficient of variation. See text for explanation.

at higher rates. Thus, virtually all of the observed COVs in our data substantially exceed the ninety-fifth percentile cutoff for the null hypothesis (no differences in underlying rates of use) in our New York data.

We added physician costs to the welfare loss measure by using the estimated ratio of total costs/hospital costs reported by Mitchell et al. (1984). The combined estimated welfare losses from variations in hospital admissions for 110 modified DRGs (which cover all hospital admissions) added up to $130 per capita in New York State. Extrapolating to the total U.S. population, the estimated aggregate annual welfare losses from variations in admissions reach $33 billion.

Within-Hospital Procedure Variability

The welfare losses discussed to this point have used the hospital admission as the unit of analysis. However, hospitalizations, even within the same DRG category, have considerable variability in their content. Our data from New York State hospitalizations (details are available from authors) allow us to explore not only the variability of hospitalizations themselves but also the variability of procedures undertaken during hospitalization. We report here our initial findings in this area, focusing on treatment of cardiac diseases, which are associated with high welfare losses at the hospital-admission level.

A series of diagnostic tests is available to determine the cardiac condition of patients who have had a myocardial infarction (MI, heart attack). In general, these tests assess different aspects of cardiac performance, and hence are not true substitutes in the sense we discussed previously. Table 7.5 displays our results for within-MI admission procedures. In each of these (all labeled "for MI" in table 7.5), the relevant denominator in calculating variations is the population of persons admitted to the hospital with a diagnosis of MI. Thus,

Table 7.5 CALCULATION OF WELFARE LOSSES FOR PROCEDURES RELATED
TO HEART ATTACK

Procedure or Admission	Spending Level ($)	Modified COV[a]	Welfare Loss ($)
MI[b] (heart attack)	496,584,013	11.20	31,145,749
ICU[c] LOS[d] for MI	42,086,475	17.34	6,327,188
Left cardiac catheterization for MI	7,682,460	35.25	4,772,968
Arteriogram for MI	9,119,090	32.23	4,736,332
Cardiac echo (ultrasound) for MI	4,892,736	28.63	2,005,231
Radioisotope studies for MI	2,638,600	29.83	1,173,951
Stress test for MI	217,562	46.49	235,111

Notes: Elasticity = − .1. Spending Level includes both hospital and physician charges,
except for ICU LOS.
a. COV, coefficient of variation.
b. MI, myocardial infarction.
c. ICU, intensive care unit.
d. LOS, length of stay.

these are conditional rates of use of these tests, and they constitute
additional variability beyond the rates of hospitalizations themselves. (MI hospitalizations have a COV of only .11).

ICU LOS

Many MI patients are admitted directly to an intensive care unit
(ICU) initially, and then are transferred to routine hospital care when
they have stabilized. Variability in length of stay (LOS) for intensive
care beds is low (COV = .17), reflecting a relatively uniform pattern
of using this resource across regions. However, because of the expense
involved, the associated welfare loss is over $6 million annually in
New York State alone, almost matching the losses associated with
hospitalization for pacemaker insertion or for other interventions
like PCTA (balloon angioplasty).

CARDIAC FUNCTIONING

Within the set of tests to assess cardiac function after an MI, variability of use seems large. Arteriograms (assessing the degree of openness
of coronary arteries) have a COV of .32, and an annual welfare loss
of $4.7 million in New York State. Stress tests occur only very infre-
quently, but with higher variability (COV = .40). Cardiac catheterization of the left heart occurs often, with about $7.6 million spent
annually for post-MI hospitalized patients, and with relatively large
variation (COV = .35). We estimate the welfare loss due to these

variations at another $4.7 million annually in New York State. Radio-nuclide studies (COV = .30) and cardiac echo (ultrasound) tests (COV = .24) add an additional welfare loss of $2 million annually in New York State. Taken together, variability in these procedures, *conditional on an MI admission,* add $19 million annually to welfare losses, compared with an estimated loss due to variability in MI admissions of about $34 million. Thus, at least for this particular illness, within-hospital differences in medical resource use appear to create welfare losses of the same order of magnitude as those associated with admission rate differences across regions. We cannot yet determine whether this finding will recur in other types of illnesses.

How Big Is "Big"?

This section attempts to place in perspective the magnitude of welfare losses associated with variations in use of the various medical interventions just estimated. Two comparisons may help place the magnitude of loss in context. First, we compare variations-induced losses with the "traditional" welfare loss from insurance, first characterized by Arrow (1963), then by Pauly (1968), and formalized by Zeckhauser (1970). The second approach compares the welfare losses with the costs of creating and disseminating information about the "correct" patterns of use.

First consider the Arrow-Pauly-Zeckhauser type of welfare loss, the combination of risk bearing and standard welfare loss triangles. Using data from the RAND Health Insurance Experiment, Keeler and colleagues (1988) estimated this combined welfare loss for various insurance plans. On a per capita basis in 1986 dollars, an uninsured person would face $1,472 of loss, all due to risk bearing.[18] A fully insured person would have $265 of loss, all due to "moral hazard" increased consumption, and would bear no financial risk. Many plans with combinations of $100–$300 deductibles and coinsurance rates of 25–50 percent created welfare losses in the realm of $50 to $60 per person, the set of relatively efficient plans. This describes the magnitude of welfare loss for the aspect of medical care use that has attracted the attention of economists over the previous several decades.[19] We can contrast this with our estimate of $130 per capita in welfare loss due to hospital admissions variations, which ignores the possibility for bias in current use rates, within-region variability, procedure-level variations within hospital admissions, and variations in medical care use outside of the hospital sector.

A second way to conceptualize these welfare losses considers the costs of finding out the correct way to use a specific medical intervention, and compares that with the welfare losses associated with variability. The procedure with the largest estimated welfare loss is the coronary artery bypass graft (CABG), with an estimated U.S. welfare loss of $.95 billion annually, *assuming that the current average rate of use is correct*. Knowledge to reduce unwarranted variance could be worth as much as the annuity value of such losses. A 25-year annuity at 5 percent, for example, is worth about 15 times the annual cost. On those grounds, an investment to understand the correct way to use CABGs could create as much as $15 billion in improved welfare, plus gains from eliminating any bias that the studies detected.

Obviously, even a perfect understanding of the optimal ways to use medical interventions will not eliminate all variability, and we emphasize that some of the variability that we attribute to "disagreement" will ultimately prove desirable. Despite these concerns, these calculations emphasize that our estimates of the welfare losses due to lack of information (or the gains from eliminating such variations) could be greatly overstated, and it would still be a good idea to invest in knowledge about the correct ways to use these interventions, even if such research only partially reduced these variations. For procedures with losses like CABG, the case is easy to make. However, even hospital admissions like carpal tunnel release, with an estimated welfare loss of $.139 per person per year, create annual welfare losses exceeding $34 million. The present value of learning when to use carpal tunnel release would exceed $.5 billion, again assuming no bias in the current average use rate of the procedure, a 5 percent discount rate, and 15 years of benefit from the knowledge. By contrast, the costs of undertaking a careful study of a procedure like this appear to be in the realm of a few million dollars. Thus, even for a procedure with low estimated welfare loss like carpal tunnel release, it seems desirable to seek better information about ways to eliminate variability. For many other procedures, eliminating even a few percent of the observed variation would create welfare gains exceeding the likely costs of conducting a careful study about the use of a specific procedure.

CONCLUSIONS

Variability in the use of various medical interventions appears to create important welfare losses. Many "explanations" of variations fail to account for much, if any, of the observed phenomena. We have demonstrated in this study that common socioeconomic phenomena cannot account for more than a trivial fraction of the observed variations for many medical interventions. We also brought to bear new data to show that substitution of one procedure for another cannot account for the observed variations.

The remnants of this analysis seem to suggest that disagreement among physicians (and their patients) across regions of the country accounts for much of the observed variation, supporting the models espoused by Bloor (1976) and Wennberg (1984). If we accept this idea even partially, the welfare losses associated with variability are large. They considerably exceed those associated with the standard "moral hazard" and risk-bearing welfare losses associated with common health insurance plans. In addition, our estimates of welfare losses do not include the effects of intraregional variability, within-DRG variability in the use of specific procedures, positive correlation of procedures that ought to be substitutes, the potential for systematic bias in the use of medical interventions, or any welfare losses from variations outside the hospital sector.

The model of physician learning discussed in this essay suggests how these variations can persist in a given community. This model also implies that aggregation across medical interventions treated by different specialties will likely distort the understanding of the importance of variations. We have presented new evidence to show that patterns of variations correspond to specialty-specific beliefs about the efficacy of medical care. Thus, our work suggests that old models of "supply creating its own demand" poorly represent what is going on, at best.

Almost all previous studies of variations in medical care have used geographic regions, and have focused on patterns of hospital admissions. This chapter offers new evidence to show that variability *within categories of admissions* in the use of specific procedures is also important, creating large additional welfare losses in addition to those calculated using hospital admission rates alone. These studies emphasize the importance of analyzing variations at a relatively microscopic level.

Many other economic aspects of variations in medical care use remain unexplored. The origination of variations is an important and unresolved problem in itself (see Phelps [1992] for some discussion of these issues). The proper approaches to modifying variable behavior also require further study. Some methods (e.g., those relying on incentives that doctors confront) may conflict substantially with approaches that seek physicians' cooperation (e.g., assuming that the problem is one of transmission of information, rather than one of perverse incentives). Until we can resolve whether the problem centers mostly on incentives or mostly on information diffusion, the proper strategies for reducing variations cannot be determined (Phelps 1993). What we *can* now say is that variations in the patterns of use of medical care seem to have high economic importance, and that research to determine the causes of variations, and to reduce inappropriate variations, should have high priority in research agendas of both governmental and private agencies.

APPENDIX 7.A: RELATIONSHIP BETWEEN THE COEFFICIENT OF VARIATION IN AN EXPLANATORY VARIABLE AND THE COEFFICIENT OF VARIATION IN A DEPENDENT VARIABLE

1. Proof that the coefficient of variation of y changes with respect to the coefficient of variation in x_i at a rate no more than η_i, the elasticity of y with respect to x_i:

Consider a model where $y = \beta_0 + x_1\beta_1 + x_2\beta_2 + \varepsilon$. Then

$\text{Var}(y) = \text{Var}(\varepsilon) + \beta_1^2\text{Var}(x_1) + \beta_2^2\text{Var}(x_2) + 2\beta_1\beta_2\text{COV}(x_1,x_2)$

$$= \sigma_e^2 + \beta_1^2\sigma_1^2 + \beta_2^2\sigma_2^2 + 2\beta_1\beta_2\sigma_{12}. \tag{7.A1}$$

If we scale the entire expression by $1/\mu_y^2$ (where μ_y = the average value of y), then σ_e^2/μ_y^2 is the coefficient of variation of the residuals squared (scaled by the average value of y). Define the coefficient of variation of x_i (σ_x/μ_x) as C_i, η_i as the elasticity of y with respect to x_i, and ρ the correlation coefficient between x_1 and x_2. Then the variance expression becomes:

$$C_y^2 = \frac{\sigma_e^2}{\mu_y^2} + \frac{\sigma_1^2\eta_1^2}{\mu_1^2} + \frac{\sigma_2^2\eta_2^2}{\mu_2^2} + \frac{2\eta_1\eta_2\sigma_{12}}{\mu_1\mu_2}$$

$$= C_e^2 + C_1^2\eta_1^2 + C_2^2\eta_2^2 + 2\rho\eta_1\eta_2C_1C_2 \tag{7.A2}$$

or

$$C_y = (C_1^2\eta_1^2 + C_2^2\eta_2^2 + 2\eta_1\eta_2\rho C_1C_2 + C_e^2)^{1/2} \tag{7.A3}$$

Then

$$dC_y/dC_1 = \frac{\eta_1[C_1\eta_1 + \rho C_2\eta_2]}{(C_1^2\eta_1^2 + C_2^2\eta_2^2 + 2\eta_1\eta_2\rho C_1C_2 + C_e^2)^{1/2}}$$

$$= \eta_1\left[\frac{C_1^2\eta_1^2 + \rho^2C_2^2\eta_2^2 + 2\,\eta_1\eta_2\rho C_1C_2}{C_1^2\eta_1^2 + C_2^2\eta_2^2 + 2\eta_1\eta_2\rho C_1C_2 + C_e^2}\right]^{1/2}$$

$$= k\eta_1, \text{ where } 0 < k \le 1. \tag{7.A4}$$

Thus, the COV of y changes with respect to the coefficient of variation of x_1 *at most* at the rate η_1, and similarly for any x_i and its associated η_i, as asserted in the text.

Notes

This research was supported by the Agency for Health Care Policy and Research, Grant R01 HS-06366. We gratefully acknowledge our University of Rochester colleagues Alvin I. Mushlin, M.D., Sc.M., Nancy Perkins, M.D., M.P.H., Ph.D. Laura Rice, M.D., and Daniel Kido, M.D. in this research project; for comments on previous versions, we are especially grateful to Randall Ellis and Myron Stano.

1. Define a region's net price as P^*, where P = actual price, s = share of population with insurance, and C = average coinsurance for those with insurance. Then $P^* = sCP + (1-s)P = P(1-s(1-C))$. The coefficient of variation in net price is calculated assuming $C = .2$; the estimated coefficient of variation is not greatly sensitive to this assumption. Obviously, variability in C across regions is not captured by this method, but this cannot add importantly to the variability in P^*, since most private insurance plans provide nearly full coverage for hospital care, and Medicare, which insures about one-quarter of all hospital days, is uniform across all regions.

2. In the health field, this "law" is attributed to Milton Roemer, M.D., who first showed the empirical relationship between hospital bed supply and per capita hospital use (Roemer 1961). The more generic economist would refer to Say's Law.

3. For example, reports of "excellent" or "good" health came from 59 percent of respondents in areas with lowest surgical rates, and 65 percent of respondents in areas of highest surgical rates (Roos and Roos 1982).

4. Diehr (1984) calculated that, with 1,000 people in each area, the extremal quotient would have an expected value of 3.2 when comparing 5 areas, and 10.9 when comparing 20 areas. Most studies of variations use many more observations than this (e.g., 40,000 to 100,000 persons), greatly reducing the problems cited by Diehr.

5. We acknowledge the assistance of Alvin Mushlin, M.D., Sc.M., Laura Rice, M.D., Dan Kido, M.D., and Nancy Perkins, M.D., M.P.H., Ph.D., in deriving the list of procedures to consider in these tests.

6. Chassin et al. (1986) estimated the substitution of two alternative therapies for hemorrhoids within Medicare data.

7. See Hogg and Craig (1970), section 8.4, for proof.

8. Stano and Folland (1988) and Folland and Stano (1989) estimated the effects of "practice style" on use on a highly aggregated variable (all ambulatory care use). They placed considerable emphasis on variations on the intensive margin of treatment (resources used per encounter), whereas most of the variations literature has demonstrated important variation on the extensive margin (number of encounters). They argued—we believe in error—that variations due to practice style should affect only the intensive margin.

9. Folland and Stano (1989) developed a model of variations on the intensive margin that requires independence of physician beliefs and location. This is clearly a risky assumption to make.

10. See Dranove (1988) for a formal model of doctors' advice-giving and patients' propensities to accept that advice.

11. This question receives more extended attention in Phelps (1992).

12. To see this, consider an aggregated variable $Y = \Sigma X_i$, with all $\mu_i = \mu$, all $\sigma_i = \sigma$, and all $\rho_{ij} = \rho$. Thus each separate variable has a COV $= \sigma/\mu$. Then $COV(Y) = (\sigma/\mu)(N + N(N-1)\rho)^{1/2}/N = (\sigma/\mu)Z$, where $0 < Z \le 1$ for $0 \le \rho \le 1$. It is easy to show that when $\rho = 0$, $COV(Y) = (\sigma/\mu)/N^{1/2}$. Also, for moderately large N (say, $N > 10$ or 20), $COV(Y)$ is approximately $(\sigma/\mu)\rho^{1/2}$.

13. Stano and Folland (1988) and Folland and Stano (1989) used a highly aggregated analysis of outpatient treatment. We show later in the chapter that correlations across

procedures and hospital admissions categories are only modestly positive, and often quite small. Thus, aggregation of hundreds of procedures is bound to mask the real variability of medical care use. To argue that variations do not exist meaningfully because of such aggregation (as Folland and Stano do) seems totally misplaced.

14. We also computed rank order correlations for the same procedures; the results show nothing different from those in table 7.3.

15. The project began March 1, 1990, under funding from the Agency for Health Care Policy and Research.

16. Randall Ellis has pointed out to us that the marginal value rapidly falls below zero when using a linear demand curve with a small elasticity (say, $-.1$) at the mean (personal communication, May 1990). However, it is easy to prove that a common alternative functional form that never produces marginal value below zero—the logarithmic transform—produces estimates of welfare loss that exceed those we estimate using the linear form, if we assume the same (constant) elasticity as we used at the average values on the linear demand curve. Intuitively, this occurs because the marginal value rapidly becomes very high for under-use with the logarithmic demand curve. Thus, our assumption of a linear demand curve may understate the true welfare losses.

17. If production costs are not constant, then an additional welfare loss arises equal to a magnitude of $.5 \, COV(Q)^2 \, PQH$, where H is the output elasticity of cost.

18. Keeler et al. (1988) assume a very large risk-aversion measure, comparable to a relative risk aversion of about 10 or greater; other estimates suggest that values in the range of 2 to 4 are appropriate. Lower risk aversion reduces the welfare losses from risk bearing proportionally. See Garber and Phelps (1992) for details.

19. The estimates from Keeler et al. refer to an under-65 population, so including an over-65 population would raise these numbers somewhat, because of the higher variance of expenditures for the elderly.

References

Arrow, K. J. 1963. "Uncertainty and the Welfare Economics of Medical Care." *American Economic Review* 53(5): 941–73.

Bloor, M. J. 1976. "Bishop Berkeley and the Adenotonsillectomy Enigma: An Exploration of Variation in the Social Construction of Medical Disposals." *Sociology* 10: 43–61.

Blumberg, M. S. 1987. "Inter-Area Variations in Age-Adjusted Health Status." *Medical Care* 25(4): 340–53.

Bowen, O. R. 1987. "Shattuck Lecture—What is Quality Care?" *New England Journal of Medicine* 316(25): 1578–80.

Chassin, M. R., R. H. Brook, R. E. Park, et al. 1986. "Variations in the Use of Medical and Surgical Services by the Medicare Population." *New England Journal of Medicine* 314: 285–90.

Daniels, M., and S. A. Schroeder. 1977. "Variations among Physicians in Use of Laboratory Tests II: Relation to Clinical Productivity and Outcomes of Care." *Medical Care* 15(6): 482–87.

Diehr, P. 1984. "Small Area Statistics: Large Statistical Problems." *American Journal of Public Health* 74(4): 313–14.

Diehr, P., K. Cain, F. Connel, and E. Volinn. 1990. "What is Too Much Variation? The Null Hypothesis in Small-Area Analysis." *Health Services Research* 24(6): 740–70.

Diehr, P., K. C. Cain, W. Kreuter, and S. Rosenkranz. 1992. "Can Small Area Analysis Detect Variation in Surgery Rates? The Power of Small Area Variation Analysis." *Medical Care* (June): 30(7): 484–502.

Dranove, D. 1988. "Demand Inducement and the Physician/Patient Relationship." *Economic Inquiry* 26: 281–98.

Dyck, F. J., F. A. Murphy, J. K. Murphy, et al. 1977. "Effect of Surveillance on the Number of Hysterectomies in the Province of Saskatchewan." *New England Journal of Medicine* 296: 1326–28.

Folland, S., and M. Stano. 1989. "Sources of Small Area Variations in the Use of Medical Care." *Journal of Health Economics* 8: 85–107

Garber A. M., C. E. Phelps. 1992. "Economic Foundations of Cost-Effectiveness Analysis," NBER Working Paper 4164. Cambridge, Ma.: National Bureau of Economic Research, September.

Glover, J. A. 1938. "The Incidence of Tonsillectomy in School Children." *Proceedings of the Royal Society of Medicine* 31: 95–112.

———. 1948. "The Paediatric Approach to Tonsillectomy." *Archives of Diseases in Children,* 1–6.

Health Insurance Association of America. 1989. *Source Book of Health Insurance Data.* Washington, D.C.: Author.

Hogg, R. V., and A. T. Craig. 1970. *Introduction to Mathematical Statistics,* 3rd ed. New York: Macmillan & Co.

Keeler, E. B., J. L. Buchanan, J. E. Rolph, J. M. Hanley, D. M. Reboussin. 1988. *The Demand for Episodes of Medical Treatment in the Health Insurance Experiment.* Report R-3454-HHS. Santa Monica: RAND Corporation, March.

Kissick, W. L., P. F. Engstrom, K. A. Soper, and O. L. Peterson. 1984. "Comparison of Internist and Oncologist Evaluations of Cancer Patients' Need for Hospitalization." *Medical Care* 22(5): 447–52.

Knox, Richard A. 1987. "Study Finds Boston Medically Spendthrift." *Boston Globe* (May 24), A-1.

Leape L. L., R. E. Park, D. H. Solomon, et al. 1990. "Does Inappropriate Use Explain Small Area Variations in the Use of Health Care Services?" *Journal of the American Medical Association* 263(5): 669–72.

Lembcke, P. A. 1952. "Measuring the Quality of Medical Care through Vital Statistics Based on Hospital Service Areas: 1. Comparative Study of Appendectomy Rates." *American Journal of Public Health* 42: 276–86.

Lewis, C. E. 1969."Variations in the Incidence of Surgery." *New England Journal of Medicine* 281(16): 880–84.

Manning, W. G., J. P. Newhouse, N. Duan, et al. 1987. "Health Insurance and the Demand for Medical Care: Evidence from a Randomized Experiment." *American Economic Review* 77(3): 251–77.

McMahon, L. F. and R. Newbold. 1986. "Variation in Resource Use within Diagnosis-Related Groups: The Effect of Severity of Illness and Physician Practice." *Medical Care* 24(5): 388–97.

McPherson L., P. M. Strong, A. Epstein, and L. Jones. 1981. "Regional Variations in the Use of Common Surgical Procedures: Within and between England and Wales, Canada, and the United States of America." *Social Science in Medicine* 15A: 273–88.

Mitchell, J. B., K. Calore, J. Cromwell, et al. 1984. "Creating DRG-Based Physician Reimbursement Schemes: A Conceptual and Empirical Analysis." Report to Health Care Financing Administration. Chestnut Hill, MA: Center for Health Economics Research.

Parente, S. T. 1989. "Measuring the Substitution of Outpatient for Inpatient Services." Master's thesis, University of Rochester.

Pauly, M. V. 1968. "The Economics of Moral Hazard: Comment." *American Economic Review* 58(3): 531–37.

Phelps, C. E. 1992. "Diffusion of Information in Medical Care." *Journal of Economic Perspectives* 6(3): 23–42.

―――――. 1993. "Medical Practice Guidelines: Compliance Issues." University of Rochester Working Paper. Rochester, N.Y.: University of Rochester.

Phelps, C. E. and C. Mooney. 1992. "Priority Setting for Medical Technology and Medical Practice Assessment: Correction and Update." *Medical Care* 31(8, August).

Phelps, C. E. and S. T. Parente. 1990. "Priority Setting for Medical Technology and Medical Practice Assessment." *Medical Care* 28(8, August): 703–23.

Phelps, C. E., C. Mooney, B. Handy, A. I. Mushlin, N. K. Perkins. 1992. "Physician-Specific Variations in the Use of Medical Resources." University of Rochester Working Paper. Rochester, N.Y.: University of Rochester.

Pineault, R. 1977. "The Effect of Medical Training Factors on Physician Utilization Behavior." *Medical Care* 15(1): 51–67.

Roos, N. P. 1984. "Hysterectomy: Variations in Rates across Small Areas and across Physicians' Practices." *American Journal of Public Health* 74(4): 327–35.

―――――. 1989. "Predicting Hospital Utilization by the Elderly." *Medical Care* 27(10): 905–19.

Roos, N. P. and L. L. Roos. 1982. "Surgical Rate Variations: Do They Reflect the Health or Socioeconomic Characteristics of the Population?" *Medical Care* 20(9): 945–58.

Roos, N. P., L. L. Roos, and P. D. Henteleff. 1977. "Elective Surgical Rates— Do Higher Rates Mean Lower Standards?" *New England Journal of Medicine* 297: 360–65.

Roos, N. P., J. E. Wennberg, and K. McPherson. 1988. "Using Diagnosis-Related Groups for Studying Variations in Hospital Admissions." *Health Care Financing Review*, 9(4, Summer): 53–62.

Roos, N. P., G. Flowerdew, A. Wajda, and R. B. Tate. 1986. "Variations in Physician Hospital Practices: A Population-Based Study in Manitoba, Canada." *American Journal of Public Health* 76(1): 45–51.

Roper, W., W. Winkenwerder, G. M. Hackbarth, and H. Krakauer. 1988. "Effectiveness in Health Care: An Initiative to Evaluate and Improve Medical Practice." *New England Journal of Medicine* 319(18): 1197–1202.

Stano, M. and S. Folland. 1988. "Variations in the Use of Physician Services by Medicare Beneficiaries." *Health Care Financing Review* 9(3): 51–57.

Vayda, E. 1973. "Comparison of Surgical Rates in Canada, England, and Wales." *New England Journal of Medicine* 289: 1224–28.

Vayda, E., W. R. Mindell, and I. M. Rutkow. 1982. "A Decade of Surgery in Canada, England and Wales and the United States." *Archives of Surgery* 117: 846.

Wennberg, J. E. 1984. "Dealing with Medical Practice Variations: A Proposal for Action." *Health Affairs* 3(2): 6–31

_____. 1987. "Population Illness Rates Do Not Explain Population Hospitalization Rates: A Comment on Mark Blumberg's Thesis that Morbidity Adjusters Are Needed to Interpret Small Area Variations." *Medical Care* 25(4): 354–59.

Wennberg, J. E. and F. J. Fowler. 1977. "A Test of Consumer Contribution to Small Area Variations in Health Care Delivery." *Journal of the Maine Medical Association* 68(8): 275–79.

Wennberg, J. and A. Gittelsohn. 1973. "Small Area Variations in Health Care Delivery." *Science* 182: 1102–08.

Wennberg, J. E., J. L. Freeman, and W. J. Culp. 1987. "Are Hospital Services Rationed in New Haven or Over-Utilised in Boston?" *Lancet* 1: 1185–89.

Wennberg, J. E., K. McPherson and P. Caper. 1984. "Will Payment for Diagnosis Related Groups Control Hospital Costs?" *New England Journal of Medicine* 311: 295–300.

Wolfe, B. L. and D. Detmer. 1984. "The Economics of Surgical Signatures." *Hospital Medical Staff* 13: 2–9.

Zeckhauser, R. J. 1970. "Medical Insurance: A Case Study of the Trade-Off between Risk Spreading and Appropriate Incentives." *Journal of Economic Theory* 2: 10–26.

Chapter Eight

AN EMPIRICAL TEST OF COMPETITION IN THE MEDICARE HMO MARKET

Roger Feldman, Catherine L. Wisner, Bryan Dowd,
and Jon B. Christianson

The spread of risk-contracting with health maintenance organizations (HMOs) was one of the most important changes in the Medicare program during the 1980s. Risk-contracting had the potential to create competition among providers within the Medicare program and to encourage an efficient style of medical practice that might spread from the HMO sector into fee-for-service (FFS) Medicare. HMO participation in the Medicare program and the number of Medicare beneficiaries enrolled in HMOs grew rapidly during 1985 and 1986, but the rate of growth in enrollment has declined substantially since 1986. Table 8.1 shows the number of HMOs by county in the United States in September 1989. Medicare HMOs are found in only 452 of 3,080 counties. However, approximately 56 percent of all individuals over age 65 live in these counties. Forty percent have access to more than one Medicare HMO. Thus, the low overall growth of HMO enrollment is due not to lack of access but to failure of Medicare beneficiaries to choose HMOs in market areas where they are available.

The failure of Medicare beneficiaries to choose HMOs is linked closely to another aspect of the Medicare HMO program. From the beginning of Medicare's experience with HMOs, policymakers have been concerned that HMOs would earn excess profits from enrolling Medicare beneficiaries. One potential source of excess profits is that the government's payment to the HMO is based on costs in the FFS sector. This payment, called the AAPCC or "adjusted average per capita cost," is an estimate of the FFS cost of basic Medicare benefits, adjusted for geographic and demographic variations. HMOs have reported hospital utilization rates as much as 40 percent below those in the FFS sector (Luft 1981). If, because of lower utilization and perhaps because of lower price per unit of service, HMOs can provide basic Medicare benefits at below-FFS costs, then the AAPCC overpays HMOs for basic Medicare benefits.[1] A second potential source of

Table 8.1 NUMBER OF MEDICARE HMOs BY U.S. COUNTY

Number of Medicare HMOs	Frequency	Percentage	Number of Elderly	Percentage of Elderly
0	2,628	85.3	12,325,546	44.5
1	267	8.7	4,182,000	15.1
2 or more	185	6.2	11,200,012	40.4
Total	3,080	100.0	27,707,558	100.0

Sources: HHS 1989a; HHS 1990.

windfall HMO profits is the possibility that HMOs obtain a favorable selection of enrollees within each of the demographic payment categories used to set the government's payment (Brown 1988).

Although the HMO program was endorsed as a way to introduce competition into Medicare, policymakers have lacked confidence that competition can be used either to determine the correct payment level for Medicare HMOs or to wring excess profits out of the system. Instead, they have relied on regulations to limit profits that HMOs can make from serving Medicare beneficiaries. This regulatory strategy was first articulated in the 1972 amendments to the Social Security Act, which authorized risk-contracting health plans to enter the Medicare program. This legislation placed HMOs at full risk for losses, but allowed them to retain only 50 percent of any savings up to a maximum of 10 percent of the AAPCC.

A fully articulated cap on excess profits became operational in the Medicare HMO risk demonstration run by the Health Care Financing Administration (HCFA) in 1980–81. The payment method used by this demonstration and now implemented in the legislation governing Medicare risk-contracting requires HMOs to compute an "adjusted community rate," or ACR. This is an estimate of the premium the HMO would charge Medicare enrollees for the standard Medicare benefit package, based on the HMO's premium-setting policies used for the non-Medicare portion of its business (U.S. General Accounting Office 1989). HMOs must apply any excess of AAPCC payments over their ACR to additional benefits, or else return the excess to the government. They are not allowed to give premium rebates to enrollees. They can, however, determine the price and number of supplementary benefits, and many Medicare HMOs offer supplementary benefits at premiums that appear attractive, relative to those charged by insurers selling Medicare supplementary policies. Although limiting HMOs' marketing options to adding benefits may account, in part, for the lackluster response of beneficiaries to HMOs when they are offered, there may still be enough maneuvering room for competition to arise.

This chapter presents a theoretical and empirical analysis of the competitiveness of the Medicare HMO market, under the current restrictions imposed by federal regulations. First, we specify a theoretical model of HMO behavior that will be used to predict how HMO premiums and supplementary benefits are determined under conditions of monopoly and competition, and how the ACR regulation affects HMO behavior under different market conditions. In addition, the model can be used to predict how HMO premiums will vary when the government pays too much or too little for basic benefits.

Second, based on the theoretical model, we estimate an equation for HMO premium-setting. This equation tests the hypothesis that observed measures of market structure (e.g., how few sellers and market shares there are) can be used to measure the theoretical concept of "monopolistic" markets. The empirical model also tests the hypothesis that HMOs are overpaid for basic Medicare benefits.

Third, we estimate the demand equation for Medicare HMO enrollment. If demand is found to be very price-sensitive, the implication is that HMOs have little leeway to earn excess profits from Medicare. Estimates of the demand equation also provide an additional test of the hypothesis that HMOs are overpaid for basic Medicare benefits.

THEORETICAL MODEL

Background

Our analysis of the competitiveness of the Medicare HMO market is based on a profit-maximizing model of HMO behavior. The HMO is assumed to maximize profits from enrolling Medicare beneficiaries, for which it receives a fixed AAPCC payment from the government, plus an optional premium paid directly by the beneficiary. The demand curve facing a monopolistic HMO is assumed to be downward-sloping, whereas the premium facing a competitive HMO is assumed to be exogenous. We write the demand curve in its inverse form as $P = P(Q,B)$, where P = premium paid by the beneficiary, Q = number of beneficiaries enrolled with this HMO, and B = HMO benefits that supplement standard Medicare coverage. The monopolistic HMO faces $P_Q < 0$ where $P_Q = 0$ for the competitive HMO.

Both firms are assumed to charge higher premiums if they offer more supplementary benefits, which implies that $P_B > 0$ regardless of market structure.

The concept of "supplementary benefits" must be explained. By law, risk-contracting Medicare HMOs are required to provide the same benefits that are available in fee-for-service Medicare. They may add supplementary benefits of their choice, such as prescription drug coverage or reduced cost-sharing for services. They may not, however, rebate any part of the government AAPCC payment to consumers.

The cost of enrolling Medicare beneficiaries equals the cost of producing basic Medicare benefits plus the cost of optional supplementary benefits provided by the HMO. For simplicity, we write the total cost function as $TC = C(B)Q$, where TC = total cost and C = average cost. Standard Medicare coverage would be denoted as $B = 0$. It is assumed that average cost increases as B increases, but does not depend on enrollment (i.e., there are no economies of scale).

It may seem odd that HMOs are constrained by not being allowed to rebate any of the AAPCC payment to consumers. Why should a firm want to give money back to consumers? A simple example can illustrate why the HMO might want to rebate part of the government's contribution. Suppose that the average cost of enrolling another beneficiary, at the current level of supplementary benefits, is $200 per month, and that the AAPCC is $400 per month. Since it is profitable to increase enrollment, the HMO will cut its supplementary premium. Even when the supplementary premium is slashed to zero, more enrollment may be profitable. To encourage people to join, the HMO might like to give back part of the government's premium contribution, but it is prevented from doing this.

An HMO can still find a way to enroll more beneficiaries, even though it cannot offer premium rebates: the HMO could add more supplementary benefits. This increases consumers' willingness to pay for HMO coverage or, at a constrained premium of zero, it increases the number of people who will enroll with the HMO. We explore later in detail how the HMO's enrollment strategy is affected by the constraint that premium rebates are not allowed.

Formal Statement of ACR Constraint

The ACR is the premium that the HMO would charge for standard Medicare benefits, according to its established premium-setting practices. If the AAPCC exceeds the ACR, the HMO must spend the excess on additional benefits or refund it to the government. Each HMO submits an application to the HCFA, which must approve the plan's proposed ACR. Plans do not disclose their commercial profit rate in the application; this rate is implicit in the commercial premium.

We begin with a simplified expression for the ACR and then develop a full statement of the ACR regulation. Let π stand for the HMO's normal profit on non-Medicare business, and let $C(0)$ be the cost of standard Medicare benefits.[2] If the HMO earned its normal profit on standard Medicare benefits, we could write $\pi = \text{ACR} - C(0)$.

Now, divide the universe of Medicare HMOs into three groups. The first group consists of all plans whose AAPCC is less than or equal to their ACR. The HCFA accepts these plans' ACR applications, and they are exempt from further regulation. Since the ACR can be written as $\pi + C(0)$, these plans face AAPCC less than or equal to $\pi + C(0)$. They can add additional benefits if they want, but this increases their average cost, so in any case the AAPCC will be less than or equal to their normal profit plus average cost.

The ACR regulation potentially affects plans where AAPCC is greater than ACR. Some of these HMOs, however, voluntarily will add benefits until normal profit plus average cost equals or exceeds the AAPCC. This group of "voluntary adders" is the second type of Medicare HMO. Finally, some plans where AAPCC is greater than ACR may not wish to add this many supplementary benefits. The ACR regulation is "binding" for this third group of HMOs (i.e., it causes a change in their behavior). The HCFA forces these HMOs to spend the excess of their AAPCC over the ACR, until the AAPCC equals the ACR plus the marginal cost of extra benefits. The marginal cost of extra benefits is $C(B) - C(0)$. Thus, the binding ACR regulation can be written as $\text{AAPCC} = \text{ACR} + C(B) - C(0)$. Using the definition of ACR, we can write $\text{AAPCC} = \pi + C(B)$, for the HMOs that are constrained by the regulation. Looking across all three types of HMOs, we see that the AAPCC can never exceed the HMO's normal profit plus its average cost. This enables us to express the regulation as $\pi + C(B) - \text{AAPCC} \geq 0$. The constraint is slack for plans not affected by the regulation and is binding for plans that are forced to add benefits.

Analyzing the ACR regulation in this way shows that it is misleading simply to use the number or percentage of plans where AAPCC is greater than ACR as a measure of regulatory stringency. For example, Porell and colleagues (1987) determined that 68 percent of Medicare

HMOs had "documented savings," that is, an excess of AAPCC over ACR in 1987. However, this percentage includes group two (voluntary adders) as well as group three. In interviews with 18 representative Medicare risk-contracting HMOs, Porell and colleagues found none who believed that the ACR requirements had any tangible impact on Medicare premiums or benefits. Rather, the HMOs consistently declared that to compete in the marketplace, they need to charge lower premiums and offer more generous benefits than prevailing comprehensive FFS Medigap policies. Another determining factor for Medicare benefits is the HMO's benefits for its employment-based policies; HMOs want to offer comparable coverage for enrollees who age into Medicare.

Formal Model for a Monopoly HMO

The HMO maximizes profit, subject to two constraints: (1) the premium charged directly to consumers cannot be negative; and (2) π + $C(B)$ − AAPCC ≥ 0. For simplicity in the second constraint, we use the letter A instead of the acronym AAPCC. The Lagrangean function for this constrained maximization is: $\mathscr{L} = [P(Q,B) + A]Q - C(B)Q + \Lambda(\pi + C(B) - A) + \lambda P(Q,B)$. Necessary conditions for a maximum are:

$$\partial\mathscr{L}/\partial Q = P + A + P_Q Q - C + \lambda P_Q \leq 0,\ Q \geq 0,\ Q\partial\mathscr{L}/\partial Q = 0 \quad (8.1)$$

$$\partial\mathscr{L}/\partial B = P_B Q - C_B Q + \Lambda C_B + \lambda P_B \leq 0,\ B \geq 0,\ B\partial\mathscr{L}/\partial B = 0 \quad (8.2)$$

$$\partial\mathscr{L}/\partial\lambda = P \geq 0,\ \lambda \geq 0,\ \lambda\partial\mathscr{L}/\partial\lambda = 0 \quad (8.3)$$

$$\partial\mathscr{L}/\partial\Lambda = \pi + C - A \geq 0,\ \Lambda \geq 0,\ \Lambda\partial\mathscr{L}/\partial\Lambda = 0. \quad (8.4)$$

There are numerous possible cases to be analyzed, depending on whether the two activity variables (Q and B) are positive, and whether the two constants are binding. However, we can safely say that both Q and B are always positive. Enrollment must be positive for the HMO to be operating in the Medicare market. Supplementary benefits must be positive because, in fact, no HMO offers just the basic Medicare benefit package; all offer reduced cost-sharing or supplementary benefits. This leaves four possible cases: (1) neither constraint is binding; (2) only the premium constraint is binding; (3) only the ACR constraint is binding; and (4) both constraints are binding. Finally, when the constraints are binding, the respective Lagrangean multipliers will be assumed to be positive. This rules out corner solutions (e.g., an HMO adjusting quantity until it finds the optimal solution exactly at $P = 0$).

CASE 1: NEITHER CONSTRAINT BINDING

In this case, λP_Q disappears from the marginal quantity condition and we can set $P + A + P_Q Q = C$. This is standard monopoly pricing: set marginal revenue equal to marginal cost. Rewriting marginal revenue in terms of the price elasticity of demand η, we get $P(1 + 1/\eta) + A = C$ or $P = (C - A)/(1 + 1/\eta)$. The monopoly pricing rule will be estimated under the assumption that the price elasticity of demand is related to observed market structure characteristics.

The point of theoretical interest concerns the role of Medicare's AAPCC payment rate in the premium equation. The AAPCC appears as a negative factor in this equation, so higher AAPCC should lead directly to lower supplementary premiums. However, the AAPCC also is related indirectly to the HMO's costs. This relationship is far from perfect, because the AAPCC is based on FFS costs. Nevertheless, it is reasonable to suppose that some factors—the prices of medical services, or a more elaborate medical practice style in a particular market — might positively affect both the AAPCC and HMO costs. The estimated coefficient of AAPCC in an empirical premium equation will capture the net effect of these factors. Should the net effect be negative, the implication is that the AAPCC is too high. Logically, an increase in the AAPCC increases the HMO's revenue at a given level of enrollment, but it also increases the HMO's costs. If the revenue enhancement is larger, then it it profitable to expand enrollment, and in order to draw in more enrollees the HMO will cut its premium.

CASE 2: PREMIUM CONSTRAINT BINDING

When the premium constraint is binding, $P = 0$ and $\lambda > 0$. The marginal quantity condition becomes $A + P_Q Q = C - \lambda P_Q$, where the extra term "$-\lambda P_Q$" is positive. This means that marginal revenue exceeds marginal cost for HMOs that are constrained by the "no-refund" condition. These HMOs need special treatment in the empirical pricing equation. Although a negative premium theoretically exists for them, they are not allowed to set that premium. Maddala (1983) referred to this model as a "censored" regression; numerous authors, starting with Tobin (1958), have proposed econometric techniques for estimating censored regressions.

Figure 8.1 MONOPOLY HMO WITH BINDING PREMIUM CONSTRAINT

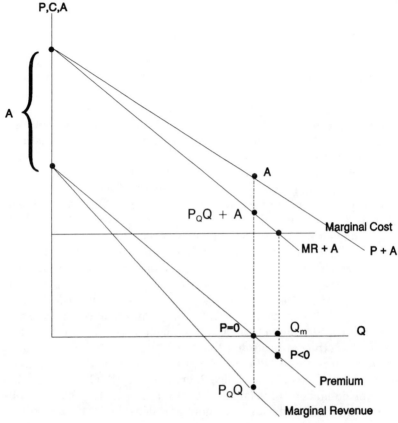

Our premium-constrained model can be illustrated by figure 8.1, which shows the monopoly HMO's downward-sloping demand and marginal revenue curves. Both of these curves are shifted upward by an amount equal to the government's AAPCC payment, denoted by A. The HMO would like to have Q_m enrollment, where marginal revenue plus the AAPCC equals marginal cost. However, the desired supplementary premium is negative at this point. This is not permitted by federal regulations, so the HMO cannot enroll Q_m beneficiaries. Instead, it must reduce enrollment until the zero-premium constraint is satisfied. The diagram of equilibrium pricing shows that marginal revenue ($P_Q Q$) is negative, but marginal revenue plus the AAPCC exceeds marginal cost. This difference motivates the HMO to attract more enrollees by offering additional supplementary benefits.[3]

Intuitively, the HMO would like to add enrollees because marginal revenue plus the AAPCC exceeds marginal cost. Because the premium is as low as it can go (zero), the only available incentive for attracting new enrollees is enhanced benefits. This incentive will cause the HMO to add supplementary benefits beyond the point where marginal revenue and marginal cost are equal. Mathematically, when the HMO chooses benefits subject to the premium constraint, the marginal condition is $P_B Q - C_B Q + \lambda P_B = 0$. Since the term "$\lambda P_B$" is positive, it follows that $P_B < C_B$, or the marginal increase in the supplementary premium from added benefits is less than the increase in cost per Medicare enrollee. This is in contrast to the unconstrained HMO that will set $P_B = C_B$.

CASE 3: ACR CONSTRAINT BINDING

This case is very similar to a binding premium constraint in terms of its effect on supplementary benefits. The marginal condition for benefits becomes $P_B Q - C_B Q + \Lambda P_B = 0$, where the added term is positive. Thus, the effect of regulation on benefits is similar to the effect of a binding premium constraint: benefits will increase. It is noteworthy, however, that the ACR constraint does not affect the monopolist's pricing rule. Both the "standard" monopoly pricing model and the ACR regulation predict that $P = (C - A)/(1 + 1/\eta)$. It is possible that the price elasticity of demand, η, depends on the level of supplementary benefits. If this is the case, then the monopolist's markup might depend on whether it is constrained by the ACR. However, without independent evidence that the ACR constraint is binding, it would be impossible to identify these cases and to control for the potential interaction between price elasticity and regulation. As shown earlier, the fact that AAPCC exceeds ACR for a particular HMO does not prove that this HMO is forced to add supplementary benefits.

CASE 4: BOTH CONSTRAINTS BINDING

In this case we would find both increased supplementary benefits and marginal revenue greater than marginal cost. Estimation methods for limited dependent variables would be needed to estimate the premium equation.

Formal Model for Competitive HMO

Individual firms in a competitive market can sell as much or as little as they want without affecting price. Formally, this means that

$P_Q = 0$ for the competitive firm. The equilibrium conditions for choosing quantity and benefits can be derived from the monopolistic model by imposing this constraint on the slope of the demand curve. In the case where the supplementary premium is positive and the ACR regulation is not binding, we have the standard conditions for competitive pricing: $P + A = C$, and $P_B = C_B$. In other words, the supplementary premium plus the AAPCC equals the marginal cost of enrollment, and the marginal increase in consumers' willingness to pay for benefits equals the marginal cost of benefits.

When only the supplementary premium constraint is binding, competition forces benefits up to the point where profits are gone. The AAPCC equals the marginal cost of enrollment at this point. However, the marginal condition for choosing benefits becomes $P_B Q - C_B Q + \lambda P_B = 0$, which is similar to the premium-constrained monopoly in which the marginal willingness to pay for benefits is less than the marginal cost of benefits.

When just the ACR regulation is binding, the equilibrium conditions are $P + A = C$ and $P_B < C_B$. We doubt whether this equilibrium will ever be observed in the real world, however. The reason is that the ACR constraint includes a positive profit in the HMO's non-Medicare business. If competition affects both Medicare and non-Medicare business equally, then we would expect profit to be zero in a competitive market. Consequently, the ACR constraint would be $C - A \geq 0$, and a binding regulatory constraint would be $C = A$. In other words, binding ACR regulation in a competitive market necessarily implies that the supplementary premium will be driven to zero. Thus, we will not observe positive supplementary premiums under binding regulation in a competitive market.

When both the ACR regulation and the zero-premium constraint are binding, the equilibrium conditions again are $A = C$ and $P_B < C_B$. Consequently, it appears that any constraint in the competitive market—either the ban on premium refunds or the ACR regulation—will result in zero supplementary premium and overproduction of supplementary benefits, on the margin.

METHODS

Our theory predicts that the jth HMO sets the premium for Medicare supplementary benefits according to factors related to the HMO's average cost, the AAPCC, and market conditions that determine the elasticity of demand for enrollment. We estimated the reduced-form premium equation by tobit analysis because the dependent variable is censored at zero for 13 of 95 observations. A reduced-form equation also is estimated for the number of supplementary benefits offered by the HMO. Because the number of benefits can be considered to be a continuous variable, this equation is estimated by ordinary least squares (OLS) regression.

The equation of primary interest in this analysis is the structural demand (enrollment) equation. Enrollment measures the quantity of HMO services demanded by the Medicare population in the market area. Demand for Medicare enrollment in the jth HMO is assumed to be a function of several exogenous characteristics of the HMO and two endogenous variables: the premium for supplementary benefits and the number of supplementary benefits offered by the HMO. To address the endogeneity of premium and supplementary benefits in the structural enrollment equation, these variables are replaced by instruments obtained by regressing premium and supplementary benefits on all the exogenous variables in the model. Our estimation method differs from standard two-stage least squares in that tobit analysis is used to obtain the premium instrument. Let the variables in the premium equation (e.g., AAPCC and market characteristics) be denoted as "X." Then the predicted premium is as follows:

$$PREDICTED\ PREMIUM = \Phi(-X'\beta_{PREM}) \cdot (X'\beta_{PREM} + \sigma\lambda), \qquad (8.5)$$

where $\Phi\ (-X'\beta_{PREM})$ is the probability that premium is positive and

$$\lambda = \Phi\ (X'\beta_{PREM})\ /\ \Phi\ (-X'\beta_{PREM}). \qquad (8.6)$$

The first-stage instrument for coverage is *Predicted Coverage* = $X'\beta_{COVERAGE}$. Therefore, the demand equation can be written as: *Enrollment* = *f(Predicted Premium, Predicted Coverage, Other Demand Variables)*. We corrected the estimated standard errors in the demand equation, as required by our substitution of instruments for righthand-side variables (Greene 1990: 624).

DATA

The data used in this analysis came from four sources: (1) the October 1989 *HCFA Monthly Report on Medicare Prepaid Health Plans* (see HHS 1989b); (2) the *HCFA Report of TEFRA HMOs by County* with 1989 and 1990 AAPCC Rates; (3) the National HMO Census (Christianson et al. 1991); and (4) the Area Resource Data File for the Population.

The *Monthly Report on Medicare Prepaid Health Plans* provided information on the status of risk-contract and cost-contract HMOs as of October 1989.[4] Medicare HMOs paid under the Diagnostic Cost Groups (DCGs) demonstration were included in the data.[5] As of October 1989, 131 HMOs were participating under Medicare risk contracts ($N = 126$) or in the HCFA DCG-payment demonstration ($N = 5$). Information utilized in this study includes supplemental premiums, additional plan benefits, date of operation, number of enrollees as of October 1989, plan model (staff, group, or independent practice association [IPA]), for-profit status, and city/state location of the plan.

The *HCFA Report of TEFRA HMOs by County* includes information on the AAPCC rates for 1989 and the number of enrollees per plan by county. The total number of HMO enrollees per metropolitan statistical area (MSA) was obtained from the National HMO Census report, and the Area Resource Data File for the Population was used to obtain the total number of HMOs per MSA. A weighted AAPCC variable was calculated for the jth Medicare HMO using the jth HMO's share of enrollees in each of the i counties in its service area:

$$AAPCC_j = \sum_i AAPCC_i \cdot \frac{\text{Enrollment in } HMO_j \text{ in County}_i}{\text{Total Enrollment in } HMO_j}. \quad (8.7)$$

The market saturation rate (SATRATE) is based on all HMO enrollment and is the percentage of the market area's population enrolled in HMOs. A weighted saturation rate, similar to the weighted AAPCC, was calculated for the jth HMO as follows:

$$SATRATE_j = \sum_i SATRATE_i \cdot \frac{\text{Enrollment in } HMO_j \text{ in } MSA_i}{\text{Total Enrollment in } HMO_j}. \quad (8.8)$$

The number of competing Medicare HMOs was determined for each HMO using a weighted average of the percentage of the HMO's enrollment in each MSA by the number of Medicare HMOs in the MSA. For those HMOs not in MSAs, county-level data were used. A similar measure of the total number of competing HMOs was calculated for each HMO.

A variable of particular interest in this analysis is the concentration of the HMO market. We hypothesized that premiums will be lower, ceteris paribus, in less-concentrated market areas. We used the

Table 8.2 HIRSCHMAN-HERFINDAHL INDEXES FOR MEDICARE HMOs BY U.S. COUNTY AND MSA

HHI Range	Number of Counties	Percentage of Counties	Number of MSAs[a]	Percentage of MSAs[a]
0.01–0.25	11	2.4	4	3.9
0.26–0.50	40	8.8	14	13.6
0.51–0.75	84	18.6	19	18.4
0.76–0.99	57	12.6	22	21.3
1.00	260	57.5	44	42.7
Total	452	100.0	103	100.0

Sources: *HCFA Report of TEFRA HMOs by County*, 1989 (Washington, D.C.: Health Care Financing Administration).
Notes: Data include only counties and MSAs with some Medicare HMOs. Hirschman-Herfindahl Index (HHI) is based on the total enrollment in Medicare HMOs and does not include the FFS Medicare sector.
a. MSA, metropolitan statistical area.

Hirschman-Herfindahl Index (HHI) to measure market concentration. The HHI index for the ith market area is defined as:

$$HHI_j = \sum_j \frac{Enrollment\ in\ HMO_j\ in\ Market\ Area_i}{Total\ HMO\ Enrollment\ in\ Market\ Area_i} \quad (8.9)$$

Tables 8.2 and 8.3 show HHIs for counties and MSAs based on Medicare HMO market shares and market shares for all HMOs. The HHIs calculated for Medicare HMOs, shown in table 8.2, indicate slightly less concentration when compiled by MSA rather than by

Table 8.3 HIRSCHMAN-HERFINDAHL INDEXES FOR ALL HMOs BY MSA

HHI Range	Number of MSAs[a]	Percentage of MSAs[a]
0.01–0.25	178	55.8
0.26–0.50	232	16.9
0.51–0.75	254	6.9
0.76–0.99	264	3.1
1.00	319	17.2
Total	452	100.0

Sources: Area Resource Data File for the Population; Christianson et al. 1990.
Notes: Data include only MSAs with some HMOs. Hirschman-Herfindahl Index (HHI) is based on the total enrollment in HMOs and does not include the FFS Medicare sector.
a. MSA, metropolitan statistical area.

Table 8.4 "HMO-BASED" HIRSCHMAN-HERFINDAHL INDEX

| | County as Market Area | | MSA[a] or County as Market Area | |
HHI Range	Number of HMOs	Percentage of HMOs	Number of HMOs	Percentage of HMOs
0.01–0.25	4	2.8	5	3.5
0.26–0.50	41	29.1	55	39.0
0.51–0.75	44	31.2	35	24.8
0.76–0.99	26	18.4	26	18.4
1.00	26	18.4	20	14.2
Total	141	100.0	141	100.0

Source: *HCFA Report of TEFRA HMOs by County,* 1989 (Washington, D.C.: Health Care Financing Administration, September).
Notes: Data include risk, DCG, and social HMOs. Hirschman-Herfindahl Index (HHI) is based on the total enrollment in Medicare HMOs and does not include the FFS Medicare sector.
a. MSA, metropolitan statistical area.

county. However, even when compiled at the MSA level, the HHI for Medicare HMOs shows substantially higher concentration than the same index computed for all HMOs.

Most of the market areas described by tables 8.2 and 8.3 are rather concentrated. However, if most Medicare HMO enrollees live in markets with low HHIs, then these tables may understate the level of competitiveness faced by Medicare HMOs. HHIs for each Medicare HMO were constructed by weighting the HHI for each market area in which the HMO had Medicare enrollees by the proportion of those enrollees found in that market area:

$$HHI_j = \sum_i HHI_i \cdot \frac{\text{Enrollment in } HMO_j \text{ in Market Area}_i}{\text{Total HMO Enrollment in } HMO_j} \quad (8.9)$$

Table 8.4 shows these weighted "HMO-based" HHIs. The first pair of columns in table 8.4 defines the market area as a county. The second pair of columns defines market areas as MSAs when the HMO's enrollees are in a county that is part of an MSA. Otherwise, the HHI for the county was used.

When the county definition of market area is used, about one-third of the HMOs face an enrollment-weighted HHI of .5 or less and about two-thirds face an HHI of .75 or less, indicating relatively dispersed market shares. When the combination county/MSA definition of market area is used, the percentage of HMOs facing HHIs of .5 or less rises to 43 percent, and the percentage facing HHIs of .75 or less rises to 67 percent. Only 14–18 percent of Medicare HMOs confine their offerings to markets in which they are the only Medicare HMO.

Tables 8.2–8.4 show that even if one lays aside competition with FFS Medicare and Medigap policies, Medicare HMOs tend not to dominate the markets in which they operate. Medicare HMO market areas exhibit relatively dispersed market shares, rather than geographically segmented markets.

Means and standard deviations for all the variables in the analysis are shown in table 8.5. The dataset was reduced from 131 cases to 95 because 29 plans had not started to enroll Medicare beneficiaries, even though they had signed risk contracts. Seven other HMOs were missing the market data needed to compute concentration measures.

The fact that HMOs set premiums over geographic areas that contain more than one market poses an empirical problem for our analysis. Some market-area characteristics that could be considered exogenous to the HMO in county-level data may be endogenous when the HMO itself is the unit of observation. In other words, the HMO cannot control the AAPCC-based payment in any county, but the HMO can determine which counties it will serve. Thus, there is some degree of endogeneity in variables such as the weighted AAPCC-based payment and weighted HHI calculated for the HMO.

RESULTS

Table 8.6 shows the estimated instruments for premium and coverage. The negative and significant coefficient of AAPCC payment in the premium equation indicates that the supplementary premium falls as the government's contribution to premiums rises. The size of this coefficient shows that a $1 increase in the AAPCC causes the supplementary premium to decrease by 26¢. According to our theory, an increase in the AAPCC increases both the HMO's revenue and costs at a given level of enrollment. If the revenue enhancement is larger, profit-maximizing HMOs should cut their supplementary premium to attract more enrollees. Therefore, the negative coefficient indicates that the AAPCC increases an HMO's revenue by more than its cost. In other words, the AAPCC payment appears to be overly generous.

The *MEDHHI* variable (Medicare HHI) measures the weighted HHI for each HMO, based on Medicare HMO market concentrations. *MEDHHI* is only one possible measure of the competitiveness of the market

Table 8.5 MEANS AND STANDARD DEVIATIONS OF VARIABLES (95 OBSERVATIONS)

Variables		Mean	Standard Deviation
PREMIUM	Supplemental premium ($/mo.)	34.55	21.02
ENROLL	Medicare HMO enrollment	11,146	21,231
TYPE	1 = HMO; 0 = CMP	0.87	0.33
STAFF	1 = Staff-model HMO: 0 = Other	0.18	0.39
GROUP	1 = Group-model HMO; 0 = Other	0.28	0.45
IPA	1 = IPA-model HMO; 0 = Other	0.54	0.50
AGE	Age of health plan in months, from operation date to October 1989	40.26	12.30
RISK	1 = Risk-contract Medicare HMO; 0 = Diagnostic Cost Group HMO	0.95	0.22
PROFIT	1 = For-profit; 0 = Not-for-profit	0.49	0.50
KAISER	1 = Plan is member of Kaiser chain; 0 = Other	0.12	0.32
HUMANA	1 = Plan is member of Humana chain; 0 = Other	0.05	0.22
FHP	1 = Plan is member of FHP chain; 0 = Other	0.04	0.20
SHARE	1 = Plan is member of Share chain; 0 = Other	0.03	0.18
QUAL-MED	1 = Plan is member of Qual-Med chain; 0 = Other	0.02	0.14

Variable	Description		
AAPCC	Weighted AAPCC for each HMO	288.55	45.40
MEDHHI	Weighted Hirschman-Herfindahl Index for Medicare HMOs	0.58	0.28
SATRATE	Saturation rate for all HMOs	0.24	0.13
MEDSAT	Interaction between MEDHHI and SATRATE	0.13	0.10
PHYS	Preventive care benefit—physicals	0.77	0.42
IMMUN	Preventive care benefit—immunizations	0.68	0.47
HLTHED	Preventive care benefit—health education	0.77	0.42
FOOT	Preventive care benefit—footcare	0.12	0.32
DRUGS	Prescription drugs benefit	0.39	0.49
EYECARE	Eye exams benefit	0.68	0.47
LENSES	Lenses benefit	0.22	0.42
EARCARE	Ear exams benefit	0.38	0.49
HEARAID	Hearing aids benefit	0.13	0.33
DENTAL	Dental exams benefit	0.17	0.38
MENTAL	Mental health services benefit	0.28	0.45
COPAY	Copayment required	−0.84	0.37
COVERAGE	Sum of supplemental benefits (PHYS through COPAY)	3.74	2.22

Notes: PHYS through MENTAL are dummy variables equaling 1 if benefit is offered and 0 if not offered. COPAY equals −1 if copayment is required and 0 if not required.

area. *SATRATE* measures the overall market penetration of HMOs for all age groups in the market area, and *MEDSAT* is the multiplicative interaction of these two variables. In regressions that contained *MED-HHI* and *SATRATE*, but not the interaction (*MEDSAT*), the effect of *MEDHHI* was positive—indicating higher premiums where market shares were more concentrated—and the *SATRATE* coefficient was negative, but neither coefficient was statistically significant. When *MEDHHI*, *SATRATE*, and *MEDSAT* are all included in the premium equation, all three variables are significant at the .05 level. The results imply that in areas of high market penetration by HMOs, a higher HHI is associated with higher premiums.

This result must be interpreted with caution. Inspection of scatterplots reveals that the significance of the interaction term is due primarily to four Medicare HMOs in the Los Angeles area with zero supplementary premium, high saturation, and low-weighted HHIs. Moreover, the result is troublesome because the negative, significant coefficient on the Medicare HHI (*MEDHHI*) implies that the HHI is negatively associated with premiums in areas with low market penetration. (The total effect of *MEDHHI* on the dependent variable is $\beta_{MEDHHI} + \beta_{MEDSAT} \cdot SATRATE$, and since β_{MEDHHI} is negative and β_{MEDSAT} is positive, the total effect of *MEDHHI* will be negative for low values of *SATRATE*.) However, the association becomes positive when more than 30 percent of the population is enrolled in HMOs. In our sample of 95 observations, about one-third of the HMOs have service areas comprising MSAs with more than 30 percent of the population in HMOs. In addition to the regressions in table 8.6, we also estimated semi- and double-logarithmic forms of the regression equations, as well as regressions using the marketwide HHI. The results of these regressions were essentially the same as those in table 8.6.

The coverage instrument indicates that HMOs with longer experience with Medicare risk contracts tend to offer more supplementary benefits. Several of the HMO-chain dummy variables also are statistically significant, but, otherwise, supplementary benefits do not appear to depend on either HMO or market-area characteristics.

The structural demand equation is shown in table 8.7. The negative coefficient of the premium instrument indicates that a $1 decrease in the monthly premium causes Medicare HMO enrollment to increase by 662 enrollees. The significance of this result is that Medicare beneficiaries are sensitive to the supplementary premium charged by HMOs. A $1 increase is small, compared with the average monthly supplementary premium of $34.55, but the loss in Medicare

Table 8.6 REDUCED-FORM EQUATIONS FOR PREMIUM AND COVERAGE

Variable	Tobit PREMIUM Equation		OLS COVERAGE Equation	
	Coefficient	T-ratio	Coefficient	T-ratio
ONE	144.635	5.431**	3.52955	1.293
STAFF	4.22056	0.734	0.954768	1.586
GROUP	−5.78154	−1.012	−0.507317	−0.830
AGE	0.258906	1.434	0.330620E-01	1.708*
PROFIT	−9.40029	−2.015**	0.294987	0.596
RISK	−10.4944	−1.244	−0.452232	−0.495
KAISER	−3.22886	−0.421	2.86663	3.474**
HUMANA	−18.1001	−1.887*	−3.18938	−3.151**
FHP	−35.6757	−2.996**	−2.02481	−1.872*
SHARE	−11.2337	−1.034	−1.55759	−1.322
QUAL-MED	4.33247	0.306	2.57746	1.687*
AAPCC	−0.263367	−4.551**	0.229610E-02	0.384
MEDHHI	−42.2547	−2.415**	−2.46092	−1.332
MEDSAT	143.388	2.598**	5.73330	1.002
SATRATE	−91.2979	−2.505**	−3.87908	−1.057
SIGMA	17.8336		1.936022	

Notes: Log-likelihood, −365.38; log-likelihood (B=0), −423.60: adjusted R-squared, .240567.
*significant at α = .10 in two-tailed test.
**significant at α = .05 in two-tailed test.

Table 8.7 STRUCTURAL DEMAND EQUATION (DEPENDENT VARIABLE = ENROLL)

Variable	Coefficient	T-ratio (corrected)
ONE	16595.1	1.904*
STAFF	17782.1	3.037**
GROUP	278.819	0.058
AGE	305.312	1.777*
YFITPREM[a]	−661.968	−4.223**
YFITCOV[a]	406.512	0.234

[a]Replaced by instruments from first-stage equations
*significant at α = .10 in two-tailed test.
**significant at α = .05 in two tailed test.

enrollment is large in relation to the average of 11,146 people. This result implies that the competitive model appears to fit best for Medicare HMOs, on average. However, there may be significant differences among subgroups of HMOs, as is discussed in the next section.

Several large, staff-model HMOs contribute to the positive and significant coefficient of STAFF. The coefficient of the COVERAGE variable is statistically insignificant, contrary to the expectation that more optional benefits should attract enrollees. HMOs appear to gain enrollees the longer their experience in the Medicare risk-contracting program, as shown by the positive coefficient of AGE (statistically significant at the .10 confidence level).

We also estimated a model that ignores the censoring problem (i.e., the PREMIUM instrument was based on ordinary least squares regression). The results were similar to those reported in table 8.7. A $1 decrease in the supplementary premium was estimated to increase enrollment by 768 enrollees in this model. The tobit method for obtaining the PREMIUM instrument is theoretically superior, and it also imparts a "conservative" (i.e., less inclined toward the competitive hypothesis) slant to the following discussion.

IMPLICATIONS OF THE FINDINGS

First, what are the implications of our results for HMOs' profit margins? Our mathematical model has identified two fundamentally different ways to compute the profit margin. For those HMOs charging a positive supplementary premium, profit maximization results in the following pricing equation: $P = (C - A)/(1 + 1/\eta)$. We can rearrange terms in this equation so that it expresses the markup of premium plus AAPCC over marginal cost, in terms of the price elasticity of demand: $(P + A - C)/(P + A) = -P/(P + A)\eta$. We calculated the percentage markup for each HMO that charged a positive supplementary premium in 1989. Eighty-two HMOs with a total enrollment of 626,712 members are included in this calculation. They represent 86 percent of the HMOs and 59 percent of total Medicare HMO enrollment in our database. The simple average markup is 3.5 percent, and the weighted average (using each HMO's enrollment divided by 626,712 as weights) is 11.4 percent. Therefore, our results show that competition among HMOs is reasonably effective in reducing the Medicare profit margin for HMOs in this group.

However, there are 13 HMOs that do not charge a supplementary premium. The HMOs in this group had 432,185 enrollees, or 41 percent of total Medicare HMO enrollment, in 1989. We have argued that these HMOs will maximize profits by adding supplementary benefits until the marginal cost of doing so exceeds the marginal revenue from another member attracted by added benefits. Descriptive data indicate that this argument is plausible, since these 13 HMOs offer 4.31 supplementary benefits, on average, whereas the HMOs that charge a supplementary premium offer an average of 3.75 supplementary benefits. The "free-to-consumer" HMOs are also much larger on average, with 33,245 enrollees, and have had TEFRA contracts somewhat longer (43.31 months versus 40.26 months, respectively) than other HMOs.

We showed earlier that the profit-maximizing conditions for these free-to-consumer HMOs could be expressed as $A + P_Q Q = C - \lambda P_Q$ for the choice of enrollment and $P_B Q - C_B Q = -\lambda P_B$ for the choice of supplementary benefits. An interesting result may be obtained by solving these two equations. This is done by eliminating λ and substituting $-P_Q/P_B = B_Q$,[6] to obtain the expression that $A = C + B_Q C_B Q$. The lefthand side, or marginal revenue from another enrollee, equals the AAPCC when the HMO is free to consumers. The righthand side, or marginal cost of another enrollee, equals C plus the cost of attracting another enrollee by adding supplementary benefits. We can rewrite this equation in terms of a markup as $(A - C)/A = B_Q C_B (Q/A)$. Unfortunately, the change in marginal cost with respect to coverage (term C_B) is not observed. Therefore, we cannot exactly calculate the markup for these HMOs. However, a lower bound on the markup can be calculated by assuming that these HMOs voluntary choose to charge zero premium (i.e., that the corner solution is an unconstrained profit-maximizing point).[7] Under this assumption, we would observe $(A - C)/A = -(P_Q Q)/A$. We calculate that the simple average markup for this group is 14.9 percent, and the weighted average (using each HMO's enrollment divided by 432,185 as weights) is 39.4 percent.

Consequently, our results indicate that competition is less effective in wringing profits from 13 large HMOs with generous benefits and no supplementary premium. It is noteworthy that the average Medicare AAPCC payment of $330.74 for this select group is considerably higher than the AAPCC for HMOs that charge consumers an extra premium. Next, we turn to the implications of these different payment levels.

We have suggested that some HMOs may be overpaid for providing basic Medicare benefits. Indirect evidence supporting our argument came from the reduced-form premium equation in which a rise in the AAPCC caused supplementary premiums to fall. Additional evidence comes from the structural demand equation where we found that some HMOs with a positive premium operate in the inelastic region of the demand curve. This is consistent with a positive premium only if the AAPCC exceeds the HMO's marginal cost. That is, the premium equation is $P = (C - A)/(1 + 1/\eta)$. If the demand curve is inelastic, the second term is negative, and P can be positive only if $C < A$. This inequality holds for the profit-maximizing level of marginal cost, which includes at least some supplementary benefits. Since marginal cost decreases as the number of supplementary benefits decreases, it follows that the AAPCC must surely exceed $C(0)$ if it exceeds the optimal C. Our empirical model indicates that eight HMOs operate in the range where the supplementary premium is positive and demand is inelastic. We believe that the AAPCC is overly generous for these HMOs.

Of more importance, however, are the 13 HMOs with no supplementary premium. It is clear that profit-maximizing C must be less than AAPCC for these HMOs, because the AAPCC is their only source of revenue. Using the same argument as in the preceding paragraph, the AAPCC must surely exceed $C(0)$ for these HMOs. Consequently, we have discovered another source of evidence indicating that Medicare overpays some HMOs for basic Medicare benefits. Some HMOs charging a positive supplementary premium, and all HMOs not charging a supplementary premium, are overpaid. HMOs in the latter group are quite large, on average, accounting for 41 percent of total Medicare HMO enrollment. The $330 monthly AAPCC payment for the basic Medicare benefit package is too high for HMOs in this group. Four of the problem HMOs are located in South Florida, and 5 are located in Southern California. We suggest that the Health Care

Financing Administration might address overpayment to HMOs on a geographic basis by concentrating on these two problem areas.

Finally, 74 HMOs charge a positive premium and operate in the range where demand for enrollment is elastic. The average cost of the *current level* of benefits for these HMOs exceeds their AAPCC, according to our pricing equation. However, we cannot determine from our model whether the average cost of *basic benefits* would be greater than the AAPCC for these HMOs.

SUMMARY

Policymakers have been reluctant to use competitive pricing to eliminate excess profits in the Medicare HMO market. Our empirical results show that these fears are largely unfounded. About two-thirds of all Medicare beneficiaries who have access to an HMO can choose among two or more such plans. Competition appears to be vigorous enough to produce an average markup of less than 4 percent (or a weighted average of 11 percent) for those HMOs that charge a supplementary premium. Future research might clarify the nature of this competitive process—for example, whether the threat of entry or competition among existing risk-contract HMOs is a more important source of pressure on HMO profits. Such research might also clarify whether our results can be generalized beyond the Medicare population. Does competition hold down profits among the HMOs serving non-Medicare enrollees as well as it seems to do for about three out of every five Medicare HMO enrollees?

We are concerned that 13 large HMOs appear to make excess profits from Medicare. It may seem paradoxical that these HMOs do not charge a supplementary premium, but this occurs because the government has been overly generous in paying them for basic Medicare benefits. The incentive to obtain more enrollees drives the supplementary premium to zero and causes these plans to offer more optional benefits than the average HMO.

Competition thus appears to wring most of the profits out of the system. However, competition over enrollment and coverage will not solve the problem that the government's premium contribution is too generous. This problem will remain so long as the AAPCC is pegged to costs in the FFS sector. We suggest that competitive pricing should be used to determine the level of the government's premium contribution as well as supplementary premiums and benefits (Dowd et al. 1992).

Notes

Funding for this study was provided by the U.S. Health Care Financing Administration (HCFA) through Cooperative Agreement No. 99-C-99169/5-02. The policy positions in this paper are those of the authors and do not necessarily reflect the opinions of HCFA staff, nor do they represent official HCFA policy.

1. One definition (Dowd et al. 1992) of the correct payment level for basic Medicare benefits is the cost of those benefits delivered by the most efficient medical care plan in a given market area.

2. "Cost" means either average or marginal cost, since one is assumed to equal the other. If marginal cost is a function of enrollment, the HMO will implicitly estimate its Medicare enrollment when it submits the ACR application. However, the actual number of Medicare enrollees is not known at this time. Once the ACR is approved, it will not vary according to how many Medicare beneficiaries actually join the HMO.

3. Mathematically, this difference is equal to $-\lambda P_Q$.

4. HMOs have the option of entering into either risk or cost contracts with HCFA. Medicare risk contractors are capitated at 95 percent of the AAPCC. Cost-contract plans are reimbursed on the basis of the actual cost of their services and, therefore, operate more like traditional FFS insurance plans than HMOs. We excluded such cost-contract plans from this study.

5. The DCG experiment used diagnostic information about previous hospitalizations to create empirically determined risk groups (Ash et al. 1989). A high incidence of hospitalizations involving little or no discretion in the decision to hospitalize was used to increase the HMO's capitation rate.

6. Totally differentiate the demand curve, holding price constant, to obtain $0 = P_Q dQ + P_B dB$. Rearrange terms to obtain $-P_Q/P_B = B_Q$, as stated in the text.

7. The first-order condition for premiums can be written as $(A - C)/A = -(P_Q Q)/A - (\lambda P_Q)/A$. The last term is zero at a corner solution, but otherwise it is positive. Therefore, the markup is at least as large as $-(P_Q Q)/A$.

References

Ash, Arlene, Frank Porell, Leonard Gruenberg, Eric Sawitz, and Alexa Beiser. 1989. "Adjusting Medicare Capitation Payments Using Prior Hospitalization Data." *Health Care Financing Review* 10 (4, Summer): 17–29.

Brown, Randall S. 1988. "Biased Selection in Medicare HMOs." Paper presented at fifth annual meeting of the Association for Health Services Research, San Francisco, June 26–28.

Christianson, Jon B., Susan M. Sanchez, Douglas R. Wholey, and Maureen Shadle. 1991. "The HMO Industy: Evolution in Population Demographics and Market Structures." *Medical Care Review* 48 (1, Spring): 3–46.

Dowd, Bryan, Jon Christianson, Roger Feldman, Catherine Wisner, and John Klein. 1992. "Issues Regarding Health Plan Payments under Medicare and Recommendations for Reform." *Milbank Quarterly* 70 (3): 423–53.

Greene, William H. 1990. *Econometric Analysis*. New York: Macmillan Publishing Co.

HHS. See U.S. Department of Health and Human Services.

Luft, Harold S. 1981. *Health Maintenance Organizations: Dimensions of Performance*. New York: John Wiley & Sons.

Maddala, G. S. 1989. *Limited-Dependent and Qualitative Variables in Econometrics*. Cambridge, England: Cambridge University Press.

Porell, Frank W., Christopher Tompkins, David Pomeranz, and Leonard Gruenberg. 1987. *Medicare TEFRA Risk Contracting: A Study of the Adjusted Community Rate*. Report prepared by Brandeis University for the Health Care Financing Administration (HFCA). Waltham, MA: Brandeis University, September 15.

Tobin, J. 1958. "Estimation of Relationships for Limited Dependent Variables." *Econometrica* 26: 24–36.

U.S. Department of Health and Human Services. 1989a. *ODAM Area Resource File*. Office of Data Analysis and Management, Bureau of Health Professionals. Washington, D.C.: Author.

_____. 1989b. *Monthly Report: Medicare Prepaid Health Plans*. HFCA. Washington, D.C.: Author.

_____. 1990. *Medicare Prepaid Health Plans by County*. HFCA. Washington, D.C.: Author.

U.S. General Accounting Office. 1989. "Medicare: Health Maintenance Organization Rate-Setting Issues." GAO/HRD-89-46, Washington, D.C.: Author, January.

Part Three

THE CASE AGAINST COMPETITION

Chapter Nine

THE IRONIC FLAW
IN HEALTH CARE COMPETITION:
THE POLITICS OF MARKETS

James A. Morone

American health care was once the envy of the world. Now, 9 out of 10 Americans are calling for fundamental change, and the U.S. health system is being referred to as an unenviable mix of "excess and deprivation" (Enthovey and Kronick 1989: 29). Roaring inflation in costs has consumed, on average, an extra one percent of the gross national product every 40 months through the 1980s (and the pace has since quickened). At the same time, 60 million citizens went without health insurance for at least part of the last 18 months of the eighties.[1] These troubles have reawakened that hardy reform perennial, health care competition. The problem is that Americans have already taken an unpleasant dose of health care competition. It is precisely what lies at the heart of America's health care troubles. Moreover, market reformers have often pursued their ideas in a government-bashing fashion that, ultimately, undermines the prospects of reforms.

Naturally, market advocates deny the charges. A true market, they correctly point out, has never really been tried—classical economic theory remains untested as a solution to our health sector maladies. The marketeers imagine a world in which health care providers jockey to satisfy consumers (and their agents, such as corporate benefits managers). They see providers who prosper because they offer better care at lower cost; in this world the market—the consumers—will discipline the others. Yet, to achieve this vision will require an intricate array of policy adjustments. To offer some examples: we must change our tax laws so consumers feel the pinch when they opt for pricey health care; we must publish data so consumers can make more-informed judgments about medical quality; we ought to provide subsidies (preferably through the tax system) so that uninsured people can purchase insurance; and we must insist that insurers do not duck the expensive patients. Market proponents insist that these changes are politically digestible. A market can be put into place, they say, one sensible step at a time, with far less political trauma than governmental health insurance schemes imported from abroad.

This chapter offers a response. We have not seen a fully articulated, carefully calibrated system of health care competition (nor has anybody else), but we have seen its fundamental dynamics at work. The tumultuous medical economy of the past decade offers a glimpse of the real-world incentives that are structured into medical markets. Recent experience offers a serious warning to those who blithely promise a simple competitive fix to our troubles. It suggests that in health care, competition perversely raises costs and leads to gaps in coverage. Moreover, the overheated health politics of the 1980s undermined our already weak prospects for controlling the deleterious aspects of medical capitalism. Why? Because, although health care competition is rooted in a skeptical view of government, to succeed competition requires extraordinarily careful and sophisticated governance.

After all, markets are political constructions. They require us to agree on rules we must then enforce. Medical markets are especially tricky because we ask them to operate in distinctly nonmarket ways. For one thing, everyone must be provided some health care, even the improvident who have lapsed in their insurance payments. In addition, information about treatments and outcomes is hard to disseminate because sick people don't often haggle with their doctors and insurance coverage (not to mention the immediate prospects of a lawsuit) distorts the exchanges that do occur. The list goes on. As a result, most market proponents propose an elaborate regulatory apparatus, either public or private: Someone has to struggle, they say, against capitalist logic and curb providers who pursue raw economic motives by avoiding less lucrative patients (ironically, the sick ones). Someone has to cull and distribute complex medical information (so consumers can calculate whether expensive hospitals actually do better). And someone has to proscribe and punish unfair market practices. In short, properly functioning medical markets place extraordinary demands on government or special private agents, or both. The task requires far more skill than the grosser judgments required by the global budgeting of national health insurance. Perhaps the most overlooked aspect of health care competition is the extent to which its rests on careful, sophisticated governance.

The great irony is that health care competition derives much of its political resonance from government-bashing. For decades, markets have been sold with an antigovernment sneer—as an all-American alternative to the bureaucratic bungling of a bloated state (in more ardent formulations, socialism enters in). For instance, Alain Enthoven and Richard Kronick's recent "Consumer Choice Health Plan for the 1990s" ends by contrasting "our historical preferences for limited government" with "something more alien and drastic" (1989: 101). Each antigovernmental bromide chips away at the necessary conditions for health care competition. Indeed, it is the very weakness of our government, eagerly held up for public ridicule in every presidential election of the past quarter century, that undermines market reform.

The following section traces the evolution of the market ideal, focusing on the interconnection between intricate policy proposals and a more bare-knuckled aversion to government. I then show how and why our health care perplexities flow from the logic of medical capitalism itself. Finally, I explore the ironic symbiosis between markets and politics.

HEALTH CARE MARKETS: AN ENVOLVING IDEA

In the world that some economists inhabit, a "market" seems unambiguous, "something as obvious as a dog" (Bowles 1991: 11). Not so in politics. In the world of politics, words are often infused with new meanings—cast and recast for different partisan purposes. Health care markets have had at least two political lives.

Before the 1970s, free markets meant leaving providers alone. The medical profession, vigilant against government incursions onto professional turf, repeatedly juxtaposed market capitalism with government tyranny. Reforms that seemed to threaten professional autonomy (such as national health insurance or even Medicare) were loudly denounced as oppressive, usurpative, and—inevitably—socialistic. Compulsory insurance was "a dangerous device . . . announced by the German emperor" (in 1918), a keystone in the arch of socialism (by the 1950s), and a "threat to every area of freedom as we have known it in this country" (by 1962). Always juxtaposed to the compulsory state was "the American Way"—markets, capitalism, free choice. These rhetorical celebrations of medical markets were, of course, merely a strategy by which the medical profession mustered allies in its struggle for professional autonomy (Morone 1990: 254–63).

The market idea was reconstructed when Americans discovered a crisis in health care costs in the early 1970s. At that time the market became a way to discipline medical providers. Consumers would force efficiency on the health system. The new usage was elaborated over two decades with increasing complexity and sophistication.

The thoughtful new market conceptions contrasted sharply with the self-interested government-bashing of the previous era. Now marketeers would rely on the state in a wide variety of ways. For example, in 1971, Martin Feldstein proposed universal catastrophic insurance, a program that would cover citizens who had spent 10 percent of their income on medical care. Alain Enthoven in 1978 (650–58; 709–20) called for "public sponsors," brokers designed to help individuals negotiate their insurance coverage. Many others invoked state assistance in fashioning health system reform.

Despite broadening recognition of the need to govern health markets, the old animus against government often lay just below the surface of promarket reform. Indeed, the market ideal was driven to the top of the health policy agenda by the most powerful political force of the late 1970s: the antigovernmental surge that pressed for deregulation and privatization throughout the American economy. In the early 1980s, Ronald Reagan's rebels articulated the sentiment with extraordinary political effect. In health care, five decades of provider vitriol gave the antigovernment rhetoric a familiar, even reassuring tone. Sophisticated market advocates knew that untangling our health care problems would take more than "removing government from the backs of the medical industry." But the celebration of markets and capitalism seemed the right attitude, a precondition for the competition experiment in medicine.

The early Reagan period proved a crossroads for the market movement. Administration officials saw a choice between two different conceptions of medical markets. One alternative linked the old antistatist vision to the essential Reagan precept that the market should be left to itself. The government would try to reduce its own expenditures, and every other payer could do the same. The other alternative was to pursue the interlocking changes proposed in much of the procompetition literature. This meant a hard fight with Congress over limiting tax breaks for rich employer health benefits; it meant government involvement to keep insurers from discriminating against the poor risks, and even, in some formulations, new programs for people without insurance. Ultimately, this second approach raised an uncomfortable paradox for Republicans: it would take government to achieve markets. The Reagan administration opted for the first route, scoring its political points through an inflated rhetorical assault on the public sector.

Proponents of health care competition rarely demurred. Even complex market schemes that relied on extensive public-sector action carried with them the older motif, a disdain of government. To this day, the two strains remain analytically independent but effectively intertwined. Writing recently in the *Atlantic Monthly*, Regina Herzlinger (1991: 19) ended a careful response to the critics of her call for competition with the following: "The government that bungled the regulation of savings and loans and banks is, ironically, the one that [my critics] would entrust with running the entire health care establishment." In a rhetorical move now familiar from constant use, a careful market scheme segues smoothly into government-bashing.

The savings and loan analogy is worth notice. This was not a case of overreaching government. Just the reverse—markets were too free, government was too weak. The lesson is that efficient markets require wise government—and nowhere more than in medicine. Even a cursory look at the current state of our health care markets suggests the daunting tasks they put before our public officials.

HEALTH CARE MARKETS IN THE REAL WORLD

Throughout the booming health-sector confusion of the 1980s, something like a systematic health policy emerged. Amid plenty of market rhetoric, payers began to compete with one another. Each insurer scrambled to reduce its own costs. In theory, the more successful private companies could pass on the savings to their enrollees and gain market share. The federal government set the pace, acting as just another insurance company. Medicare and Medicaid looked after their own costs: they developed elaborate price-setting mechanisms (Medicare's Diagnostic Related Groups [DRGs], for instance), they froze reimbursement levels (Medicaid is notorious in many states), and they raised copayments. In good market fashion, other payers were left to mind their business as they saw fit.[2]

Health care payers and providers scrambled to lower their costs with entrepreneurial gusto. Corporations encouraged employees to enroll in health maintenance organizations (HMOs), which, in turn, marketed promises of savings and efficiency. Many large companies left their traditional carriers and insured themselves; some negotiated deals with health care providers through preferred provider organizations (PPOs), which also marketed promises of savings and efficiency. Blue Cross touted case management, then hedged its bets by sponsoring HMOs. Commercial insurers responded with managed-care plans of their own, along with all kinds of new "insurance products."

At first, in the mid-1980s, this flush of activity was met with cheers. Here was activity and innovation, flowing from the private sector. As one observer reflected:

> The system appears to be reshaping itself to respond to an era of constrained resources yet undiminished demands for quality . . . . The restructuring of the U.S. health care delivery system now under way appears to be producing a clinical and management structure that diverges increasingly from the centrally managed . . . systems of other countries (Jeffrey Goldsmith, in Ginzberg 1986: 69).

By the end of the decade, competition among payers had produced more pain than even the gloomiest critics had forecast. Although this was (and is) only partial competition, it illuminates the logic of capitalist energy in the marketplace. Consider two major health policy problems we now face: costs and the uninsured.

1. **Costs** Health care costs continue to rise at a dizzying pace, representing 8.4 percent of gross domestic product in 1975, 9.1 percent in 1980, and over 12 percent today (Scheiber and Poullier 1991). The unexpected news is that price competition among payers raises costs, for three reasons. First, the many cost-control devices wielded by our payers (managed care, preferred provider organizations, DRGs) amount to institutional devices through which each bargains with providers about price and volume—one of the keys to Western European cost-control strategies as well. However, Americans undermine their bargaining strategy by establishing a multitude of bargainers in the name of choice and competition. Providers maintain their income by shifting costs from payers who are more effective at squeezing costs (Medicare, Medicaid) to those who are least effective (so far, business corporations have been the losers.) In effect, providers get multiple safety valves through which to escape tough cost-control programs. Many payers, each competing to keep their own costs down, create inflationary pressure on everyone.[3]

Second, new kinds of health providers, especially HMOs, were to be "the workhorses of the market revolution." Because patients generally pay a fixed annual fee, these organizations were thought to have clear incentives to provide less costly care. Once HMOs entered the market, predicted the procompetition faithful, they would swiftly attract patients away from payers and providers who failed to control costs.

Instead, as HMOs penetrated local markets, costs jumped. The new organizations skimmed off the best risks (the charitable argue that this was not a conscious strategy, that sicker patients have stronger ties to their physicians and health plans). This left traditional plans like Blue Cross with a pool of clients whose average costs are higher; thus premiums of traditional plans rose. The HMOs then appeared to shadow-price Blue Cross. A segmented market leads to higher premiums for everyone.

The third reason that price competition among payers raises costs is that all this activity creates a great administrative apparatus. Employment opportunities in medical administration surge as each hospital department and physician's office hires specialists designed to volley paper back and forth to counterparts working for insurance companies and corporations. Each new cost-containment program swells their ranks. Calculating the costs of all this administrative activity has itself grown into a flourishing trade among policy researchers—estimates range from $31 billion (former Office of Management and Budget Director Richard Darman's lowest estimate, in Office of the President [1992: chap. 3]) to $100 billion (the U.S. General Accounting Office's highest).[4]

The conclusion violates every microeconomic bone of every American health policy apparatchik: in health care, competition among payers raises costs. And that is not the worst of its problems.

2. **The Uninsured** In theory, consumer choices drive the market. Providers and payers jockey to satisfy consumers (and their agents such as corporate benefits managers). All things being equal, those who provide better care at lower cost will win; more-efficient providers will swiftly attract clients away from the less efficient.

In practice, both payers and providers have learned a simpler way to win the American health care competition: insure and treat less-expensive patients. The result has been a great race for patients who are less likely to be ill. Payers have swiftly improved their capacity to identify good and bad bets. What follows is market segmentation, risk selection, the refusal to insure many individuals and small groups, the refusal to insure preexisting medical conditions, and the disenrollment of people who are likely to be (or have been) sick. Some of these consequences were forecast by competition's critics;

others (like the fast spread of preexisting condition clauses) are unanticipated results of the creative energy of managers in a competitive environment.[5]

After all, a relatively small number of patients consume a large portion of medical resources. The most effective way to reduce premiums is not through tough negotiating or managerial techniques or more efficient forms of service delivery, but simply by avoiding the "poor risks." In the world of payer competition, the incentives are clear: insure the healthiest possible segment of the market and, above all, do not pay anybody else's costs. Medical providers have similar incentives passed on to them. Find patients who pay relatively more; shift costs from the payers who pay less to those who pay more; seek patients who are less ill (for they are relatively less costly to treat—an especially important consideration for those under price schedules or capitation arrangements); and, above all, avoid the nonpayers (who will wreck your reputation for efficiency). A decade of competition among payers has given every actor the same incentives: seek the healthy, shun the sick.[6]

The widely lamented army of uninsured people is a direct result. An elaborate system of hidden cross-subsidies—the very concept of a pooled risk, the basic idea of insurance—is eroding under the pressure of competition among payers. The consequences run wide and deep: uninsured, underinsured, uninsurable, labor management tensions, and—our most recently discovered medical malady—"job lock" (3 out of 10 workers recently reported that the fear of losing insurance coverage deterred them from seeking new jobs).[7] As costs continue to rise, many employers exacerbate these troubles by reducing or eliminating health benefits.

Market advocates offer elaborate political concoctions to address this trouble. Before delving into the details, it is important to emphasize the larger point: competition offers both payers and medical providers powerful incentives to avoid expensive patients. Market proponents would set up incentives to compete, and would then block off the surest winning strategy. In theory, there are plenty of ways to do so. In the real world of politics and markets, the American entrepreneur (often struggling for survival, with jobs at stake and political connections in line) is not easy to control.

Can market advocates seriously tackle these problems? Can the difficulties of costs and coverage be addressed with more (or better, or smarter) competition? How? These questions lead us back to the skill and power of our regulators.

MARKETS AND REGULATORS

Like any system of rules, markets promote some values and subordinate others, advantage some participants and disadvantage others. This is true, of course, for any market. Health care markets, however, are so complex because of the many social demands we make of our health care system: as suggested earlier, we expect some care for all citizens; we bail out some hospitals; we want physicians with the best possible training; and we want high technology, low costs, and plenty of choice.

Over the past 15 years, proponents have made their systems more complicated by trying to address other deviations from the market ideal: people do not obviously "shop" for medicine. They certainly do not do so when they are ill. Even if they wished to behave like proper economic men and women, they often have insufficient information. Providers appear to shape (if they do not outright induce) demand for their own services.[8] Beyond these familiar matters lie the challenges adumbrated in the preceding section—extending coverage (in the teeth of real world incentives) and cutting costs (ditto). To make it all work, marketeers have restlessly tinkered with their markets.

Take, for example, the most important current challenge. How do we halt the chase for patients who are less likely to be sick? Perhaps the best known proposed solution is Enthoven and Kronick's (1989) risk rating—consumers are rated by their risk factor and providers are paid more for treating patients who are apt to cost more. But what is simple in theory is enormously complicated in political reality. Which risks will be addressed, which overlooked? Age? Income? Race? Previous illness? Hazardous occupation? Environmentally hazardous hometown? Disabilities? The accounting rapidly gets extraordinarily complex. And who sets the rules? How are they monitored? Enforced? Changed over time?[9] All of which raises the nub of the matter: in the real world of health politics, there is no archimedean point from which these choices can be made in a rational and dispassionate manner. On the contrary, such choices are fundamentally political. Groups will lobby. So will payers with an economic stake in the outcome. Picture the scene when the risk raters take up the question of people who have tested HIV positive. And what will they say to the Blue Cross contention that telephone workers (whom it happens to insure) cost more to cover and should be reimbursed at a higher rate? Will elected public officials sit quietly through the process?

Other market proposals raise similar issues. The Bush administration version would have gathered the uninsured into large risk pools, then calculated the (presumably higher) costs of these groups and required other insurance pools to cross-subsidize part of the difference. It would have proscribed insurers from excluding employee groups, individuals, or people with expensive illnesses (Office of the President 1992, chapter 3). All in all, the proposal was a roundabout creation that would require armies of nimble regulators.

Opening the markets to as many individuals as possible is only one adjustment away from the free interplay of market forces. Other questions turn on the difficulty of distinguishing good medicine from bad. Again, creative tinkerers have been hard at work. Walter McClure (1988), for example, has stumped for a "buy-rite" proposal whereby hospitals would be rated (from 1.1 to 5.0) on multiple quality-of-care dimensions. The Health Care Financing Administration stumbled in the same general direction when it published hospital mortality statistics (producing much heat but little discernible light). Others have suggested institutes for health care evaluation (Bunker et al. 1982a, 1982b). The efforts all face an enormous challenge: reducing the enormously complex world of medicine into data that are simple enough to turn patients into wise consumers. These interventions are just the beginning. Someone has to worry about the citizens who fall between the private sectors' cracks, those usually relegated to a public program of last resort. And some agent would have to watch for frauds—such as individuals "sneaking" into welfare categories, providers making misleading claims, and managed care programs that cut corners.

In sum, markets require extraordinary—extensive, subtle, steady—regulation. It may come from either public or private regulators (I touch upon the difference in the following paragraphs). In either case, this is the unwritten section of almost all procompetitive proposals. Regulation is simply ignored or waived away ("fine-tuning," "oversight," a "local" question," say the various proposals). But this is no detail. It is at the heart of the matter. Poorly regulated competition yields precisely the kind of trouble that now plagues American health care.

The regulatory imperative is often obscured by a feckless trust in "incentives." Market proposals always come groaning under the weight of new *incentives*—operating independently, interacting smoothly, moving predictably (pick any promarket proposal and count the usages of the word). Once the proper incentives are in place (presumably put there by some wise political agent), the health care market will run by itself. But we are a long way from your apples for my oranges. The elusive incentives are asked to reshape the behavior of consumers, physicians, employers, hospitals (from administrators to house staff), payers, health care organizations, local governments, states, and on and on. As Marmor, Mashaw, and Harvey (1990) pointed out in *America's Misunderstood Welfare State,* incentives are not behavior. Those simple prods to sensible action repeatedly lead in entirely unexpected directions. Thus, competition to reduce costs led, willy-nilly, to competition for less-expensive patients. And this is a straightforward case, for it was simply an unanticipated strategy in the predictable race for success. Fixing on incentives often reduces a complex series of crosscutting desires to a simple reflex. The unexpected response comes because a simple change in economic incentive does not always tap the real motives in peoples' behavior. (For example, fiddling with financial incentives will not get patients shopping for new doctors when they value longstanding relationships with their present ones.) Trying to change the behavior of many different kinds of actors—all simultaneously— is an extraordinary aspiration. For thoughtful market advocates, one of the lessons of the 1980s is that it is neither desirable nor, in practice, possible to simply organize correct incentives and step aside. In health care, the unguided pursuit of self-interest is thick with troubles.

Moreover, regulating private markets is difficult. The freer the market—and the greater the social demands we place on it—the more demanding the regulatory task. Recall Herzlinger's (1991) comment on the savings and loans: liberating the bankers put new pressures on the regulators. That innovation collapsed partially because the regulators were not up to the job. In health care markets, the regulator's job is far more exacting, the social demands are far more extensive, the values we pursue so much more crosscutting. Health care markets are not—cannot be—any better than those overseeing them: setting the rules, ensuring some access for everyone (possibly against the self-interest of many), forbidding the creative techniques designed to sidestep sick customers, disseminating consumer information. In short, health care competition requires regulation that is both precise and sweeping.

Ironic Flaw in Health Care Competition

This leads to one of the great ironies of recent American history: health care competition is only as good as the government that competition advocates have so long and loudly deprecated. Even as the meaning of markets evolved over the years, they were steadfastly defined and celebrated as an alternative to the public sector. Sustained state-bashing has had the intended result: a weaker, less popular state. The unexpected consequence is that the state is less capable of organizing and running an effective market. The very rhetoric that made markets more popular now renders them less plausible. Market proponents have helped undermine (perhaps destroy) the essential conditions of their own success.

Market advocates have an answer, although it is distinctly innocent of American political history and thought: apolitical oversight. Where public authority is necessary (say, for rating risks), organize it to be independent and nonpolitical. Wherever possible, turn to private-sector regulators: for example, private organizations can produce information or rate quality.

The idea of decisions beyond (or better, *above*) politics is one of the most tarnished reform grails in American politics. It is, after all, precisely the ideal that James Madison and Alexander Hamilton attacked in *The Federalist*.[10] The roots of the contemporary aspiration for apolitical decisions lie in the late 19th century. Since the Progressive era, reformers have tried again and again to wrestle public decisions away from politics. The American civil service was structured on that principle—sold with the promise that independent administrators meant efficient and honest government in perpetuity. The independent regulatory commissions were introduced with the same faith. So were the Bureau of the Budget (now the Office of Management and Budget) and the Health Care Financing Administration (Morone 1990: chap. 3).

The history of reform movements in America echoes with repetitions of the "goo-goo" experience: the aspiration to get beyond politics only makes the American government more incoherent. As each reforming generation discovers, there is no decision-making platform outside politics. For one thing, when officials make value judgments, some groups are helped, other harmed. In a democratic society, the losers come forward and lobby. (Indeed, American political history can be read as a long lesson in the biases of an interest group society.) Oddly, analysts who revere the incentive power of self-interested capitalism expect the incentives to stop working at the government's edge. Somehow, self-interested groups won't pursue their incentives into the public sector or government officials won't pursue theirs by responding.

Moreover, each generation of reform has discovered that science and objective information offer an illusory guide to policy. The very definition of issues to be addressed (and ignored), the delineation of possible alternatives, the modes of searching for information, the organization of public commentary, the selection of officials and countless other matters are (again, fundamentally) political choices: they set some values over others, help some interests at the expense of others. The call for "getting beyond politics" continues to beguile reformers. It is not a realistic aspiration.

Worse, the search for governance beyond politics (even beyond government) renders our political institutions less effective and less accountable. Each new independent agency (created to chase the apolitical chimera) simply exacerbates the main tendency of our public institutions: fragmentation, overlap, duplication, stalemate, confusion, uncertain accountability, unclear lines of authority. Created to be independent, agencies pursue their own self-interest, form alliances with other organizations (public and private), and make judgments uncontrolled by any form of public accountability. In short, the distrust of government that triggers the search for apolitical governance only renders the government weaker. It is that weakness which creates the confusion and incoherence that market advocates have so long critiqued.

The Health Policy Lesson of the Eighties

The call of the market is not hard to understand. But the health policy lesson of the 1980s is that markets are not possible without subtle and extensive government regulation. Perhaps the most disregarded feature of the many competition proposals is the many demands they put on the state. American government may not be up to the task. The Republican ascendancy of the past two decades made it even less so. Market advocates will find no lasting relief in either government-bashing or the scramble to leave politics. On the contrary, they face a task they are unlikely to pursue and for which they are ill equipped to succeed: improving the capacity of American government.

All health care reformers—liberal and conservative, those who advocate national health insurance and those pursuing markets— face the same difficult proposition: building a better, more effective, stronger, government. That inescapable political fact turns our great health reform debates inside out. The charge that Americans do not like government sinks the market idea. The claim that America's genius lies in private-sector competition only restates the challenge, for in medicine, competition produces soaring costs and shrinking coverage.

It is time to be less oblique about health care reform. Americans ought to stop searching for ways to sidestep their government—the government will be in the middle of any successful health care system, market systems most of all. We ought to end the quest for ways to unleash the power of private enterprise—too much private enterprise in health care has caused us enormous pain. Once we abandon the lost market cause, we can get on with a useful debate: Which of the many alternative (yes, public) programs will best control costs while offering all Americans decent health care?

Whatever the final answer, the first step is reconstructing the community—the pool of shared risk—that years of partial competition has destroyed. There is a simple, incremental, fully American, politically popular way to begin: expand Medicare to the entire population. There are also far more elaborate ways to achieve a more just, efficient health care system. But none is more complex—to describe, to legislate, to implement, or to administer—than the ostensibly simple notion of health care competition.

Notes

1. On inflation, see Scheiber and Poullier (1991, 1987). On the uninsured, see Swartz (1990) and Swartz and McBride (1990).

2. For a discussion of Medicare DRGs as competition, see Morone and Dunham (1985).

3. For discussion, see Morone (1990). The same point is made in Enthoven and Kronick (1989:30).

4. On administrative costs, see Woolhandler and Himmelstein (1991), Himmelstein and Woolhandler (1986), and Evans (1990).

5. See Brown (1990).

6. For elaboration, see Morone (1990).

7. On job lock, see Eckholm (1991).

8. For recent entries into the voluminous debate on this matter, see Rice, Nelson, and Colby (1992) and Kronick (1992).

9. For a broadly analytic account of the point made in this paragraph, see Stone (1988). For a critical discussion of risk rating, see Dunham, Morone, and White (1983).

10. For discussion, see Morone (1990: chap. 1).

References

Bowles, Samuel. 1991. "What Markets Can—and Cannot—Do." *Challenge* 14: 11.

Brown, Lawrence. 1990. "The Medically Uninsured: Problems, Policies, and Politics." *Journal of Health Politics, Policy and Law* 15: 413–26.

Bunker, John et al. 1982a. "Evaluation of Medical Technology Strategies: Effects of Coverage and Reimbursement." *New England Journal of Medicine* 306: 620–24.

_____. 1982b. "Evaluation of Medical Technology Strategies: Proposal for an Institute of Medical Care Evaluation." *New England Journal of Medicine* 306: 686–92.

Dunham, Andrew, James Morone, and William White. 1982. "Restoring Medical Markets: Implications for the Poor." *Journal of Health Politics, Policy and Law* 7 (Summer).

Eckholm, Erik. 1991. "Health Benefits Found to Deter Switches in Jobs." *New York Times* September 26: A1.

Enthoven, Alain. 1978. "Consumer Choice Health Plan." *New England Journal of Medicine* 298: 650–58; 709–20.

Enthoven, Alain, and Richard Kronick. 1989. "A Consumer Choice Health Plan for the 1990s: Universal Health Insurance in a System Designed to Promote Quality and Economy, Parts I and II." *New England Journal of Medicine* 320 (1): 29–37, 94–101.

Evans, Robert. 1990. "Tension, Compression, and Shear: Directions, Stresses, and Outcomes of Health Care Cost Control." *Journal of Health Politics, Policy and Law* 15: 101–28.

Feldstein, Martin. 1971. "A New Approach to National Health Insurance." *Public Interest* 23 (Spring).

Ginzberg, Eli, ed. 1986. *Health Care in the 1990s*. Totowa, N.J.: Rowman & Allanheld, 1985.

Herzlinger, Regina. 1991. "Healthy Competition." Letters to the Editor. *Atlantic Monthly* 268 (November): 19.

Himmelstein, David, and Steffie Woolhandler. 1986. "Cost without Benefit: Administrative Waste in U.S. Health Care. *New England Journal of Medicine* 314: 441.

Kronick, Richard. 1992. "Commentary: Can Consumer Choice Reward Quality and Economy?" *Journal of Health Politics, Policy and Law* 17 (Spring): 25–33.

Marmor, Theodore, Jerry Mashaw, and Philip Harvey. 1990. *America's Misunderstood Welfare State* (New York: Basic Books).

McClure, Walter. 1988. "The Buy-Rite Proposal." Paper presented at the annual meeting of the New York Academy of Medicine, May 1–2.

Morone, James A. 1990. "American Political Culture and the Search for Lessons from Abroad." *Journal of Health Politics, Policy and Law* 15: 129–43.

————. 1990. "Beyond the N Words." *Bulletin of the New York Academy of Medicine* 66(4): 344–365.

————. 1990. *The Democratic Wish: Popular Participation and the Limits of American Government.* New York: Basic Books.

Morone, James A., and Andrew Dunham. 1985. "Slouching to National Health Insurance: The Politics of Health Care." *Yale Journal of Regulation* 2(2): 263–91.

Office of the President. 1992. *The President's Comprehensive Health Reform Proposal.* Washington, D.C.: U.S. Government Printing Office, February 6.

Rice, Thomas, Lyle Nelson, and David Colby. 1992. "Will Medicare Beneficiaries Switch Physicians? A Test of Market Competition." *Journal of Health Policy and Law* 17 (Spring): 3–24.

Scheiber, George, and Jean-Pierre Poullier. 1990. "International Health Spending: Issues and Trends." *Health Affairs* 10(1): 106–16.

————. 1987. "International Health Care Spending." *Health Affairs* 6(3): 105–12.

Stone, Deborah. 1988. *Policy Paradox and Political Reason* (New York: Harper/Collins).

Swartz, Katherine. 1990. "Why Requiring Employers to Provide Health Insurance Is a Bad Idea." *Journal of Health, Policy and Law* 15(3): 779–92.

Swartz, Katherine, and Timothy McBride. 1990. "Spells without Health Insurance: Distributions of Durations and Their Link to Point in Time Estimates of the Uninsured." *Inquiry* 27: 281–85.

Woolhandler, Steffie, and David Himmelstein. 1991. "The Deteriorating Efficiency of the U.S. Health Care System." *New England Journal of Medicine* 324: 1253.

Chapter Ten

COMPETITION AND THE NEW ACCOUNTABILITY: DO MARKET INCENTIVES AND MEDICAL OUTCOMES CONFLICT OR COHERE?

Lawrence D. Brown

A health policy Rip Van Winkle who nodded off in 1973 and woke up 20 years later might be disoriented indeed. In 1973 a new competitive strategy for cost containment was in its infancy: by encouraging health maintenance organizations (HMOs), the federal government would move the health care system toward efficiency by means of markets, incentives, and consumer choice. The year 1993 finds the federal government sponsoring agencies and experts to study medical outcomes and the effectiveness of medical procedures. From these studies, it aims to derive practice guidelines that give physicians helpful norms—norms to which they may in time be held accountable by peers, the public, and purchasers. Meanwhile, proponents of market strategies increasingly rally under the banner of "managed competition," a complex and carefully articulated system in which efficiency-minded executives in managed-care plans might employ guidelines and outcomes research to extend the micromanagement of the providers they are determined to put squarely at risk for utilization decisions in their integrated organizational networks. Moreover, to sharpen the paradox, those inclined toward more regulatory interventions in 1993 proffer global budgets. Such budgets might be sold to providers as part of political bargains relieving them of the more onerous clinical intrusions generated by managed care and related schemes that depend on financial risk in a framework of tight administrative oversight.

William D. White has pointedly summarized the paradox of policy evolution: "How did we move from policies declaring allegiance to competition to what is becoming the most clinically regulated system in the world"? (Personal communication to author.) There is no obvious resolution to the paradox. Are competition and guidelines the strategic antinomies they once seemed to be? Are there latent or manifest points of compatibility? Are they parallel and nonintersecting roads to a common end? These are the questions this essay tries to elucidate.

MARKET COMPETITION AND ACCOUNTABILITY

Competition as a health-cost-containment strategy has always been understood as, among other things, a theory of how to induce desirable behavioral change in physicians. Since health care costs became a broad social concern (that is, since the late 1960s when the federal government began agonizing over the rising costs of Medicare and Medicaid), there has been a fairly stable consensus among analysts that the basic source of the problem is excessive, inappropriate use of health care resources. Various culprits have been identified, including: surplus hospital capacity (Roemer's Law); extravagant consumer expectations (born of first-dollar coverage and the American's boundless faith in technological progress); technologies that are too quickly introduced, too widely diffused, and too easily applied; legal stimuli to defensive medicine (overdoctoring) as a protection against malpractice claims; and unconstrained specialization by physicians and consequent overuse of high-intensity services. But many observers would doubtless agree that the key variable underlying and sustaining all these and other various ills is the ominous conjunction of third-party payment and fee-for-service practice.[1] Providers use too many services across the board because the more they do, the more they get paid by insurers, leaving neither them nor their patients with a tangible stake in holding costs down. Provider (especially physician) accountability has for 20 years been the central theme and challenge of the cost-containment debate.

Economic accountability was precisely the target at which HMOs aimed. The superior incentives embodied in HMOs meant putting physicians newly at financial risk for their treatment decisions, which meant holding them accountable to an organized system that integrated the delivery of care with its financing. In 1970 Paul Ellwood explained to academic and governmental audiences that prepaid group practice plans such as Kaiser Permanente had been reaping and sharing the rewards of such efficiencies for years, and conjectured that the conceptual skeleton of Kaiser and kindred plans—prepaid financing linked to group practice in an integrated organizational setting—might be implantable in a variety of institutional forms. In 1971, Richard Nixon (the American Medical Association's preferred presidential candidate in 1968) endorsed Ellwood's reasoning in a historic message to the U.S. Congress, blasting the prevailing system as inefficient and replete with illogical incentives, and urging federal encouragement to HMOs as a corrective.[2] Organized medicine, of course, protested that "corporate" medicine was a recipe for under-service and poor-quality care. Given the growing preoccupation with overuse, however, reformers were confident that efficiency-enhancing measures could be pushed quite a distance before quality was systematically jeopardized.

This theory of provider accountability to an encompassing organizational system envisioned several distinct mechanisms that worked in the same direction, that is, lowering costs without sacrificing quality. One mechanism was flatly financial: if the HMO's physician group was frugal over the year, it might rack up a surplus to divide among group partners as a bonus to their salaries. A second device was peer review in the goldfish bowl of group practice, where peers continually saw each others' work, would identify overuse (or under-use), and could intercede with problem partners. A third control was hierarchical: the executive and medical directors of the plan reviewed the utilization of the groups' physicians and challenged questionable admissions, diagnostic tests, lengths of stay, and referrals. A fourth source of accountability was informal but was perhaps most important of all: "well-socialized" physicians, devoted both to the general norms of prepaid group practice and to the well-being of their group in particular, were widely viewed as vital to the success of plans that neither underserved (imperiling subscribers' health and damaging the plans' reputations) nor overprovided (threatening the plans economic survival). In concert these mechanisms theoretically constituted a powerful framework for accountability (Brown 1983, chaps. 3, 4; Luft 1987). It is worth noting, meanwhile, that notwithstanding their prominent financial trappings, these mechanisms were mainly purposive, contextual, and indirect, depending little on the codification of practice norms and styles into formal guidelines or outcome-based benchmarks.

These basic ingredients of physician accountability in an HMO—financial incentives, peer review, utilization review, and commitment to the group's corporate well-being—were controversial in the eyes of the AMA and other entrenched defenders of fee-for-service medicine, but few others doubted that, if properly implemented, they would do more good than harm. Whether accountability thus institutionalized within HMOs would also successfully drive a competitive dynamic of system wide cost containment was, and remains, quite another question, however. These plausible intra-organizational measures sustained a policy strategy only to the degree that they helped trigger, in turn, a range of desired inter-organizational dynamics. Specifically, they pointed to cost containment's promised land only if sizable numbers of insured people joined HMOs (which implied a large number of well-working plans available for them to join); if the HMOs did in fact compete with each other (or with traditional plans) on price (otherwise the motives to incur the organizational costs of tough utilization review and other controls would weaken); and if plan managers found that vigorous enforcement and refinement of the mechanisms of accountability were necessary for maintenance and enhancement of the plan.

In fact, these elements of pro-market logic proved to be problematic. HMOs proliferated slowly, and subscribers were slow to join. (In 1980 about 235 HMOs nationwide enrolled about 4 percent of the population. Ten years later almost 600 plans enrolled about 15 percent of the population, a significant but still rather minor penetration.) Some plans discovered that they could avert the risks and threats of sharp price competition by avoiding poorer risks, capturing market segments delimited by area or social group, shadow-pricing with an eye on their main competitors (including other HMOs), and substituting genteel "rivalry" for head-to-head price warfare (McLaughlin 1988).[3] In principle, chief executive officers (CEOs) get paid both to take risks and to secure the financial well-being of their organization. In practice, when the risk-taking objective threatens well-being, the former tends to be sidelined rather quickly. Even the more aggressive and expansionist plans found that competition need not be more than a sometime thing: discount deeply, grab a big market share, wait out the shakeouts and mergers, and then declare a huge premium increase. In principle, purchasers buy health coverage much as they buy ice cream, shopping around more or less continually for the best value for money. In practice, few CEOs or benefit managers want to upset their workers' settled attachments to payers and providers by switching them regularly in and out of alternative health plans.

Moreover, the implementation of the mechanisms of accountability within HMOs proved to be variable and contingent as such plans expanded. Some used bonus incentives, others rejected them. In some, peer review was carefully cultivated; others were more casual. In some, the executive and medical directors monitored utilization closely and steered firmly toward efficiency; others ran a looser ship, which sometimes sank. Some recruited physicians with a professional and purposive allegiance to prepaid group practice; others made do with grumbling fee-for-service denizens who had concluded that the federal government was serious about promoting HMOs, had pondered the financial implications of the looming physician surplus, and had signed on to protect their flanks from closed panel competitors with unknown potential penetration. As HMOs inspired such looser-jointed mutations as independent practice associations (IPAs), preferred provider organizations (PPOs), and alternative delivery and managed-care systems more broadly, the organizational guarantees of accountability grew still less reliable. And no one had—or has—much reliable evidence on what the diffusion of organizational types and the dilution of organizational controls mean for the quality of care. In short, the original position notwithstanding, observers (including anxious policymakers in Washington, D.C.) could see that the system was becoming more competitive (that is, populated by miscellaneous entities that combined financing and delivery in diverse ways and sought to lock up market shares) but not necessarily more efficient or accountable.

MEDICAL CULTURE AND ACCOUNTABILITY

That the connections between competition and accountability proved to be something less than syllogistic was no major revelation to the many analysts and policymakers who had never accepted assurances that market forces were the best and only path to responsible physician behavior. Not that these skeptics were any less devoted to promoting provider accountability or any less convinced of its centrality in the cause of cost containment. They were merely unpersuaded that competition was the best means to this widely shared end.

While theorists of competition were promoting HMOs as the cure for the ills of fee-for-service medicine, John Wennberg and others adept in the art of small-area analysis were unearthing extraordinary differences in treatment rates among areas and populations with comparable demographic and other properties, and were wondering what accounted for these patterns (Wennberg 1984; Wennberg and Gittelsohn 1982).[4] Nothing around which a regression equation could easily be wrapped seemed to explain them. Apparently, physicians in different communities learned and disseminated different practice styles—embodied different medical cultures, so to speak. The small-area analysts recognized that these variations carried high economic—and probably quality-of-care—costs and were as eager as the competition advocates to suggest means of repairing them. As Wennberg (1984: 31) noted, elimination of the use of hospitals for "marginal services which many physicians feel can be treated in the ambulatory setting or not at all" would save significant sums.

The incorporation of large numbers of physicians within organized systems such as HMOs was but one way to effect this convergence. In the mid-1970s a systemwide HMO strategy was still a gleam in Washington policymakers' eyes, and no one could be sure how many physicians would come under the discipline of HMOs, nor when, nor exactly what it all might mean. Both cost and quality considerations, therefore, argued that physician reform leaders and health service researchers should learn all they could about actual and desirable practice patterns and about who practiced how. If information were both abundant and specific, physicians might be moved to heal themselves.

As these arguments were gaining force among small-area analysts and other researchers, the federal government was launching a related effort of its own, the Professional Standards Review Organizations (PSROs), created in 1972. These groups were born of the same basic challenge that inspired virtually all cost-containment programs in the 1970s: Physicians, the undisputed captains of the medical team, used too many resources, and costs could be controlled only if these captains were somehow persuaded to adopt more frugal practice styles. The federal government, nervous about Medicare costs, was no longer content to sit and do nothing, but it could not engineer such reforms itself. Direct federal promulgation of guidelines and such would be assailed as cookbook medicine forced on furious physicians by pointy-headed bureaucrats. The government could, however, create a framework in which local physicians, using the best available data, sought consensus on performance standards and norms for various diagnoses and then used these to review each other's work. The goal was exactly what Wennberg was urging: bring the high rollers closer to the norms and thereby save money and enhance quality in one fell swoop.

For a host of reasons, the PSROs, over a troubled 10-year life, failed to please their federal masters or anyone else. Workable local physician review organizations proved to be remarkably difficult to build and sustain. The operational goals of the program were never clear to those implementing it in the field: was cost containment the central focus, or quality improvement, or if the two together, in what concrete combinations and subject to what trade-offs? The enthusiasm of local physicians (including medical societies and their leaders of course) for the program varied greatly across the 200-odd PSROs. A few leaders warmed to their mission, some sullenly resolved to use the program to block change, while most muddled along at a snail's pace, tinkering with their workplans and conducting inconclusive reviews of the data and literature. Pertinent data and professional consensus on norms and standards were often elusive. Sophisticated staff leadership and analytical expertise were frequently wanting. Implementation of the program in the hospitals was regularly impaled on organizational thickets such as the respective merits of delegated versus nondelegated reviews. Reviewers were reluctant to deny continued stays in (not to mention admission to) the hospital when concrete cases confronted statistical generalities (Brown 1982).

The Reagan administration, pointing to studies that suggested that overall the PSROs cost at least as much to run as they saved, called for their elimination. Unwilling to abandon hope that government could encourage behavioral change by means of education, dialogue, and physician self-scrutiny, Congress transformed the PSROs into Peer Review Organizations (PROs)—single-state bodies concentrated more clearly on cost containment and funded by competitive federal contracts, not grants. The more the federal government tried to sharpen the mission and teeth of physician peer review bodies, however, the more rank-and-file doctors complained about red tape and bureaucratic meddling, and the more they muttered about the unhappy effects of government's intrusions on quality of care. Moreover, the health services research community neither embraced the PSROs and PROs as a promising vehicle for the changes they hoped to induce nor showed significant interest in studying them or explaining their checkered careers.

Looking askance at these fumbling federal efforts and the hostility they inspired, physicians, researchers, and reformers bent on promoting behavioral change by means of knowledge and education began formulating an alternative voluntary strategy that would circumvent and surpass the PROs. Their plans turned on the development, codification, and dissemination of two basic types of knowledge. First, before one could decide what medical practice patterns were desirable, one had to know the results of existing patterns (that is, what impact do medical procedures have on health status outcomes?). Second, once a body of knowledge about outcomes was at hand, analysts could examine means in the light of ends and try to formulate practice guidelines indicating the circumstances in which one or another procedural alternative made sense. (Some analysts contended that guidelines need not wait upon definitive outcome studies but rather could proceed—at least to a point—by developing informed professional consensus on the acceptable range of choice in concrete cases.) As the 1980s wore on, outcomes, effectiveness research, and medical practice guidelines generated growing enthusiasm among an increasingly cohesive coterie of physician reformers, health service researchers, and policymakers and their staffs. Here was a voluntary, intra-professional route to cost containment and better quality, one that promised to escape the frustrations of the 1970s because it depended neither on the organizational exigencies of competition nor on the government's maladroit ventures in peer review.

PRACTICE GUIDELINES AS PUBLIC POLICY

The efforts to investigate the impact of medical procedures on health outcomes and to derive sound practice guidelines for the edification of rank-and-file physicians might have stayed aloof from the policy frays engulfing competition and regulation. Health services researchers might have acquired existing datasets and, perhaps assisted by modest foundation grants, milked their meaning. The AMA and various specialty societies might have taken the lead in developing guidelines, then disseminating them mainly through professional channels to their particular constituencies. Modest doings on the sidelines proved, however, incompatible with the ambitions of two key elements of the new accountability coalition—entrepreneurial researchers and policymakers, who came to see in outcomes studies and guidelines development means to advance ends of their own.[5]

For certain researchers (especially economists and clinicians who bridged the worlds of medical practice and cost-effectiveness analysis) explicit governmental endorsement of their work meant large sums of money and national visibility—two goods they could never have attained, at least not on such a scale, within the walls of academe. Second, for some policy reformers, outcomes and guidelines promised to complement and advance their accelerating attempts to expose the flaws of the prevailing system and to use research findings as a resource in the struggle for political clout. These latter individuals expected that the analysis of outcomes and the generation of guidelines would produce large bodies of highly corrosive knowledge. Deep exploration of what providers do and what they achieve would doubtless expose vast overuse and questionable quality, which would further discredit providers in the eyes of payers, the public, and politicians, and thereby soften up the system for further change. In short, knowledge about outcomes and guidelines could be a kind of empirical jiujitsu that used the weight of professional practice to throw the providers off balance and topple them.

To the policy reformers this corrosive knowledge might be especially useful in extending the case for budgetary regulation, which had arrived belatedly but forcefully on the federal scene with the adoption in Medicare of the Diagnosis Related Group-based Prospective Payment System for hospitals in 1983 and the system of Resource Based Relative Value Scales for physician payment in 1989. The design of the new payment systems and the rates embodied in them rested on certain assumptions about provider behavior and how it ought to change. But one need not leave these crucial matters to the invisible hand of economic incentives if health researchers were prepared to play both bad cop (discovering with scientific authority the errors of professional ways) and good cop (showing practitioners the light in the form of guidelines and other analytically derived vehicles of improvement) while policymakers looked on and drew their own conclusions. As mentioned earlier in this book, in the Omnibus Budget Reconciliation Act of 1989 (OBRA—PL 101-239), Congress replaced the National Center for Health Services Research with an Agency for Health Care Policy and Research (AHCPR). The AHCPR housed a Forum for Quality and Effectiveness in Health Care that was charged with, among other things, leading a national effort to develop medical practice guidelines and sponsoring patient outcome research teams (PORTS).

Practice guidelines and PORTS are classic examples of a policymaking style that political scientist Charles O. Jones (1975: 176) has called "speculative augmentation." With a snap of the legislative fingers the musings of academics on the possible contributions of research on effectiveness and outcomes to behavioral change had been enshrined as a public policy quest backed by millions of ardently sought federal dollars. Implementing the policy may, however, hold some surprises and disappointments, because there is considerable uncertainty about exactly what guideline development, performance measures, and so forth, mean and how they should proceed.

A laconic Congress told the AHCPR and its Forum for Quality and Effectiveness in Health Care little more than that they were to "arrange for" the development of "clinically relevant guidelines" that would help providers decide "how diseases, disorders, and other health conditions can most effectively and appropriately be prevented, diagnosed, treated, and managed clinically" as well as the construction of standards, measures, and criteria useful for quality assessment and assurance (PL 101–239, Title IX, Sec. 912). Unsure what to do, the agency sought advice from the Institute of Medicine (IOM), which formed a committee whose staff set about making sense of it all. The committee's report began by noting that the field of guideline development is "a confusing mix of high expectations, competing organizations, conflicting philosophies, and ill-defined or incompatible objectives." It then unveiled its own version of the ever-growing laundry list of "attributes" of good guidelines. The IOM's attributes, eight in number, emphasized validity, reliability, clinical applicability, clinical flexibility, clarity, scheduled review, documentation, and, intriguingly, development by a multidisciplinary process, meaning one that features "participation by representatives of key affected groups and disciplines." Of course, each of these individual terms embraces a long list of definitional qualities of its own (Institute of Medicine 1990: 24, 59, 70, 74–75). And participation by representatives of key affected groups—providers, consumers, private purchasers, and governmental budgetmakers should do for a start—would seem to give group politics a strong hand in their explication.

Alas, if agreement is ever reached, no one may know precisely what was defined: the IOM (Institute of Medicine 1990: 8–9) maintains that the law does not equate practice guidelines with standards of quality, performance measures, and medical review criteria, but a leading academic expert has opined that guidelines are basically indistinguishable from algorithms, appropriateness standards, parameters, and protocols (Greenfield 1991). And once these momentous distinctions are clarified, other problems remain. One study found that goals for the development of guidelines tend to be vague and lacking in evaluative criteria; that there is slight consensus on which of the several methods for developing guidelines is best; that their implementation in real practice settings has had little attention; and that neither the developers nor the users of guidelines show much commitment to evaluating their influence on behavior, costs, or outcomes. Consequently, the authors argue, practice guidelines "may lack the crucial characteristics (clarity, specificity, flexibility, reliability, validity, and others) that are likely to affect both their acceptance by practitioners and their impact on clinical practice" (Audet et al. 1990: 713). These considerations lead some analysts to contend that outcomes deserve scholarly and practical priority over guidelines (Greenfield 1991), an issue much in dispute between the camps.

As is often the case, the primary significance of the new enterprise seems to be as much political as medical and scientific: OBRA 1989 witnessed the birth of a new iron triangle linking an influential segment of the health research community, the AHCPR and its Forum, and the legislative staff that promoted these "speculative augmentations."

AND WHAT BECAME OF COMPETITION?

While health services researchers and policy reformers were cementing their alliances and concerting their influence on behalf of federally sponsored outcomes research and guideline development, the theory of competition, which had more or less peacefully coexisted with this parallel image of physician accountability, was steadily approaching a crossroads. The 1980s showed that although American health care mechanisms might sustain a high degree of laissez-faire competition, they probably could not make market forces fulfill their promise without moving to a coherent competitive *system*.

Part of the problem was that competition, like outcomes and guidelines, means different things to different people. Some equate it with enhanced consumer cost-consciousness: if only the baleful effects of first-dollar coverage were reversed by means of cost sharing and changes in tax provisions so as to make the insured pay more for their care, the system would quickly become more competitive and better disciplined. To others it denotes increasing numbers of managed-care systems challenging each other for market share; more HMOs, more PPOs, and the like mean more competition essentially by definition. To still others—for, instance, Alain Enthoven and other supporters of "managed competition"—it entails a carefully crafted set of rules, a national policy framework that would encourage health plans to contest for market share but would also close off such socially harmful shortcuts as creaming good risks and rejecting poor ones (Enthoven 1980; Enthoven and Kronick 1989). Not surprisingly, these three images of competition point in different policy directions.

In the late 1970s many procompetitive reformers thought they shared a common, concrete agenda for change. Employers would be required to offer a multiple choice of health plans (including supposedly more efficient managed-care schemes) and would be obliged to limit their premium contributions to the price of the "most efficient" plan (presumably a managed-care alternative), so that employees who stubbornly insisted on "Cadillacs" would have to hit their own wallets for the extras. Legislation would also limit the exclusion of the value of employers' contributions to employees' health coverage from the latter's taxable income, forcing workers to think twice about where they wanted to spend money now newly perceived as their own. This agenda, however, papered over major practical differences among divergent images of a competitive system.

The basic problem became clear when one pondered the consequences of adopting only this short list of reforms. Better risks—younger, healthier types who expected to use little care—might gravitate to the "poorer" plans, that is, those with low premiums but abundant cost sharing, exclusions, and limitations, while the poorer risks—older, sicker people planning to use many services—might move into the "better" plans, those with higher premiums but little or no cost sharing, and few exclusions or limitations. If this segmentation played out over time the HMOs and other "good" plans could drown in a sea of adverse selection. Those who never met a market they did not like were happy to let the chips fall where they may. Markets honor the free play of consumer preferences and should not be rigged to favor the designs of social theorists. Others—most notably Alain Enthoven (1980)—argued that unleashing such market dynamics would be disastrous. Competition should meet basic criteria of social responsibility, which in turn required a host of procompetitive regulations governing premium setting, benefit packages, rates, enrollment, and more, all designed to ensure that the competitive game had a level playing field. The free marketers (including, evidently, health decision makers in the Reagan administration) thought these regulatory safeguards too prescriptive and too redolent of national health insurance to be acceptable. But the problems of not going all the way were clearly daunting, and the split within the competitive camp gave befuddled policymakers sound reasons to keep the market-building agenda at arm's length.

Even as these disagreements among advocates of competition persuaded policymakers to hesitate, they also gave ammunition to a range of interest groups that would be discomfited by a new competitive order. Physicians, labor, business, the elderly, insurers, and hospitals all chimed in at one point or another with caveats on procompetitive reform (Enthoven 1980b). By the early 1980s the evident disarray among market theoreticians plus the near-total absence of a supportive constituency had virtually buried the notion of systematic procompetitive change.

The poor prospects for competition de jure did not mean, however, that the existing system was not growing more competitive de facto. Several variables owing little to competitive theory were indeed accentuating competition (or rivalry) among more or less organized entities that were (more or less) evolving into "systems" over time. What emerged was the predictible result of the selective tightening of resources in a system organized around multiple players and payers with huge financial stakes in protecting themselves from each other's depredations in the absence of a constraining policy framework designed to protect social ends.

Federal and some private purchasers, seeking relief from rising costs, tried unilaterally to redefine terms and levels of payment to providers or to strike prudential deals with insurers who offered them discounts. Insurers tried to secure discounts to extend to purchasers by allying with "preferred" providers (doctors and hospitals) who assumed some of the financial risk of care or otherwise promised to hold the line on costs. Providers cooperated in these hitherto despised arrangements because they feared that the talk of cost containment might soon take an ugly (income-threatening) turn, because governmental and academic prognosticators had convinced them that HMOs and managed care were a major wave of the future, and because they feared that the much-discussed surplus of physicians and beds might leave them on the outside looking into closed-panel or other exclusive groups if they failed to join them. Relatively few consumers, providers, or purchasers showed a taste for group- or staff-model HMOs (see chapter 5, this volume), but all these players hoped to realize some of the HMOs' benefits while averting many of their constraints by launching looser-jointed entities like IPAs and PPOs. In time the earlier parsimonious, coherent notion of the PGP (prepaid group practice)/HMO—an encompassing organizational system that integrated the delivery and financing of care within a framework with the will and power to plan and steer—dissolved into the mists of "managed care," which came to mean anything and everything from a PGP such as Kaiser Permanente to an indemnity insurance plan with a utilization review component, to a list of physicians capitated to style themselves as "gatekeepers" for plan enrollees, with many procedural variations along the way.

By the early 1990s managed care was much in vogue for the same reasons that HMOs became fashionable in the early 1970s. In both cases, no one knew what the terms really meant, they could be given virtually any meaning by any interested party, and they extended the promise of significant cost containment without threatening major changes in the provision or consumption of care. Alain Enthoven and the stalwart editorial page of the New York Times (1992) continued to insist that an articulated system of managed competition was the system's sole salvation. What had emerged in fact, however, was essentially the reverse of managed competition—the proliferation of "competitive management" in which a motley crew of managed-care semisystems labored to sign up weary purchasers eternally (and for the most part vainly) in search of durable discounts. In 1990 as in 1970, some observers were convinced that, given time, these ventures in competitive management would slow costs. Others dismissed them as more of the tired competitive follies whose only prominent legacy over the 1980s was aggravated cost shifting, higher administrative costs, more unabashed avoidance of poor health insurance risks, and—the bottom line—costs that rose more sharply in the "competitive era" than they had before.

MANAGED COMPETITION AND GLOBAL BUDGETS: RAISING THE ANTE ON ACCOUNTABILITY

In November 1992 the parameters of the health policy debate, and the positions of competition and outcomes research in it, changed dramatically with the election of Bill Clinton to the presidency. The election ratified propositions that had grown evident since Harris Wofford's surprise senatorial victory in Pennsylvania in 1991 and that public opinion polls were driving home daily—the U.S. public was fed up with many aspects of the health care system, demanded change, and would register its demands in the voting booth. Clinton responded by raising the strategic ante in both the competitive and regulatory sweepstakes. His campaign proposals and early utterances in office suggested that he would supplant laissez-faire competition with an improved managed brand and would move beyond limited federal efforts to set payment rates and sponsor guidelines and outcomes research and toward national and state budget caps.

When Clinton took office in January 1993, Alain Enthoven had been arguing for 15 years that anything less than his carefully crafted managed-competition plan would merely aggravate market failures in the name of market forces. His contention had fallen on deaf ears in the Reagan and Bush administrations, which would not embrace the extensive procompetitive regulations the scheme presupposes. Clinton, however, both understands and accepts the need for such a federal regulatory framework and evidently also sees the appeal of market strategies in a society that wants big change in health care but fears Big Government. His election, therefore, may signal a heightening of both the plausibility and complexity of competitive reforms.

Plausibility will increase because managed competition both sharpens the mechanisms of accountability that link providers to purchasers and shuts off the antisocial circumventions (preferred risk selection and the like) that accompany unmanaged competition. But complexity increases, too, because managed competition invents a range of new institutional forms and networks that raise questions of accountability that are all the more perplexing for the intellectual sweep and boldness of the proposed new system. Health insurance purchasing would largely be channeled through "sponsors" including health insurance purchasing cooperatives (or health alliances) which would be advised by various boards with expertise in quality assessment and other important matters. The functions and virtues of these entities as shoppers and buyers are reasonably clear, at least in economic theory, but their governance structures, and their attachments (if any) to the larger political system, rarely get the sustained discussion they deserve. Although the ascendancy of managed competition is a striking departure, in this respect the state of policy thinking is unhappily continuous with the past: all eyes (mainly economic) are trained on the capacities of the new system to hold providers accountable to purchasers, and larger, broader issues of control get short shrift.

Global budgets also raise questions of accountability that are no less pressing but no better understood. During the presidential campaign Clinton spoke favorably of national and state caps on health spending—caps that must not be exceeded. Perhaps to ease fears of political control of the health budget, however, he added that the caps would be set not by government directly but by multimember boards with representatives of business, consumers, and other groups. How these boards are to be constituted, who will appoint them, and to whom they are to stand accountable are good questions that remain as yet poorly explored. And although advocates hope that global budgets will be a more reliable means of making providers accountable to purchasers than are the speculations of market theory, they seldom explain which of several possible images of provider accountability they foresee for the United States. Cross-national experience shows budget limits brought to bear on providers in publicly owned facilities (Great Britain), in solo fee-for-service practices and private hospitals (Canada), through the self-discipline of professional associations (Germany), through taxes raised and allocated locally for local institutions (Sweden), and more. Each mechanism embodies a distinct cultural-structural theory of provider accountability. None takes root easily or plays out unproblematically, but each offers insights that have yet to be carefully mined in the U.S. debate.

In many ways U.S. deliberations seem to be flying off in all directions precisely when the public would presumably like to see them settle down toward a consensual, workable reform model. The pursuit of practice guidelines and outcomes research may offer a promising, though limited, area of convergence. Managed competition and global budgets both squeeze resources and by doing so raise constant, pointed questions of how to identify and reward cost-effective practices. Foreign systems face a similar challenge: despite cost-containment records far better than that of the United States, they too suspect that substantial overuse and numerous ineffective medical procedures inflate costs and might yield to better information on what works and what should be discouraged as marginal or useless. Guidelines and outcomes, then, are likely to grow more prominent in any future regime, competitive or regulatory. The very power of their consensual appeals, however, may sow seeds of policy disappointment. The production of guidelines and outcome findings achieves little by itself; everything depends on how they are plugged into and disseminated throughout the world of rank-and-file practitioners. The desired results require structures of professional and political accountability that are intensely controversial, scientifically unspecifiable, of little interest to the clinicians and economists drawn to guidelines and outcomes research—and, in consequence, badly underanalyzed and underdeveloped. In health policy, such clinical consensus restates, with heightened urgency, accountability questions that inspire sharp social conflict.

ACCOUNTABILITY, LOWER AND HIGHER

This chapter has discussed two models that seek to increase physicians' accountability to higher authority. The first tries to enfold them in, and constrain them by, organizational structures that themselves obey the discipline of the laws of market competition. This enfolding and constraining entail putting physicians at financial risk for the costs of unnecessary care. Risk takes various forms, including loss of bonus, the withholding of a portion of expected salary or a share of group revenues, capitated payments, and dismissal from a closed-panel network. The degree of risk that physicians will assume depends, however, on the organizational options open to them and the organizational demands made on them. These choices and demands depend, in turn, on the public's tolerance for systems that rely heavily on risk-bearing providers to control costs. The physician who is modestly capitated for a wide range of enrollees' services must, for example, guard the gates closely or face significant financial loss. The public's apparent preference for retaining considerable freedom of choice among providers who are not pressured constantly to consult the bottom line has generated an emerging social compromise whose modal form is a modicum of control maintained by managed-care plans that impose moderate levels of risk on participating providers. Nor—at least until now—need they do more to compete successfully in their own narrow terms: unable to agree on a formal model of systemwide competition in which government sets clear rules of the game, purchasers have encouraged de facto competition, an unchoreographed cost shifting that defeats true accountability. Government, which has cast its lot with prudent purchasing and regulation, has so far not been moved to change this outcome, and business, which is highly averse to conflict with workers and providers, and highly resistant to cooperation with government, does not yet dare to change it. Whether managed competition will end the impasse remains to be seen.

The second model hopes to promote accountability by means of information, education, and professional self-scrutiny and self-regulation. Clinicians and health services researchers have joined in search of information about health outcomes and the effectiveness of medical procedures, information that will inform practice guidelines expected to enhance quality and contain costs too. The education mavens laboring to harvest information and disseminate findings on desirable practice patterns often assume that useful information will reach rank-and-file practitioners, that it will move them to ponder, and change, the errors of their ways, and that such behavioral change will be prompt and broad enough to forestall the need for greater governmental regulation. Some policymakers supporting these efforts anticipate the opposite, however: the work on guidelines and outcomes may expose vast waste in the prevailing system, while attempts to implement correctives will reveal the profession's unwillingness to reform itself and thereby strengthen the case for sharper public interventions, including global budgets, that accelerate the quest for insights into cost-effectiveness that guidelines and outcomes hope to convey. Whether this venture in enhanced accountability to scientific and professional knowledge will end up increasing provider autonomy or public authority remains to be seen.

Although these two models differ in their mechanisms and philosophies of change, they display at least five similarities that are arguably, in aggregate, far more important than their differences. First, both derive from a common inspiration and problem diagnosis, namely the premise that profligate provision in the heady world of fee-for-service practice and third-party payment is the basic source of the cost problem and that the proper policy objective is to promote a more frugal medical style that will slow costs without sacrificing quality. The two models are parallel roads to a common end.

Second, in both instances, policy analysts have played matchmaker between two parties, purchasers and providers, who are interdependent but also averse to direct bargaining. The organizational structures of managed care and the scientific apparatus of practice guidelines can be viewed as "mediating institutions" that promote bargaining between skittish buyers and sellers of health services.

Third, in both cases, public purchasers were the first to arrive at the party, while their private-sector counterparts came fashionably late. Today many corporate purchasers still pledge allegiance to simple competitive images the federal government seems to be transcending, and have little idea how to insert themselves into, or make constructive use of, the outcomes and guidelines "movement."

Fourth, for all the fanfare and controversy surrounding them, both models represent reform efforts that have been timid, catalytic, indirect, and—quite possibly—effete. The agitated debate about a competitive system has left the nation with a competitive nonsystem that amounts to one more economic weapon with which the system's diverse stakeholders frustrate and torment each other. The requisites of "true" competition—extensive procompetitive regulation in which government sets the rules of the game—may find a constituency, but has not done so yet. Likewise, the new commitment to practice guidelines is the latest flowering of the long-held hope that information and education can change the hearts and minds of physicians. Beyond lie the anxieties and aspirations of the movement's strange political bedfellows: Will the evidence about outcomes and practice guidelines be seized by the federal government as a stimulus and an accompaniment to more stringent budgetary regulation? In both cases, the models were advanced as alternatives to, bulwarks against, increased regulation. In both cases, an unsatisfactory evolution may help to build the case for more regulation. If so, the competitive agenda may fare the poorer: making it work means institutional reform that ignites conflict across the whole system, whereas the tightening and toughening of practice guidelines in reimbursement systems require only that physicians be branded incorrigible and then assigned to take the political fall. (Global budgets are, of course, another story.)

Fifth, and perhaps most important, the central concern of both models has been enhanced provider accountability to *purchasers*. Neither model has paid much attention to the larger health care system in which provider-purchaser relations are set or to the larger social purposes to which these players presumably stand accountable.

One can easily picture another image of accountability, one highlighting the larger systemic dimensions that these two models ignore. Some systems—indeed those of all Western industrial democracies save the United States—start from the conviction that health care is a right of all citizens, and that it is a social duty, fulfilled through the polity (meaning government), to invent institutional arrangements securing this right. Purchasers enter such a system with a clear set of social expectations and obligations, and providers understand that they are laying claim to *social* resources. In such a system, accountability takes on layers of related connotations very different from the American pattern. It means, first, that government is obliged to ensure universal entitlement to uniform benefits at a cost that society deems affordable. Second, it means that purchasers (employers, workers, government) expect to bear a fair share of the costs of meeting that basic social objective. Third, it means that providers' inevitable and legitimate pursuit of economic gain should be effectively balanced against purchasers' capacities, just as society's pursuit of the basic humane objective should be contemplated in the larger social picture, including the fiscal demands of policy arenas other than health care.

These normative notions of accountability imply certain institutional forms. These include strategies to limit the aggregate social resources flowing into health care (for example, global budgets, limits on government appropriations, caps that link growth in health spending to the growth of gross domestic product, or negotiated ceilings on percentage increases or monetary amounts in various spending categories) and structured negotiations between purchasers and providers to decide how such socially constrained sums are to be apportioned among hospitals, regions, specialities, disease types, and personnel categories. Such systems reject the foreshortened models of accountability that dominate policy in the United States, because these American palliatives scarcely acknowledge the humanitarian purposes that health care systems supposedly exist to advance.

Notes

1. For example, according to Alain Enthoven (1992: 807), "Much of the economic failure of our system can be ascribed to the traditional model of fee-for-service, solo medical practice and remote third-party payment. The incentives inherent in this model are inflationary."

2. For background see Lawrence D. Brown (1983: chap. 5).

3. The distinction comes from Catherine McLaughlin. On the limits of competition see quartet of articles in the *Journal of Health Politics, Policy and Law*, vol. 10 (Winter 1986), pp. 613–697. (See references.)

4. For a useful bibliography on small area analysis, see Pamela Paul-Shaheen et al. (1987).

5. For background, see Gray (1992) and Wennberg (1992).

References

Audet, Anne-Marie, Sheldon Greenfield, and Marilyn Field. 1990. "Medical Practice Guidelines: Current Activities and Future Directions." *Annals of Internal Medicine* 113 (1 November): 709–714.

Brown, Lawrence D. 1982. "Political Conditions of Regulatory Effectiveness: The Case of PSROs and HSAs." *Bulletin of the New York Academy of Medicine* 58 (Jan.–Feb.): 77–90.

———. 1983. *Politics and Health Care Organization: HMOs as Federal Policy.* Washington, D.C.: Brookings Institution.

Enthoven, Alain. 1980a. *Health Plan: The Only Practical Solution to the Soaring Cost of Medical Care.* Reading, Mass: Addison-Wesley.

Enthoven, Alain. 1980b. "How Interested Groups Have Responded to a Proposal for Economic Competition in Health Services." *American Economic Review, Papers, and Proceedings* 70 (May): 142–48.

———. 1992. "Commentary: Measuring the Candidates on Health Care." *New England Journal of Medicine* 327 (Sept. 10): 807–809.

Enthoven, Alain. 1993. "The History and Principles of Managed Competition." *Health Affairs* 12 (supplement): 24–48.

Enthoven, Alain, and Richard Kronick. 1989. "A Consumer-Choice Health Plan for the 1990s: Universal Health Insurance in a System Designed to Promote Quality and Economy, Parts I and II." *New England Journal of Medicine* 320: 29–37, 94–101.

Institute of Medicine. 1990. *Clinical Practice Guidelines: Directions for a New Program*, edited by Marilyn J. Field and Kathleen N. Lohr. Committee to Advise the Public Health Service on Clinical Practice Guidelines, Institute of Medicine. Washington, D.C.: National Academy Press.

Feldman, Roger, Bryan Dowd, Don McCann, and Allan Johnson. 1986. "The Competitive Impact of Health Maintenance Organizations on Hospital Finances: An Exploratory Study." *Journal of Health Politics, Policy and Law* 10 (Winter): 675–697.

Gray, Bradford H. 1992. "The Legislative Battle over Health Services Research." *Health Affairs* 11 (Winter): 38–66.

Greenfield, Sheldon. 1991. "Guidelines or Outcomes: Which Will Prevail?" Lecture delivered at conference of Health Services Improvement Fund of Empire Blue Cross and Blue Shield, New York, October 24.

Johnson, Allan and David Aquilina. 1986. "The Competitive Impact of Health Maintenance Organizations and Competition on Hospitals in Minneapolis/St. Paul." *Journal of Health Politics, Policy and Law* 10 (Winter): 659–674.

Jones, Charles O. 1975. *Clean Air: The Policies and Politics of Pollution Control.* Pittsburgh: Pittsburgh University Press.

Luft, Harold S. 1987. *Health Maintenance Organizations: Dimensions of Performance.* New Brunswick, N.J.: Transaction Books.

Luft, Harold S., Susan C. Maerki, and Joan B. Trauner. 1986. "The Competitive Effects of Health Maintenance Organizations: Another Look at the Evidence from Hawaii, Rochester, and Minneapolis/St. Paul." *Journal of Health Politics, Policy and Law* 10 (Winter): 625–658.

McLaughlin, Catherine C. 1988. "Market Responses to HMOs: Price Competition or Rivalry?" *Injury* 25 (Summer): 207–218.

Merrill, Jeffrey and Catherine McLaughlin. 1986. "Competition versus Regulation: Some Empirical Evidence." *Journal of Health Politics, Policy and Law* 10 (Winter): 613–623.

New York Times. 1992. "The Answer: Managed Competition for America's Health." December 2, 1992, p. A22, and "The Answer: Managed Competition—How to Make It Work." December 3, 1992, p. A24.

Paul-Shaheen, Pamela, Jane Deane Clark, and Daniel Williams. 1987. "Small Area Analysis: A Review and Analysis of the North American Literature." *Journal of Health Politics, Policy and Law* 12 (Winter): 741–809.

Wennberg, John E. 1984. "Dealing with Medical Practice Variations: A Proposal for Action." *Health Affairs* 3 (Summer): 6–32.

————. 1992. "AHCPR and the Strategy for Health Care Reform." *Health Affairs* 11 (Winter): 67–71.

Wennberg, John, and Alan Gittelsohn. 1982. "Variations in Medical Care among Small Areas." *Scientific American* (April): 120–134.

White, William. 1991. Personal Communication to author.

Chapter Eleven

THE POLITICAL CONSIDERATIONS OF PROCOMPETITIVE REFORM

Theodore R. Marmor and David A. Boyum

During the 1970s, the discourse of American health policy shifted dramatically. The health debates of the early 1970s were marked by an atmosphere of urgency; indeed, the sense of trouble was so widespread that Republicans and Democrats, liberals and conservatives competed over which form of national health insurance to offer in response. Perhaps more significantly, it was widely assumed that the necessary tools of reform were intensified planning and broader regulation. By the end of the 1970s, however, this approach had, for many, been discredited. To pro-market advocates, the answer was less regulation, not more, and competitive reforms became a dominant feature of health policy debate.

At least three factors made the increased attention to competition an understandable development. First, traditional concerns about access to medical care and the distribution of its costs began to take a backseat to worries about controlling the total cost of care. Problems of the uninsured and poorly protected could not compete for the public's attention with the genuinely ominous numbers on medical inflation. In 1970, the United States, possessing a strong and growing economy, spent 7.4 percent of its gross national product (GNP) on health care. In 1980, with a weak economy still reeling from the twin oil shocks of the previous decade, the proportion was 9.1 percent (U.S. Bureau of the Census 1990: 92, table 134).[1]

A second factor was the general ascendance, in academic writing, of economic approaches to analyzing public policy—or more accurately, as Evan Melhado (1988: 35) has pointed out, the ascendance of economic analysis that had a deregulatory mission.[2] Obviously the Chicago School comes to mind, but others who would hardly be associated with that movement, like economist Charles Schultze and political scientist Theodore Lowi, were also influential (Melhado 1988: 41–45). All of this provided the intellectual groundwork for procompetitive health care reforms. Indeed, Melhado (1988: 87, n. 65) cited a personal telephone conversation in which "Alain Enthoven reports that he had read Schultze's book [*The Public Use of Private Interest*] shortly before devising his Consumer-Choice Health Plan and that he regards his [own] book as the 'working out' in the health care economy of an example of Schultze's general propositions."

A third factor bolstering the competitive movement was the spread of such antigovernment, antiregulatory sentiment to the wider political arena. Although this sentiment has become synonymous with Ronald Reagan, it in fact had earlier roots. Americans often forget the extent to which Jimmy Carter ran for president on an anti-Washington, antigovernment platform, portraying himself as a down-home farmer who, pitchfork in hand, was headed to the nation's capital to slay the federal leviathan.

More than a decade after Carter's presidency, the intellectual themes of health policy debate remain remarkably similar. At the outset of the 1980s, many politicians and policymakers were looking to competition because health care costs had soared to over 9 percent of GNP. Now, in the early 1990s health care costs absorb something like 13 percent of GNP (*New York Times* 1991)[3] and many are still looking to one or more of the many competitive approaches to health insurance and provision as the answer.[4]

To most of those who oppose competitive reforms, these numbers provide ample evidence that market forces simply cannot constrain health care costs. But these very same data on rising health expenditures are also presented as crucial evidence of the need for more competition—either among providers or insurers—in American medical care. Competition's advocates argue that a genuinely competitive market has never really been tried in the United States, and that our unabated inflation shows just how urgent the need for market competition is. For example, in the recent survey by the *Journal of the American Medical Association* of health care reform proposals, Alain Enthoven and Richard Kronick (1991: 2532) argued that "contrary to a widespread impression, America has not yet tried *competition* of alternative health care financing and delivery plans, using the term in the normal economic sense, i.e., *price* competition to serve cost-conscious purchasers."

Enthoven and Kronick are right that a competitive market for health plans has never been implemented on a comprehensive scale. Instead, piecemeal, uncoordinated, and largely unsuccessful attempts have been made to introduce more competition into the delivery of health care. A case in point was, in the 1970s, the invigor-

ated application of antitrust law to the medical (and other) professions and the concomitant lifting of the ban on advertising.[5]

Enthoven and Kronick may also be right that, if fully implemented,
certain competitive plans, like their Consumer Choice Health proposal,[6] might well restrain the growth of health care costs. It does
not necessarily follow from this, however, that such competitive
schemes are the answer to our health care woes.

Many procompetitive advocates offer plausible, yet debatable, economic arguments to support their particular proposals. But intelligent
policy ideas require a sound political grounding as well. Indeed,
where medical care reform is concerned, any thoughtful policy analysis must address a whole host of issues, ranging from questions of
political feasibility and practical implementation to concerns about
distributional consequences and compatibility with professional
ideals. It is to these matters that procompetitive advocates have generally paid insufficient attention.

PROBLEMS OF IMPLEMENTATION

Historical Evidence

Henry Kissinger is fond of telling the following story. The president's
national security adviser asks one of his top military analysts to
develop a policy to deal with the problem of Soviet submarines. A
few months later the analyst reports back to his boss, who promptly
asks, "What is your recommendation?" "Heat up the world's oceans
and boil the Soviet subs to the surface." "And how do you propose
to implement this strategy?" questions the national security adviser.
"Look," replies the analyst, "you asked me to come up with the
policy—it's your job to implement it."

The point of the story is not to suggest that procompetitive reform
proposals are as quixotic as plans to boil the oceans. Rather, the aim
is to illustrate the need for policy ideas to have reasonable plans and
prospects for implementation. Unfortunately for backers of procompetitive reform, historical experience—both international and
domestic—is not reassuring.

On the international front, there is not a single country in the world
to which procompetitive advocates can point as a model. They do,
of course, use foreign medical care systems as negative models—as
evidence of the failure of government-run insurance or care. But

although it is undoubtedly important to examine and highlight the inadequacies of these systems, one always has to be careful comparing a hypothetical scheme (procompetitive) with actualized systems. As stock brokers and commodities traders are fond of saying: "Anyone can trade on paper."

By contrast, proponents of alternative strategies of reform—like a single-payer approach—can look to a host of countries that provide their citizens with universal access to medical care at relatively lower costs. Even more important, these policymakers can use international experience to help answer the most important of all implementation questions: How do we get there from here? After all, countries like Canada and Australia have fairly recently made the transition from a U.S.-style system to a single-payer design.

Nor should domestic experience make anyone hopeful about the prospects for procompetitive reform. Consider the case of HMOs, which many procompetitive advocates see as essential to combating the perverse incentives and informational asymmetries of fee-for-service medicine. Despite all the rhetoric about managed competition and legislative efforts to encourage the establishment and expansion of HMOs since 1973, only 15 percent of the U.S. population, or 36.5 million people, were enrolled in HMOs by 1990. One problem has been that throughout the 1980s, HMOs and other managed-care insurance plans failed to earn a reasonable rate of return. In 1989, 66 percent of established HMOs and only 46 percent of new HMOs were profitable. In both 1987 and 1988, HMOs reported average losses of over 4 percent on revenue; although 1989 showed an improvement, even in that year HMOs earned on average less than 1 percent on revenue.[7]

Another obstacle is that, plain and simple, doctors prefer fee-for-service. Eli Ginzberg (1988) has suggested that many HMOs have been forced to rely on individual or independent practice associations, and not on the pure HMO form as envisioned by Ellwood, Enthoven, and others. This claim is backed by Marsha Gold's (1991: 193) findings: "Network and individual practice associations (IPA)-model plans . . . increased from 97 to 433 between 1980 and 1990. Their share of HMOs increased from 41 percent to 76 percent, and of enrollment from 19 percent to 58 percent."

The Need for Regulation

It is worth emphasizing that there are two broad theories of procompetitive reform. One approach presumes that there is insufficient price competition in medicine and that first-dollar insurance (insurance, that is, without deductibles and cost sharing) induces wasteful and financially costly patient demands. This view argues that individuals should bear a greater share of their medical expenses and that doing so would encourage them to shop around for services and avoid needless care. The mechanisms for putting these policies into practice are increased deductibles and copayments, as well as the careful monitoring of medical services to counteract the fee-for-service incentives of providers.

By contrast, the "managed-competition" approach rejects the notion that competition is feasible at the point of treatment. For example, Enthoven (1979: 147) has asserted that the "conditions under which the competitive market produces an efficient allocation of resources cannot be well satisfied by a market in which the 'product' the consumer buys is the individual medical care service." He has argued:

> First . . . increasing numbers of insurance policies include an upper limit on the family's out-of-pocket cost above which all costs will be paid by insurance. At that point, the weak economic incentive introduced by insurance is removed altogether.
>
> Second, for most illnesses, the physician cannot quote a fixed price for treatment in advance. . . . Until he has done some work, he does not know whether you have indigestion or a heart attack. . . .
>
> Third, the individual episode of medical care is not good material for rational economic calculation. If the patient is in pain or urgent need of care, the transaction is not entirely voluntary. The sick patient is in a poor position to make an economic analysis of treatment alternatives or negotiate with the doctor over fees.
>
> Fourth, it is very costly for the patient to become well-informed about the costs and benefits of alternative treatments. (1979: 144–45)

All of this leads Enthoven to advocate competition among health plans (most of which would ideally be HMOs) rather than among doctors.

Although these two approaches differ greatly in their theory of competition, both employ the procompetitive label. Indeed, advocates have carefully chosen this label, as an explicit contrast to other reform approaches. The implication is that the other "approaches" are not procompetitive, but anticompetitive and proregulation. And much of the intuitive appeal of procompetitive proposals is that they are somehow self-regulating, not dependent on public regulation and management in which so many have so little faith.

Note, however, that some managed-competition plans backed by some procompetitive advocates favor competition that is far from unfettered—to the contrary, these plans necessitate extensive regulation, since they are hardly self-governing. For example, in the kind of competition between insurance plans advocated by proponents of managed competition, some plans might thrive by only attracting the young and healthy; while in rural areas, where it is often difficult to get even one medical provider to cover the population, competition among plans, whatever the encouragement, might be totally unfeasible. To avoid such imbalances, managed competition sets up detailed rules to govern the system. These rules require all citizens to enroll through specified purchasing agents in one or another of a limited number of pre-approved plans. Participating insurance companies, for their part, are forced to offer several predetermined varieties of plans.

But it is not only managed competition that is managed. Despite the procompetitive rhetoric, even more market-based reform proposals presume an extensive regulatory framework to combat market failures. For example, the plan proposed by the Bush administration forbids insurance firms from using experience-rating in pricing their policies; the Heritage Foundation's proposal accepts experience-rating, but relies on state-regulated and state-administered insurance pools to cover high-risk individuals (Marmor and Barr 1992).

Robustness

In arguing against government-financed or government-provided medical care, advocates of procompetitive reform often claim that governments are not sufficiently competent to manage such systems. For starters, it is claimed, the inevitable concessions of the political process ensure that, when finalized, policy programs will bear scant resemblance to their initial design. Then inefficiency sets in, as governments are slow and ineffectual at responding to the results of their actions (which regularly include consequences the opposite of those that were intended).

Yet, as noted in the previous section, procompetitive advocates have proposed a variety of detailed government programs, laws, and regulations designed to address and eliminate the kind of market failures that might occur in unregulated medical markets. What happens when government incompetence contaminates these efforts? What happens to Enthoven's plan when only half of its provisions get enacted and implemented, when insurance companies are not required to offer specific types of plans, when the government increases, rather than eliminates, the tax deductibility of medical insurance? What happens if experience rating is allowed, but the government sets up no provision for high-risk pools?

The answer may be that procompetitive plans are not robust, that they do not perform well unless conditions are just right. After all, by detailing those government actions required to eliminate current market failures, backers of procompetitive reform implicitly acknowledge that without these remedies, a competitive system does not work very well. (Indeed, few would claim that our current system, plagued by skyrocketing costs and large numbers of uninsured, works well.)

ISSUES OF VALUES

Choice

In support of their policies, advocates of competition stress as well the rhetoric of free choice. For instance, as stated earlier, Enthoven has labeled his procompetitive plan the "Consumer Choice Health Plan." He explained: "The patient still has 'free choice of doctor' in the sense that he can join the health plan in which his favorite doctor participates. But now he also has the right to agree to get his care from a limited set of providers who offer him a lower premium and/ or better benefits" (1979: 147). Not only is this a debatable notion of consumer choice—as Paul Starr (1992) points out—but even if it were not, the idea of a favorite doctor is itself somewhat arcane. Could Enthoven himself tell us the name of his favorite otolaryngologist? How about his favorite gastroenterologist? And what is the likelihood that his favorite internist, cardiologist, neurologist, ophthalmologist, urologist, and proctologist are all members of the same health plan?

Enthoven and others seem to imply that Americans value the choice of an insurance company more than they prize the choice of a doctor. Surveys and common sense, however, both dispute this conclusion.[8] Consider the mindset of someone faced with a choice between two health plans. One is a traditional Blue Cross/Blue Shield plan that allows unrestricted selection of physician and hospital. The other, an HMO, has lower premiums, but provides no reimbursement for physicians outside its network. Most people regard such a choice as burdensome, as being forced to opt unfairly for either money or the quality of their medical care. Clearly this is not a straightforward "free" choice. Indeed, if the HMO is selected, the subscriber does not feel that his or her freedom has been enhanced, but, rather, that some of that freedom has been lost.

Access and Distribution

Most Americans agree that medical care should not be allocated primarily on the basis of ability to pay, and that everyone should receive a decent minimum standard of care. They are right; medical care is no ordinary commodity. Not only is it, like food and shelter, a basic prerequisite for life, but the need for it is not just a matter of behavioral choices but substantially a function of luck.

Few advocates of competition believe that medical care should be allocated solely on ability or willingness to pay. And their plans generally guarantee access to a "reasonable" or "decent basic minimum" of health care services. But at some point above this minimum, all procompetitive programs allow, and depend on, price-conscious behavior. In other words, they allow for some inequality of access or distribution based on willingness to pay.

As philosophers like Norman Daniels (1985) have emphasized, it is open to question whether such market-based plans meet the requirements of justice. Nor is it clear to most Americans that a "decent basic minimum" is sufficient. A recent survey found that 91 percent of Americans polled think that "everybody should have the right to get the best possible health care," and 66 percent believe it unfair that some people can afford better health insurance than others (Callahan 1988, quoted in Oswalt 1990: 1165). And, in another survey, despite concerns over the cost of care, 63 percent of Americans favored making health care more available to everyone who does not yet have it, rather than lowering the nation's health care spending (Fitzpatrick 1987, cited in Blendon and Edwards 1991: 3588).

Professional Ideals

Despite the increasing rewards afforded American medical practitioners, they are increasingly dissatisfied. Because of managed care—an inevitable development under most procompetitive plans—doctors complain they no longer enjoy the autonomy they once had. Rather, elaborate and expensive procedures, including utilization reviews, requirements for pre-admission certification, and other forms of second-guessing, have proliferated. American Medical Association surveys have found that 60 percent of physicians strongly oppose third-party reviews of their hospitalization decisions (Harvey 1986). In a 1991 article in the *Atlantic Monthly*, Regina Herzlinger reported that more than 30 percent of current physicians say they would not have attended medical school had they known what their futures had in store.

If doctors were concerned about these developments only to the extent that their incomes are threatened, we would not lose any sleep over it. But managed care has the potential to—indeed it already has—dramatically alter the relationship between doctors and patients. That relationship has always been considered special. It is not simply one of seller and buyer, or provider and consumer, as some economists crudely describe it. Doctors are asked to abide by a professional ethic to do whatever they can to assist their patients. And patients, who are at their physically and emotionally most vulnerable when they require medical care, expect this from their doctors. It is hardly reassuring for patients to have their physician's medical judgment second-guessed (by the patient's employer or insurance company) on grounds of cost-effectiveness.

CONCLUSION

It is not the purpose of this essay to reject procompetitive approaches. Indeed, a primary theme of this discussion is that issues of implementation are so important that no one could intelligently claim one plan is superior to another simply because it is labeled procompetitive, as opposed to, say, single-payer. Consider, for example, two proposals for American medical care, the first, a single-payer scheme, and the second, a procompetitive design. Both appear promising in theory, but the first, one surmises on the basis of its implementation details, is destined to become a poorly structured, badly managed program— a kind of Medicaid writ large. The second, in contrast, has features that promise to work more effectively when implemented, resulting in a carefully and skillfully regulated program of managed competition. No responsible advocate of Canadian-style, single-payer plans, however committed to government insurance, would favor the first proposal, given its practical ineffectiveness. Similarly, if we compare a well worked-out single-payer plan with a poorly implemented procompetitive scheme, no thoughtful proponent of market-based reform would favor the latter, however intense his or her commitment to the theory.

Many advocates of competition have thoughtfully diagnosed the various market failures that plague our current medical care arrangements. And many have offered intelligent proposals to remedy these shortcomings. This chapter contends, however, that the arguments of most procompetitive reformers are, to date, inadequate because they fail to explore issues of implementation, especially doubts about the government's capacity to do what their plans would require. They also overlook important questions of whether their proposals are compatible with certain values—not just of access and distribution, but also of choice and professional ideals. Until advocates of competition address more thoroughly these political and philosophical questions, their analyses must be considered narrow and insufficient.

Notes

1. A frequently expressed, but ignored, concern over the overall cost of health care has been the more important question of the marginal benefit derived from each additional dollar of health spending. Although it is often assumed that the goods and services purchased in the name of health care remain the same over time, this assumption overlooks the profound changes in medical technology and practice that have occurred in the past 20 years.

2. It may be hard to remember, but at one time economics helped to justify government intervention and regulation: "The principal motive for the increased application of economics to public policy after World War II was the expanding of government as a purveyor of large public programs entailing major expenditures" (Melhado 1988: 35).

3. The *New York Times* (see Hilts 1991) reported U.S. Department of Commerce predictions based on actual yearly costs to November 1991; health expenditures rose 11 percent in 1991 to a total of $738 billion. The department estimated 1992 expenditures would be around $817 billion, or 14 percent of GNP.

4. See, for example, "Dialogue: The Great Health Care Debate" (1992).

5. For a discussion of the hopes and philosophies underlying the antitrust approach, see Marmor, Boyer, and Greenberg (1981).

6. See Enthoven and Kronick (1989).

7. Data from Group Health Association of America's Annual HMO Industry Survey, cited in Gold (1991: 196).

8. See Taylor and Leitman (1991).

References

Callahan, D. 1988. "Allocating Health Resources." *Hastings Center Report* 18: 14–20.

Daniels, Norman. 1985. *Just Health Care.* Cambridge, England: Cambridge University Press.

Enthoven, Alain C. 1979. "Consumer-Centered vs. Job-Centered Health Insurance." *Harvard Business Review*, 57 (1, Jan./Feb.): 147.

Enthoven, Alain C., and Richard Kronick. 1992. "Dialogue: The Great Health Care Debate: Will Managed Competition Work?" *New York Times*, January 25: sec. 1, p. 23.

———. 1991. "Universal Health Insurance through Incentives Reform." *Journal of the American Medical Association* 265 (May 15): 2532.

———. 1989. "A Consumer Choice Health Plan for the 1990s: Universal Health Insurance in a System Designed to Promote Quality and Economy, Parts I and II." *New England Journal of Medicine* 320: 29–37, 94–101.

Fitzpatrick, T. B. 1987. *Changes and Choices in the Health Care System.* Report no. 116. Cambridge, Mass.: Cambridge Reports.

Ginzberg, Eli. 1988. "U.S. Health Policy—Expectations and Realities." *Journal of the American Medical Association* 23 (Dec. 30): 3648.

Gold, Marsha R. 1991. "HMOs and Managed Care." *Health Affairs* 10 (4, Winter): 193.

Harvey, L. 1986. *AMA Surveys of Physician and Public Opinion: 1986.* Chicago: American Medical Association.

Herzlinger, Regina. 1991. "Healthy Competition." Letters to the Editor. *Atlantic Monthly* 268 (1, August): 71.

Hilts, Philip J. 1991. "U.S. Health Bill Expected to Rise by 11% for '91: Spending to Increase in Each of Next 5 Years." *New York Times*, December 30: A 10.

Marmor, T. R. and Michael S. Barr. 1992. "Making Sense of the National Health Care Reform Debate." *Yale Law and Policy Review* 10 (2): 228–82.

Mamor, T. R., Richard Boyer, and Julie Greenberg. 1981. "Medical Care and Procompetitive Reform." *Vanderbilt Law Review* 34: 1003–28.

Melhado, Evan M. 1988. "Competition versus Regulation in American Health Policy." In *Money, Power, and Health Care*, edited by Evan M. Melhado, Walter Feinberg, and Harold M. Swartz. Ann Arbor, Mich.: Health Administration Press.

Oswalt, Charles E. 1990. "Expensive Health Care: A Solvable Problem?" *Archives of Internal Medicine* 150: 1165.

Starr, Paul. 1992. *The Logic of Health Care Reform.* Knoxville, Tenn.: Whittle Books.

Taylor, Humphrey, and Robert Leitman. 1991. "Consumers' Satisfaction with Their Health Care." In *System in Crisis: The Case for Health Care*

Reform, edited by Robert J. Blendon and Jennifer N. Edwards. Washington, D.C.: Faulkner & Gray's.

U.S. Bureau of the Census. 1990. *Statistical Abstract of the United States: 1990,* 110th ed. Washington, D.C.: U.S. Government Printing Office.

Part Four

CHANGING THE ASSUMPTIONS

DOES THE MARKET CHOOSE THE CORRECT INCENTIVES TO GET TO THE DESIRED OUTCOMES? MARKET FAILURE REEXAMINED

Frank A. Sloan

The political debate about the proper role of government in the health care sector is nothing new. The health care policies of much of this century have been responses to perceived market failures.

DISTINGUISHING CHARACTERISTICS OF HEALTH CARE AND MARKET FAILURES

Asymmetric Information

The first concern addressed at the beginning of the century was consumer ignorance. Policymakers accepted the notion that consumers were not well-positioned to make choices about the personal health services they purchased. Because of asymmetric information between buyers (patients) and sellers (physicians, hospitals, and others), the buyers were thought to be easy prey. Responses were accreditation of schools in the health professions and hospitals, licensure of health facilities, enactment by states of practice acts for various health professions, advertising bans, codes of ethics of medical associations, and peer review by hospital medical staff. In place of reliance on markets came reliance on professional norms and self-regulation by health care professionals and by institutions such as hospitals. Both buying and selling were entrusted to sellers who, conforming to professional norms, would make the right choices for patients.

Even today, this worldview has a following among critics of what is perceived as rising commercialization of medical practice and the demise of professionalism (see, e.g., Relman 1991). Other developments that address inadequacy of health care consumer information, such as Professional Standards Review Organizations and their replacements, Peer Review Organizations, and tort law as applied to medical malpractice, are much more recent developments.

In general, high information cost to consumers is a source of monopoly power that means higher prices, lower output, and, possibly, lower product quality as well. Information may be costly to health care consumers when services are purchased infrequently, because of the technical nature of some types of medical care, and because of patient anguish and/or haste at the point of service. Although society is generally worse off when sellers possess market power, in health care, matters may be still worse to the extent that information asymmetries confer the ability to generate demand for their services on providers. The extent to which providers of health care services can in fact generate demand has been a topic of considerable debate among specialists in health care economics.[1] To the extent that suppliers of medical care have this potential, information deficiencies are that much more of a problem.

It is easy to be cynical about the professional model, particularly because it elevates medical care to a special status in which there is no need to balance the benefits to devoting resources for personal health care services against alternative uses. Incidental aggrandizement of one's own and professional colleagues' incomes in the absence of countervailing pressures is an added, if unspoken, consideration. The fatal flaw of the professional model, however, is not that it seems to support personal aggrandizement by health professionals, but, rather, that it asks that physicians make judgments based on medical necessity without having to consider the opportunity costs. At a minimum, the professional model should be coupled with a budget constraint. In fact, many who espouse a professional model would prefer a constraint (dollar ceiling) that would allow physicians to allocate resources among patients without being subject to external controls on the way they practice.

However, inadequate information need not be a given. An appropriate role for government is to improve the flow of accurate information. Some information will only be provided with public support. Further, various private mechanisms, such as managed health care, by substituting knowledgeable agents for ill-informed patients can, in principle, enhance availability of adequate information to consumers. In practice, decision making by such agents is impeded by lack of clinical knowledge about the efficacy of various diagnostic and therapeutic modalities.

Externalities in Consumption

A second important characteristic and source of market failure is that, unlike the case for the vast majority of goods and services, individuals' consumption of medical care is a matter of social concern. With some major exceptions—alcohol treatment, mental health services, infectious diseases such as AIDS—the concern is not that failure to prevent, treat, and isolate individual cases of disease will cause its spread to others. Rather, as a matter of equity, there is widespread consensus that medical care should be available to all, irrespective of ability to pay.

Although the generality is universally accepted, or practically so, the consensus breaks down at the next level of specificity. Does equity imply equality in use or even equality in health outcomes? Certainly equality in outcomes would realistically require much more massive outlays for personal health services. Since poor outcomes reflect many factors, not just insufficient use of medical care, the expenditure increase to achieve this objective would produce massive inefficiencies in resource allocation. Much more modest objectives would be to achieve minimumly adequate levels of health outcomes and, even more attainable, minimumly adequate levels of use of medical care. Even the most modest objective is difficult to operationalize, since health care is multidimensional. Does, for example, equality of use extend to amenities of service that are legitimate dimensions of quality, such as patient waiting time and private hospital rooms? Or to access to the latest, most sophisticated, expensive technologies?

There is certainly no national consensus about the equity objectives that we as a society desire to achieve or that are attainable in fact. A century ago, we relied on private philanthropy and donated care by health professionals. In the 1930s, Blue Cross plans, the first prepaid health plans, promoted community rating. All persons paid the same premium irrespective of their health. After World War II, public policy focused on expansion of the numbers of personnel and hospital facilities, especially in areas in which low-income and geographically remote persons lived. Since the mid-1960s, the vehicle for assuring equity in the delivery of health care services has been health insurance. Lack of such insurance and underinsurance of others are seen as major sources of inequity in use and in health outcomes. Much of the public support for universal single-payer health insurance has its origin in the notion that only if the poor and otherwise disadvantaged individuals have the same coverage as everyone else, will equity be achieved (Schroeder and Cantor 1991).

We can be certain that competition cannot achieve equity in health services consumption on its own. In particular, competition eliminates sellers' market power to charge higher prices to some patients just to subsidize the services provided to others—in the jargon of the industry, to shift cost (Dranove 1988b; Phelps 1986). Conferring market power on sellers to achieve equity in consumption is a flawed idea. Thus, its demise is to be applauded.

The approach of granting suppliers monopoly profits so that some services may trickle down to the poor is objectionable for two reasons. First, there is no guarantee that the poor will be served. Second, as already mentioned, monopolies produce distortions in the allocation of resources. The not-for-profit hospital that must break even raises its price of services for which it has unexploited market power, such as for a well-insured service as coronary bypass surgery, to subsidize the care of uninsured patients.[2]

Uninsured patients as a fraction of all hospitalized patients actually increased during the 1980s (Sloan, Morrisey, and Valvona 1988b). However, if competition truly evolves, one may expect the trend to be reversed. There will be no surplus for cross-subsidizing care of the uninsured. The need for governmental intervention to achieve equity under a regime of competition is inescapable.

Uncertainty

A third distinguishing characteristic of personal health services is that individuals are exposed to the risk of catastrophic expenditures on health services. When faced with large stochastic expenditures, risk-averse individuals demand insurance. Health is not unique in this regard.

Several phenomena may lead to distortions in insurance markets and institutional arrangements, many of them private mechanisms to deal with these distortions (see Arrow 1963; Pauly 1968).

MORAL HAZARD

One of these phenomena is moral hazard. There is considerable empirical evidence that insured persons demand more health care services (Manning et al. 1987). Evidence that insurance affects choice of provider/quality is somewhat weaker (see, e.g., Marquis and Holmer 1986; Marquis and Rogowski 1991; Short and Taylor 1989), even though such a relationship plausibly exists. Increased cost-sharing is one solution, but it may result in use patterns considered to be "inequitable," and, depending on how cost-sharing is imple-mented, will to a lesser or greater degree, reduce protection against individual risk. Also, in one important study, a substantial amount of inappropriate hospital use was detected, but cost sharing did not selectively reduce inappropriate hospitalization (Siu et al. 1986).

Martin Feldstein (1973) estimated that the welfare cost of overuse of services offset by far the benefits of risk reduction provided by complete insurance, but his calculations were based on an assumed degree of responsiveness of use to price that empirical research conducted later showed to be too high. Also, he did not account for the possibility that some of the additional services may have been just as effective as the ones cost sharing would eliminate. The trade-off between equity and efficiency is much more difficult to calculate. The nearly universal demand for complete insurance suggests that societies place considerable weight on equity considerations.

Price incentives to combat moral hazard need not be implemented at the point of service. Experience-rated premiums are one mechanism. Experience rating is common in certain lines of insurance, such as automobile insurance, where insurance tends to be sold on an individual basis. Drivers with chargeable automobile accidents are surcharged about 40 percent on average. Accidents and/or convictions that involve drunk driving are surcharged many times this (Sloan and Githens 1992). Probably the main reason that health insurance premiums are not experience rated is that such insurance is generally provided through groups. This reason is not fully satisfactory, since it should be possible to do some experience rating of individual members within groups. Unfortunately, there is a lack of information on experience rating and underwriting practices in individual health insurance.

Another reason that experience rating is common in automobile insurance is that much of automobile insurance is third-party coverage, which necessarily involves determination of liability. Causation of the expenditure is more readily determined in automobile accidents than in medical care use. But equity considerations are also a factor. There is a seeming reluctance to surcharge the victim of cancer in the same manner as one surcharges the automobile owner with chronic losses, because many forms of cancer are beyond the patient's control, and, even for preventable forms of cancer, there is a reluctance to charge patients for their past errors. The reluctance to surcharge policyholders goes beyond this, however. Health insurance policyholders typically do not face varying premiums for readily observable characteristics that predict health expenditures, such as age and family size.

One explanation for why healthy persons may be willing to cross-subsidize the care of less-healthy individuals by means of a community-rated premium structure is that the healthy face a good chance that their health will deteriorate in the future, at which time they, too, will be the recipients of a cross-subsidy. By contrast, the riskiest automobile insurance policyholders are often young. An older policy-holder is not likely to become as risky, at least until he or she becomes very old. Thus, there is widespread reluctance to cross-subsidize premiums of high-risk automobile insurance policyholders (Cotter and Jensen 1989).

Utilization controls provide another mechanism for coping with moral hazard. Various managed-care plans represent private mechanisms for established utilization rules before the fact. Utilization controls necessarily involve administrative cost. Recent criticism of the high administrative cost incurred by health insurers in the United States obscures the fact that some administrative expenditure may yield reductions in the use of some services that a well-informed but uninsured individual in a similar health state would not purchase.

Moral hazard may also exist on the supply side. First, when price does not vary with the quantity of services provided, as in capitated plans or even under Medicare's Prospective Payment System (PPS), there may be underprovision of service (Ellis and McGuire 1990). Second, once premiums have been collected, insurers may take excessive risks in managing the income from premiums, leading to bankruptcy risk. States have implemented guaranty funds to protect insureds against bankruptcy. This is less of a problem in health insurance than in other lines. Many employer groups are self-insured, only relying on insurers to administer their plans. Group purchasers are presumably more knowledgeable about insurers' insolvency risk. Health insurance is a very "short-tail" line, meaning that benefits follow premium payments by a few months on average—not years, as in certain property-liability lines.

ADVERSE SELECTION

Another source of failure in insurance markets is adverse selection, a consequence of which is that coverage may not be available. In health insurance, the adverse selection problem had been "solved" by the predominance of group insurance. In recent years, it has become "unsolved" by a proliferation of plans offering multiple insurance plan options to persons covered by groups. Although not all studies investigating the issue agree, there is some empirical evidence of adverse selection on the part of individuals when given a choice among health insurance plans offering different amounts of coverage.[3] However, insurers have various mechanisms for coping with adverse selection in multiple option plans, such as by limiting open enrollment periods.[4] If anything, there is current concern that insurers may be becoming too aggressive in classifying risks, thus leaving unhealthy individuals without insurance at affordable prices.[5]

OVER- AND UNDERINSURANCE

Unlike other types of insurance, premium payments for health insurance are given special tax treatment. Of particular importance, contributions to health insurance provided as a fringe benefit are a tax-deductible business expense for employers and are excluded from personal income taxation. In general, the tax subsidy exceeds the loading on group insurance, with the consequence that it is less expensive after taxes to pay for one's medical care through a health insurance plan than it is to purchase it directly (Pauly 1986). Empirical studies of the demand for insurance consistently show that insurance purchases are sensitive to price, even though the studies reveal a broad range of responses (elasticities from -0.2 [Taylor and Wilensky 1983] to over -1.0 [Ginsburg 1981; Phelps 1985; Long and Scott 1982; Woodbury 1983; Sloan and Adamache 1985]).

One may infer that eliminating the tax subsidy, or at least limiting it, would increase relative demand for less-complete insurance (insurance with more cost-sharing provisions) and for various forms of managed care. It is only possible to speculate about the precise form of the response to an appreciable increase in the price of insurance. Even if insurance purchases were unresponsive to a change in price, a strong argument can be made for changing the form of the tax subsidy, since current tax treatment provides a disproportionate benefit to the affluent. Economists seem to be in universal agreement that this subsidy should be eliminated or at least limited. Its persistence can probably be explained by practical politics ("read my lips" about tax increases, lobbying by the health insurance industry).

Some would oppose limiting the subsidy out of concern that it would lead to more uninsured persons. This is really not a legitimate criticism, since the current subsidy could be replaced by a fixed-dollar refundable tax credit that would give less-affluent families greater ability to acquire health insurance than they now have (Enthoven 1980, 1988).

In contrast to acute care, private insurance for long-term care services is virtually nonexistent. This is not because families face no expenditure risk for such care. There are probable impediments on both demand and supply sides of the long-term care insurance markets. Medicaid may have crowded out private demand for such insurance. Pauly (1990) suggested that the elderly fear that, with insurance, their children would have an incentive to institutionalize them against their will. Insurers may be reluctant to supply such coverage, because, among other reasons, they cannot predict the price of nursing home care far in advance at the time it would be necessary to collect premiums. Further, the prevalence of diseases leading to institutionalization varies over time and is difficult to predict far in advance (e.g., the increased prevalence of Alzheimer's disease).[6] Supply-side market failures argue for government provision of long-term coverage.

Public Goods

The productivity of medical care has been greatly increased by scientific advances. Much of the technological change has been motivated by firms hoping to make a profit from their investments. Since knowledge is a public good, much of the private investment is only forthcoming with patent protection. Conferring monopoly status on new products is justified to the extent that firms have a comparative advantage over government-sponsored research in producing new findings. However, in fundamental research undertakings, relative to publicly funded research, the cost of patent protection appears to outweigh any perceived benefit.

Governments have also had an active role in funding education in the health professions. The public-good features of these investments are distributional. They relate to providing persons from moderate- and low-income families access to careers in the health professions and, by augmenting supply of persons with degrees in the health professions, improving access of the population to health care.

ROLE OF INCENTIVES IN HEALTH CARE MARKETS

Probably no one would argue that incentives do not matter at all in health care markets, but there is plenty of debate—not all informed—about the effect of incentives. More precisely, the debate focuses on several types of issues.

First, how do various incentives affect the behavior of the partici-pants in the market? Many of these incentives involve prices. Largely because of an assumed lack of information and/or motivation on the part of market participants, many observers have argued that the effects of prices have been either vitiated or take a form that is untypical of most markets.[7] As a result of considerable empirical research, we now know much more about effects of price on behavior of both providers and consumers than we did a couple of decades ago.

Second, given that incentives matter, can markets be expected to provide appropriate incentives to achieve desired outcomes?

Third, to the extent that market failure is unavoidable, what kinds of public interventions are indicated?

This section addresses the first two issues, relying in part on comments already made. In the next section, I discuss the role of governments in health care in view of my comments on the first two questions.

Effects of Price on Behavior of Individuals and Organizations in Health Care Markets

Taken as a whole, the empirical evidence strongly supports the view that prices matter a great deal. Absent this evidence, decisions made by consumers of personal health care services were thought to be guided by factors other than price, because such individuals do not possess the requisite information. Yet, largely because of the Health Insurance Experiment conducted by researchers at the RAND Corporation, we now have conclusive evidence that demand for medical care is responsive to price (cited in Manning et al. 1987), as is demand for long-term care (Nyman 1989). As indicated earlier, there is evidence that price affects demand for health insurance. Empirical results from several studies point to the influence of price on demand for cigarettes and alcoholic beverages (Chaloupka 1991; Coate and Grossman 1988; Cook and Tauchen 1982).

The majority of hospitals in the United States are operated on a not-for-profit basis. Not-for-profit status affects the nature of hospitals' response to price, but such institutions are responsive to price incentives nonetheless. There is now considerable empirical evidence that Medicare's change from paying on a retrospective cost to a prospective basis caused major changes in hospital behavior, such as hospital input use and length of stay (Sloan, Morrisey, and Valvona 1988a). Reimbursement method affects other aspects of hospital behavior as well, such as the debt-equity mix selected (Wedig et al. 1988).

Effects of price on physician behavior are more uncertain. On the one hand, the evidence is clear that physicians' willingness to participate in programs such as Medicaid is responsive to price (Sloan, Cromwell, and Mitchell 1978). Further, physicians have diffused to smaller communities as their aggregate numbers have increased, presumably because of limited earnings opportunities in more populous areas (Newhouse et al. 1982). Yet, work hours appear to be fairly price insensitive (Sloan 1974), and advocates of placing expenditure limits on physicians' services point to the increases in quantity of service following imposition of price controls.[8] To the extent that prices are held below their market clearing level, one would expect patients to demand more care, but, at the same time, physicians should be less willing to supply as much as when price is allowed to reach its equilibrium level. Thus, controlling price might ordinarily be expected to create excess demand and lower the quantity of services provided.

Some have interpreted the evidence of increased output in response to price controls as evidence that physicians have substantial ability to generate demand for their services (e.g., Holahan and Scanlon 1978). But the argument that quantity increases in response to price ceilings means that physicians will generate demand for their services to achieve income targets when prices are limited is not airtight (Feldman and Sloan 1988). Further, various other empirical evidence, such as the responsiveness of physician participation in insurance programs to price, the diffusion of physicians to less-populous areas, and findings on patient demand for health care services, are inconsistent with the view that market forces place no meaningful limits on physician-generated demand. More important, imposing expenditure limits, the policy advocated by some who interpret the experience with price controls as prima facie evidence of supplier-induced demand, is only one approach for dealing with the phenomenon of physician-generated demand. The alternative is to find mechanisms for empowering consumers.

Can Markets Be Expected to Provide Appropriate Incentives?

The market system relies on decentralized, private decision makers—consumers and producers—for allocative choices. When the parties to a transaction are the sole or primary interested persons, society tends to take a noninterventionist position, unless it has reason to believe that the transaction is unfairly structured. Such unfairness would occur if the consumer is incapable of making informed choices. Thus, putting aside equity concerns for now, the adequacy of consumer information is a logical place to start in addressing the appropriateness of incentives provided by health care service markets.

Consumer information appears to be better for some types of services than for others (Pauly 1978, 1988), and there are differences among consumers in the amount of information they possess. Lack of information need not lead to higher use of medical care. In an empirical study of the link between consumer information and use, Kenkel (1990) found that more-informed patients had comparatively higher rates of use of physicians' services, including laboratory services.

For an important subset of services—expensive, infrequently used services, sometimes used in life-threatening situations—information available to the patient at the point of service may be inadequate. For example, the patient in need of coronary bypass surgery on an emergency basis may be ill-positioned to make informed choices.

Yet, matters are not nearly so bleak as they might first appear. To continue the example, insurers are frequent purchasers of coronary bypass surgery, and there are appreciable differences among suppliers in both price and outcome (Hannan et al. 1991). At least part of the differences in outcome can be attributed to quality differences. Insurers should be well-positioned to make comparisons on price and quality of such services. Consumers or employers on their behalf, in turn, should be able to select those insurers who perform such comparisons ably.

Some would question whether insurers can do the job. Although price variation is observable, measuring case-mix and quality differences accurately is admittedly much more difficult. Only during the last decade or so has meaningful progress been made in case-mix and quality measurement, and much of the important work remains to be done.

But, while recognizing that these comparisons are often difficult to make, the same argument certainly applies to the alternatives as well. Would physicians working for a regulatory agency really be better positioned to make such choices for patients than would physicians working for an insurance company? Traditionally, the patient's personal physician has been charged with making these choices for the patient, and organized medicine has argued loud and hard to maintain this prerogative for its members. But the personal physician's comparative advantage is in knowing about the patient rather than about the price-quality combinations in the marketplace. Given widespread insurance coverage, excess utilization would arise even if personal physicians were perfect agents for perfectly informed patients. Hence, utilization controls are necessary, but in a market system, they are implemented by private insurers. Because of the tax subsidy and other reasons, including lack of consensus about appropriate diagnostic and therapeutic regimens among physicians and the public-good nature of cost containment, such controls may be undersupplied.

Society has developed a number of second-best private safeguards under the assumption that consumers cannot be sufficiently well informed (Arrow 1963), such as not-for-profit institutions and peer review by medical staff. If, indeed, consumers are not and cannot be informed, it is doubtful that these safeguards will suffice. Hansmann (1980) has aptly included hospitals in his list of "entrepreneurial" not-for-profit organizations. The subsidies these organizations enjoy are simply insufficient to permit them to behave much differently from their for-profit counterparts (Institute of Medicine 1986). Peer review by hospital medical staff, as currently structured, has had a mixed record. Elsewhere, James Blumstein and I have suggested ways to strengthen the peer review process (Blumstein and Sloan 1988).

The public safeguards implemented to protect ignorant consumers have at best a mixed track record. Licensure of health professionals has an abysmal record. To illustrate, in a study of medical malpractice claims in Florida, for example, the professional licensure board did not investigate physicians who had incurred large medical malpractice losses (Sloan et al. 1989). Tort liability is justified when patients misperceive the risks of alternative courses of treatment. In principle, a liability rule can be devised to give physicians incentives to take the due care that would be demanded by informed patients (Danzon 1985). In practice, no reliable evidence exists on tort law's deterrent effect in the health field, and, in spite of much theorizing, there is not much evidence of its deterrent effect in any other field either.[9]

The prospect for relying on markets to achieve an equitable distribution of resources is bleak. Even if private cross-subsidies from more-affluent to less-well-off individuals were desirable, competitive forces, if allowed to operate, inevitably eliminate producers' ability to make such subsidies. To produce equitable outcomes in a market, one needs an equitable distribution of resources to obtain the services. Only government has the ability to achieve an equitable distribution of resources in a comparatively distortion-free way. Thus, the bottom line is that markets can provide many of the correct incentives, but ensuring an adequate distribution of purchasing powers in health care is an appropriate role for governments.

APPROPRIATE ROLES FOR GOVERNMENT IN A MARKET SYSTEM

There are several appropriate roles for government in a health care system that is basically reliant on market forces. These roles are all important, but I make no attempt here to rank them in order of priority.

First, although government has a responsibility to support basic biomedical research, it also has a role in supporting research on the effectiveness of alternative treatment modalities. Lack of the latter type of information is an impediment to decision making by insurers and other private organizations. Health maintenance organizations (HMOs) achieved cost savings by eliminating (presumably) low-benefit hospital admissions (Luft 1981), but once these savings have been realized, finding other sources of savings has been a hard act to follow. Without public subsidies, the market will undersupply such outcomes research.

Second, government can disseminate information on supplier characteristics, including price, diagnostic- and therapeutic-procedure-specific outcomes, and disciplinary actions taken against individual physicians. Such information can be obtained by private organizations, but it is costly to do so. Health care providers vigorously oppose such information dissemination on grounds that such comparisons cannot be performed accurately. But it is doubtful that individual physicians typically have the requisite information on price and outcomes when they refer their patients to other physicians. The Health Care Financing Administration's decision to release hospital-specific mortality information was a positive step.

The Health Care Quality Improvement Act of 1988 required that a National Practitioner Data Bank be established. The bank contains information on disciplinary actions and medical malpractice claims against individual physicians. Information from the bank is not available to consumers, but is housed in a secure Department of Defense facility in Camarillo, California ("Data Bank, Heal Thyself" 1991). Such security precautions are ironic, since information on cases filed is available in every county courthouse in the nation. The reason for maintaining a data bank is to reduce the cost of information. It is certainly possible to improve procedures for gathering and analyzing such information, but the principle itself is sound.

Third, I identified certain areas where the market has failed to provide insurance—long-term care insurance and acute-care coverage for 15 percent of Americans currently uninsured. These are areas where the government might directly provide or subsidize coverage. Such a policy has two justifications. First, to the extent that lack of coverage now reflects impediments on the supply side—including high nondiversifiable risk of providing certain types of coverage and/or a high load for providing insurance to individuals or employees of small firms or in the presence of adverse selection—no market will evolve even if the uncovered persons would have been willing to pay considerable amounts for such insurance. This set of reasons provides a rationale for public provision of coverage. Second, other persons may prefer that the uninsured be covered because the former underwrite the cost of such care. This consideration provides a reason for subsidization. Weighing in against such government involvement is the possibility that the uncovered would not demand such insurance even if they were fully informed (Pauly 1990).

Fourth, although governments are involved in support of private insurance via the tax subsidy, much more important are the programs it operates itself. No matter what is said in scholarly debates, as a practical matter, public provision of insurance is here to stay. This is not all bad, and, in fact, is probably good.

Although public organizations are relatively good at redistributing resources, they are said by some to be inefficient, uninnovative, and unresponsive to consumer wants. On at least the first two dimensions, the major public insurers have performed at least as well as their private counterparts and probably better. On the innovation front, Medicare implemented the Prospective Payment System (PPS), has promoted capitation plans, has released hospital-specific information on mortality, and is experimenting with competitive bidding. Medicaid has actively engaged in selective contracting in California (Zwanziger and Melnick 1988). Many of these innovations have not only benefited these programs but have had beneficial effects system-wide.

Public provision of insurance is potentially consistent with the use of private market mechanisms. A case in point is private contracting/competitive bidding. Unless facilities are to be government-owned and physicians and other health care personnel are to be government employees, prices must be established. In the past, public payers reimbursed providers on the basis of retrospective costs or charges. During the past decade, there has been a shift to administered prices. In one important sense, the shift represents an improvement. With prices fixed, inefficiency in production is not rewarded.

But a major problem remains. There is no guarantee that the price be set at a level that just covers the underlying cost of an efficiently produced outcome of adequate quality. PPS bases hospital prices on historical charges stepped down to cost. Medicare's new pricing system for physicians has a Resource Based Relative Value Scale that was rigorously developed on the basis of expert physician opinion (Hsiao, Braun, Dunn, et al. 1988; and Hsiao, Braun, Yntema, and Becker 1988). We cannot be sure that a market unencumbered by imperfections, such as consumer ignorance and overinsurance in some parts, would have generated similar price schedules. For one thing, the physician pricing system was developed to be budget neutral, with prices for so-called cognitive services rising and prices for many surgical services falling in absolute value. It is doubtful that a "perfect" market would have produced this result. Administered prices tend to be rigid in the downward direction. Providers tell the government when price is too low, but not when, as a result of a technological advance or a drop in an input price, the price is too high.

In general, markets do a better job of ferreting out the true cost of production. In this context, however, existing price structures may be distorted by consumer ignorance and insurance. Also, any pricing system must cope with heterogeneity of patients and the risk of quality degradation. A serious impediment to reliance on market-determined prices, such as would be forthcoming if government used various competitive bidding approaches, is the principle that every insured person be guaranteed full freedom of choice of health care provider without bearing any financial consequences of selecting the "gold-plated" alternative. If a producer faces no loss of business, why should it submit a low bid?

Important questions remain about the potential of competitive bidding/negotiation approaches in health care (Hoerger and Waters 1991). Empirical evidence on the subject accumulated to date is meager. First of all, the extent to which such market-driven prices would fall below the administered ones is not known. Also, the winners might let quality deteriorate after they have won the contract and/or reject disproportionate and unacceptable numbers of expensive-to-treat people. The proof of the pudding is ultimately in empirical evidence on these approaches. Anecdotal arguments should not foreclose securing such evidence. It should be possible to reduce the threat of quality degradation by ensuring that the provider has other patients than those covered by the contract with the payer. This is a valid reason, for example, against nursing homes with all Medicaid residents and, more broadly, a reason to reject a single-payer financing system. Providers' desire to treat more profitable private patients under a multipayer system may lead to a general upgrading of quality of service and responsiveness to patient references. To combat selective acceptance of the payer's insureds, one can include a take-all-comer provision in the contract or prespecify the terms at which the contractor can opt out.

CONCLUSION

Finally, if we are not to rely on market incentives to achieve the desired outcomes, what are the alternatives? One is public provision of personal health care services, such as in the United Kingdom, but this is highly unlikely in this country. Another is a mixed public-private financing system with reliance on capacity and expenditure ceilings, causing resources to be allocated on a nonprice basis. The latter alternative is a much more realistic possibility. A third is a return to the professional model briefly described earlier; this alternative is even less likely than direct public provision.

Although proponents of caps emphasize the failings of markets, both theory and empirical evidence make me pessimistic about the potential of caps. This country's major attempt to limit capacity, certificate-of-need legislation enacted by the states, was a failure when judged on its own terms—cost containment as opposed to improved allocation of resources (Sloan 1988). All-payer setting of hospital prices/revenues achieved at most the savings attributable to Medicare's PPS (Robinson and Luft 1988; Sloan et al. 1988a). Even supporters of price controls point to their shortcomings in cost containment as implemented in the United States under the Nixon administration's Economic Stabilization Program (Holahan and Scanlon 1978), not to mention the allocative distortions such controls would have produced had they been retained for long. Further, removing the market's major equilibrating instrument, price, does not eliminate underlying market forces. Rather, administered prices with reliance on capacity and expenditure limitations is just an invitation for jury-rigged regulations on entry, utilization, technology adoption, and the like.

Perhaps, the context for successful controls was wrong in the United States. But, realistically, policymaking must reflect the context in which it operates.

Notes

I wish to thank Professor Thomas Hoerger, of Vanderbilt University, and Willard Manning, of the University of Minnesota, for helpful comments on an earlier version of this paper.

1. See, for example, Dranove (1988a), Feldman and Sloan (1988), Phelps (1986), Reinhardt (1985), and references cited in these articles.

2. If the hospital is a price-taker, it might perform more of the overpriced procedures.

3. See Ellis (1985), Price and Mays (1985), Price (1985), Short and Taylor (1989), and Marquis (1992).

4. For a more extensive discussion of ways that insurers can cope with adverse selection, see Sloan (1992).

5. See, for example, Kolata (1992).

6. See Blumstein, Bovbjerg, and Sloan (1991) and Newhouse (1990).

7. See, for example, Hsiao, Braun, Yntema, and Becker (1988).

8. See Feldman and Sloan (1988) for discussion of this point.

9. See, for example, Bruce (1984).

References

Arrow, Kenneth J. 1963. "Uncertainty and the Welfare Economics of Medical Care." *American Economic Review* 53: 941–73.

Blumstein, James F., and Frank A. Sloan. 1988. "Antitrust and Hospital Peer Review." *Law and Contemporary Problems* 51 (2, Spring): 8–92.

Blumstein, James F., Randall R. Bovbjerg, and Frank A. Sloan. 1991. "Beyond Tort Reform: Developing Better Tools for Assessing Damages for Personal Injuries." *Yale Journal on Regulation* 8 (1, Winter): 149–86.

Bruce, Christopher J. 1984. "The Deterrent Effects of Automobile Insurance and Tort Law: A Survey of the Empirical Evidence." *Law and Policy* 6 (1, January): 67–100.

Chaloupka, Frank. 1991. "Rational Addictive Behavior and Cigarette Smoking." *Journal of Political Economy* 99 (4, August): 722–42.

Coate, Douglas, and Michael Grossman. 1988. "Effects of Alcoholic Beverage Prices and Legal Drinking Ages on Youth Alcohol Use." *Journal of Law and Economics* 31 (1, April): 145–71.

Cook, Philip J. and George Tauchen. 1982. "The Effect of Liquor Taxes on Heavy Drinking." *Bell Journal of Economics* 13 (2, Autumn): 379–90.

Cotter, Kevin D., and Gail A. Jensen. 1989. "Choice of Purchasing Arrangements in Insurance Markets." *Journal of Risk and Uncertainty* 2: 405–14.

Danzon, Patricia M. 1985. *Medical Malpractice: Theory, Evidence, and Public Policy.* Cambridge, Mass: Harvard University Press.

"Data Bank, Heal Thyself." 1991. *Medical Benefits* 8 (19, Oct. 15): 6.

Dranove, David. 1988a. "Demand Inducement and the Physician-Patient Relationship." *Economic Inquiry* 26 (2, April): 281–98.

———. 1988b. "Pricing by Non-Profit Institutions: The Case of Hospital Cost-Shifting." *Journal of Health Economics* 7 (1, March): 47–57.

Ellis, Randall P. 1985. "The Effect of Prior Year Health Expenditures on Health Coverage Plan Choice." In *Advances in Health Economics and Health Services Research*, vol. 6, edited by Richard M. Schleffler and Louis F. Rossiter. Greenwich, Conn.: JAI Press.

Ellis, Randall P., and Thomas G. McGuire. 1990. "Optimal Payment for Health Services." *Journal of Health Economics* 9 (4): 375–96.

Enthoven, Alain C. 1980. *Health Plan: The Only Practical Solution to the Soaring Cost of Medical Care.* Reading, Mass.: Addison-Wesley.

———. 1988. "Managed Competition of Alternative Delivery Systems." In *Competition in the Health Care Sector: Ten Years Later*, edited by Warren Greenberg. Durham, N.C.: Duke University Press.

Feldman, Roger, and Frank A. Sloan. 1988. "Competition among Physicians, Revisited." In *Competition in the Health Care Sector: Ten Years Later*, edited by Warren Greenberg. Durham, N.C.: Duke University Press.

Feldstein, Martin S. 1973. "The Welfare Loss of Excess Health Insurance (Part 2)." *Journal of Political Economy* 81 (1, March/April): 25–80.

Ginsburg, Paul G. 1981. "Altering the Tax Treatment of Employment-Based Health Plans." *Milbank Memorial Fund Quarterly* 59 (2, Spring): 224–55.

Hannan, Edward L., Harold Kilburn, Harvey Bernard, Joseph F. O'Donnell, Gary Lukacik, and Eileen P. Shields. 1991. "Coronary Bypass Surgery: The Relationship between Inhospital Mortality Rate and Surgical Volume after Controlling for Clinical Risk Factors." *Medical Care* 29 (11, November): 1094–1107.

Hansmann, Henry B. 1980, "The Role of Nonprofit Enterprise." *Yale Law Journal* 89 (5, April): 835–901.

Hoerger, Thomas J., and Teresa M. Waters. 1991. "Competitive Bidding for Health Care Services." Paper presented at the 61st annual conference of the Southern Economic Association, Nov. 25, Nashville, Tenn.

Holahan, John, and William Scanlon. 1978. *Price Controls, Physician Fees, and Physician Incomes under Medicare and Medicaid.* Washington, D.C.: Urban Institute.

Hsiao, William C., Peter Braun, Daniel Dunn, Edmund R. Becker, Margaret DeNicola, and Thomas R. Ketcham. 1988. "Special Reports: Results and Policy Implications of the Resource-Based Relative-Value Study." *New England Journal of Medicine* 319 (13, Sept. 29): 881–88.

Hsiao, William C., Peter Braun, Douwe Yntema, and Edmund R. Becker. 1988. "Estimating Physicians' Work for a Resource-Based Relative-Value Scale." *New England Journal of Medicine* 319 (13, Sept. 29): 835–41.

Institute of Medicine. 1986. *For-Profit Enterprise in Health Care,* edited by Bradford Gray. Washington, D.C.: National Academy Press.

Kenkel, Don. 1990. "Consumer Health Information and the Demand for Medical Care." *Review of Economics and Statistics* 72 (4, November): 587–94.

Kolata, Gina. 1992. "New Insurance Practice: Dividing Sick from Well." *New York Times,* March 4: A1, A7.

Long, James, and Frank Scott. 1982. "The Income Tax and Nonwage Compensation." *Review of Economics and Statistics* 64 (2, May): 211–19.

Luft, Harold S. 1981. *Health Maintenance Organizations: Dimensions of Performance.* New York: John Wiley & Sons.

Manning, Willard G., Joseph P. Newhouse, Naihua Duan, Emmett B. Keeler, Arleen Leibowitz, and M. Susan Marquis. 1987. "Health Insurance and the Demand for Medical Care." *American Economic Review* 77 (June): 251–77.

Marquis, M. Susan. 1992. "Adverse Selection with a Multiple Choice among Health Insurance Plans: A Simulation Analysis." *Journal of Health Economics* 11 (August): 129–51.

Marquis, M. Susan, and Martin R. Holmer. 1986. *Choice under Uncertainty and the Demand for Health Insurance.* Report prepared for Health Care Financing Administration. Santa Monica, Calif: RAND Corp.

Marquis, M. Susan, and Jeannette A. Rogowski. 1991. *Participation in Alternative Health Plans: The Role of Financial Incentives in Medicare Beneficiaries' Decisions.* Report for Health Care Financing Administration. Santa Monica, Calif: RAND Corp.

Newhouse, Joseph P. 1990. "Comment on 'Nursing Home Utilization among the High-Risk Elderly' by Alan M. Garber." In *Issues in the Economics of Aging,* edited by David M. Wise. Chicago: University of Chicago Press.

Newhouse, Joseph P., Albert P. Williams, Bruce W. Bennett, and William B. Schwartz. 1982. "Does the Geographical Distribution of Physicians

Reflect Market Failure?" *Bell Journal of Economics* 13 (2, Autumn): 493–505.

Nyman, John A. 1989. "The Private Demand for Nursing Home Care." *Journal of Health Economics* 8 (2, June): 209–31.

Pauly, Mark V. 1968. "The Economics of Moral Hazard." *American Economic Review* 58 (3, June): 531–37.

————. 1978. "Is Medical Care Different?" In *Competition in the Health Care Sector*, edited by Warren Greenburg. Germantown, Md.: Aspen Systems Corp.

————. 1986. "Taxation, Health Insurance, and Market Failure in the Medical Economy." *Journal of Economic Literature* 24 (2, June): 629–75.

————. 1988. "Is Medical Care Different? Old Questions, New Answers." In *Competition in the Health Care Sector: Ten Years Later*, edited by Warren Greenberg. Durham, N.C.: Duke University Press.

————. 1990. "The Rational Nonpurchase of Long-Term Care Insurance." *Journal of Political Economy* 98 (1, February): 153–68.

Phelps, Charles E. 1985. "Large Scale Tax Reform: The Case of Employer-Paid Premiums." Working Paper 20, Applied Economic Workshop. Rochester, N.Y.: University of Rochester.

————. 1986. "Cross-Subsidies and Charge-Shifting in American Hospitals." In *Uncompensated Hospital Care: Rights and Responsibilities*, edited by Frank A. Sloan, James F. Blumstein, and James M. Perrin. Baltimore: Johns Hopkins University Press.

Price, James R. 1985. "Selections and the Competitive Standing of Health Plans in a Multiple-Choice Multiple-Insurer Market." In *Advances in Health Economics and Health Services Research*, vol. 6, edited by Richard M. Scheffler and Louis F. Rossiter. Greenwich, Conn.: JAI Press.

Price, James R., and James W. Mays. 1985. "Biased Selection in the Federal Employees Health Benefits Program." *Inquiry* 22 (Spring): 67–77.

Reinhardt, Uwe E. 1985. "Editorial. The Theory of Physician-Induced Demand: Reflections after a Decade." *Journal of Health Economics* 4 (2, June): 187–93.

Relman, Arnold S. 1991. "Shattuck Lecture—The Health Care Industry: Where Is It Taking Us?" *New England Journal of Medicine* 325 (12, Sept. 19): 854–59.

Robinson, James C., and Harold S. Luft. 1988. "Competition, Regulation, and Hospital Costs, 1982 to 1986." *Journal of the American Medical Association* 260 (18, November): 2676–81.

Schroeder, Steven A., and Joel C. Cantor. 1991. "On Squeezing Balloons: Cost Control Fails Again." *New England Journal of Medicine* 325 (15, Oct. 10): 1099–1100.

Short, Pamela Farley, and Amy K. Taylor. 1989. "Premiums, Benefits, and Employee Choice of Health Insurance Options." *Journal of Health Economics* 8 (4, December): 293–311.

Siu, Albert L., Frank A. Sonnenberg, Willard G. Manning, George A. Gold-berg, Ellyn S. Bloomfield, Joseph P. Newhouse, and Robert H. Brook. 1986. "Inappropriate Use of Hospitals in a Randomized Trial of Health Insurance Plans." *New England Journal of Medicine* 15 (20, November): 1259–66.

Sloan, Frank A. 1974. "A Microanalysis of Physicians' Hours of Work Decisions." In *The Economics of Health and Medical Care*, edited by Mark Perlman. London and Basingstoke, England: MacMillian Press.

————. 1988. "Containing Health Expenditures: Lessons Learned from Certificate-of-Need Programs." In *Cost, Quality, and Access in Health Care: New Roles for Health Planning in a Competitive Environment*, edited by Frank A. Sloan, James F. Blumstein, and James F. Perrin. San Francisco: Jossey-Bass Publishers.

————. 1992. "Adverse Selection: Does It Preclude a Competitive Health Insurance Market?" *Journal of Health Economics* 11 (October): 353–56.

Sloan, Frank A., and Killard Adamache. 1985. "Fringe Benefits: To Tax or Not To Tax?" *National Tax Journal* 38 (1, March): 47–64.

Sloan, Frank A., and Penny B. Githens. 1992. "Drinking, Driving, and the Price of Automobile Insurance." Photocopy.

Sloan, Frank A., Jerry Cromwell, and Janet B. Mitchell. 1978. *Private Physicians and Public Programs*. Lexington, Mass.: D.C. Heath and Co.

Sloan, Frank A., Michael A. Morrisey, and Joseph Valvona. 1988a. "Effects of the Medicare Prospective Payment System on Hospital Cost Containment: An Early Appraisal." *Milbank Quarterly* 66 (2): 191–220.

————. 1988b. "Hospital Care for the 'Self-Pay' Patient." *Journal of Health Politics, Policy, and Law* 13 (1, Spring): 83–102.

Sloan, Frank A., Randall R. Bovbjerg, Paula M. Mergenhagen, and W. Bradley Burfield. 1989. "Medical Malpractice Experience of Physicians: Predictable or Haphazard?" *Journal of the American Medical Association* 262 (23, December 15): 3291–97.

Taylor, Amy, and Gail R. Wilensky. 1983. "The Effect of Tax Policies on Expenditures for Private Health Insurance." In *Market Reforms in Health Care* edited by Jack Meyer. Washington, D.C.: American Enterprise Institute.

Wedig, Gerard, Frank A. Sloan. Mahmud Hassan, and Michael A. Morrisey. 1988. "Capital Structure, Ownership, and Capital Payment Policy: The Case of Hospitals." *Journal of Finance* 43 (1, March): 21–40.

Woodbury, Steven. 1983. "Substitution between Wage and Nonwage Benefits." *American Economic Review* 73 (1, March): 166–82.

Zwanziger, Jack, and Glenn A. Melnick. 1988. "The Effects of Hospital Competition and the Medicare PPS Program on Hospital Cost Behavior in California." *Journal of Health Economics* 7 (4, December): 301–20.

Chapter Thirteen

IS CANADA REALLY DIFFERENT? A COMPARISON OF HEALTH CARE SPENDING IN SELECTED U.S. STATES AND CANADIAN PROVINCES

Kenneth E. Thorpe

Growth in health care spending is a continuing concern among public and private payers. During the 1980s, health care spending increased at an average (nominal) annual rate of 10 percent. During the same time period, the U.S. gross national product (GNP) increased 6.8 percent. Many view the growing share of health care as a percentage of GNP as evidence of our inability to control growth in health care spending. This concern has escalated with the recent sluggish expansion in the U.S. economy.

International comparisons are also cited to show that, relative to other countries, the United States has been unable to control growth in health spending. For instance, health spending relative to GNP has increased at a slower pace in both Canada and Germany relative to that in the United States (for data on Canada and United States, see figure 13.1). Between 1975 and 1987, health consumed an additional 1.6 percentage points of total GNP in Canada, 0.6 percentage points in Germany, and 2.5 percentage points in the United States (Schieber, Poullier, and Greenwald 1992). According to some, the inability of the United States to maintain a constant ratio of health to GNP results from its reliance on multiple sources of health insurance, high administrative costs, and relatively high payments to providers.

Some observers doubt that, within our current multiple-payer system, the United States can successfully control the growth in health care spending. In contrast, the monopsony purchasing/negotiating power, single-payer approach of the Canadian and German health care systems is often credited for, and seen as a requirement to, controlling the growth in health care spending. This apparently lower rate of cost growth is achieved in Canada without measurable reductions in the quality of medical care delivered to citizens.

Previous international studies that have examined the growth in health spending have focused on the national experience (i.e., they examine Canadian and U.S. averages). These analyses overlook, how-

Figure 13.1 HEALTH SPENDING AS PERCENTAGE OF GNP, CANADA AND
UNITED STATES, 1970–87

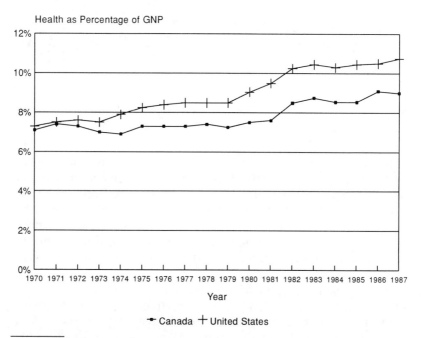

Sources: Health Care Financing Administration, Washington, D.C. and Health and
Welfare, Canada, 1991.

ever, the substantial variation in cost-growth experience within each
jurisdiction. (See, for example, Schieber, Poullier, and Greenwald
1992; and Schieber and Poullier 1989.) For instance, a number of
U.S. states have adopted innovative regulatory and competitive
approaches to adress the growth in health care spending.

This chapter examines the cost-containment record of the Canadian
health care system relative to that of the United States. I specifically
address four groups of questions, as follows.

1. When adjusting for inflation and population growth, how different is the experience in Canada and the United States? How do
   the experiences of these countries compare to those of the
   United Kingdom and Germany?
2. Where different rates of growth are evident, are they limited to
   certain types of spending, or do they persist across all categories?

3. How do experimental payment systems, both competitive and regulatory, within the United States compare to payment approaches used in Canada? In addition, do the Canadian provinces experience the same degree of variation in cost growth as observed in the United States?
4. How does the experience of public and private payers compare to the experience among the Canadian provinces?

INTERNATIONAL COMPARISONS: UNITED STATES, CANADA, GERMANY, AND UNITED KINGDOM

Most international comparisons of health care spending examine the ratio of health spending to gross national product. Another approach is to examine real per capita growth in spending. Measurement issues are important in this case, as the analysis of comparative spending trends yields different results. For instance, Barer, Welch and Antioch (1991: 230) have noted that:

> In the long run, rising real GNP per capita increases real wages in the health care sector, causing health care costs per capita to rise. In judging the comparative international performance of one sector of the economy, such as health care, it is inappropriate to use a measure that is heavily influenced by the comparative performance of entire economies.

These conclusions, however, are not supported by the simple example. In a competitive market, with no growth in total factor productivity in health care, the relative price of health care will rise at the economywide rate of increase in productivity, and deflating by GNP is likely appropriate. However, substantial changes in productivity have occurred in the health care sector (e.g., cataract and ambulatory surgery). Thus, if total factor productivity also rises in the health care sector (say, by 10 percent) along with the rest of the economy, prices in the health care sector would not rise; relative prices would remain constant except that 10 percent more would be produced. In this case, examining the health sector by itself would be appropriate.[1] I present results using both approaches in the following section.

Focusing on the relative growth in health spending among the United States, the United Kingdom, Canada, and Germany yields some interesting observations. When controlling for changes in population and the growth in health and medical prices,[2] the United States

Figure 13.2 REAL PER CAPITA GROWTH IN HEALTH CARE, 1970–87

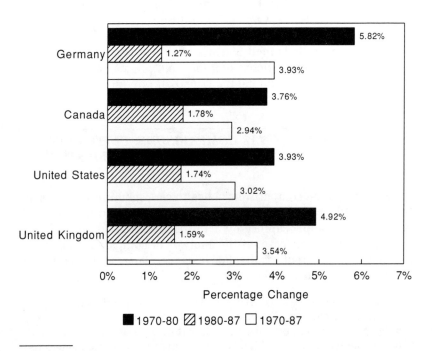

Sources: Health Care Financing Administration, Washington, D.C. and Health and Welfare, Canada, 1991.

had a lower annual average rate of per capita health growth than either the United Kingdom or Germany between 1970 and 1987 (see figure 13.2). During this time period, health spending in constant dollars per capita increased 3.02 percent in the United States, 2.94 percent in Canada, 3.93 percent in Germany, and 3.54 percent in the United Kingdom. These relative rankings change when using more recent data (1980–87). In particular, the health spending in constant dollars per capita is *lower* in the United States (1.74 percent) than in Canada (1.78 percent), but is higher than either Germany or the United Kingdom. These data provide a substantially different picture of the cost-containment performance of these countries than that suggested when health spending is indexed by GNP. Although real per capita health spending has increased at similar rates between the United States and Canada, real per capita GNP has increased 0.4

Table 13.1 AVERAGE ANNUAL RATE OF REAL PER CAPITA HEALTH CARE
GROWTH, CANADA AND UNITED STATES, 1970–87

	Canada (%)		United States (%)	
	1970–80	1980–87	1970–80	1980–87
Per capita total spending	3.8	1.8	3.9	1.7
GNP per capita	3.2	2.1	2.4	1.7
Inpatient care per capita	3.9	0.8	5.2	1.1
Ambulatory spending per capita	3.6	2.3	3.8	3.8
Pharmaceutical spending per capita	1.6	5.5	0.4	0.2

Sources: *Health Care Financing Review*, 1989 Annual Supplement, 111–94; Health
Insurance Association of America, 1990, "Canadian Health Care: The Implications of
Public Health Insurance," table 2 (Washington, DC: Edward Neuschler).

percentage points faster in Canada than in the United States (see
Table 13.1).[3]

Constant per capita health spending during the past several years
is actually lower in the United States than in Canada. Much of the
different rate of growth between the United States and Canada can
be traced to lower real per capita growth in pharmaceutical spending
in the former. Between 1980 and 1987, such spending increased at
an average annual rate of 0.2 percent in the United States compared
to 5.5 percent in Canada (see table 13.1).[4] Real per capita spending
on inpatient care grew 0.3 percentage points less in Canada than in
the United States during the 1980s. This is, however, substantially
less than the 1.3 percent annual difference between the United States
and Canada in the growth in inpatient spending observed during
the 1970s. Growth in ambulatory care spending per capita has been
substantially higher in the United States relative to Canada during the
1980s. The difference in annual growth rate in ambulatory spending
between Canada and the United States was 1.5 percent during this
period (see table 13.1).

As displayed in table 13.2, constant dollar per capita growth in
health spending decreased in the United States during the 1980s.
Three possible explanations account for this decrease. The first was
the advent of state all-payer rate-setting programs and selective con-

Table 13.2 AVERAGE ANNUAL REAL PER CAPITA GROWTH IN HEALTH
SPENDING, BY TYPE OF PAYER, UNITED STATES, 1970–87

Source of Insurance	1970–80 (%)	1980–87 (%)
Medicare per enrollee	6.0	2.4
Medicaid per recipient	3.9	1.2
Private insurance per covered life	5.9	4.1
Out-of-pocket spending per uninsured	N.A.[a]	−3.0

Sources: "National Health Expenditures, 1989." Health Care Financing Review, 1990,
Winter, 1–26; and U.S. Bureau of the Census, Current Population Survey.
a. N.A., not available.

tracting in California. Second, Medicare introduced its Prospective
Payment System (PPS) during the early 1980s. Third, private payers
increased the scope of managed-care efforts. The following is a cursory examination of the comparative effects of these interventions.[5]

Relative to the 1970s, constant dollar per capita spending decreased
among all third-party payers in the United States between 1980 and
1987 (see table 13.2) Out-of-pocket spending per uninsured person
decreased at an average annual rate of 3 percent.[6] The most impressive reduction occurred within the Medicare program. During the
1970s, constant dollar growth in per beneficiary spending increased
6 percent, higher than increases observed among private insurers or
Medicaid. During the 1980s, however, annual growth in the Medicare
program fell substantially, increasing at an average annual rate of
2.4 percent (see table 13.2). A number of published reports have
documented the cost-containing impact of Medicare's PPS during
the mid- to late 1980s. (See, for example, Coulam and Gaumer 1991;
and Feder, Hadley, and Zuckerman 1987). The role of the PPS relative
to other factors accounting for the decrease in real growth is not
clear, however.

The growth in spending among private insurers also fell, although
the difference during the 1980–87 time period was not as pronounced
as was the reduction in Medicare spending. This reduced rate of
growth coincided with the widespread adoption of managed care
and increased use of copayments by health plans and employers.
The relative contribution of these approaches to addressing moral
hazard cannot, however, be determined by these data.

HOW DO STATE PAYMENT EXPERIMENTS IN THE UNITED STATES COMPARE WITH THOSE IN CANADA?

This section examines variations in health spending within the United States and Canada to compare the effectiveness of state experiments in controlling costs with those found in Canada. The Canadian system has been widely touted for its ability to control the growth in health spending.[7] Their success is apparently vested in centralized control exerted by the Canadian provinces with respect to negotiating hospital spending (i.e., setting budgets), and the coordinated system of fee negotiation with physicians. Implicit in these comparisons is the notion that a single health plan acting as a monopsony purchaser is better positioned to control aggregate spending than a system with multiple health plans. As noted earlier, the faster growth in health spending as a percentage of GNP in the United States relative to that in Canada or Germany is often used as evidence to support this view. What these studies overlook (in addition to the GNP indexing issue) is the enormous diversity in cost growth within the United States. This diversity can be attributed partially to the adoption of state rate-setting programs, as well as selective contracting adopted by a handful of U.S. jurisdictions. At issue is whether these competitive and regulatory efforts within our current pluralistic insurance system can achieve results (i.e., growth in health spending) similar to those found under the Canadian single-payer system. Some preliminary comparisons are presented next.

During the 1970s and 1980s, four states, New York, New Jersey, Massachusetts, and Maryland, introduced all-payer hospital rate-setting programs. In general, these efforts were also accompanied by relatively rigorous certificate of need (CON) laws, tight Medicaid payments for physicians, and in some cases, utilization review (UR).[8] In addition, the state of California developed its selective contracting program during the 1980s, an approach that has since altered dramatically the nature of the health insurance marketplace in that state. Both of these efforts (rate setting and selective contracting) retained multiple sources of health insurance and health plans within each state. The key difference was the degree of government restructuring or new control over the contracting rules between payers and providers. In both cases, state governments (or in some cases, commissions) expanded their powers, therefore assuming a central role in shaping the delivery systems in their respective states. In the case of California, the state acted as a catalyst to alter the relative bargaining powers of public and private health plans and providers. The all-payer states assumed a direct role by coordinating payment rates across all payers.

In addition to the state efforts just mentioned, the market share of alternative competitive delivery systems increased dramatically in some states. For comparative purposes, I examine two such states, Minnesota and Wisconsin, and two time periods: 1976 through 1982 and 1980 through 1990 (I only have data through 1987 for the Canadian provinces).

As noted earlier, constant dollar per capita cost growth was slightly lower in Canada than in the United States during the mid-1970s and early 1980s. This comparison masks considerable diversity in experience within both countries, however. During this first time period, the most successful state and provincial cost-containment records were posted by New York State and Ontario, respectively.[9] Between 1976 and 1982, constant dollar per capita health spending (all personal health spending) increased 3.1 percent in New York and 4.1 percent in the United States nationwide (see table 13.3). Only Ontario experienced a similar annual growth rate (3.0 percent) during this same time period; no other province in Canada experienced a growth rate as low as that in New York State. Indeed, with the exception of Maryland, each of the all-payer rate-setting states posted lower rates of growth than the average Canadian province during this time period.

The experience among the Canadian provinces differed widely in the late 1970s. Constant dollar per capita growth ranged from a high of 7 percent in the territories to 3 percent in Ontario. Many provinces experienced higher constant dollar rates of growth in spending than either the rate-setting states or the "competitive" states in the United States.[10]

Cost growth during the 1980s in the most aggressive U.S. states relative to the Canadian provinces revealed similar results. Again, constant dollar per capita cost growth was lowest in New York State (3.9 percent, tied with that in Wisconsin, table 13.3). This rate of growth was substantially lower than that found in Ontario (5.9 percent) and was lower than every province except British Columbia, Prince Edward Island, and Newfoundland. Constant dollar cost growth within each of the all-payer rate-setting states was lower than the national average in Canada during the 1980s. With the exception of Wisconsin, the more competitive approaches provided mixed results. Constant dollar growth in California increased 4.8 percent, slightly higher than that observed in Canada, although lower than many of the Canadian provinces. Interestingly, constant dollar cost

Table 13.3 AVERAGE ANNUAL RATE OF REAL PER CAPITA GROWTH IN HEALTH CARE SPENDING, SELECTED U.S. STATES AND CANADIAN PROVINCES

States with Rate Setting	Years (%)		Provinces with Rate Setting	Years (%)	
	1976–82	1980–90		1976–82	1980–87
New York	3.1	3.9	Newfoundland	6.0	3.7
Maryland	4.2	4.3	Prince Edward Island	3.4	1.3
Massachusetts	3.8	4.4	Nova Scotia	4.7	6.5
New Jersey	3.3	4.6	New Brunswick	7.3	5.0
			Quebec	4.2	4.1
			Ontario	3.0	5.9
Competitive states:			Manitoba	3.7	4.5
California	3.9	4.8	Saskatchewan	4.4	5.6
Wisconsin	3.9	3.9	Alberta	3.3	4.1
Minnesota	4.3	*	British Columbia	4.7	2.6
			Territories	7.0	7.3
Border states:			Total Canada	3.9	4.7
Washington	3.9	6.0			
Montana	4.2	4.6			
Idaho	3.1	4.8			
Michigan	4.1	4.4			
Total United States	4.1	5.2			

Sources: Health Care Financing Administration, Washington, D.C.; and Health and Welfare, Canada, 1991. *National Health Expenditures in Canada, 1975–87*. Ottawa.
Note: Data are deflated by each country's implicit GNP price deflator.

Table 13.4 AVERAGE ANNUAL PERCENTAGE INCREASE IN REAL PER CAPITA
HOSPITAL AND PHYSICIAN SPENDING, SELECTED U.S. STATES
AND CANADIAN PROVINCES, 1976–82

States/Provinces with Rate Setting	Percentage Change in Hospital Care	Percentage Change in Physicians' Services
New York	2.0	4.9
Maryland	4.5	3.9
Massachusetts	3.9	3.9
New Jersey	3.3	3.0
Competitive States:		
California	5.2	4.7
Wisconsin	3.9	4.5
Minnesota	3.7	4.2
Total United States	5.4	5.6
Newfoundland	4.6	3.1
Prince Edward Island	3.2	3.4
Nova Scotia	3.7	2.8
New Brunswick	5.1	6.0
Quebec	3.8	1.2
Ontario	2.0	3.2
Manitoba	2.6	3.6
Saskatchewan	2.9	4.1
Alberta	3.0	4.0
British Columbia	3.7	4.9
Territories	7.2	5.6
Total Canada	3.1	3.3

growth in Washington (a border state) was substantially higher than that of its neighbor to the north, British Columbia, during the 1980s. Factors accounting for the relatively high (by U.S. standards) growth in health spending in the state of Washington are not immediately clear.

As expected, the impressive experience of the all-payer states relative to the Canadian provinces is primarily the result of lower growth in hospital spending. Between 1976 and 1982 (the only dates where comparative spending by sector exists), constant dollar hospital spending increased at the same rate in both Ontario and New York State (2 percent, see table 13.4). Hospital growth among the other rate-setting states was also lower than the U.S. average, although except for New York, each was slightly above the Canadian average. Since selective contracting was not adopted in California until 1982, the data in table 13.4 do not provide a true picture of the ability of selective contracting to control hospital spending relative to the budget-based systems in California.

CONCLUSION AND OBSERVATIONS

My preliminary analysis comparing the cost-containment experience within selected U.S. jurisdictions and Canadian provinces yields some interesting insights. In particular, within the United States, state all-payer rate setting generates similar, and in some cases lower, rates of constant dollar per capita growth in health care spending than the Canadian single-payer system. Competitive approaches, such as those developed by California, also seem to achieve similar, although slightly higher, rates of aggregate growth in spending relative to the all-payer states. Although these approaches seem effective in controlling the growth in spending, the results indicate that a single health plan/payer is not a prerequisite to generating "lower" growth in health spending. The analysis suggests, however, that government must assist in restructuring the contracting rules between health plans and providers, and, furthermore, that these restructured rules could include coordinated rates of payment across health plans or creation of a forum for competitive interactions among health plans and providers. Finally, the results indicate that national proposals addressing the issue of cost growth based either on the Canadian single-payer system or on those retaining private insurance with a quasi-public agency coordinating rates of payment across health plans, and encouraging competitive delivery systems, may generate similar rates of future health spending.

Notes

1. See Abramowitz and David (1973: 431). I also thank Joseph P. Newhouse for pointing out the nature of these arguments.

2. I use the medical care and health services price index specific to each country to calculate real per capita spending growth. See *Health Care Financing Review*, 1989 Annual Supplement, table 13.

3. The difference in annual growth is calculated as $d = (1 + $ percentage change in Canada)$/(1 + $ percentage change in United States$) - 1$.

4. It is not clear, however, how much of these large observed differences may reflect variations in how such spending is categorized and defined within Canada and the United States.

5. A more rigorous econometric test may yield different results, although a simple regression of real per capita spending on a time trend, and dummy variables for Canada and the United States, did not provide any additional insights.

6. This is not to suggest, however, that all out-of-pocket spending is traced to the uninsured. A substantial portion of such spending results from out-of-pocket spending among those with health insurance for (noncovered) long-term care services, spending among the insured for noncovered services, and so on.

7. See, for example, Evans et al. (1989).

8. The correlation between rigorous CON laws and the existence of state rate-setting programs have made empirical efforts to understand the separate contributions of the interventions on reducing cost growth difficult, if not impossible.

9. This analysis does not, however, discuss any dysfunctional or unintended effects of cost-containment efforts in either country.

10. The constant dollar figures for Canada and the United States differ from earlier tables. Here I used the implicit price deflators to adjust current dollars, and previously I used medical- and health-sector-specific indicators. My preliminary calculations for earlier years indicate that the results outlined next are not sensitive to this choice.

References

Abramowitz, Moses, and Paul David. 1973. "Reinterpreting Economic Growth: Parables and Realities." *American Economic Review* 63 (May): 428–39.

Barer, Morris, W. Pete Welch, and Laurie Antioch. 1991. "Canadian/U.S. Health Care: Reflections on the HIAA's Analysis." *Health Affairs* (Fall): 229–36.

Coulam, Robert F., and Gary L. Gaumer. 1991. "Medicare's Prospective Payment System: A Critical Appraisal." *Health Care Financing Review, 1991 Annual Supplement*: 45–77.

Evans, Robert G., Jonathan Lomas, Morris Barer, et al. 1989. "Controlling Health Expenditures—The Canadian Reality." *New England Journal of Medicine* 320 (9): 571–77.

Feder, J., J. Hadley, and S. Zuckerman. 1987. "How Did Medicare's Prospective Payment System Affect Hospitals?" *New England Journal of Medicine* 317 (14): 867–73.

Health Care Financing Review. 1989. *1989 Annual Supplement*, table 13. Author.

Schieber, G., and J. P. Poullier. 1989. "International Health Care Expenditure Trends: 1987." *Health Affairs* (Fall): 169–77.

Schieber, G., J. P. Poullier, and Greenwald. 1992. "U.S. Health Expenditure Performance: An International Comparison and Data Update." *Health Care Financing Review* 13 (4): 1–87.

Chapter Fourteen

THE POLITICAL ECONOMY OF HEALTH CARE REFORM IN THE UNITED KINGDOM

John Posnett

In January 1989 the British government published plans for the most radical reform of the National Health Service (NHS) since its inception in 1948. These plans, embodied in the White Paper "Working for Patients" (Her Majesty's Stationery Office 1989), represented the outcome of a review of health service finance instituted by Prime Minister Margaret Thatcher in 1988 in response to persistent criticism of cash shortages and underfunding in the NHS.

Despite the initial emphasis on finance, most of the proposals in the White Paper relate to the structure of health care provision in the United Kingdom. It is no secret that the prime minister favored proposals designed to reduce the burden of the NHS on the exchequer by encouraging greater reliance on health insurance in place of direct public expenditure financed by taxation. Partly as a result of experience from elsewhere, most notably the United States, this proposal was quickly dismissed on the grounds that any substantial expansion of insurance would carry with it the risks of nonprice competition and cost escalation.

What remained was a void, and the political process abhors a void. The review was thus extended to include new proposals to reform the system of health care delivery. The proposals outlined in the White Paper owe as much to a political imperative to reform as to a careful analysis of the relative merits of alternative means of provision. Under the circumstances, the White Paper is a remarkably coherent and plausible document.

The reforms referred to in this paper were implemented by the NHS and Community Care Act of 1990 and became operational in April 1991.

BACKGROUND OF REFORM

Underfunding in the NHS

Between 1979 and 1988, government spending on the NHS increased from £10 billion to £26.5 billion ($15 to $40 billion), an 18 percent increase in real expenditure per capita. At the same time, the number of hospital beds fell by 16 percent, from 446,000 (8.2 per 1,000 population) to 374,000 (6.7 per 1,000), while hospital deaths and discharges increased by almost 22 percent, from 86.2 to 105.7 per 1,000. Despite these increases in real funding and levels of activity, criticism of NHS underfunding has continued to rise. The public's perception of the NHS is based in part on visible and politically sensitive indicators such as waiting lists; between 1981 and 1988 the total number of patients waiting for treatment increased by almost 10 percent, from 728,000 to 798,000. In some regions, particularly in the South East and East Anglia, the increase was even greater. In the North East Thames region, for example, waiting lists increased by 61 percent in this period. Although waiting times (rather than numbers waiting) is a better indicator for policy purposes, the persistence of the problem has been a major underlying cause of discontent.

The funding debate has also been fueled by international comparisons of health care expenditure showing the United Kingdom near the bottom relative to other countries of the Organization for Economic Cooperation and Development (OECD). Table 14.1 shows per capita health expenditures in U.S. dollars and as a percentage of gross domestic product (GDP) for OECD countries in 1987. In the United Kingdom, total health spending represented 6.1 percent of GDP ($758 per capita) compared to 11.2 percent of GDP ($2,051 per capita) in the United States and a mean of 7.3 percent of GDP ($934 per capita) for the OECD overall.

An empirical relationship between per capita health spending and GDP is well established in the literature, with an estimated elasticity of expenditure at or around unity (Leu 1986; Newhouse 1977; Parkin, McGuire, and Yule 1987). However it seems clear that even allowing for differences in GDP, health spending in the United Kingdom is relatively low. A recent study based on a large sample of pooled time-series and cross-section data for 20 OECD countries over 28 years (Hitiris and Posnett 1992) confirms the importance of GDP as a determinant of per capita health spending, but also indicates that the relationship is not homogeneous. In particular, the introduction of country-specific shift dummies into the expenditure equation suggests that the 20 countries in the sample fall into three broad groups: a group of five countries (Australia, Finland, France, Italy, and the United States), for which the shift dummy is found to be statistically significant and positive, suggesting that in these countries health expenditure is higher than would be expected from GDP alone; a further 14 countries for which the shift dummy is not significant; and 1 country (the United Kingdom) for which the dummy variable

Table 14.1 TOTAL HEALTH EXPENDITURE OF OECD COUNTRIES, 1987

	Dollars per Capita	Percentage of GDP[a]		Dollars per Capita	Percentage of GDP[a]
United States	2,051	11.2	Australia	939	7.1
Canada	1,483	8.6	Japan	915	6.8
Iceland	1,241	7.8	Belgium	879	7.2
Sweden	1,233	9.0	Italy	841	6.9
Switzerland	1,225	7.7	Denmark	792	6.0
Norway	1,149	7.5	United Kingdom	758	6.1
France	1,105	8.6	New Zealand	733	6.9
Germany	1,093	8.2	Ireland	561	7.4
Luxembourg	1,051	7.5	Spain	521	6.0
Netherlands	1,041	8.5	Portugal	386	6.4
Austria	982	8.4	Greece	337	5.3
Finland	949	7.4	Turkey	148	3.5
OECD[b] mean				934	7.3

Source: Schieber and Poullier (1990: tables 1, 3).

a. GDP, gross domestic product.
b. OECD, Organization for Economic Cooperation and Development

is significant and negative. A similar result was reported by Leu (1986), who suggested that the presence of a centralized health system in the United Kingdom and New Zealand reduces per capita spending by 20–25 percent for a given level of GDP.

This sort of evidence cannot be used to support the claim that the National Health Service is underfunded, if only because the link between health expenditure and improvements in health status is still a matter of conjecture. Conventional (political) wisdom asserts that the lower levels of health spending in the United Kingdom are not associated with inferior health outcomes—and it is certainly true that crude indicators such as infant mortality rates or life expectancy do not appear to differ in any systematic way from OECD norms. Nonetheless, for each of the three main causes of death in the United Kingdom—diseases of the circulatory system, malignant neoplasms, and diseases of the respiratory system—the age-standardized mortality rate in the United Kingdom is higher than the mean of all OECD countries (table 14.2). The overall age-standardized mortality rate is also higher in the United Kingdom: 915.8 per 100,000 compared with an OECD mean of 855.4. Hitiris and Posnett (1992) found weak evidence of a significant positive relationship between crude mortality rates and GDP per capita, and a significant negative relationship between mortality rates and health spending after allowing for differences in the age structure of the population. Nonetheless, the elasticity of mortality with respect to health spending is low: less than 0.1 in absolute value. It is also interesting to note that a country-specific shift dummy for the United Kingdom in the mortality equation proved to be positive and significant, suggesting that mortality is higher in the United Kingdom even after the effects of income, health spending, and demographic factors are taken into account.

Although it may be suggestive, none of this proves that the NHS is underfunded. The evidence weakly supports the proposition that the marginal product of health care is positive, but without further evidence on the marginal cost of health spending, it is impossible to say whether the level of funding in the United Kingdom is too low, any more than it is possible to say that the level of funding in the United States is too high. Ultimately, the correct level of funding of the NHS is a political question that hinges on the willingness of taxpayer-voters to devote more resources to health at the expense of higher taxation and/or lower spending on other public services.

The Reform Proposals

The pre-reform NHS is financed from general taxation (82.6 percent), National Insurance contributions (14.6 percent), and patient charges

Table 14.2 AGE-STANDARDIZED DEATH RATES PER 100,000 (TOTAL POPULATION)

	Year	Diseases of the Circulatory System	Malignant Neoplasms	Diseases of the Respiratory System	All Causes
Australia	1983	414.0	191.5	58.4	820.8
Canada	1984	339.6	199.1	55.3	761.8
Finland	1983	476.5	186.7	69.1	912.9
France	1983	274.7	205.5	51.5	825.4
Germany	1984	423.0	205.2	52.1	877.4
Italy	1981	401.7	197.7	62.7	869.5
Netherlands	1984	341.2	220.9	53.2	784.5
New Zealand	1983	442.3	213.7	104.3	922.5
United Kingdom	1983	435.2	217.6	130.5	915.8
United States	1982	407.0	193.3	53.2	842.4
OECD mean (23 countries)		394.8	197.5	65.8	855.4
Range		261.9	102.6	103.4	355.0
Standard deviation		62.4	25.7	25.5	94.6

Source: Organization for Economic Cooperation and Development (1987, table 15).

(2.8 percent). Funds are allocated from the center to Regional Health Authorities and through them to the smaller and more numerous District Health Authorities (DHAs), whose function is to plan and manage service delivery for their catchment population. One of the responsibilities of the DHA is to manage NHS hospitals and community facilities within the geographical boundaries of the Authority.

The reforms contain no proposals to change the basic financial structure of the NHS. What will change, however, is the structure of health care supply. The NHS and Community Care Act (1990) contains provisions designed to create a quasi-market in the NHS in which the functions of purchasing and providing health care are to be separated, and in which the relationship between purchasers and providers is mediated by a system of contracts. The new structure of the NHS is heavily influenced by Alain Enthoven's critique of the United Kingdom's health care system (Enthoven 1985), and by other features of the U.S. health market—notably, health maintenance organizations (HMOs) and the process of selective (or competitive) contracting introduced into the Medicaid system in a number of states.

The key elements underpinning the creation of a quasi-market in the NHS are the separation of the roles of purchasers and providers, the introduction of budget-holding GP (general practitioner) practices, and the establishment of self-governing NHS trusts.

Purchasers and Providers

In the pre-reform NHS the functions of purchasing and providing health services were effectively combined in the District Health Authority. The most significant impact of the reforms will be a move away from this vertical integration of roles, and the substitution of a set of contracts between hospital suppliers and the DHA (as purchaser) in place of direct management control. The primary function of the DHA will now be to identify health care needs and to purchase services from competing suppliers through a process of selective contracting.

GP Budgets

As of April 1991, GP practices with 9,000 or more patients may apply to hold budgets for the purchase of diagnostic procedures and other (mainly elective) treatments on behalf of their patients. At the same time, as the relative importance of the capitation element in GPs' salaries is increased, GPs are to be encouraged to compete for patients. Both GP budget-holders and the DHA purchaser will be funded by cash-limited budgets allocated on the basis of a weighted capitation formula. Patients of non–budget-holding GPs will have all of their health care purchased by the DHA.

SELF-GOVERNING TRUSTS

In the long run, it is envisaged that all of the major provider units (including hospitals, community units, and ambulance services) will become self-governing trusts within the NHS. Self-governing units will be freed from direct DHA management and will be run instead by a board of trustees, including representatives of medical staff groups. All of the assets of the unit will be transferred to the trust, and surplus revenues may be retained for use within the business, subject to a nondistribution constraint. Independent trust units will also have the power to set terms and conditions for staff, including rates of pay.

In the first wave of self-governing trusts (April 1991) 57 provider units were granted trust status, with a second wave approved in April 1992. Hospitals and other provider units that do not obtain trust status will continue to be managed by the relevant District Health Authority, but these providers, like the trusts, will have to compete for contracts with other local units.

NHS INTERNAL MARKET

Apart from the conceptual distinction between purchasers and providers, the most important behavioral changes are likely to result from the fact that provider units can no longer rely on guaranteed prospective funding irrespective of the cost or quality of services. Providers must now compete for contracts from cash-limited purchasers, and the expectation is that this competition will improve the cost-effectiveness of provision, and make suppliers more responsive to the demands of patients. Self-governing units will also have the added incentive that surplus revenues may be retained and used to expand facilities.

Benefits are also expected to result from the refinement of the purchasing role. Purchasers will have a responsibility to identify the health care needs of their resident population, and to plan the purchase of services in such a way that those needs are met. This is a substantial undertaking that is, as yet, only partially understood. Purchasers will have to begin to set priorities for treatment, to evaluate the cost-effectiveness of alternative procedures, and to develop measures of health care outcomes as part of the process of monitoring and evaluating the performance of suppliers. The information demands of the internal market will be substantial, and far exceed the capacity of the present system.

OPERATION OF THE NHS INTERNAL MARKET

Since the underlying aim of the reforms is to improve the efficiency of health care delivery in the United Kingdom, any constructive evaluation of the performance of the post-reform NHS hinges on the meaning of *efficiency* in this context. The NHS is motivated by the fundamental egalitarian principle that resources for health care should be allocated according to need (defined as ability to benefit), rather than on the basis of ability to pay (Culyer 1991; Williams 1990). It follows that the objective of the NHS is to maximize improvements in health status subject to a global budget contraint, and the achievement of efficiency in meeting this objective implies: (1) that resources should be allocated between medical procedures in such a way as to maximize the resulting improvement in health. This condition, which is analogous to allocative efficiency, requires that only those health care procedures that have a positive impact on health should be produced, and that the mix of services produced will be such that the value of improvements in health is maximized; and (2) that all health care procedures and services should be produced at least-resource cost.

In the NHS quasi-market, the achievement of *allocative efficiency* is the primary responsibility of purchasers, and in particular of the District Health Authorities. DHAs will be responsible for assessing the health care needs of their resident population and for deciding on the best ways to meet those needs. Purchasers will then articulate the demands of consumers through the specification of bids for service delivery. However, although purchasers may have the primary role in determining service priorities, responsiveness of providers to consumer demands is also an important requirement.

The reforms offer a real prospect of improvement in allocative efficiency, but the information requirements are substantial (Culyer 1991; Maynard 1991). In particular, DHA purchasers will require information about the current health needs of the population. Descriptive epidemiological studies of the incidence and prevalence of medical problems may be a starting point, but such studies are not sufficient. Since the emphasis is on need as ability to benefit, rather than on ill health per se, attention must also be directed to identifying those states of health that are amenable to medical intervention.

Purchasers will also require information on the cost-effectiveness of medical interventions. Efficiency requires that all of the health care services that are contracted by purchasers be shown to be clinically effective in the sense that they actually generate improvements in health status. But clinical effectiveness is not enough. Purchasers also need to determine that the specific services purchased are the most cost-effective available. If this condition is not met, the net effect on health status could be increased by an appropriate reallocation of the total budget.

Finally, purchasers must also seek information on the value of improvements in health offered by alternative medical services. So long as the total budget is constrained, purchasers will not be able to buy all of the cost-effective services available, and priority setting becomes essential. Information on the relative value of alternative health interventions, as reflected in QALY (Quality Adjusted Life Year) gains for example, is an input into the process of priority setting. At present, most of the day-to-day rationing in the NHS is done by clinicians and is reflected, if at all, in the composition of waiting lists. One of the implications of the reform is that these decisions will become explicit in the contracts negotiated by purchasers.

Achievement of *technical efficiency* depends on the behavior of the supply side of the market, and in particular on the impact of competition between providers. In the NHS internal market, provider units compete for contracts from cash-limited purchasers. The emphasis on price competition in the proposed mechanism for selective contracting is expected to generate incentives to reduce costs and to enhance technical efficiency. The extent to which this expectation is likely to be realized depends on a number of features of the operation of the internal market. The following features are likely to be of particular importance: the nature of contracts, the actual extent of competition in the market, and the nature of regulation.

Contracts

The nature of the contract between purchaser and provider influences the incentives facing providers and the extent of risk sharing between the two parties. Three types of contracts have been proposed: block contracts, cost-per-case contracts, and cost and volume contracts.

1. *Block contract.* A block contract is similar to a capitation contract in which the purchaser buys access to an agreed range of facilities for a given period at a fixed fee. The contract does not specify workload volume or the precise range of services to be supplied to individual patients. Most of the inherent risk involved in the contingent nature of health care demand falls on the provider, and for this reason the cost of a block contract may be expected to be higher than one in which contingencies are more completely defined.

The incentives inherent in a block contract are well known (Bartlett 1991). Since revenue is effectively fixed, the provider has an incentive to minimize actual expenditure. For this reason, block contracts typically also include target indicators such as length of stay, as well as detailed procedures for monitoring performance.

2. *Cost-per-case contracts.* The majority of the contracts negotiated in the first period of the NHS quasi-market have been block contracts, which reflects both the lack of detailed cost data and the dominance of the DHA purchaser. However, for referrals from GP budget-holders, and for some other referrals outside the DHA, contracts have been negotiated on a cost-per-case basis, with prices set at average procedure cost. The distribution of risk in this type of contract is more favorable to the provider, and most such contracts contain maximum acceptable workload levels to enable purchasers to control total expenditure.

3. *Cost and volume contracts.* Cost and volume contracts, which combine elements of both block and cost-per-case contracts, are uncommon in the NHS. Purchasers buy access to facilities up to a maximum agreed workload, and then purchase additional cases beyond the agreed maximum at a cost-per-case rate.

Competition

One of the aims of the health care reforms is to increase competition between health care suppliers in the hope of achieving the benefits of reduced cost and enhanced efficiency.

In the NHS internal market, it is inevitable that there will be significant elements of monopoly power in the short run, given the legacy of service planning that has been designed to avoid duplication and to take advantage of available economies of scale. The most likely outcome is that the NHS market will be characterized by varying degrees of competition, both between areas and between specialties. Contract prices are to be set on the basis of a competitive bidding process, and in markets that are genuinely competitive, this process may be expected to lead to some improvement in technical efficiency. However, in a market characterized by a significant degree of monopoly power, costs (and, hence, prices) may be expected to rise as providers seek to maximize surplus revenues (in the case of self-governing trusts) or merely to increase discretionary expenditure. With a fixed budget constraint, any increase in cost is likely to result in reductions in activity and increased waiting times.

Regulation

In view of the likely characteristics of the internal market, the need for some form of regulation is recognized. In the short run, when local monopoly may be expected to be the norm, the primary objective of regulation will be to curtail the abuse of monopoly power. In the long run, the objective will be to facilitate competition both by improving the flow of information and by ensuring the contestability of markets (Ferguson and Posnett 1991). An important consideration, therefore, is the need to ensure that policies designed to restrain the operation of the market in the short run do not at the same time stifle the incentives necessary for development of the competitive process. In particular, the imposition of rigid pricing rules or a central price schedule may be expected to constrain rather than facilitate the operation of the market.

The main element in the government's regulatory strategy is the imposition of an average cost pricing rule. Provider units are required to set prices on the basis of the cost of providing an expected volume and mix of workload in the coming year. The total revenue generated from all current contracts (whether block or cost-per-case contracts) should be just sufficient to cover total costs, including an imputed return on capital. In the event of "unplanned" excess capacity, providers will be able to sell additional units at marginal cost, but cross-subsidization of services is prohibited.

The imposition of what is, in effect, a cost-plus pricing rule generates no inherent incentive for providers to minimize the cost of provision. The relevant regulation provides for hospital accounts to be audited to prevent overt exploitation of purchasers, but the fundamental impossibility of determining the "correct" cost of providing health care services appears not to have been recognized. In a cost-plus environment, monopoly producers have an incentive to increase costs to maximize retained surpluses and thus facilitate discretionary expenditure. This sort of behavior cannot be detected by financial audit. Monopoly providers will be expected to offer higher levels of amenity, more up-to-date technology, and more resource-intensive treatment. The only restraint on this sort of behavior will be the availability of comparable cost data from more competitive markets, combined with effective sanctions on suppliers and, crucially, the development of adequate indicators of output quality.

The process of competitive bidding also opens up the possibility of product differentiation. So long as the preferences and/or budgets of purchasers differ, a hospital may enter into a number of contracts for the supply of the same basic service at different levels of amenity. Waiting times may differ between patients of different purchasers, or access to certain diagnostic procedures may be offered to some patients and not others. The NHS has always embodied elements of inequality of access between patients of different District Health Authorities, but the introduction of an internal market offers the prospect of similar inequalities for patients in the same hospital.

The proposed pricing rules offer no solution to this problem. In addition, the opportunity for providers to charge for excess capacity at marginal cost is a potential source of abuse. For example, suppose a provider sets the price of a block contract with the local DHA in order to cover the total costs of projected workload. Capacity above the expected level can then be sold at marginal cost and, since average costs will typically be falling, a second purchaser will be able to buy access to the same facilities at a lower cost because the DHA purchaser has already covered all of the fixed costs of provision. This has already led to situations in which patients of budget-holding GPs are able to gain quicker access to hospital facilities than patients of the local DHA, because the GP is able to purchase access at marginal cost. This is probably an inevitable consequence of the creation of GP budgets, given the fact that the DHA purchaser will be the main source of demand for most providers, but the impact on the equity aims of the NHS could be important.

Finally, the pricing rules allow scope for constructive cost allocation to take advantage of local monopoly power. Most provider units will hold a block contract from the DHA for the supply of local services, and will compete for contracts from other purchasers. By their very nature, the supply of local services will be less competitive than the supply of, for example, elective procedures or diagnostic tests, and this creates incentives for providers to load as much as possible of the fixed costs of provision onto the DHA purchaser to reduce the price of the more competitive product. The average cost rule does not specify the principles by which capital and overhead costs should be allocated, but alternative possible bases such as total patient volume or total revenue costs offer exploitable opportunities for distortion in both the input and output mix of hospital provision.

Operation of the Market in the Long Run

In the long run, the effects of the operation of a quasi-market in the NHS will depend on the *interaction* of the contract (reimbursement) regime, the extent of competition, and the nature of regulation.

Against the background of an average cost-pricing rule, a combination of block contracts and competitive markets will generate incentives for providers to reduce total projected expenditure in order to reduce bid prices. However, in a system in which contracts are awarded at the price of the winning bid, providers have no incentive to *minimize* costs, except where this is dictated by the behavior of other competing providers. The availability of comparative cost data enhances the opportunities for strategic behavior and collusion.

Reducing expenditure by restricting admissions is unlikely to be a winning strategy, because the total number of cases treated is a highly visible and politically sensitive variable easily monitored by purchasers. A more likely response will be for providers to seek to contain costs by reducing inpatient resource use (e.g., drugs, skilled staff inputs, and diagnostic procedures), by reducing length of stay by earlier discharge to home or to subacute facilities, and by reducing case-mix severity. Within the same total admissions, hospitals will face incentives to select-out those cases that are expected to be more difficult (and, hence, more costly) to treat.

The observed effects of competition are likely to be reductions in length of stay, earlier discharge, and lower costs. Hospitals may even have some incentive to increase total admissions in an attempt to maintain turnover in the face of reductions in length of stay. Unobserved effects may be expected to include patient selection and reductions in case-mix severity, cost-shifting, and (potential) adverse effects on patient outcomes as a result of reduced inpatient stays and early discharge.

A monopoly provider faces weak incentives to reduce projected costs. Indeed, a provider with significant market power may be expected to seek to increase total costs to maximize revenues (recall that contract price, and hence hospital income, is to be based on recorded costs). The payoff is in terms of retained surplus (in the case of a self-governing trust), or in the opportunity for enhanced discretionary spending. A monopolist may be expected to increase expenditure on those items that generate utility for consultants and managers, and on those that enhance the market position of the hospital by making it more attractive to patients. Conversely, expenditures that increase cost without improving utility will come under pressure. Thus, a monopoly supplier may be expected to increase expenditure on the physical environment of the hospital, to maintain excess capacity in order to reduce waiting times, and to invest in high-technology diagnostic and therapeutic facilities while at the same time seeking to reduce inpatient resource use and length of stay. To the extent that more difficult cases are also more interesting to clinicians, the tendency in competitive markets for case-mix severity to fall may be partly offset.

The observed effects of the introduction of contracting in a monopoly market will be increased amenity (both clinical and nonclinical), greater variety of services, reduced length of stay, and higher costs. Unobserved effects might be expected to include overinvestment in high technology and excess capacity, as well as cost-shifting and potentially adverse patient outcomes, although the magnitude of these effects might be expected to be less than in a competitive environment.

Where cost-per-case contracts are substituted for block contracts, the underlying incentives facing both competitive and monopolistic suppliers will be essentially unchanged, with the qualification that attention will be directed to cost per case rather than to total costs. However, since total income is now positively related to the number of cases treated, providers have an incentive to expand workload up to the ceiling specified in the contract. In addition, where payment rates are related to patient diagnosis, opportunities for "DRG (Diagnosis Related Group) creep" emerge. Hospitals will now face incentives to select patients at the less severe end of a particular diagnostic group, and to reclassify patients wherever possible into more expensive (and more lucrative) groups.

REFLECTIONS ON THE FIRST YEAR

In the first full contracting period (April 1991 to April 1992), the substantive effect of the changes has been small. District purchasers have been funded to provide the same or enhanced levels of activity as in the previous year, and the budgets of fund-holding GP practices have been closely related to existing patterns of referrals. Most of the contracts negotiated in the first period have been block contracts based on existing capacity and workloads, and the overall objective has been to ensure a stable transition to the new system.

In future periods, beginning in April 1992, budgets to purchase health services are to be allocated on the basis of a weighted capitation formula designed to reflect the different health care needs of different districts. Some districts will be major losers under capitation, and changes in overall levels of activity between districts and between providers appear inevitable. In addition, as hospital costing procedures become more sophisticated, block contracts will be replaced by cost-per-case or cost and volume contracts, which will also highlight differences in efficiency (and service quality) between providers. Already a major review of London hospitals has pointed to the extent of excess capacity and higher costs in the city, and has recommended the closure or amalgamation of a number of well-known London hospitals (Tomlinson 1992).

Changes in the real budgets of local purchasers and improved hospital costing procedures will sharpen the operation of the contracting process. In the United States, selective contracting is now a feature of Medicaid administration in a number of states. For example, the Arizona Health Care Cost Containment System established (in 1982) a selection process in which health care providers are invited to bid for Medicaid enrollees in prepaid group plans at an all-inclusive capitation rate. However, the potential benefits of selective contracting in reducing health care costs depend crucially on the presence of competing bidders. In the NHS, most providers will operate in two distinct markets: the market for local (core) services, and the market for elective (noncore) procedures. Core services (e.g., emergency treatment) are those that must be purchased locally, and in this market most of the major providers enjoy a relatively high degree of monopoly power in their dealings with the DHA purchaser. The market for elective procedures is likely to be more competitive, with a major role for GP fund-holding practices, and the benefits of selective contracting are most likely to emerge in this sector.

Nonetheless, experience in the United States suggests that over time the number of competing bidders declines, and financial viability assumes increasing importance because of the potential disruption and cost of insolvency among providers. In the Arizona scheme, for example, in the fourth year of the program (by which time the number of bidders had reduced from 50 to 15), bids were evaluated on a 200-point scoring scheme in which only 40 points were related directly to bid prices (McCall et al. 1987). One implication for the United Kingdom is that even in those markets that are competitive, it will be in the interests of both providers and purchasers to enter into long-term contracts, rather than into an unstable annual bidding process. Not only is this likely to be more productive in ensuring the viability of major providers, it will also be expected to reduce the costs of contract enforcement and monitoring.

From April 1991 to April 1992, 306 GP practices obtained fund-holding status. These practices covered 3.7 million patients (an average list size of 12,000), and controlled £404 million ($600 million) (1 percent of the total Hospital and Community Health Services [HCHS] budget). In the second contracting year (1992–93), the number of fund-holding practices has increased to 600, controlling 4 percent of the total HCHS budget.

The fund-holding concept is similar to an HMO-type arrangement in which the practice assumes responsibility for the provision of hospital diagnosis and investigation, outpatient visits, and a range of elective surgical procedures in exchange for a capitation payment. Depending on the geographical distribution of practices, patients are free to choose between competing primary care providers. Unlike most HMOs in the United States, GP fund-holders are not responsible for the full range of hospital treatments; emergency treatment, and most medical procedures are funded directly (through contracts) by the local DHA purchaser.

Evidence from the operation of HMOs in the United States (e.g., Manning et al. 1984) suggests that the introduction of GP budgets will generate incentives for development of a less hospital-intensive style of medical care, and for a reduction in hospital referrals and inpatient admissions. So far, the experience of fund-holding in the NHS supports these expectations. GPs are providing more diagnostic facilities in local practice premises, and the amount of minor surgery performed by GPs has increased (Boyle and Smarje 1992). In addition, fund-holders are using their competitive position as marginal purchasers of hospital facilities to improve patient access and quality of service. A number of fund-holders have arranged for consultants to hold outpatient clinics in GP surgeries, and some providers have offered reduced waiting times for the patients of fund-holders willing to pay the marginal cost of additional sessions. This arrangement, in particular, has caused considerable criticism, to the point where the Department of Health has issued specific guidance designed to eliminate "preferential" treatment of this sort (EL [91] 84), despite the fact that pricing unplanned excess capacity at marginal cost is perfectly acceptable within the pricing rules.

Despite the relatively small proportion of the overall HCHS budget controlled by fund-holding practices, their position as marginal purchasers of competitive (noncore) services has given them significant influence, and as the number of fund-holding practices expands, this influence will increase accordingly. In the longer term as DHA budgets are reduced (fund-holder budgets are deducted directly from the DHA allocation), some district purchasers will lose control of all but core services, and the role of the purchaser in local planning efforts to achieve allocative efficiency will inevitably be weakened. Budgetary control by the DHA is also compromised by the fact that nonfund-holding GPs are, in principle, still free to refer patients to any provider of their choice, even if the provider does not hold a contract with the district. The cost of these extracontractual referrals remains the responsibility of the local DHA purchaser, and in the first contracting period, districts held an average of 1.5 percent of total budgets in reserve to cover the cost of unplanned referrals. Proposals have been made to constrain the referral behavior of GPs, but as yet the implicit conflict between a GP's clinical freedom to refer in the best interests of the patient, and the need for the DHA to retain budgetary control of a cash-limited allocation has not been resolved.

Other features of the operation of HMOs in the health care market in the United States are also becoming evident. Faced with a capitated budget, some fund-holding practices have attempted to reduce financial risk by cream-skimming. Since open enrollment is not a requirement of the contract between a GP practice and the NHS, this sort of patient selection is quite feasible, although the force of local public opinion has proved a powerful deterrent. It remains to be seen whether in future periods, when the allocation of fund-holder payments is more closely linked to a true capitation system (rather than to existing referral behavior as in the first period), the incentives for cream-skimming become more powerful.

Compared with average HMO enrollment, the average list size of existing fund-holders (12,000) appears low. As financial constraints begin to bite, some fund-holding practices may be pushed to the edge of financial viability, although compared with their U.S. counterparts, GP fund-holders are less exposed to risk because of the limited range of their purchasing responsibilities. Nonetheless, individual practices have already begun to form joint-purchasing consortia in an attempt to reduce exposure to risk, and to enhance their competitive position. This development is already well advanced among DHA purchasers, and major providers have also been quick to see the benefits of mergers with potential competitors. The trend toward larger units on both sides of the market appears well set.

Of the 57 self-governing trusts that were approved in the first wave in April 1991, most were large acute hospitals (with an average of 720 beds). These trusts controlled £1.8 billion ($2.7 billion) accounting for 13.5 percent of total U.K. hospital expenditure. It is too early to determine whether the internal market has had any discernible effect on hospital costs, or on the overall quality of care. Certainly, activity levels in 1992 rose over those in the previous year, with an increase of 3.5 percent in inpatient cases, a 31 percent increase in day cases, and a 3 percent reduction in waiting lists. However, since NHS spending increased by over 9 percent in the period, it is difficult to judge whether any of this increase in activity has been due to enhanced performance on the part of providers.

The reforms have at least highlighted the wide differences in costs between different hospitals. A study of the range of prices (cost-per-case rates) facing one GP fund-holding practice in London found wide differences between highest and lowest quoted costs. For example, in a sample of 5 hospitals the price of a cataract operation varied between £250 and £3,622 ($375–$5,433), while the price of a hysterectomy varied between £969 and £2,300 ($1450–$3450) (Glennerster, Matsaganis and Owens 1992). Part of these differences is undoubtedly due to variations in costing procedures rather than to genuine differences in efficiency. Nonetheless, a study designed to establish a baseline against which to monitor future trends in cost found that the 57 hospitals granted trust status in the first wave had unit ward costs 9.2 percent lower than nontrust hospitals after correcting for bed size and case mix (Bartlett and Le Grand 1992). This suggests a process of self-selection in which hospitals granted trust status are already more efficient. It will be important in subsequent analysis not to overestimate any possible efficiency gains among these hospitals.

One of the new freedoms available to the self-governing trusts is that of setting the wages and conditions of staff; this represents a weakening of the traditional monopsony power of the NHS as the effective sole buyer of medical and nursing manpower in the United Kingdom. So far, the trusts have shown no desire to compete for staff on the basis of wages, but there is evidence of a change in skill-mix, with a substitution of support workers for more highly trained nursing staff. In the long run, the effect on hospital costs of the erosion of the monopsony position of the NHS will depend on the extent of excess demand for personnel. Current evidence suggests that, at least in the case of medical staff, this is not likely to be a problem in the foreseeable future.

Further reform of the structure of the NHS is very unlikely in the medium term, and there are even indications that the government is seeking to constrain the full effects of the reforms to ensure a period of relative stability *(Health Care UK, 1991* [1992]). With the internal market in place, however, it is possible to envisage a time when competition between purchasers for patient affiliation might also be encouraged. By replacing the current system of direct exchequer funding with a system of (supplementable) capitated vouchers, consumers could be offered a greater degree of choice between competing health maintenance agencies (including GP fund-holders, DHAs, insurance companies, major hospital providers, and others). The benefit, from the point of view of the exchequer, is that with supplementation a voucher scheme may offer an opportunity to achieve the government's original goal of increasing the share of private funding in the NHS.

Note

This chapter is a revised version of a paper originally presented at the symposium on "Competitive Health Policy Reforms: Appraisal and Prognostication," at the University of Illinois at Urbana-Champaign, in November 1991.

References

Bartlett, W. 1991. *Quasi-Markets and Contracts: A Markets and Hierarchies Perspective on NHS Reform.* Studies in Decentralisation and Quasi-Markets, no. 3, School of Advanced Urban Studies. Bristol, England: University of Bristol.

Bartlett, W., and J. Le Grand. 1992. *The Impact of NHS Reforms on Hospital Costs.* Studies in Decentralisation and Quasi-Markets, no. 8, School of Advanced Urban Studies. Bristol, England: University of Bristol.

Boyle, S., and C. Smarje. 1992. "Minor Surgery in General Practice: The Effect of the 1990 GP Contract." In *Health Care UK, 1991,* edited by A. Harrison. London: King's Fund Institute.

Culyer, A. J. 1991. "The Promise of a Reformed NHS: An Economist's Angle." *British Medical Journal* 302: 1253–56.

Enthoven, A. C. 1985. *Reflections on the Management of the National Health Service.* London: Nuffield Provincial Hospitals Trust.

Ferguson, B., and J. Posnett. 1991. "Pricing and Openness in Contracts for Health Care Services." *Health Services Management Research* 4: 46–52.

Glennerster, H., M. Matsaganis, and P. Owens. 1992. *A Foothold for Fund-holding.* London: King's Fund Institute.

Harrison, A., ed. 1992. *Health Care UK, 1991.* London: King's Fund Institute.

Her Majesty's Stationery Office. 1989. *Working for Patients.* Pub. no. CM 555. London: Her Majesty's Stationery Office.

Hitiris, T., and J. Posnett. 1992. "The Determinants and Effects of Health Expenditure in Developed Countries." *Journal of Health Economics* 11: 173–181.

Leu, R. 1986. "The Public-Private Mix and International Health Care Costs." In *Public and Private Health Services,* edited by A. J. Culyer and B. Jönsson (41–63). Oxford, England: Basil Blackwell.

Manning, W. G., A. Leibowitz, G. Goldberg, W. H. Rogers, and J. P. Newhouse. 1984. "A Controlled Trial of the Effect of a Prepaid Group Practice on Use of Services." *New England Journal of Medicine* 310: 1505–10.

Maynard, A. K. 1991. "Developing the Health Care Market." *Economic Journal* 101: 1277–86.

McCall, N., D. Henton, S. Haber, L. Paringer, M. Crane, W. Wrightson, and D. Freund. 1987. "Evaluation of Arizona Health Care Cost Containment System, 1984–85." *Health Care Financing Review* 9: 79–90.

Newhouse, J. P. 1977. "Medical Care Expenditure: A Cross-National Survey." *Journal of Human Resources* 12: 115–25.

Organization for Economic Cooperation and Development. 1987. *Financing and Delivering Health Care: A Comparative Analysis of OECD Countries.* Paris: Author.

Parkin, D., A. McGuire, and B. Yule. 1987. "Aggregate Health Care Expenditures and National Income." *Journal of Health Economics* 6: 109–27.

Schieber, G., and J. P. Poullier. 1990. "Overview of International Comparisons of Health Care Expenditures." In *Healthcare Systems in Transition: The Search for Efficiency.* Paris: Organization for Economic Cooperation and Development.

Tomlinson, B. 1992. *Report of the Inquiry into London's health service, medical education and research.* London: Her Majesty's Stationery Office.

Williams, A. H. 1990. "Ethics, Clinical Freedom, and the Doctors' Role. In *Competition in Health Care: Reforming the NHS,* edited by A. J. Culyer, A. K. Maynard, and J. Posnett (178–91). Basingstoke, England: Macmillan.

Chapter Fifteen

POLICIES FOR THE 1990s: RATIONING HEALTH CARE

Mary Ann Baily

Rationing is the health policy issue for the 1990s. According to conventional wisdom, health expenditures are growing so rapidly that Americans must accept health care rationing or watch their entire gross national product (GNP) be swallowed up by the health care sector. This is a major change, since only a few years ago, few were even willing to use the word *rationing* in a policy context. Nevertheless, although open discussion of rationing has begun, its role in the health care system remains controversial. Everyone agrees that rationing means that people do not get some health care that would benefit them, and that it would be nicer if it could be avoided. Everyone does *not* agree on just what limits on beneficial care should be called rationing, the extent to which such limits are necessary, and the degree of urgency needed to impose them.

This chapter briefly discusses the meaning of *rationing*, placing it in the broad context of limiting beneficial care; explains why beneficial care must be limited; argues that rationing is the central issue for American health policy; considers competitive strategies for health care reform from the perspective of this issue; and concludes with observations for the future.

RATIONING DEFINED

Webster's dictionary says that "to ration" is "to distribute equitably" or "to use sparingly"; a "ration" is "a share especially as determined by supply" (*Websters' Ninth New Collegiate Dictionary* 1986: 977). The important elements in this definition are *scarcity* and *equity*. Scarcity implies that there isn't enough for people to have all they want, so *beneficial* care is limited (rationing is not about eliminating useless or harmful care). Equity implies that care is distributed according to judgments about what is fair: for example, in line with the benefit to the recipient—the recipient's *need*.

From an economist's perspective, rationing is part of the normal allocation process in a world of scarce resources. Market economies distribute goods through a system of prices; in economic terminology, prices "ration" the available goods to those willing and able to pay for them. This may not seem to have much to do with equity, but if the distribution of income is reasonably fair, the goods go to the people who value them the most—those who "need" them the most, with need assessed by the person concerned, not some bureaucrat.

When prices fail to ration for some reason, or the result of price-rationing is unacceptable (for example, because the distribution of income isn't equitable, or because society wants a specific distribution of a good, such as health care) then the rationing must be done some other way.

Nonprice rationing of health care can be obvious or unobtrusive. It can result from the decisions of private actors, such as insurance companies and health care providers, or those of government actors, such as federal, state, and local legislative bodies and the administrators of Medicare and Medicaid. It can occur through waiting time, first-come-first-served, random drawing, ration tickets, priority rules imposed on providers, or the priorities that providers decide themselves. Often, nonprice rationing comes about through a combination of mechanisms. For example, a local government cuts a public hospital's budget, the hospital's administrators ration the diminished resources across departments within the hospital, and the physicians in each department ration the available resources to individual patients.

The economist's definition of rationing is very inclusive. It is too inclusive for some, who prefer to identify only some actions that limit beneficial care as rationing, focusing on aspects such as the level at which the action is taken, who takes it, whether it is part of a conscious policy, and if it is, how the policy was formed and what values it incorporates (Etzioni 1981; Evans 1983; Hadorn 1991; and Reagan 1988).

For example, some consider decisions about the quantity of resources to provide for an entire category of patients or a type of health service to be "allocation" decisions, reserving "rationing" for decisions about how resources are applied to individual patients (Evans 1983). For example, deciding how much to spend on computerized tomography (CT) scanners is allocation; deciding which patients get CT scans is rationing. Some say "rationing" applies only to policies developed deliberately by the whole community to serve the public interest, not to policies developed by interested parties to serve their own interests (Reagan 1988). Therefore, insurance companies are not rationing when they decide to cover liver transplants for children with biliary atresia but not to cover transplants for adults with other liver diseases. Some do not call it rationing when a policy that restricts the number of health facilities causes people to decide not to seek care because they can't afford the cost in money and travel time (Reagan 1988).

The definition of *rationing* has more than semantic significance. Since the term has a strong negative connotation, policies labeled as such automatically seem undesirable. This skews debates about cost containment. One policy may be rejected on the grounds that it is rationing, only to be replaced by a policy that does not receive the label but produces a worse outcome.

The economist's definition (the definition used in this chapter) has the advantage of neutrality. It considers all the features of the health care system that together result in limiting the beneficial care received by an individual, whether price or nonprice, explicit or implicit. From this perspective, rationing is neither good nor bad in itself; it is evaluated by looking at both the *outcome* (the ultimate distribution of health care and of its cost) and the *process* (the means used to bring about that distribution) and asking whether they are consistent with societal values of equity and liberty.

REASONS FOR LIMITING BENEFICIAL HEALTH CARE

Why ration health care at all? Everyone understands that scarcity requires limits on goods in general, but shouldn't health care be an exception?

The answer is no, because the benefits from health care form a continuum, from saving a life to eliminating a minor inconvenience. Exempting health care from limits would require too great a sacrifice in benefits from alternative uses of resources, uses that might even have more impact on health (for example, through better nutrition or safer transportation) than some health care.

Both efficiency and equity dictate that there be limits on beneficial care, and further, that these limits take the form of nonprice rationing. Efficiency requires limits to control moral hazard, so the benefits of risk-pooling through health insurance can be gained at reasonable cost. When insurance pays the bill, people consume health care as if it were free, rather than weighing the benefits against the cost, yet the cost falls on the group as a whole through their insurance premiums. A homely analogy is the situation that arises when people dining out together decide in advance to split the bill evenly. Each person has a financial incentive to order a more expensive meal, yet the group as a whole must pay the total cost. If the check is to be evenly divided, it would be prudent to agree also to choose from a limited menu—to submit to some nonprice rationing.[1]

The equity argument comes from acknowledgment of a societal obligation to ensure access for all to some basic level of health care (an "adequate level" or "decent minimum"), without having to bear an excessive burden in money, time, or travel costs, and further, to ensure a fair distribution of the cost of achieving this. Since the societal obligation does not extend to everything of benefit, limits are necessary on the care provided at public expense.

The efficiency and equity arguments mean there are two different kinds of limits (nonprice rationing) to consider: limits people should want as rational participants in voluntarily formed risk pools; and limits on the care provided to fulfil the social obligation. The logic in either case implies that the limits be specific to health state. In Mark Pauly's (1968) classic article on moral hazard, the extent of moral hazard depends on which of two illness states the consumer is in. People may disagree on how much care society should guarantee someone who is ill, but they surely agree that the amount of care should depend on what is wrong with him.

Therefore, setting the entitlement in public or private insurance/delivery systems is complex. It is not sufficient to define "a basic package" as a list of services, such as physician visits, hospital services, prescription drugs, and so on. Such a list is no more an adequate level of health care than a list of foods is an adequate diet. There must be some process of patient and provider decision making that determines how much people actually get. Note, also, that the question is not just *whether* a health condition should be treated, but also *how*—in other words, the standard of care to be provided for all possible adverse health states.

RATIONING IN AMERICAN HEALTH POLICY

What people receive in a health care system is clearly fundamental. Yet surprisingly little attention has been paid in past American policy debate to the determination of the standard of care. Rather, the focus has been on insurance: expanding coverage for the privately insured, extending private insurance to more people, and setting up public insurance for groups excluded from the private insurance system. The coverage itself was expressed almost entirely in terms of the types of services included and the extent of cost sharing, not the adequacy and cost-effectiveness of the care received for different medical conditions.

This focus had its roots in a simplistic view of medicine and of consumer and provider behavior. Insurance was provided for "medically necessary care" without appreciation of the term's inherent ambiguity. It was understood that more health care would be used if people paid less than the full cost out-of-pocket, but this was not seen as a serious problem. If the care was medically necessary, well, wasn't the whole point of insurance to ensure access to necessary care? Medically unnecessary care was a different story, but ethical doctors would not provide it. (Of course, some attention would have to be given to preventing fraud by the unscrupulous few who would try to abuse the system.)

This view ignores the variability in the way episodes of illness can be handled, as well as the role of financial incentives in influencing how patients and providers perceive medical necessity. In the United States, the ambiguity of the term *medically necessary* was usually resolved by defining it as "everything beneficial."[2] In a private insurance market characterized by comprehensive coverage and fee-for-service or cost-based reimbursement, both consumers and providers liked this definition. The effect, however, was an exorbitant bill for insured medical care that included care of only minimal benefit.

The bill would have been even more exorbitant had the "everything of benefit" ideal actually been achieved. In fact, such a standard of care was too expensive even for the well insured. The beneficial health care a patient received was always limited by price, by the structure of insurance, by the availability of resources, and by the decisions of health care providers. Certain types of care, such as long-term care, were not privately insured at all. Other types were insured but subject to deductibles, copayments, quantitative limits, and other forms of cost sharing. The number and geographical distribution of physicians, hospitals, and other facilities rationed access by distance and waiting time for appointments. Reimbursement incentives led physicians to direct their efforts in some directions and not others, justifying the result by the way they defined necessary care.

An "everything of benefit" definition was even less a reality for publicly provided care, although this was not official policy, since Americans resisted open acceptance of a different standard of care for the publicly insured ("two-tier" medical care). If care was either medically necessary or unnecessary, how could they admit that the poor were to be deliberately denied medically necessary care, or justify differences in the definition of medical necessity depending on who was paying? Nevertheless, they were not willing to fund an "everything of benefit" standard for the publicly insured.

Under public programs, spending was limited by restricting eligibility, excluding some services and arbitrarily limiting the covered amounts of others, restricting the budgets of public providers, setting low reimbursement levels and thereby discouraging providers from serving program clients, and other strategies. These strategies often resulted in severe limits on beneficial care—a standard of care clearly lower than the standard considered "medically necessary" by the privately insured—yet, when the consequences of the strategies were exposed (in a Medicaid clinic or a public hospital, for example) the reaction was to see the situation as a shameful, anecdotal failure, rather than as an inherent failing in the structure of the financing system.

For both the publicly and privately financed, there could be no open debate on what care was worth having when all medically necessary care was supposed to be provided, with cost playing no role in the definition of medical necessity.[3] Since there was no process for fine-tuning the standard of care to bring the benefits of care in line with the costs, some people got too much and others too little in both the private and public sectors.

The extent to which there was actual rationing (the limiting of care understood to be beneficial) is controversial, especially for the privately insured. It is an important issue, because if rationing can be shown to be something that already occurs and the goal is simply to do it better, it may seem more acceptable than if it represents a new departure.

The debate can only be resolved by empirical evidence, and unfortunately, such evidence is difficult to find and interpret. Since the need for limits was not openly accepted, restrictions were imposed as unobtrusively as possible. No one wanted to know about limits on beneficial care, especially those systematically related to the structure of the financing system. Moreover, even when data exist on disparities in what people received, our lack of knowledge of the effectiveness of much of medical care makes it difficult to determine whether one person was getting too little or the other person too much. As the need for limits on care has begun to be openly acknowledged, however, people have started to look for and find evidence of the extent of limits on beneficial care.[4]

American reluctance to acknowledge the necessity for rationing has led to serious inefficiency and inequity. More important, it has become the major obstacle to achieving universal access to health care. No country, not even the United States, can afford a health care system that provides everything of benefit to everyone. When the check for expanding access to the system had to be a blank check, it is not surprising that the country was reluctant to sign.

COMPETITIVE STRATEGIES AND THE RATIONING ISSUE

Advocates of competition-based health care reform played a major part in thrusting the rationing issue onto the policy stage. Their approach arose out of concern for cost containment in private insurance, and their main contribution was an appreciation of the importance of moral hazard. (See the works of Pauly, Havighurst, Enthoven, Ellwood, and McClure listed in the references.) This made the rationing issue central, since the essence of moral hazard *is* the failure of prices to ration and the need for other mechanisms to replace them.

Their analysis explained why consumers should *want* insurers to control moral hazard and thus hold down insurance premiums. Cost sharing, especially for routine care, was one method.[5] Its use was inherently limited, of course, since the purpose of insurance was to protect against large medical bills. Also, consumers lacked information about medical care, and thus were not always able to make efficient rationing decisions for themselves. Premium competition could, however, be expected to lead insurers to develop other rationing methods such as utilization review and "gatekeeping" by physicians, as well as to foster the development of alternative insurance-delivery systems that were better suited to weighing the benefits and costs of care than the standard combination of traditional insurance and fee-for-service medical practice.[6]

Several reasons were advanced to explain why such developments were not occurring: the tax subsidies to employment-related insurance insulated consumers from the effects of moral hazard on premiums; consumers had little choice in health insurance anyway, since employers offered one or at most a few plans; and providers were able to organize effective resistance against cost-reducing changes.[7] If these features of the market were corrected, it was argued, consumers would want rationing and the market would respond with a choice of rationing strategies. Consumers would be limited to the "choices on the menu" if they got sick, but at least their preferences would shape the menu.

Health economists all agree that these features of the market are obstacles to achieving efficiency and equity. But even if they were eliminated, it is unlikely that a competitive insurance market would solve the rationing problem so easily.

This chapter argues that competition advocates recognized the centrality of the rationing issue, but then failed to appreciate its complexity. As a result, their policy analysis is flawed. At the least, their proposals must pay much more attention to the rationing issue, and there is real doubt that it can be handled satisfactorily within the framework of a market competition approach. This thesis is discussed next in regard to five areas: information about rationing strategies, the social insurance objective in health policy, the role of physicians, the role of employers, and the role of government.

Information about Rationing Strategies

In a competitive health insurance market, buyers select a coverage option by weighing the rationing strategy it represents against the premium cost, taking into account their personal risk profiles and health care preferences. Sellers offer the rationing strategies buyers want, at premiums related to the buyers' expected use of care. Both sides of the market face formidable information problems in carrying out these tasks.

Sellers must ensure that the buyer's risk profile and propensity to use care match the premium paid, or risk experiencing adverse selection (insuring a pool of people at higher than expected risk). Getting information on individual buyers is costly, especially since it is to the buyers' advantage to understate their health risks and their propensity to use care.

Buyers must learn the advertised rationing strategy that goes with each coverage option and enough about medicine to appreciate the strategy's implications for their own utility. Then they must determine whether what is advertised is what actually happens. It is to the insurer's advantage to understate the extent to which an option limits beneficial care.

Both opponents and advocates of competitive strategies have raised these issues.[8] Most of their attention has been focused on the biased selection problem. It has been argued that the effect on profits of the composition of the risk pool will swamp the effects of producing care efficiently and controlling utilization, and that firms will therefore compete by managing their risk pools rather than by offering an efficiently produced, cost-effective standard of care at the lowest possible price. (See, for example, Newhouse 1982). All agree that competition strategies must be structured to minimize this.

Considerable attention has also been given to the problem of consumer information. This problem has usually been seen as one of understanding an insurance policy—services covered, cost-sharing provisions, and so on. Health insurance policies are complicated, and advocates of competition recognize that consumers need some help. But consumers must do more than understand the policy; they must understand the entire standard of care they are buying, a far more difficult task. Insurers and providers themselves are hard put to specify the standard of care and communicate it. For example, health maintenance organizations (HMOs) find it a challenge to determine whether their own organizations meet internal quality standards, and to compare their standards of care with those of other HMOs.[9]

Moreover, insurers can gain by concealing the extent to which beneficial care is limited, and the scope is extremely broad for rationing care in ways hard to detect. For example, a small fraction of the members of a risk pool uses a large fraction of the resources. Money can be saved by rationing those people tightly.[10] Since these individuals rely on their providers for information, they themselves may not even realize they have been denied beneficial care, let alone their fellow subscribers. If this strategem is combined with easy access to inexpensive routine care, subscribers may be misled about the nature of the rationing.

Using rationing strategies to compete can dovetail nicely with achieving favorable selection. The subscribers who are best informed about the real rationing strategies are likely to be those affected by them, who are, in turn, likely to be those who are more costly than average. The rationing rules can be deliberately manipulated to manage the composition of the risk pool. In sum, when the rationing issue is considered, managing the information problem in a competition-based health care system is even more difficult than commonly supposed.[11]

Social Insurance Objective in Health Policy

Although advocates of competition emphasize efficiency, they recognize that there is a social insurance dimension to health policy, also. Americans want a safety net of guaranteed access to adequate care from a mixture of altruism, moral obligation, and self-interest. They care about the suffering of others, they believe it is morally right to ensure access to at least a decent minimum, and they recognize that there are limits to their own ability to provide against financial and medical reversals of fortune.

Competition advocates see the social insurance task as primarily one of plugging everyone into the private insurance market. This leads to a focus on the two kinds of people who tend to be excluded, the poor and the high risk. The poor can't afford coverage for an adequate level of care because their incomes are too low, and high-risk people can't afford it because their premiums are too high (since premiums vary with risk).

According to standard microeconomic theory, the most efficient way to improve the access of a particular group to a good is to give them dollars and let them purchase their own preferred level of access. The public has never been convinced by this in the case of health care, and maintains a strong preference for good-specific redistribution (all parties to the current debate on health care reform seem to accept as a given that there must be guaranteed access to a decent minimum of care). Accordingly, competition advocates propose to give the poor and the high risk earmarked dollars—vouchers for the purchase of health insurance policies of their choice. Competitive strategies devote considerable attention to how to determine a subsidy structure so all are insured. They devote much less attention to what people are insured for, seeming to take for granted the value of allowing people freedom of choice in the details of their insurance coverage.[12] Yet, the rationing strategy cannot be left entirely to voluntary choice, or it may ration away care that is part of the decent minimum.

When the rationing issue is addressed, it is with a requirement that all have coverage for at least a "basic package" of services. Of course, there must also be a process that determines the actual amounts of care received, to avoid making the "list equals adequate diet" mistake. Alain Enthoven's Consumer Choice Health Plan did this by assigning a key role to HMOs (Enthoven 1980). A minimum list of services was specified, to be delivered by an organization with the financial incentive to set a cost-conscious standard of care, serving a population that voluntarily enrolled in the HMO and in which poor people were not in the majority. Other analysts (and Enthoven's later writings) have been less specific. Essentially, they rely on the market to produce satisfactory methods for setting the standard of care in a way that controls moral hazard and satisfies the adequacy criterion, without specifying the details.

It is implicitly assumed that the market behavior of the nonpoor will set a standard of care that is at least adequate, and perhaps more than adequate.[13] The rationale is that if consumers of average income choose not to be insured against the cost of some treatment, what better indication can there be that society does not consider it part of the adequate level?

But this is far from clear. The market result is the answer to the wrong question. It is the standard of care for which a person chooses to insure given his own risk profile, not his estimate of the decent minimum to be provided everyone. The choice is made in a world in which the risk of ill health varies with genetic endowment and over time; there is periodic recontracting for insurance; income varies widely; and claims on income vary over time and across individuals for people at the same income levels. A rational consumer may choose a plan that provides more than adequate coverage for a situation he or she expects to occur within the relevant time period, but omits coverage for something unlikely. For example, one might believe that schizophrenics should be able to get treatment, but might also believe one's own risk of schizophrenia is negligible and choose a health insurance plan that excludes it.[14] A standard of care set in this manner does not protect people against changes in their risk profiles over time, nor does it ensure that the system as a whole satisfies the moral obligation to ensure access to a decent minimum.

Protection against a change in risk profile could be secured by making a long-term contract for health insurance early in life. If consumers could not change plans, however, there would be far less market pressure on insurers to compete on quality and price. There is, in other words, a market failure argument for constrained choice of rationing strategy that parallels the original moral hazard argument for nonprice rationing (Newhouse 1984).

More important, long-term contracts would not address the issue of moral obligation. Allowing people unconstrained choice of rationing strategies is fundamentally at odds with the social insurance objective. The decent minimum approach to equity is based on the belief that there are health services so basic that everyone should have access to them, regardless of ability to pay and regardless of individual purdence or folly in insurance decisions. Accordingly, society has a moral obligation to guarantee access to these services and to spread the cost over all its members so no one faces an excessive financial burden to obtain them. But this means people must choose to insure themselves for at least this level of care, and accept the obligation to pay, on an income-related basis, for their coverage.

What is the adequate level, or decent minimum? This is a moral question to which there is no simple answer, especially in a secular, pluralistic society with no universally accepted moral framework.[15] Although it is a moral question, as a practical matter, it must be answered through some combination of economic and political processes. These comments are not meant to suggest that a decent minimum approach leaves no room for diversity of preferences and freedom of choice, or for competition-based financing strategies. Allowing people to purchase more than the adequate level at their own expense is compatible with the approach, but more important, the guaranteed standard of care itself would reasonably include, for many health conditions, a range of treatment options from which a patient could choose based on his or her preferences and particular circumstances. Also, given the difficulty of devising a practical process for reaching a consensus on an adequate level, the average market outcome could well be a useful starting point, since the market behavior of average citizens spending their own money to protect themselves against the financial risk of ill health can provide valuable information about trade-offs. Such a standard is, however, likely to contain systematic biases (in both directions, depending on the health condition) as an answer to the real question: What level of care does the average American of goodwill believe should be guaranteed to all?

Note, also, that the social insurance issues raised here interact with the information problems discussed in the previous section. Health plans that skimp in subtle ways on care that is part of the adequate level but not likely to be used by most of the plans' members will face little corrective market pressure even if members become aware of it—and will have a cost advantage.

Role of Physicians

The physician, by the nature of medical care and by law, plays a key role in advising the patient about what care to have and granting the patient access to that care. Physician cooperation, or at least acquiescence, in rationing is therefore essential.

There is a long standing problem in our health care system of conflicting messages from society to physicians about what they are supposed to do. For instance, the physician should:

☐ Do everything that can benefit the patient medically without regard to cost;
☐ Do what benefits the patient, given both the medical benefit *and* the cost the patient bears;
☐ Weigh the needs of patients competing for the same resources— for example, intensive care unit beds, dialysis machines, the physician's time—and decide whose need is greater;
☐ Be the steward of societal resources, weighing health against other societal goods;
☐ Seek personal fulfilment—a satisfying professional life, a good living for self and family.

Physicians traditionally have dealt with these conflicting duties on an ad hoc basis, with help from features of the system already described. Often they have been able to do everything medically beneficial for well-insured patients without worrying about the cost to the patient and still do well financially, since private insurers defined medical necessity as everything of benefit and reimbursed physicians on a fee-for-service basis. Physicians could allow financial incentives to subtly shape their definition of medical necessity when (as has so often been the case) there was insufficient information about the effect of an intervention. They could avoid hard choices about patients who could not afford important care by not taking on such patients in the first place.[16] They could make triage decisions in the emergency room, the intensive care unit, or a transplant program when forced to, but push for more resources to minimize the need for such difficult decisions. They could refuse any broader responsibility as steward of societal resources, whether private insurance funds or public funds, by emphasizing their role as patient advocate and warning against any interference in the doctor-patient relationship. These tactics have not eliminated conflicts, but have kept them from getting hopelessly out of hand.

Physicians who care for the poor have experienced conflicts in more intense form than other physicians, since resources have been more limited. The resulting inefficiencies and inequities in the distribution of care have been more difficult to overlook, and personal financial well-being more elusive. Nevertheless, the tendency has been to see the problem as one of anecdotal failure, a matter of persuading the public to allocate more resources to a particular disease, program, or service, not one inherent in the nature of health care financing.

Now, however, the escalating cost of health care and the policies introduced to respond to it have sharpened the longstanding contradictions in society's expectations of physicians and brought them out into the open. There is a profound malaise in the medical profession as it finds itself pressured from all sides—through changes in organization and financial incentives—to limit beneficial care, even though many physicians see this as unethical.

The competition advocates pay little attention to this. The market model leads them to a narrow view of the motives that influence the relationship between physician and patient. They collapse the multiple conflicting objectives just outlined to those in the literature on principal-agent relationships. The patient (the principal) wants the agent to maximize patient utility subject to patient budget constraints. The physician (agent) has an ethical duty to pursue the patient's best interest but also seeks his own self-interest. The presence of insurance complicates the agency role, admittedly, since insured patients want all beneficial care when they are ill, yet it is in their long-term interest to bind themselves and their physicians to nonprice rationing methods of their choice. Nevertheless, through market competition, a mix of organizational and financial constraints on patients and physicians will develop to bring their goals into reasonable harmony, with only limited government intervention to establish the "rules of the game."

There is no place in this analysis for an "ethical duty" of physicians to ignore cost in their clinical decisions (for example, to advise patients to have medical care for which the benefits are not worth the patients' cost, or to resist insurers' efforts to limit low-benefit care) or for the discomfort physicians feel in violating this duty. There is no recognition that for American physicians, to ration at all is uncomfortable, and administering an array of rationing strategies that differ with source of payment is even worse.[17] There is also no guidance on how physicians should resolve conflicts in duty to their own patients, duty to the patients of others, and duty to society. In fact, there is no explicit recognition that such conflicts will occur.

The competition advocates perform a valuable service in showing why physicians who care about their patients' welfare should abandon the "everything of benefit without regard to cost" ideal—why physicians serve their patients better by participating in rationing, provided the rationing process is efficient and fair. This point is very important. Some who accept the necessity for rationing nevertheless believe that physicians should not actively participate in it.[18] Rationing, they say, should be done by external constraints, with physicians as "patient advocates" pursuing everything of benefit for their own patients within the constraints. Such an approach is impractical. Insurers would have great difficulty designing a rationing strategy that is sensitive to the specifics of each person's medical situation and allows some scope for personal preferences, yet permits a physician to pursue one patient's good in total disregard for the consequences for other patients or society. For their patients' sake, physicians must accept some responsibility for acting as stewards of communal resources.

The competition advocates also perform a valuable service by emphasizing the role financial incentives have always played in physician behavior. They encourage a healthy skepticism about the extent to which physicians have subordinated self-interest to professional and ethical values in the past, and highlight the importance of aligning individual incentives with communal goals.

They are not convincing, however, when they imply that the competitive process can do the whole job of conveying to physicians how to balance the interests of their patients, society, and themselves. At the very least, more explicit attention must be given to this. What part do physicians play in setting the standard—or rather the choice of standards—of care? Do they have a responsibility to ensure that care is always at least adequate? If so, how do they know what is adequate? Do they have any responsibility to make sure their patients understand the rationing process? How much must they tell an individual patient who is failing to receive beneficial care?

If physicians are to accept any social responsibility, it must be defined for them in a manageable way. Otherwise, they may simply abandon the professional ideal of physician as patient advocate, pursuing the patient's good without regard to cost, and move directly to the ideal of physician as businessperson, maximizing profit subject to third-party payer and government constraints. Our nation's experience with the results in other imperfect markets when business persons pursue profit without regard for the common good should make us uncomfortable with this prospect. This is the basis for the concern expressed by leaders of the medical profession about the "commercialization" of medicine and the participation of physicians in the "medical-industrial complex."[19]

Role of Employers

As previously noted, competition advocates recognize that consumers and insurers need help with their respective tasks if market competition is to take place on price and quality. In most versions of competitive reform, employers are assigned to help. Employers are expected to act as agents for their employees, helping to manage both adverse selection and moral hazard in their employees' best interests. To some extent, this is a pragmatic decision to build on existing structures, since employers already play a major role in the health insurance market. There is, however, something more at work—the tension between the realization that consumers need such an agent and a profound lack of confidence in the ability of government to act in their interest. Yet, the expectation that employers can and will do so effectively seems inconsistent with the market model.

First, the task itself is ill-defined. Preferences with respect to health care rationing vary with characteristics such as age, sex, health status, family structure, education, and income. These are unlikely to be homogeneous in an employee group, so a single option is unlikely to satisfy, yet allowing choice creates administrative costs and the complexities of managing selection bias. What set of options is in the best interests of an employee group?

Second, the employers may be unqualified to perform the task. Since managing employee health insurance is complex, it requires specialized expertise. Expertise can be purchased, but then employers must be able to evaluate the quality of the expertise. Even large firms find managing health insurance difficult and expensive; small firms find it prohibitive.

Third, it is questionable whether employers can be trusted to perform the task. Employers seek to maximize the firm's profits. The link between employer profits and being a perfect health insurance purchasing agent for employees is not very direct. Employers and employees are likely to have divergent interests in health insurance matters. Economic theory predicts that employers will choose the health coverage that maximizes their profits while letting employees think they have the health insurance they want. Workers cannot easily detect this; they need agents in the first place because of their inability to evaluate their options. Moreover, if they do detect it, what can they do? They can change jobs, but there are many constraints on job choice; workers often do not have the luxury of allowing the details of health insurance coverage to be the determining factor in their decisions.

Employers have a less than exemplary record in looking after their employees' interests in other areas. When it comes to safety in the workplace, for example, employees are more likely to have similar interests than in health care, yet there are many abuses. Consider, for example, the recent fire in a chicken processing plant in the South, in which workers died because fire doors were locked, allegedly to prevent the workers from stealing chickens.

Fourth, and most important, assigning this task to employers conflicts with the underlying rationale for reliance on competitive markets to allocate goods. One of the great advantages of the market system, economists teach their students, is decentralization. Suppliers can concentrate on managing their own businesses, with all the information they need about the rest of the economy embodied in the prices for their inputs and outputs. Given this, it seems odd that free-market economists should be expecting employers not only to make and sell their own products but to perform this complicated health insurance task, too, and do it well.

Finally, linking health insurance to employment interferes with the operation of the labor market. Another basic tenet of microeconomics is the superiority of paying workers in dollars rather than in specific goods. Many aspects of a job that affect utility cannot be separated from it: for example, specific duties, location, physical environment, work hours, vacation and sick leave policies, salary. Why add this extraneous element to the worker's job choice? The adverse effects are already visible in today's labor market: people whose employment decisions are seriously constrained by their particular health care situations ("job-lock").

Linking health insurance to employment also distorts the employer's hiring decision. Employers have an incentive to avoid persons of higher than average health risk and to interfere in employee lifestyle decisions outside of the workplace, not because of effects on job performance but because of effects on health care costs. This, too, is a phenomenon that is already observable in the market and is getting worse.

These problems have been acknowledged in the competition literature to some extent. Havighurst (1982), for example, recognized limitations of employers as agents for consumers, but considered them preferable to government. Enthoven, on the other hand, originally argued that linking employment and health insurance was undesirable. He designed his Consumer Choice Health Plan with no special role for employers, and assigned the role of controlling adverse selection and ensuring the availability of accurate information about insurance alternatives to government (Enthoven 1980). Over time, the failure of the political system to adopt his entire plan, a growing realization of the complexity of the consumer's information problems in making the best choice of plan, and the desire to identify pragmatic ways of building on existing structures led him to advocate a role for employers. He recognized that many employers may be unable or unwilling to perform it adequately, however, and identified employers as only one of a number of possible organizations (including government agencies) that could serve as "sponsors"—agents for a group of consumers (Enthoven 1988a, b).

Linking the performance of competitive strategies to the behavior of "sponsors"—whether employers, with known goals and characteristics that are at odds with their role of agency, or other organizations whose goals and abilities to serve in this role are unspecified—introduces a certain indeterminacy into the system.[20] Moreover, a market characterized by large organizations "competing" with each other by bi- and multilateral bargaining is a long way from the competitive market model on which the usual efficiency claims of market organization are based.

Role of Government

Competitive strategists recognize the powerful financial incentives for employers, insurers, and providers to subvert the social goals, even if they are inclined to deemphasize them. There is a role for government—to limit the extent to which insurers, providers, and employers (or sponsors) use manipulation of the information given to consumers and the composition of risk pools to compete with each other instead of the more socially desirable strategies of producing health care efficiently and setting the right benefit-cost trade-offs in the standard of care. Government also serves, in some versions, as sponsor for those who cannot otherwise be incorporated into the private system. There is already an extensive literature, by those on both sides of the debate on competition strategies, revealing the importance and complexity of these tasks.[21] The preceding discussion argues that these tasks are even more difficult when the rationing issue is fully understood.

The case for markets is based on lack of confidence in the ability of government to carry out its responsibilities. There is some basis for this. After all, there is government regulation of worker safety, but the factory fire doors were still closed. Nevertheless, in health care, all agree that markets will not produce the desired outcome without optimal government regulation. It seems odd that it is considered easier to teach incompetent bureaucrats how to stop competent private agents from successfully pursuing profit to the detriment of the social good than it is to teach bureaucrats how to pursue the social good themselves.

RATIONING IN THE FUTURE

How beneficial care is limited—that is, rationed—is the critical design feature in any proposal to reform the health care system. It is important that the public understand this, so that health care reform can reflect its preferences about rationing.

In evaluating the rationing implications of reform proposals, it is essential to take the broad perspective. In the past, there has been too much emphasis on dramatic "lifeboat" rationing examples—like the choice of candidates for organ transplants or kidney dialysis—and not enough on the way the entire system limits beneficial care.

In rationing, both the outcome and the process are important. The outcome is the distribution of care and of its cost. Who gets what? Who pays? How does this match societal values? For example, what is the trade-off between benefit and cost, and the distribution of benefit and cost by race, ethnicity, gender, geographic location, income, education, medical condition, and age?

Proposals for reform do not, of course, come with this information attached. Rather, they define a structure that produces the outcome, and only some features of the outcome can be readily predicted in advance. Consequently, the processes that determine the outcome must also be examined. Of particular importance is the extent to which there is accountability to society for the way care is rationed. Accountability can take the form of market, political, or administrative processes. Competition strategies emphasize market accountability, and other proposals emphasize political and administrative accountability, but all incorporate elements of all three.

The way individual patients and providers are treated within a rationing system is also important. How much respect is there for the autonomy of patients? Rationing constrains health care choice by definition, but there can still be some flexibility in the standard of care to allow for individual preferences. Other aspects of choice are also vital: How much freedom is there to choose one's physician and the location and timing of one's care? To what extent does the structure of the system place constraints on choices unrelated to health—for example, the choice of employment, place of residence, marital status?

Likewise, how much respect is there for the autonomy of physicians and other health care providers? Again, rationing constrains physician choice by definition, but the standard of care can still leave them room to exercise their own judgment. Moreover, they are likely to feel less constrained if they have a role in defining the standard of care they administer. As with patients, other aspects of choice are also significant: How much freedom do physicians have to choose specialty, location, hours of work, and the patients they serve?

CONCLUSION

Achieving an efficient and fair distribution of health care and of its cost, while preserving important aspects of freedom, is a difficult problem. To solve it, society must use some combination of market and political behavior to set the decent minimum, the range of variation in standards of care, and the distribution of health care cost.

In the United States, advocates of competition-based health care reform start from the premise that health care is fundamentally a private entreprise, albeit one with special public policy significance. They begin with the private markets for health care and health insurance, ask how they fail as markets, and look for the minimum amount of government intervention that will produce the usual efficiency benefits of well-functioning markets. Competition advocates devote attention to the social insurance goal, but as an afterthought. Their approach is to graft a social insurance dimension onto the private market.

In other countries, policymakers start from the premise that health care is fundamentally a social enterprise. They place primary importance on establishing a process to determine a cost-conscious standard of care to be guaranteed to everyone. Figuring out how people who want more can have it without interfering with the achievement of the social insurance goal is of secondary importance. Equity comes first, with efficiency the afterthought.

The task of getting the markets for health care and health insurance to function well as private markets, let alone fulfill the social insurance goal, turns out to be surprisingly complex. To implement competition strategies for health care reform, the organization of existing markets would have to change substantially, and there would have to be government regulation of a peculiarly delicate kind. Moreover, there is no prior experience with such a system, and it is by no means clear how well it would work, even under the most favorable of circumstances. One cannot help wondering whether it is worth the effort.

Americans clearly have inconsistent values. They say they want affordable health insurance but object to any limits on their own access to beneficial care. They give lip service to the desirability of a single-tier system that guarantees access to quality care for everyone, yet they are reluctant to vote the funds to pay for it. They are troubled by the concept of health care as "just another private good," to be bought and sold like soap—yet they are afraid of the consequences of accepting the concept of health care as a social good, to be distributed through a government-supervised nonmarket process. Pressure is building to resolve these contradictions.

The competition strategies for health care reform resolve these contradictions in favor of individualism and the market. But is this the choice a fully informed American public would make? Do Americans really want an elaborate market apparatus to allow them to choose from an array of standards of care? This is, after all, a country in which, until recently, the prevailing social myth was that there was a single standard of care, that of "medically necessary care." Freedom of choice was highly valued, but it meant the freedom to choose the providers believed most likely to understand one's personal medical situation and to deliver that medically necessary care effectively and humanely. Isn't it possible that Americans would prefer to guarantee themselves and others a single cost-conscious standard of care, so long as it was not *too* cost-conscious and allowed some room for variation in individual preferences, in care options, and choice of provider?[22]

However these questions are answered, one thing is clear. The solution to health care reform (and a number of other pressing policy problems) requires new attention to the performance of the public sector—to the improvement of its ability to set the right goals and achieve them, whether the goals relate to the supervision of a private system based on competition or the administration of national health insurance.

Notes

1. Of course, this does not mean *any* nonprice rationing is more efficient than price rationing. If a nonprice rationing method is sufficiently inaccurate and unresponsive, limited price rationing (e.g., in the form of copayments) can dominate it.

2. See, for example, Chassin (1991).

3. In theory, one could work to eliminate useless or harmful care, believed by many to be a major problem in the United States. In practice, it was often impossible to get everyone to agree that a procedure was of no benefit, and with an "everything of benefit" standard of medical necessity, patients and physicians could and would continue to use it.

4. See, for example, Braveman et al. (1991), Hadley, Steinberg, and Feder (1991), Hand et al. (1991), Hayward et al. (1988), Young and Cohen (1991), Burstin, Lipsitz, and Brennan (1992), Wenneker, Weissman, and Epstein (1990), Javitt et al. (1991).

5. Early proponents of competition-based reform emphasized the importance of consumer incentives, advocating increased cost sharing. See, for example, Feldstein (1971), Pauly (1971), and Seidman (1977, 1980).

6. Others in the debate on competition-based reform acknowledged the importance of consumer incentives but placed the emphasis on distorted consumer incentives in the purchase of insurance, and on changing provider incentives through changes in the structure of health insurance and the delivery of care (for example, see Ellwood 1971, McClure 1976, 1978, Havighurst 1978, 1982, and Enthoven 1980).

7. Havighurst, especially, emphasized the role of aggressive antitrust enforcement in fostering competition in the health care sector (see, for example, Havighurst 1978, and 1983a).

8. See, for example, Enthoven (1980, 1988a), Newhouse (1982, 1984), Pauly (1984), Rushefsky (1981), and Sofaer (1993).

9. See, for example, Siu et al. (1991) and Brook and Kosecoff (1988).

10. See Newhouse (1982), Luft (1980), and Luft and Miller (1988).

11. Pauly has raised many of these issues (e.g., Pauly 1988a), but has argued that market forces will lead providers to be concerned about their reputations and therefore to furnish accurate information about the standard of care they provide. This argument seems unconvincing, especially since Pauly does not explicitly discuss the strong financial incentive providers have to mislead if they can do it successfully.

12. Havighurst (1982: 6) has gone so far as to say ". . . consumer choice is an ethical imperative . . . . the competitive process, precisely because it is based on choice, validates the outcome whatever it may turn out to be. Thus the only relevant empirical issues would be those relating to the process itself—whether people were freely choosing with correct incentives and had a meaningful range of choice available to them."

13. It is also implicitly assumed that consumers are reasonably knowledgeable about the risks of illness and the benefits of medical treatment. Enthoven (1988c) has stated explicitly that the decent minimum should be "a standard of care that equates marginal benefits and costs for people of average incomes in that society." Others (e.g., Pauly 1988a) have implied that a lower standard would be acceptable for the decent minimum.

14. Annually, a Washington, D.C., consumer magazine (Washington Consumers' Checkbook) publishes an issue for federal employees on choosing health insurance coverage. It advises them to identify the health care needs they and their dependents are likely to have before the next open season (a one-year period) and to find the plan that will minimize their total health care cost given those expectations. Obviously, that plan may well not be the plan the purchaser thinks guarantees an adequate standard of care for everything that could happen.

15. For discussion of this question, see Baily (1986) and the references cited therein.

16. Physicians are free to choose the patients for whom they will be responsible (except in emergency situations) without violating ethical standards.

17. One issue of significant practical importance in competition strategies is the implication of the coexistence of an array of standards of care for the malpractice litigation system. Most observers agree that major change is required in the malpractice system to make it compatible with cost containment, whatever system of health care reform is adopted. Nevertheless, competition strategies would require adjustments of unusual complexity, since the current system is based on a relatively uniform standard of care, with a limited number of distinctions (e.g., between generalist and specialist providers). For discussion, see Havighurst (1983b) and Epstein (1976).

18. See, for example, Angell (1985).

19. See, for example, Relman (1991).

20. Since the 1992 presidential election, there has been increased (and much-needed) attention to sponsors, with discussion of the various types of organizations that might serve as sponsors, and how they should be structured and held accountable for their activities. See, for example, Zelman (1993), Starr (1993), Robinson (1993), Sofaer (1993), and Kronick (1993).

21. See, for example, the articles by Enthoven, Havighurst, and Pauly in the references; also Jones (1989, 1990), Newhouse (1982, 1984), Feldman (1987), Feldman and Dowd (1991), Weisbrod (1978, 1983), and Rushefsky (1981).

22. This would be even more likely if there were some provision for the wealthy to obtain additional care clearly labeled "nonessential" and paid for fully out of their own pockets.

References

Aaron, Henry J. 1991. *Serious and Unstable Condition: Financing America's Health Care.* Washington, D.C.: Brookings Institution.

Aaron, Henry J., and William B. Schwartz. 1984. *The Painful Prescription: Rationing Hospital Care.* Washington, D.C.: Brookings Institution.

Altman, Stuart H., and Marc A. Rodwin. 1988. "Halfway Competitive Markets and Ineffective Regulation: The American Health Care System." *Journal of Health Politics, Policy and Law* 13 (2, Summer): 323–39.

Angell, Marcia. 1985. "Cost Containment and the Physician." *Journal of the American Medical Association* 254: 1203–7.

Baily, Mary Ann. 1986. "Rationing Medical Care: Processes for Defining Adequacy." In *The Price of Health*, edited by George J. Agich and Charles E. Begley (165–84). Dordrecht, Holland: D. Reidel Publishing Co.

Braveman, Paula A., Susan Egerter, Trude Bennett, and Jonathan Showstack. 1991. "Differences in Hospital Resource Allocation among Sick Newborns According to Insurance Coverage." *Journal of the American Medical Association* 266(23): 3300–8.

Brook, Robert H., and Jacqueline B. Kosecoff. 1988. "Competition and Quality." *Health Affairs* 7 (3, Summer): 150–61.

Brown, Lawrence D. 1988. "Afterword." *Journal of Health Politics, Policy and Law* 13 (2, Summer): 361–63.

Burstin, Helen R., Stuart R. Lipsitz, and Troyen A. Brennan. 1992. "Socioeconomic Status and Risk for Substandard Medical Care." *Journal of the American Medical Association* 268(17): 2383–87.

Chassin, Mark R. 1991. "Quality of Care: Time to Act." *Journal of the American Medical Association* 266(24): 3472–73.

Crandall, Robert W. 1981. "The Impossibility of Finding a Mechanism to Ration Health Care Resources Efficiently." In *A New Approach to the Economics of Health Care,* edited by Mancur Olson (29–43). San Francisco: Pacific Research Institute for Public Policy.

Eddy, David. 1991. "Rationing by Patient Choice." *Journal of the American Medical Association* 265(1): 105–8.

Ellwood, Paul, Nancy N. Andersen, James E. Billings, Rick J. Carlson, Earl J. Hoagberg, and Walter McClure. 1971. "Health Maintenance Strategy." *Medical Care* 9 (3, May–June): 291–98.

Enthoven, Alain. 1978. "Competition of Alternative Delivery Systems." In *Competition in the Health Care Sector: Past, Present, and Future,* edited by Warren Greenberg (255–77). Germantown, Md.: Aspen Systems Corp.

―――――. 1980. *Health Plan: The Only Practical Solution to the Soaring Cost of Medical Care.* Reading, Mass.: Addison-Wesley.

―――――. 1988a. "Managed Competition: An Agenda for Action." *Health Affairs* 7 (3, Summer): 25–47.

―――――. 1988b. "Managed Competition of Alternative Delivery Systems." *Journal of Health Politics, Policy and Law* 13 (2, Summer): 305–21.

―――――. 1988c. *Theory and Practice of Managed Competition in Health Care Finance.* Amsterdam: North-Holland.

―――――. 1989. "Effective Management of Competition in the FEBP." *Health Affairs* 8 (3, Fall): 33–50.

―――――. 1990. "Multiple Choice Health Insurance: The Lessons and Challenge to Employers." *Inquiry* 27 (Winter): 368–75.

Epstein, Richard A. 1976. "Medical Malpractice: The Case for Contract." *American Bar Foundation Research Journal* 1 (January): 94–95.

Etzioni, Amitai. 1991. "Health Care Rationing: A Critical Evaluation." *Health Affairs* 10 (2, Summer): 88–95.

Evans, Roger W. 1983. "Health Care Technology and the Inevitability of Resource Allocation and Rationing Decisions, Part II." *Journal of the American Medical Association* 249(16): 2208–19.

Feldman, Roger. 1987. "Health Insurance in the United States: Is Market Failure Avoidable?" *Journal of Risk and Insurance* 54(2): 298–313.

Feldman, Roger, and Bryan Dowd. 1991. "Must Adverse Selection Cause Premium Spirals?" *Journal of Health Economics* 10: 349–57.

Feldstein, Martin. 1971. "A New Approach to National Health Insurance." *Public Interest* 23 (Spring): 93–105.

Frech III, H. E. 1981. "The Long-Lost Free Market in Health Care: Government and Professional Regulation of Medicine." In *A New Approach to* the Economics of Health Care, edited by Mancur Olson (44–66). San Francisco: Pacific Research Institute for Public Policy.

Fuchs, Victor R. 1984. "The 'Rationing' of Medical Care." New England Journal of Medicine 311(24): 1572–73.

————. 1988. "The 'Competition Revolution' in Health Care." Health Affairs 7 (3, Summer): 5–24.

Ginsburg, Paul B. 1984. "The Competition Debate Five Years Later." Journal of Health Economics 3 (3, December): 307–11.

Hadley, Jack, Earl P. Steinberg, and Judith Feder. 1991. "Comparison of Uninsured and Privately Insured Hospital Patients: Condition on Admission, Resource Use, and Outcome." Journal of the American Medical Association 265(3): 374–79.

Hadorn, David C. 1991. "The Health Care Resource Allocation Debate: Defining Our Terms." Journal of the American Medical Association 266(23): 3328–31.

Hand, Roger, Stephen Sener, Joseph Imperato, Joan S. Chmiel, JoAnne Sylvester, and Amy Fremgen. 1991. "Hospital Variables Associated with Quality of Care for Breast Cancer Patients." Journal of the American Medical Association 266(24): 3429–32.

Havighurst, Clark C. 1974. "Speculations on the Market's Future in Health Care." In Regulating Health Facilities Construction, edited by Clark C. Havighurst (249–69). Washington, D.C.: American Enterprise Institute.

————. 1978. "The Role of Competition in Cost Containment." In Competition in the Health Care Sector: Past, Present, and Future, edited by Warren Greenberg (285–323). Germantown, Md.: Aspen Systems Corp.

————. 1980. "Prospects for Competition under Health Planning-cum-Regulation." In National Health Insurance: What Now, What Later, What Never? edited by M. V. Pauly (329–59). Washington, D.C.: American Enterprise Institute.

————. 1982. Deregulating the Health Care Industry: Planning for Competition. Cambridge, Mass.: Ballinger.

————. 1983a. "The Contributions of Antitrust Law to a Procompetitive Health Policy." In Market Reforms in Health Care: Current Issues, New Directions, Strategic Decisions, edited by Jack A. Meyer. Washington, D.C.: American Enterprise Institute, 295–322.

————. 1983b. "Decentralizing Decision Making: Private Contract versus Professional Norms." In Market Reforms in Health Care: Current Issues, New Directions, Strategic Decisions, edited by Jack A. Meyer (22–45). Washington, D.C.: American Enterprise Institute.

————. 1988. "The Questionable Cost-Containment Record of Commercial Health Insurers." In Health Care in America: The Political Economy of Hospitals and Health Insurance, edited by H. E. Frech III (221–58). San Francisco: Pacific Research Institute for Public Policy.

Hayward, Rodney A., M. F. Shapiro, H. E. Freeman, and C. R. Corey. 1988. "Inequities in Health Services among Insured Americans: Do Working-Age Adults Have Less Access to Medical Care than the Elderly?" New England Journal of Medicine 318(23): 1507–12.

Javitt, Jonathan C., A. Marshall McBean, Geraldine A. Nicholson, J. Daniel Babish, Joan L. Warren, and Henry Krakauer. 1991. "Undertreatment of Glaucoma among Black Americans." New England Journal of Medicine 325(20): 1418–22.

Jones, Stanley P. 1989. "Can Multiple Choice Be Managed to Constrain Health Care Costs?" Health Affairs 8 (3, Fall): 51–59.

_____. 1990. "Multiple Choice Health Insurance: The Lessons and Challenge to Private Insurers." Inquiry 27 (Summer): 161–66.

King, Kathleen. 1990. "Rationing Health Care." CRS Report for Congress, 90-346 EPW. Washington, D.C.: Congressional Research Service, Library of Congress, July 12.

Kirkman-Liff, Bradford L. 1991. "Health Insurance Values and Implementation in the Netherlands and the Federal Republic of Germany: An Alternative Path to Universal Coverage." Journal of the American Medical Association 265(19): 2496–2502.

Kronick, Richard. 1993. "Where Should the Buck Stop: Federal and State Responsibilities in Health Care Financing Reform." Health Affairs 12(Supplement): 87–98.

Luft, Harold S. 1980. "Health Maintenance Organizations, Competition, Cost Containment, and National Health Insurance." In National Health Insurance: What Now, What Later, What Never? edited by M. V. Pauly (283–306). Washington, D.C.: American Enterprise Institute.

Luft, Harold S., and Robert H. Miller. 1988. "Patient Selection in a Competitive Health Care System." Health Affairs 7(3, Summer): 97–119.

McClure, Walter. 1976. "The Medical Care System under National Health Insurance: Four Models." Journal of Health Politics, Policy and Law 1(1, Spring): 22–68.

_____. 1978. "On Broadening the Definition of and Removing Regulatory Barriers to a Competitive Health Care System." Journal of Health Politics, Policy and Law 3(3, Fall): 303–27.

McLaughlin, Catherine G. 1988. "Market Responses to HMOs: Price Competition or Rivalry?" Inquiry 25(Summer): 207–18.

Mechanic, David. 1979. Future Issues in Health Care: Social Policy and the Rationing of Medical Services. New York: Free Press.

Merrill, J., and A. B. Cohen. 1987. "The Emperor's New Clothes: Unraveling the Myths about Rationing." Inquiry 24(Summer): 105–9.

Newhouse, Joseph P. 1982. "Is Competition the Answer?" Journal of Health Economics 1: 109–16.

_____. 1984. "Cream-Skimming, Asymmetric Information, and a Competitive Insurance Market." Journal of Health Economics 3 (1, April): 97–100.

Pauly, Mark V. 1968. "The Economics of Moral Hazard: Comment, Part 1."
    American Economic Review 58 (3, June): 531–37.
————. 1971. An Analysis of National Health Insurance Proposals. Wash-
    ington, D.C.: American Enterprise Institute.
————. 1978. "Is Medical Care Different?" In Competition in the Health
    Care Sector: Past, Present, and Future, edited by Warren Greenberg
    (11–35). Germantown, Md.: Aspen Systems Corp.
————.1980. "Overinsurance: The Conceptual Issues." In National Health
    Insurance: What Now, What Later, What Never? edited by M. V.
    Pauly (201–19). Washington, D.C.: American Enterprise Institute.
————. 1984. "Is Cream-Skimming a Problem for the Competitive Medical
    Market?" Journal of Health Economics 3 (1, April): 87–95.
————. 1988a. "Is Medical Care Different? Old Questions, New Answers."
    Journal of Health Politics, Policy and Law 13 (2, Summer): 227–37.
————. 1988b. "A Primer on Competition in Medical Markets." In Health
    Care in America: The Political Economy of Hospitals and Health
    Insurance, edited by H. E. Frech III (27–71). San Francisco: Pacific
    Research Institute for Public Policy.
Reagan, Michael D. 1988. "Health Care Rationing: What Does It Mean?" New
    England Journal of Medicine 319(17): 1149–51.
Relman, Arnold S., 1991. "Shattuck Lecture—The Health Care Industry:
    Where Is It Taking Us?" New England Journal of Medicine 325(12):
    854–859.
Robinson, James C. 1993. "A Payment Method for Health Insurance Purchas-
    ing Cooperatives." Health Affairs 12(Supplement): 65–75.
Rushefsky, Mark E. 1981. "A Critique of Market Reform in Health Care: The
    'Consumer-Choice Health Plan.' " Journal of Health Politics, Policy
    and Law 5(4): 720–41.
Seidman, Laurence S. 1977. "Medical Loans and Major-Risk National Health
    Insurance." Health Services Research 12 (Summer): 123–28.
————. 1980. "Income-Related Consumer Cost Sharing: A Strategy for the
    Health Sector." In National Health Insurance: What Now, What
    Later, What Never? edited by M. V. Pauly (307–28). Washington,
    D.C.: American Enterprise Institute.
————. 1981. "Consumer Choice Health Plan and the Patient Cost-Sharing
    Strategy: Can They Be Reconciled?" In A New Approach to the
    Economics of Health Care, edited by Mancur Olson (450–66). San
    Francisco: Pacific Research Institute for Public Policy.
Siu, Albert L., Elizabeth A. McGlynn, Hal Morgenstern, and Robert H. Brook.
    1991. "A Fair Approach to Comparing Quality of Care." Health
    Affairs 10 (1, Spring): 62–75.
Sofaer, Shoshanna. 1993. "Informing and Protecting Consumers Under Man-
    aged Competition." Health Affairs 12(Supplement): 76–86.
Starr, Paul. 1993. "Design of Health Insurance Purchasing Cooperatives."
    Health Affairs 12(Supplement): 58–64.

Webster's Ninth New Collegiate Dictionary. 1986. Springfield, Mass.: Merriam-Webster.

Weisbrod, Burton A. 1978. "Comment [on Pauly]." In *Competition in the Health Care Sector: Past, Present, and Future,* edited by Warren Greenberg (37–42). Germantown, Md.: Aspen Systems Corp.

————. 1983. "Competition in Health Care: A Cautionary View." In *Market Reforms in Health Care: Current Issues, New Directions, Strategic Decisions,* edited by Jack A. Meyer (61–71). Washington, D.C.: American Enterprise Institute.

Wenneker, Mark B., Joel S. Weissman, and Arnold M. Epstein. 1990. "The Association of Payer with Utilization of Cardiac Procedures in Massachusetts." *Journal of the American Medical Association* 264(10): 1255–60.

Young, Gary J., and Bruce B. Cohen. 1991. "Inequities in Hospital Care: The Massachusetts Experience." *Inquiry* 28 (Fall): 255–62.

Zelman, Walter A. 1993. "Who Should Govern the Purchasing Cooperative?" *Health Affairs* 12(Supplement): 49–57.

Part Five

COMPETITIVE REFORM AND THE FUTURE

Chapter Sixteen

COMPETITIVE REFORM AND THE FUTURE

Richard J. Arnould, Robert F. Rich, and William D. White

Over a decade of experimentation with competitive reforms is now behind us. The essays in this volume have variously examined the context and scope of these reforms, evidence on their impacts, and their possible implications. This concluding chapter considers what has been learned about competitive reforms in the 1980s that could help guide health care policy in the 1990s and beyond.

Current debate over health care policy focuses on issues of comprehensive reform. As discussed in chapter 1, no single comprehensive agenda existed for implementing competitive reforms in the 1980s. Experimentation occurred on a piecemeal and often disparate basis. Efforts encompassed market-oriented strategies to improve performance on both the demand and supply sides of markets for medical services and health insurance, and to solve a range of informational problems. Evaluation of the impact of these strategies has necessarily also been piecemeal. The implications of fully implementing these programs remain a matter of conjecture. However, based on the essays in this volume, three important lessons emerge from the reforms of the 1980s.

First, based on experiences with "payer-driven" competition, competitive forces can be successfully harnessed to improve performance in health care markets. Second, competitive mechanisms cannot be relied on to address equity problems. Third, elements of competitive reforms may be compatible with a wide range of alternative reform schemes. The next section considers these lessons in more detail, then discusses the future of competitive reforms under a range of alternative scenarios and closes with a discussion of the feasibility of reform under current political conditions.

THREE LESSONS FROM COMPETITIVE REFORMS

The basic premise of competitive reforms has been that competitive forces in health care markets can be successfully harnessed to solve problems with "market failure" by improving incentives for health care consumers and producers to more efficiently allocate resources. Following the taxonomy presented in chapter 1, reform efforts can be broadly classified into four types: (1) those operating on the demand side of markets for health services; (2) those operating on the supply side of markets for health services; (3) those involving insurance markets; and (4) those seeking to improve information flows.

Longstanding skepticism has existed about the comparability of health markets to those for other goods and services. A major contention of Part Two of this volume is that competitive reforms on the supply side of markets for health services, through a shift from "patient-driven" to "payer-driven" competition, are having an impact on provider performance in ways consistent with economic predictions. Thus, Zwanziger and Melnick (chapter 6) and Dranove (chapter 4) report that following restructuring of hospital markets in California, there has been a relative decrease in prices in more competitive markets.

Evidence for the ability of other types of competitive reforms to improve market performance, although generally positive, is less convincing. For example, opportunities for the majority of consumers to directly exercise their preferences in insurance markets remain limited. Feldman and colleagues' finding (in chapter 8) that rents are squeezed out of firms in more competitive markets for Medicare health maintenance organizations (HMOs) suggests that real potential exists for linking "payer-driven" competition in service markets to "consumer-driven" competition in insurance markets. Unfortunately, there has not been the kind of large-scale experimentation with consumer-driven competition analogous to experiments with payer-driven competition. Information-oriented strategies discussed by Freund (chapter 3) and Brown (chapter 10) are still largely in their infancy. Although such strategies could serve to improve quality while cutting costs, this has yet to be demonstrated. Based on experiences in markets for medical services, however, competitive strategies are a powerful potential tool to promote efficiency.

The same cannot be said for promoting equity. As discussed by Sloan (chapter 12), competitive strategies are poorly suited to address issues such as the uninsured. Americans have yet to reach a consensus on the matter of access to health care. But virtually no one advocates allocating health care services purely through the market. Provisions for improving access to care on equity grounds are a component of all the major proposals for reform, albeit in varying degrees.

The third lesson to be derived from the essays in this volume is that competitive strategies are best conceived of as a set of mechanisms for improving market performance, rather than as a monolithic prescription. Thus, competitive strategies have been implemented in the context of private insurance markets, as well as the Medicare system (see Feldman et al., chapter 8), the California MediCal system (Zwanziger and Melnick, chapter 6), and experiments that are underway by the British National Health Service (Posnett, chapter 14). Accordingly, use of these strategies should not be treated as an either/or proposition, but as a mechanism for potentially improving efficiency under *any* proposal for health care reform.

FUTURE OF COMPETITIVE STRATEGIES

Proposals for competitive reforms have been closely identified with market-oriented schemes such as Pauly and colleagues' (1992) *Responsible National Health Insurance* plan. Our third lesson suggests that the future of competitive reforms is not necessarily tied to any particular approach; competitive strategies and "managed competition" could be elements of a wide range of scenarios.

Although individual proposals for comprehensive health reform are too numerous to review in detail here, they can be grouped into three main types—voucher/tax credit schemes, mandated employer benefits, and universal national health insurance (NHI). In addition, "rationing" of health care is sometimes put forward as a fourth option. However, problems with ensuring equitable access to care through a purely competitive approach almost certainly require that competitive strategies under any of the first three scenarios be accompanied by an element of nonmarket allocation. Accordingly, we consider rationing as a general issue.

When comparing alternative strategies for reform, it is important to examine both their intrinsic merits and their potential for implementation. Many of the concerns raised in this volume about implementing competitive strategies are quite broad. For this reason, we largely defer discussion of implementation issues until the end of this section.

Rationing

Scarce resources may be "rationed" in many ways. Using markets and the price system is one option, but in health care the term usually refers to nonmarket schemes (Baily, chapter 15). Historically, the U.S. health care system has eschewed "rationing" for the insured population. Thus, the purported standard of care has been "flat-of-the-curve" medicine—provision of any and all care that may yield positive benefit to a patient regardless of cost.

Competitive reforms and proposals for "rationing" share the common premise that at the margin, benefits and costs should be equated (i.e., that allocation should be "efficient" in an economic sense). The two approaches are often contrasted as alternative means of achieving this objective. But there is a potential for significant complementarity between competitive strategies and rationing. As a practical matter, rationing is an issue in terms of implementing such strategies in at least three important respects: (1) rationing may be necessary if we are to provide equitable access to care; (2) because of the merit good dimensions of health care (i.e., dimensions of health care that are deemed to be intrinsically desirable by society even though consumers might not freely consume adequate amounts of these goods and services) rationing may be necessary to provide appropriate access and availability of health care; and (3) because of problems with moral hazard, rationing may be necessary to control excess utilization of health care services.

Rationing is inherent in any sort of redistributive scheme attempting to assure some "minimum" level of access to care below that required to practice "flat-of-the-curve" medicine (i.e., in essence below maximal care). Directly or indirectly, this implies some sort of societal comparison of costs and benefits.

Moreover, in providing minimum access, an open-ended voucher for any type of health insurance coverage a consumer might care to purchase is rarely an option under either existing or proposed voucher schemes. Generally, particular services are identified as meritorious and their consumption encouraged (e.g., vaccinations). Consumption of other services may require special approval (e.g., organ transplants). Finally, for some procedures reimbursement may not be provided at all (e.g., cosmetic surgery, use of a nongeneric drug where a generic is available). Implicitly, such reimbursement restrictions amount to an additional form of nonprice rationing made explicit in proposals such as those recently introduced in Oregon.

Finally, even where the level of insurance coverage may be market determined, moral hazard raises issues potentially resolved through nonprice rationing. In essence, "managed-care" strategies (Arnould et al., chapter 5), may be viewed as mechanisms for precommitting consumers to a style of care and enforcing this style on providers.

Despite efforts at standardization, medical care remains far too complex to spell out every possible contingency in a contract. As a result, the "appropriateness" of care must often be evaluated on an individual basis. Enrolling in an HMO or preferred provider organization (PPO) amounts to precommitting to some sort of implicit or explicit algorithm for administrative rationing of care.

Voucher/Tax Credit Schemes

Under voucher/tax credit schemes, consumers satisfying selected criteria receive vouchers or tax credits that allow them to purchase approved insurance in the private market where a public plan may also be offered to assure access to a minimum level of care. In its simplest form, the primary impact of this type of scheme would be to supplement existing purchases of coverage. However, plans such as the *Responsible National Health Insurance* plan (RNHI) proposed by Pauly and colleagues (1992) seek to combine vouchers and tax credits with "managed competition."

The underlying goals of such plans are to restructure markets for medical services to foster payer-driven competition, and to restructure insurance markets and link "payer-driven" competition with undiluted consumer-driven competition in insurance markets. Equity concerns would be addressed by adjusting the cost of obtaining a minimum package of benefits to ability to pay. Everyone, regardless of ability to pay, would be required to purchase coverage equivalent to this minimum package. No limits would exist on supplemental coverage, but purchases of insurance not covered by vouchers or tax credits would no longer be tax deductible.

These reforms are intended to align costs and benefits to promote efficient allocation of health care resources, eliminating the need for any proactive form of cost containment. Accordingly, government "rationing" of services would not be needed except, implicitly, at the level of the minimum plan; supplemental levels of coverage would be determined by market forces, albeit in conjunction with "management" of care by private insurers.

Concerns about the voucher/tax credit/managed competition approach have focused on four issues. First, there are major concerns that the level of access to coverage for the uninsured would be insufficient. Yet, proposals other than the RNHI plan do not generate universal access. Second, unless the basic voucher is quite large, a voucher/tax credit plan would almost certainly lead to sharp inequities in spending for care between those with coverage restricted to the basic voucher and the rest of the population. Third, there are concerns about adverse selection in insurance markets. In current proposals, employment-based group insurance would remain a primary vehicle for obtaining coverage. Experience rating has been advocated by Pauly and colleagues (1992) as a solution. But it seems possible that large numbers of individuals could be forced into a residual public plan, undermining competition.

Finally, there are concerns about the effectiveness of market forces in controlling costs. Dranove (chapter 4) and Zwanziger and Melnick (chapter 6) point to mounting evidence that payer-driven competition can contribute to cost containment in conjunction with managed care. But evidence that payer-driven competition can be successfully linked to consumer-driven competition in insurance markets is less clear.

Mandated Benefits

Mandated benefit schemes (referred to as play or pay), like voucher/tax credit schemes, generally imply continued purchases of private insurance. Typically, employers are required to offer employees a minimum level of benefits (play) or bear a tax (pay) to finance public insurance. This type of scenario can also be linked to managed competition. For example, at this writing managed competition plays an important role in mandated benefit schemes being considered by the Clinton administration.

Play-or-pay/mandated benefit schemes raise many of the same concerns discussed earlier for voucher/tax credit schemes, including universal access, adequacy of the minimum benefit package, and the ability of competition to control costs. Adverse selection is also an important issue; if employers prefer to "pay" rather than "play," this type of approach could lead to rapid growth in public provision of insurance, which would undermine competitive dimensions.

An additional concern is that mandated benefit plans would increase compensation costs. Higher employee compensation costs could have the perverse impact of reducing employment of low-wage workers, who currently are among those experiencing the greatest difficulty obtaining health insurance and are a target group for expanded benefits.

Universal National Health Insurance

Universal national health insurance (NHI) schemes are commonly viewed as the antithesis of competitive schemes. Under Canada's single-payer system, for example, the market for private health insurance has been eliminated by regulatory fiat, as have most forms of out-of-pocket payments. Both the scope of insurance coverage and the level of provider budgets are politically determined. Competition for patients, to the extent it exists between providers, is on the basis of the quality of care rather than price.

A universal, single-payer scheme does not necessarily rule out competitive elements, however. As discussed by Posnett (chapter 14), extensive experimentation is being undertaken with competition in the United Kingdom by the National Health Service. These experiments are very new. However, they suggest that price competition between providers under a universal scheme should not be ruled out. For example, a voucher/managed competition scheme could exist in which everyone has a fixed voucher and can select between a range of plans offered by provider networks.

IMPLEMENTATION ISSUES

Essays in this volume raise two key considerations about the implementation of competitive reforms under all the scenarios discussed here. A ubiquitous concern raised by Morone (chapter 9), Brown (chapter 10), and Marmor (chapter 11) is that the costs of implementing competitive reforms of any type on a comprehensive basis may be high. A second concern, articulated by Posnett (chapter 14) and implicit in other essays, is that the local nature of health care delivery may make fostering competition difficult.

Administrative costs have clearly been rising in the U.S. health care system. The degree to which this is attributable to competitive reforms is unclear. At least two issues may be involved. One is marketing costs in a more competitive environment. The other is costs associated with achieving regulatory goals. Debates have long raged in economics about whether expenditures on advertising and other marketing costs are wasteful (see Carlton and Perloff 1989, ch. 18; and Friedman 1983). Without taking a position in this debate, there is no obvious reason to view health as a unique case per se; Dranove (chapter 4) points out that the same issue exists in many other industries.

Regulatory costs pose a more complex issue. Morone (chapter 9) argues that addressing problems of adverse selection and the quality of care associated with mounting competition could prove extremely costly given broad concerns about equitable access to care. Available evidence does not point to massive problems (see Zwanziger and Melnick, chapter 6). However, concern remains first because under current piecemeal reforms, mediating mechanisms exist that could be swept away under a fully comprehensive system. For example, opportunities for hospitals to perform a buffering function through cost shifting to cross-subsidize care could be largely eliminated. Second, analysis typically assumes that the goodwill and professionalism of providers can be taken for granted. It may not be true that in an increasingly competitive environment this would necessarily be the case, potentially increasing the need to more closely oversee their activities.

In chapter 14, Posnett's discussion of the English experience highlights another problem with competitive strategies implicit in analyses of payer-driven competition in the United States. Providers not located in large urban areas often have substantial market power because health care markets tend to be local. Posnett emphasizes the possibility that providers may be able to use this market power to stymie competitive strategies, exercising monopoly power when permitted to do so.

FEASIBILITY OF REFORM

This volume has focused primarily on solutions to a health care "crisis" regarding costs and access in the United States. Issues of cost and access do not fully account for the crucial problems facing the U.S. health system; however, several factors are exacerbating the current situation. First, Americans have shown a fascination and preoccupation with development of state-of-the-art technology; we *expect* each local hospital to have the best and most up-to-date equipment. Moreover, we, as citizens, expect the federal government to invest heavily in the research and technology that will continue to provide the United States with a competitive advantage in technology development, production, and application. Consequently, the overall cost of delivering health care is driven up.

Second, we similarly *expect* that each of us will have access to state-of-the-art care. Consequently, social expectations represent a very important dimension of the crisis in rising health care costs. It is not sufficient for those interested in solving these problems to propose changes in the structure or organization of the system or reimbursement practices. The level of expectations of citizens also must be changed.[1]

Finally, demographics, along with state-of-the-art technology mentioned above, account for the fact that we have a population with an increasingly large number of elderly people who are living longer and demanding more health care services. This puts great pressures on the long-term care system. These factors may have led to a "policy crisis" that is linked to the health care "crisis." For the third time in the post–World War II era, comprehensive health care reform is a critical item on the national agenda. Major reform efforts failed in the 1950s and in the 1970s. There is a real possibility that major reform will fail once again, for cost and access problems cannot be jointly resolved so long as policymakers fail to address the expectations of consumers and providers.

ORIGINS/IMPLICATIONS OF THE POLICY CRISIS

The failure of past reform efforts cannot be fully explained by the nature and substance of the problems facing the health care system. Failure associated with the "policy crisis" may occur in the presence of one or more of the following conditions: (a) policymakers cannot agree on the approach to take to solve a problem; (b) policymakers cannot agree on the nature and magnitude of the problem to be addressed; and/or (c) policymakers cannot agree on what would constitute a "successful" outcome of a particular approach or intervention. Historically, these conditions have produced controversy over the goals or objectives of a program, the way a program is to be organized, the strategy used to implement a program, and the approach used to evaluate a program.

The health care arena is in a policy crisis not just because it displays *all* of these characteristics, but because it has displayed them for many decades. The federal government has neither the will nor the capacity to respond to the "crisis." "Capacity" should be thought of as a combination of tested procedures, past precedents, and structures/organizations that can effectively respond to a problem or set of problems. In most cases, when a problem reaches the agenda, a policymaker looks for precedents to serve as the foundation for formulating an appropriate response. The policymaker might ask: How is this problem similar to other problems we have faced in the past? and What measures or procedures could we adopt that have been used successfully in the past? For example, the testing and contact tracing procedures used in fighting hepatitis and tuberculosis have served as models for public health officials in the AIDS crisis.

The lessons explored in the earlier chapters of this volume bear directly on this policy crisis. Competitive reforms do improve the efficiency of health care markets. They also provide a yardstick against which the success of policy can be measured. However, implementation of competitive reforms has been limited. They do not resolve issues of equity, yet they are tools that can provide efficiency in implementing a voucher or play-or-pay system and may be useful in a universal system (e.g., the British National Health Service). Furthermore, while the evidence drawn from the competitive health reforms provides substantial bases for the positive roles these tools can play in resolving our health care policy problems, this same evidence does not address other aspects of these problems directly. It does not provide for differentiation of the "workability" among the alternative policies, it does not address access, and it continues to sweep under the carpet such critical issues as the development of a long-term care policy.

As we experience yet a new wave of health care reform in the 1990s, it is critical to recognize that we have both a health care crisis and a policy crisis; dual crises that make implementation of major reform difficult. However, we do know that competition can play a major role in any policy chosen.

Notes

1. Although not dealt with elsewhere in this volume, we would be remiss if we failed to mention that tort laws in the United States are contributing to the rising costs of health care. Physicians are paying high premiums for malpractice insurance; in turn, juries and judges are making large awards to patients.

References

Carlton, Dennis W., and Jeffrey M. Perloff. 1989. *Modern Industrial Organization.* Glenview, Ill.: Scott, Foresman.

Friedman, James. 1983. *Oligopoly Theory*. Cambridge, England: Cambridge University Press.

Pauly, Mark, Patricia Danzon, Paul Feldstein, and John Hoff. 1992. *Responsible National Health Insurance*. Washington, D.C.: American Enterprise Institute.

ABOUT THE EDITORS

Richard J. Arnould is professor of economics in the Department of Economics and the College of Medicine at the University of Illinois at Urbana/Champaign and director of the Program in Health Economics, Management and Policy. He has authored numerous studies on the impact of incentives on levels of efficiency in health services markets, causes of market failure in health services markets, and on the impact of various regulatory mechanisms such as antitrust and product safety on a variety of industries. He is co-editor of the *Quarterly Review of Economics and Finance* and serves on the editorial board of the *Review of Business Studies*.

Robert F. Rich is director of the Institute of Government and Public Affairs and professor of political science, health resources management, community health, and medicine at the University of Illinois. His areas of interest include health and mental health policy, science and technology policy, and environmental policy.

William D. White is an associate professor at the department of economics at the University of Illinois at Chicago and associate professor and associate director of the Institute of Government and Public Affairs at the University of Illinois. He is author of studies on the structure and performance of markets for hospital services, the design of health care payment systems, and the economics of professional regulation. He is a member of the editorial board of the *Journal of Health Politics, Policy and Law*.

ABOUT THE CONTRIBUTORS

Mary Ann Baily has been adjunct associate professor of economics and public policy at the George Washington University since 1983. She taught at Yale University from 1973 to 1979, and served as the staff economist for the President's Commission for the Study of Ethical Problems in Medicine and Biomedical and Behavioral Research from 1980 to 1983. Her research interests include health care rationing, access to care, and the implications of HIV infection, organ transplantation, and Alzheimer's Disease for health care financing.

David A. Boyum is a policy analyst with the Botec Analysis Group in Cambridge, Massachusetts. He recently published (with Theodore R. Marmor) "American Medical Care Reform: Are We Doomed to Fail?," which appeared in Fall 1992 edition of *Daedalus*.

Lawrence D. Brown is professor and head of the Division of Health Policy and Management in the School of Public Health at Columbia University. He writes on competitive and regulatory issues in health policy and on the politics of health care policymaking more generally. He (and Catherine McLaughlin) evaluated the Robert Wood Johnson Foundation's Community Programs for Affordable Health Care and their Program for the Medically Uninsured. He was editor of the *Journal of Health Politics, Policy and Law* from 1984–1989.

Jon B. Christianson, professor in the Institute for Health Services Research at the University of Minnesota, has extensive experience in evaluating HMOs. Since 1986, Dr. Christianson has examined the organization and delivery of mental health, alcohol, and chemical dependency services in HMOs. He was an investigator on an AHCPR-funded grant that examined the determinants of HMO foundings, failures, mergers, and acquisitions. Recently, he completed a study of the desirability of allowing HMOs to offer an open-ended option under their TEFRA risk contracts.

Craig Copeland is a graduate assistant and doctoral candidate in health economics at the Department of Economics, University of Illinois/Urbana-Champaign. He received a B.S. in Economics from Purdue University.

Bryan Dowd, associate professor in the Institute for Health Services Research at the University of Minnesota, specializes in research relating to the structure and performance of health care markets. He has published extensively on the effects of HMOs on health care costs and utilization of services, and the effects of government regulation on health care markets. Recently, he completed a study of biased selection in Twin Cities Medicare health plans.

David Dranove is associate professor of management and strategy and health services management at Northwestern University's Kellogg School of Management, and faculty associate at Northwestern University's Center for Urban Affairs and Policy Research. He is on the editorial boards of the *Journal of Health Economics* and the *Journal of Medical Practice Management*. He is widely published in both economics and health services research journals and received the 1993 John Thompson Prize in Health Services Research.

Roger Feldman is professor of health services research and economics at the University of Minnesota. Recently, he has completed studies of competition among private health insurers, hospitals, and HMOs, including a study of HMO mergers. Dr. Feldman is a regular contributor to journals in health services research and economics and is on the editorial boards of several journals, including *Health Services Research* and *Inquiry.*

Deborah A. Freund is professor of public affairs and associate dean for academic affairs of the School of Public and Environmental Affairs at Indiana University. She currently is the chairman of the Board of the Association of University Programs in Health Administration and sits on the board of directors of the Association for Health Services Research. She has published extensively, and is particularly noted for her research on Medicaid case management and hospital length of stay.

Kathryn M. Langwell is Deputy Assistant Director for Health for the Congressional Budget Office. From 1983 through 1989, while a senior economist at Mathematica Policy Research, Inc., she was project director and co-principal investigator of the National Evaluation of the Medicare Competition Demonstrations. Her current research interests include issues related to the performance of the health insurance market, impacts of cost containment and competition on the market for health services, and the implications of AIDS for public and private health care expenditures.

Theodore R. Marmor is professor of public policy and management at the Yale School of Organization and Management. He is a fellow of the Canadian Institute of Advanced Research, a member of the Institute of Medicine of the National Academy of Sciences, and a founding board member of the National Academy of Social Insurance. His most recent book, co-authored with Jerry L. Mashaw and Philip L. Harvey, is *America's Misunderstood Welfare State: Persistent Myths, Enduring Realities.*

Glenn A. Melnick is associate professor in the School of Public Health at UCLA and a resident consultant at the RAND Corporation. His research interests include the effects of competition on hospital and physician behavior and international health services.

Terri Menke is a research specialist, Department of Veterans Affairs, in Houston, Texas, and holds a concurrent appointment as assistant professor at the Baylor College of Medicine. She has been a principal analyst at the Congressional Budget Office, where she specialized in issues related to health reform and comparative health systems. Prior to joining CBO, she was an analyst at the Center for Health Economics Research in Needham, Massachusetts.

Cathleen Mooney is an associate in the Department of Community and Preventive Medicine at the University of Rochester, where she has carried out research since 1987. Trained in public policy analysis, she specializes in the study of medical practice variations (both at the regional and individual physician level) and in medical technology assessment. She teaches a graduate course in clinical decision and cost effectiveness analysis for graduate students, medical students, and post-doctoral fellows at the University of Rochester.

James A. Morone is associate professor of political science at Brown University. His latest book, *The Democratic Wish: Popular Participation and the Limits of American Government* won the American Political Science Association's 1991 Gladys M. Kammerer Award for the best book on the United States and was named a "notable book of 1991" by the *New York Times*. Morone has been editor of the *Journal of Health Politics, Policy and Law* since 1989. He has written extensively on both health care policy and on American political culture and institutions.

John Posnett is senior lecturer in economics and director of the graduate program in health economics at the University of York, U.K. His main research interests are in the areas of health economics and the economics of philanthropy. Recent publications include papers on the tax deductibility of contributions to charity, on the theory of neutrality, and on the determinants of international differences in health spending.

Charles E. Phelps is (since 1984) professor, Department of Political Science and Department of Economics and (since 1989) professor and chair, Department of Community and Preventive Medicine, at the University of Rochester. From 1971 to 1984, he was a member of the Economics Department of the RAND Corporation, where he carried out research in health care, natural resources, energy, and regulatory policy. His current research interests focus on medical technology assessment (particularly diagnostic technologies), variations in medical care use, and the role of these studies in efficient allocation of medical care resources. He is associate editor of the *Journal of Health Economics*. He was elected to the Institute of Medicine in 1991 and published a textbook titled *Health Economics* in 1992.

Frank A. Sloan is Alexander McMahon Professor of Health Policy and Management at Duke University. Previously he was employed by the RAND Corporation (1968–71), the University of Florida (1971–76), and Vanderbilt University (1976–93). He is a member of the Institute of Medicine of the National Academy of Sciences and has served as a member of several public advisory groups. His most recent book, coauthored with a team of researchers at Vanderbilt, is *Suing for Medical Malpractice*, University of Chicago Press, 1993.

Kenneth E. Thorpe is Deputy Assistant Secretary for Planning and Evaluation in the U.S. Department of Health and Human Services. Prior to joining DHHS, he held positions at the University of North Carolina at Chapel Hill and at the Harvard School of Public Health. He has written widely on issues in health care finance.

Catherine L. Wisner is currently employed as a Health Research Methodologist for Park Nicollet Medical Foundation in Minneapolis, Minnesota, and serves on the Minnesota Health Planning Advisory Committee, addressing the contribution of health care technology to the cost of health care in Minnesota. Her research interests include health plan effects on the health status of plan enrollees and the effects of conflict and abuse in the workplace on health status and health care utilization.

Jack Zwanziger is assistant professor in the Department of Community and Preventive Medicine at the University of Rochester and a consultant at the RAND Corporation. His research has focused on the multiple effects on the performance of the health care system of recent changes in the structure of the health insurance industry. He has published the results of these studies (coauthored with Glenn Melnick) in a variety of journals.